AF361252

COLLECTIVE FARMERS, MASTER SCIENCE!

Collective Farmers, Master Science!

Youth, Education, and Inequality in the Russian Countryside, 1960s–1970s

TATIANA VORONINA

TRANSLATED BY MAEVE ZIMMERBAUM

UNIVERSITY OF TORONTO PRESS
Toronto Buffalo London

© University of Toronto Press 2025
Toronto Buffalo London
utppublishing.com
Printed in Canada

ISBN 978-1-4875-5038-7 (cloth)   ISBN 978-1-4875-5041-7 (EPUB)
                                   ISBN 978-1-4875-5039-4 (UPDF)

Library and Archives Canada Cataloguing in Publication

Title: Collective farmers, master science! : youth, education, and inequality
   in the Russian countryside, 1960s–1970s / Tatiana Voronina ; translated by
   Maeve Zimmerbaum.
Names: Voronina, Tatʹiana (Tatʹiana I︠U︡rʹevna), author
Description: Includes bibliographical references and index.
Identifiers: Canadiana (print) 20250182491 | Canadiana (ebook)
   20250182580 | ISBN 9781487550387 (cloth) | ISBN 9781487550394 (PDF) |
   ISBN 9781487550417 (EPUB)
Subjects: LCSH: Youth—Government policy—Russia (Federation)—
   Vologodskai︠a oblastʹ—History—20th century. | LCSH: Youth—Russia
   (Federation)—Vologodskai︠a oblastʹ—Social conditions—20th century. |
   LCSH: Education—Russia (Federation)—Vologodskai︠a oblastʹ—History—
   20th century. | LCSH: Equality—Russia (Federation)—Vologodskai︠a
   oblastʹ—History—20th century. | LCSH: Country life—Russia (Federation)—
   Vologodskai︠a oblastʹ—History—20th century. | LCSH: Socialism—Russia
   (Federation)—Vologodskai︠a oblastʹ—History—20th century. | LCSH: Oral
   history—Russia (Federation)—Vologodskai︠a oblastʹ. | LCSH: Vologodskai︠a
   oblastʹ (Russia)—Rural conditions—History—20th century.
Classification: LCC HQ799.R92 V65 2025 | DDC 305.2350947/1909046—dc23

Cover design: Val Cooke
Cover image: Youth! Jump on the Tractor (1976). Ruben Suryaninov. Gamborg
Collection/Bridgeman Images.

We wish to acknowledge the land on which the University of Toronto Press
operates. This land is the traditional territory of the Wendat, the Anishnaabeg,
the Haudenosaunee, the Métis, and the Mississaugas of the Credit First Nation.

University of Toronto Press acknowledges the financial support of the
Government of Canada, the Canada Council for the Arts, and the Ontario Arts
Council, an agency of the Government of Ontario, for its publishing activities.

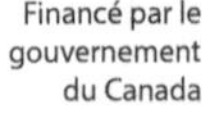

For my parents

Contents

Part Four: The Rural Komsomol and the Reproduction of Inequality

List of Illustrations

Translator's Note

Due to the prevalence of technical terminology in the following study (administrative divisions, institutions, official programs, and initiatives), a few clarificatory words are in order. I have attempted to balance readability with the reader's potential need to have access to precise names for further research, as well as fidelity with customary translation choices.

For administrative divisions, cities, towns, and geographical regions, I have chosen to use the names as they appear in Google Maps in order to facilitate easy Internet searches. For this reason, oblast names appear without adjectival suffixes, while district names contain them (for example, "Vologda Oblast" but "Vologodsky District").

The names of collective farms (*kolkhozes*) and state farms (*sovkhozes*) have generally been translated into English in order to convey a sense of the symbolic nature of the named environment. Thus, the reader will find the *kolkhozes* and *sovkhozes* "Stalin's Path," "Red Banner," "Dawn," "Sunrise," and "Red Star." The exception to this rule is those farms that are named after population centres, such as "Vorobyevsky," "Maisky," "Kirovsky," "Nikolotorzhsky." In such cases, the names of state farms have been placed in quotation marks, while the names of population centres have not. It is important to note that although a farm might share the name of a population centre, this did not indicate that all of the farm's workers belonged to that village. A *sovkhoz* was an agricultural enterprise that managed farms, fields, and production facilities belonging to many settlements and villages. Thus, the territory of the *sovkhoz* "Maisky" covered the population of multiple *selsoviets* and dozens of villages in addition to the Maisky settlement that served as its centre.

For acronyms and abbreviations, I have based these on the English translation when referring to institutions more or less specific to this book. Thus, I use "VDI" to refer to the Vologda Dairy Institute rather than "VMI" for the Russian Vologodskii Molochnii Institute. However, acronyms or abbreviations referring to more general types of institutions of have been rendered in their customary form; thus, for example, oblast public education committees are referred to as "Oblono."

There were a few instances in which I took creative liberty while translating initiative or program names. In such cases, the name of the program in Russian is provided in parentheses. For example, I chose to translate *vseobuch* as "gen-comp," indicating general compulsory schooling.

It is inevitable that there will be some slippage when attempting to describe the reality of one culture in the language of another. And while reaching consensus agreement on questions of translation and transliteration is impossible, I hope nevertheless to have provided a generally clear translation of an essentially complicated and technical subject.

Maeve Zimmerbaum

Preface

My work on this book can be compared to a marriage of convenience that, over the course of years, became a marriage of love. In 2017 I received an invitation to participate in a project dedicated to the late-Soviet countryside conducted by the Department of Eastern European History at the University of Zurich under the auspices of the Swiss National Scientific Foundation and the leadership of Ekaterina Emeliantseva Koller. By that time I already had a rich background of research experience, but my interests were far removed from the countryside. I agreed to join the research team, seeing as the position granted me the benefits of academic affiliation in Switzerland, which had become my second home, a salary, and the opportunity to continue my academic career. The invitation, moreover, came at a time when my previous research project was coming to an end, and I was thinking about starting something new.

Rather quickly, my interest in the village past ceased to be a tribute to the institute financing me and grew into an engaging dialogue with questions about the character and structure of Soviet society. Immersing myself in a new world of research, I was able to draw on my past experience studying Soviet history and the sincere interest in personal biographies that I developed in the early 2000s when I was still working at the Oral History Centre at the European University at Saint Petersburg. It was also a serendipitous coincidence that the story of my family is intimately connected with the countryside and that my parents live in Vologda to this day. This had a positive effect not only on the logistical aspects of the project, seeing as it facilitated long-term work in the Vologda archives and allowed my son and young daughter to take frequent visits to their Russian grandmother and grandfather, but also allowed me to discuss my findings with the people I was writing about. The book took on a personal dimension and became very dear to me, if not familial.

I am deeply grateful to the project head and to my colleagues Benjamin Kaelin, Anna Sokolova, and Alexandra Kasatkina for their fruitful cooperation within the walls of the University of Zurich, where my academic endeavours and initiatives were given financial support on multiple occasions. Additionally, I would like to thank the Salomon David Steinberg Foundation for awarding me a grant in July 2022 that allowed me to complete my research. I am thankful to the Graduate School of the Faculty of Arts and Social Sciences at the University of Zurich for financing the international workshop "Landscapes of Late Soviet Modernity," which we organized in Zurich on 9–10 September 2020, and which served as a breath of fresh air during a period of pandemic lockdown. It is gratifying to know that papers that were presented at the workshop were published in a special issue of *Canadian Slavonic Papers*, under the title "The Feelings of Progress: Peripheral Temporalities during Late Socialism."

Several sections of my work were read and commented upon by friends and colleagues who provided invaluable advice: Alexei Yurchak, Nikolay Mitrokhin, Alexandr Kaplunovsky, Tatiana Borisova, Sergei Oushakin, Ben Eklof, Ekaterina Melnikova, Svetlana Adonieva, Inna Veselova, Zinaida Vasilieva, Olga Malinowa-Tsiafeta, Benjamin Tromly, Alexis Peri, Catriona Kelly, Zuzanna Bogumil, Xenia Cherkaeva, Galina Orlova, Pavel Kupriyanov, Olga Voronina, and Elena Campbell. Their advice, comments, and recommendations played a significant role in improving the text. I am especially thankful to Olga Shevchenko, whose intellectual generosity, friendly disposition, goodwill, and sincere interest in my endeavours gave impetus to the project.

Also extremely beneficial were Kate Brown's recommendations on academic writing, which I was lucky to receive during a week-long workshop in 2021. I hope that they helped make my text interesting and stylistically varied. The talented translator Maeve Zimmerbaum, fearlessly battling with the participial constructions and bureaucratic specificity of academic Russian, was able to make the book easily readable in English. I would also like to extend my thanks to my husband, Aron P. Mueller, and to Stephen Shapiro, the tactically skilled and thoughtful editor at University of Toronto Press who read over and commented on my manuscript while providing sage guidance in the final stages of preparing it for publication.

My periods of work in Vologda, in the settlements Maisky and Molochnoe, owe much to the efforts of Anton Liutynsky, Larisa Chernova, Elena Alexeevna Avdeeva, Yulia and Anton Beliaev, Elena Beliaeva, Larisa Guch, my sister, Natasha Voronina, and my parents. They helped simplify the organizational hustle and bustle necessary for accessing oblast archives, the search for interviewees, and providing living accommodations. The

"Molochnoe Amateurs' Club" headed by Liubov' Khanova and the "Centre for Museum Work for the Vologda Molochnoe Dairy Institute and Vologda Butter," under the leadership of Liubov' Belova, helped me collect material on local history and allowed me to immerse myself in the history of Vologda's dairy institute. Alexandr Filin, from the history museum at the *sovkhoz* "Maisky," and Elena Vorobieva were my guides into the world of Maisky settlement.

I am also grateful to Elena Korkina for assisting with transcribing more than one hundred hours of recorded interview material. Special thanks go to the librarians at the Vologda Oblast I.V. Babushkin Universal Scientific Library, the archivists at the Vologda Oblast State Archive, the Vologda Oblast Archive of New Political History, and the Russian State Archive of Socio-Political History in Moscow for providing me access to research materials.

I am grateful to all of the respondents who agreed to share the stories of their lives with me: Alexander Ivanovich Korshunov, Evgenii Nikolaevich and Galina Nikolaevna Khokhlovy, Zinaida Alexseevna Staroverova, Tatiana Veniaminovna and Sergei Nikolaevich Kuznetsovy, Evgenii Gennadievich Guliaev, Galina Vasilievna Shikhova, Irina Alexandrovna Barintseva, Nina Ivanovna Sokolova, Sergei Ivanovich Trifonov, Elena Ivanovna Vorobiova, Zoya Fiodorovna Loktikova and Alexander Anatolievich Varfolomeev, Elena Alexeevna Avdeeva, Tatiana Leonidovna Rumiantseva, Olga Viktorovna Bezborodova, Irina Konstantinovna Shazkova, Elena Stanislavovna Zolotova, Genrikh L'vovich Paranichev, Sergei and Valentina Andreevy, Igor Pavlovich Lebedev, Antonina Alexandrova Kuznetsova, Tatiana Stepanovna and Vladimir Alexandrovich Semenovy, Alexander Iliich Abramov, Valentina Nikolaevna Belova, Olga Vasiliievna and Alexander Alexeevich Beliaevy, Liudmila Vladimirovna Smirnova, Vladimir Petrovich Puchkov, Evelina Alexandrovna Medvedeva, Liudmila Nikolaevna Makarova, Rimma Leonidovna Fedotova, and Kapitolina Fedorovna Kharlamova.

Finally, I wish to thank my parents, Iya Leonidovna and Yuri Mikhailovich Voronin, to whom I dedicate this book.

List of Abbreviations

CPSU	Communist Party of the Soviet Union
DOSAAF	Volunteer Society for Cooperation with the Army, Aviation, and Navy
GAVO	State Archive of Vologda Oblast
KP	Komsomol Projector
RGASPI	Russian State Archive of Socio-Political History
RSFSR	Russian Soviet Federal Socialist Republic
USSR	Union of Soviet Socialist Republics
VDAI	Vologda Dairy Agricultural Institute
VDI	Vologda Dairy Institute
VLKSM	All-Union Leninist Young Communist League, or "Komsomol"
VOANPI	Vologda Oblast Archive of New Political History
VPI	Vologda Pedagogical Institute

COLLECTIVE FARMERS, MASTER SCIENCE!

Introduction

Not everyone can boast that their cousin works at Facebook – but I can. We met up in Berkeley in the winter of 2012, after my father called from Vologda and announced that Alexei (or Alyosha) had finished his master's degree at Simon Fraser University in Vancouver and was moving to San Francisco. At the time, I was working on my postdoctoral fellowship at the University of California, Berkeley, and waiting for my daughter to be born. In the days leading up to meeting my cousin, I was worried that I would not to be able recognize him. The last time we had seen each other had been at a family meal in Vologda more than ten years earlier; he had been only ten years old then, and I had no idea what he would look like now. But when I caught sight of him on the train platform, I recognized him instantly. He looked like all the men in our family, gazing out from the pages of our family photo album. The unlikeliness of this meeting would be lost on those who do not know that Alyosha and I come from deep within the Russian provinces. I was born in Vologda, he in Severodvinsk. Our shared ancestors from two generations before us had lived in a small village in the Kirillovsky District of Vologda Oblast. All had been illiterate. Sitting under the shade of a lemon tree, we savoured our meeting and shared in a sense of surprise at the unpredictable twists and turns of our family biography.

I have told this story to friends many times as proof that the world is small and that God works in mysterious ways. But, then again, if we look at it from a slightly different angle, was our meeting really so unpredictable? What if we reject for a moment the notion that Alyosha and I are the sole stewards of our own fates, and instead view ourselves as the continuation of a family stretching back many generations, a family that had painstakingly chosen specific life strategies that had helped us come together thousands of kilometres from home?

The circumstances that brought my cousin and me together on a new continent in 2012 were connected to education, which is an important theme of this book. After all, was it not the hope for a better life that had justified the cult of education among Vologda peasant families? As I contemplate this, I remember that, when I was a schoolgirl, the question of whether my sisters and I would go to university was not up for discussion; it was one of the few but strict demands my parents made of us. Alexei's parents were equally emphatic.

There is a certain irony, however, in the fact that our family had come to understand the value of education relatively recently. Although my grandparents were semi-literate and could barely sign their own names, they nevertheless encouraged my father to study diligently because they had come to see education – rather than peasant labour, as had been the case earlier – as the key to the future. As a result, after graduating from a rural school in 1966, my father enrolled in the Department of Agricultural Machine Mechanization at the Vologda Dairy Institute (VDI). After graduating from the institute in 1971, he was assigned to work as the chief engineer on the *sovkhoz* where he was raised.[1] That year, he met my mother, who at the time was a young agronomist who had been dispatched to the same sovkhoz after graduating from an agricultural technical college.

In photographs from that time, my mother appears as a slender young woman dressed in a miniskirt and a playful headband with a stylish, transparent visor. In 1971, at the age of eighteen, she was already an agricultural specialist and the secretary of the sovkhoz's Komsomol organization (the All-Union Leninist Young Communist League, or VLKSM in its Russian-language abbreviation). My father, the twenty-two-year-old chief sovkhoz engineer, posed for the correspondent of *New Life*, a Kirillovsky District newspaper, in horn-rimmed glasses, with tousled hair and a charming smile. After just two years, in 1973, my parents would move from the sovkhoz "Vorobyevsky" to Molochnoe, near Vologda. My father had received an offer to work there as a lab technician and assistant teacher in the Cybernetics Department of VDI. A few years later, he moved to Leningrad to write his dissertation. In 1978, my father's parents moved to Molochnoe. My sister and I would come into the world in the same place. During those years, my mother completed her studies at VDI and went on to work first as an agronomist specializing in seeds, and then as a senior research associate at the RSFSR North-West Scientific Research Institute for Meadow Management and Dairy Farming. In other words, my parents' decision to move to a student city near Vologda was directly connected with education and their understanding of its importance for their careers and their family's well-being.

My parents' life stories are, in all likelihood, atypical for rural-born residents of Vologda Oblast. There were a number of serious barriers limiting the scope of educational possibilities for rural youths in the USSR between the 1960s and the 1980s. However, the general educational progression (rural school, then a technical school or institute), the choice of profession and specialization, a work assignment to a farm, and then migration to a city comprised the familiar stages of the collectivist experiment in the USSR's rural regions. This book is focused on this experiment and its implications for Soviet society. For this reason, I have made my parents full-fledged characters, giving the history I tell here a deeply personal character.

Rural Youths

One reason that it is difficult to write about young people in the USSR is that so many brilliant works have already been written on the subject. Thanks to the research of Juliane Fürst, Alexey Golubev, Elena Omelchenko, Hillary Pilkington, Donald Raleigh, Benjamin Tromly, Gleb Tsipursky, Alexei Yurchak, and Sergei Zhuk, we know that young people in the post-war USSR were members of the Komsomol, took part in unofficial youth groups, dreamed of jeans, danced the twist to rock and roll, studied in schools, technical institutes, and universities, got together in the entranceways of buildings, and in many ways differed from their parents.[2] However, as is the case in the majority of descriptions of late socialism, these works create a picture of only those youths who lived, in various decades, in large Soviet cities. Only a small number of articles focus on young people outside of big cities,[3] as do certain books written by Soviet sociologists during the heyday of "rural sociology" more than fifty years ago.

Thus, it is not surprising that the post-war USSR is strongly associated with Soviet urban culture, even if this is not completely fair, for two reasons. First of all, a large number of young people in urban areas in the Soviet Union had initially started life as rural schoolchildren and later moved into cities to continue their studies or to work. Second, in many Russian regions (such as in Vologda Oblast, which I will investigate in this work) the rural population continued to predominate over the urban population. In such places, there were many fewer young people in urban areas than in rural ones. Nevertheless, the experience of rural people was considered atypical and backward in late-Soviet society. As a result, rural people were often understandably ashamed of or reluctant to speak about their backgrounds. I know from my own experience how unpleasant it is to have your regional accent and intonation become the subject of attention and belittlement (in Vologda, for instance, people *okat*, meaning they pronounce their *o*'s without vowel reduction, while "properly speaking" city folk pronounce *a*'s instead).

Unsurprisingly, people who moved into cities from rural areas hid their rural upbringing and found it strange that someone might be interested in their pre-urban experiences. A few times during the course of this project people I approached refused to be interviewed. When interviews did take place, however, they were typically enjoyable for all involved. I fondly remember how Ludmila S., while attempting at my request to convince her neighbour to agree to an interview, exclaimed over the phone, "Say yes! You'll like it!" This exclamation contained not only praise for my abilities as a careful listener, but also the joy Ludmila felt at the realization that her autobiography is important and interesting, that a rural upbringing can be an object of pride rather than a stigma. The open format of a biographical interview allowed people to tell their stories on their own terms, without encountering a condescending sneer directed towards their rural background.

Why is it, though, that young people, rather than some other rural demographic, serve as the focus of this book? The primary reason is that young people were a driver of change in late-Soviet Russian villages. Rural young people were placed by the Soviet leadership at the centre of a colossal social experiment that led to the depopulation of rural regions and their eventual urbanization, as well as to the transformation of the life trajectories of those who lived there. These momentous processes transpired when young people in the countryside heeded the party's advice to become educated. Once they became immersed in the new Soviet education system, brought about by Nikita Khrushchev's reforms, they adopted the attitudes and outlook of Soviet modernity and abandoned the long-standing customs and ways of life that had defined the world of their parents and grandparents. Previously, peasants retained their way of life even in the complete absence of material stimuli for agricultural production. Like a phoenix, rural communities were resurrected after sudden disasters, hunger, wars, collectivization, and failed harvests. But post-war changes brought down the curtain on the agrarian history of the Russian North and led to the near-complete disappearance of what was once the most populous class in Russian society.

Collectivization, for all the violence it unleashed, did not destroy these elements. But after the educational reforms and program of urbanization of the 1960s and '70s, all these steadfast customs and habits of mind vanished. They vanished because of Soviet educational institutions that planted new notions of progress and exacerbated the differences – economic, cultural, and perspectival – between the urban and rural. In other words, I show that rural youth left the countryside during these decades not only because of poor living conditions there, but out of a desire to become modern. Thanks to their new education, they obtained the opportunity to uproot their lives in order to pursue this desire. Peasants, one might argue, were already marginalized under a regime of urban modernity, but this was greatly exacerbated by the educational reforms because it was the villagers' own children who were ostracizing them. These very personal rifts cut into peasant families, culture, individuals' sense of self-worth, and even their spatio-temporal perceptions. Local identity, local knowledge, and local culture were all sacrificed to an ideal of social progress associated with urban concepts of socialism. That final blow fell when many of the newly educated youth chose to leave the countryside altogether. Rural Vologda was able to weather the bloody perils of collectivization, but the cultural transformation of its youth was a shift that its society was unable to withstand.

These outcomes were connected only partially with Soviet economic policy in villages. Scholars have explained rural inequality in late-Soviet society by pointing to collectivization, failed economic reforms, gender, and the subsequent neglect of the countryside.[4] I argue that the destruction (through abandonment) of the peasant way of life in rural north-western Russia was the result not of related economies – at least not directly – but of cultural transformation.

These developments began with the announcement of the Program for Building Communism at the Twenty-Second Congress of the Communist Party of the Soviet Union (CPSU) in October 1961, which set the course for the country's development over the coming decades and prioritized the elimination of class distinctions and the merging of the city and the countryside. It was precisely at this time that Vologda region villages were drawn into Soviet modernity at the cost of losing local systems of knowledge and a future based on peasant culture and the agricultural autonomy of its farms.

Despite its stated aims, the Program for Building Communism exacerbated the inequality between the urban and rural populations in the USSR by imposing urbanized conceptions of progress onto rural young people.[5] Whereas in the pre-war period rural localities experienced inequality as a result of the uneven distribution of resources and the limited representation of the peasantry within the government, with the implementation of the Program for Building Communism rural localities were stripped of the very possibility of differing from cities. From that time on, the government began to conceptualize rural problems not on the basis of class inequality or the relationship of the peasantry to private property, but according to the specifics of the rural landscape and the position the village occupied on the path to social development. This approach allowed the state to close its eyes to the enduring inequality between the country's urban and rural populations by writing it off as a consequence of the uneven development of Soviet territories.

It is revealing that the magazine *Rural Youth*, relaunched in 1962 with coloured inserts, illustrations, and a stylish design, was as widely read in cities as in the countryside. It was "rural" only insofar as it contained short feature stories about sovkhoz Komsomol organizations, and these seemed the price to be paid for publishing the popular detective stories that brought the magazine record-breaking sales.[6] In official Soviet discourse, young people were viewed as a single group. Distinctions such as Komsomol member, schoolchild, and young worker created only minor differences of shading in the collective portrait. The Soviet bureaucracy, of course, distinguished between Komsomol members and those who were not members of the VLKSM ("non-union" youths, in the terminology of the era), as well as between schoolchildren and university students, and between those who worked on a *kolkhoz*, or collective farm, and those who worked elsewhere. Nevertheless, the "Moral Code of the Builder of Socialism," which was adopted in 1961, was intended to apply to all young people without distinction.[7] These rules of conduct for life in the classless society of the future applied to everyone universally. As Catriona Kelly has argued, being young in the Soviet Union during this period was more closely tied to an ideological concept than one's biological age, a situation quite different from what young people experienced in the West.[8]

In the USSR, the concept of "youth" covered the years between 14 and 35 years of age, in accordance with social milestones.[9] Thus, in the 1960s and '70s, children joined the Pioneers beginning at the age of 9 and the Komsomol at 14. As my research relies on the records of Soviet educational institutions, it is these documents that define the boundaries of the age category I study. As a result, my research focuses on boys and girls from the age of 7, when Soviet schoolchildren began their studies, to 27, when young people officially aged out of the Komsomol.

Not all rural inhabitants, or rural youth, were peasants. The founders of Russian peasant studies focused on the history of agriculture and assumed that the behaviour of rural producers was predetermined by economic interests. I propose a different lens through which to examine the rural experience, drawing on cultural geography and oral history. People living in rural areas in the late Soviet period had various and sometimes conflicting interests. In addition to the collective farm peasantry, the Vologda region was home to members of the rural intelligentsia (paramedics, librarians, teachers), "specialists" (agronomists, veterinarians, and engineers who were sent to the countryside on fixed-term contracts from universities or technical schools), white-collar employees (managers, accountants), students and teachers from rural technical schools, as well as workers from logging enterprises, flax mills, brick factories, and other enterprises located in rural areas. These people were united not by class, kinship, or common interests, but by their place of residence. Methods of cultural geography bring these rural but not agricultural workers into the analytical frame. They also help me to reconstruct the distances, spaces, and terrain of the countryside this diverse population inhabited. By broadening the collection of peoples and spaces that are considered rural, I can examine how various subcultures and forms of rural identity took shape during the period under study.

Chronologically, this study spans two decades: the 1960s and '70s. The earlier boundary is connected with the announcement of the Program for Building Communism at the Twenty-Second CPSU Congress in October 1961, which set the course for the country's development over the coming decades and prioritized the elimination of class distinctions and the merging the city and the countryside. The upper boundary is set tentatively to mark the end of Brezhnev's reign and the start of the political and economic perturbations that would relegate the problems of the countryside, its population, and agriculture to the peripheries of state attention.

Modernity

Among the various concepts informing my book's theoretical framework, a prominent place is given to the notion of modernity. From the point of view of the creators of modernity, faith in progress, which gave rise to the European notion of "New Time," as opposed to the conception of time that tended to characterize the medieval period, created a new temporal framework and new hierarchies.[10] The concept of modernity as it is was understood by political philosophers during the twentieth century served as an alternative to the "civilization approach," and proved to be more flexible.[11] In the opinion of Reinhart Koselleck, one of the theorists of this concept, people of the "New Time" viewed progress as a linear process in which human societies moved from lower stages of development to higher ones. The past leads to the present, and the present leads to the future.[12] Despite the many differences between the political regimes of the USSR and those in the countries of the "capitalist bloc," their respective visions for the future shared many commonalities. Both envisioned a fairer, more technologically advanced and urbanized future.[13] The primary differences were in the methods by which this future was to be realized. In the USSR, building socialism served as such a method. Multiculturalism inspired some philosophers, starting with Shmuel Eisenstadt, to talk about the existence of multiple modernities, or about different types and trajectories of modernity.[14] In most European countries, the rejection of tradition in favour of modernity came with the emergence of a market economy and liberal thought.[15] However, in Russia modernity was triggered by state-initiated cultural initiatives aimed at integrating rural worlds into the global order.[16] In historical, sociological, and anthropological research on Russia and the Soviet Union, the topic of modernity has so far been addressed almost exclusively in the context of the history of the Russian Empire and, as it pertains to the Soviet period, in the context of Stalinism.[17] I apply it to the late Soviet period.

Considering a variety of modernities allows me to reject the view that rural localities are peripheral to cities, always lagging behind them developmentally, and instead analyse them as territories with their own spatio-temporal properties.[18] This approach resonates with the conception of modernity that Teodor Shanin used to ground his study of the peasantry as a class possessing persistent characteristics and its own conception of the future.[19] At the same time, this approach alludes to the conception of modernity formulated by James Scott, one in which local "modernities" are contrasted with state modernization, or "high modernity."[20] In other words, I conceive of modernity as the vision for the future that people experience, one that influences their choices in the present and is formed under the influence of group and class values.

If we view modernity as a society's ideas about the future, then it can inform us about why decisions are made in the present.[21] Koselleck calls this the "horizon of expectation" that forms the agenda for a society living with a conception of linear time.[22] With this in mind, I analyse the desire to change one's life trajectory by leaving the countryside as a means of rejecting one scenario of modernization (rural) for another (urban).

It is important to note that Soviet modernity was manifested not only in social hierarchies and the conceptualization of territories, but also in the nature of knowledge. It is not coincidental that Michael David-Fox associated the beginning of the USSR's path to modernization with the replacement of academic faculties in Soviet academies at the end of the 1930s rather than with the political upheavals of 1917.[23] It was at that time that the concept of Soviet modernity replaced the European model of modernity in the USSR. However, the shift from the European to the Soviet model occurred primarily in Soviet cities, with almost no effect on everyday life in the countryside. In rural areas, modernity, understood as a shift in the nature of knowledge, came much later than the 1930s. At first, the emphasis was placed not so much on changing the nature of knowledge in villages from European to specifically Soviet as it was on replacing local knowledge with any sort of modern, global knowledge, be it Soviet or European.[24] In the USSR, the process by which state global knowledge came to eclipse local knowledge occurred, in essence, over the course of a single generation in the 1960s and '70s and was largely connected with schooling reforms.

Another important concept for this work comes from Michel Foucault.[25] Utilizing its control over schooling, the Soviet government, by transforming school curriculums and introducing them to rural areas, offered the population its own "modern" conceptions of reality, a form of what Foucault labelled "dominant knowledge."[26] Foucault theorized that actors forming a discourse create and preserve power by maintaining control over the dissemination of knowledge. Knowledge always retains a trace of power relations and is tied to the position from which it is produced and spread. In the Soviet countryside, dominant knowledge was opposed to local knowledge formed from within rural communities – that is, the "subjugated knowledge" marginalized by the state. In this system, schools can be regarded as an instrument of control over knowledge and as an instrument of social and political domination. Following in Foucault's footsteps, modern researchers working on education tend to view schooling and education as instruments of such domination and the colonization of certain systems of knowledge by others.[27] Viewed in this light, the choice of some rural schoolchildren to reject their studies ceases to be a purely pedagogical issue and becomes a form of social protest.[28]

Paying attention to the social and class nature of Soviet educational inequality allows us to account for the problematization of "rural youths" as a group in the 1960s and '70s, especially as the object of contradictory state policies. Oriented towards the future, Soviet socialism always pinned its hopes on the younger generation, but state and party authorities were at a loss when it came to rural youth. On the one hand, they regarded rural young people through a class lens and treated them as backward, unenlightened second-class citizens whom they barred from cities, denied passports, and forced to work on collective farms. On the other hand, the regime saw all young people as a group embodying the promise of the revolution and the elimination of differences between city and countryside as one of its core mandates. The way to make rural youth "Soviet" was to immerse them in the world of Soviet modernity, which was inherently urban in its values and outlook. The way to achieve this was through education. While this might seem like a straightforward course of action, the regime did not concretely formulate and execute it until the 1960s. This is where my story begins.

One last concept that informs my work on this book is Alexei Yurchak's notion of a "performative shift." He has argued that, despite the seemingly regimented nature of Soviet life, the lack of political freedoms, and state disregard for human rights, Soviet people nevertheless found ways to live autonomously by forming their own communities that did not enter into direct confrontation with the government.[29] In his opinion, when young people entered the Pioneers, the Komsomol, or even the Communist Party, such actions did not mean that they were "Sovietized" or indoctrinated. By contrast, because the state was only interested in preserving formal ("performative") duties and ensuring the continuity of external discourse, it was often unable to control the meaning that people bestowed on official spaces and initiatives. When it created structures meant to bolster Soviet ideology in the countryside, the government did not ensure that these structures actually functioned. All that mattered was the production of official reporting documentation. As a result, the pieces of infrastructure the state created (clubs, sport facilities, musical collectives, forums for political discussion, etc.) were as likely to exist only on paper as to actually be realized and play an important role in young people's self-expression. In other words, Soviet modernity imposed by the state did not become an essential condition of life for people in rural localities. Moreover, it was the varied and diverse combinations of progressive and conservative, urban and rural, Soviet and non-Soviet that characterized Soviet rural localities in the period studied here.

The multitude of theories and approaches that inform this book are not meant to scare the reader away with excessive theorization; rather, they reflect the difficulty inherent in conceptualizing the phenomenon of inequality that links the various themes and subjects of this work.

The Rural Worlds of the Vologda Region

Collective Farmers, Master Science! immerses the reader in the pastoral world of the Vologda region. Vologda Oblast is just a single region, of course, but it is a vast one. It is located in the north-western part of European Russian, and forms part of the Russian North. Before the revolution, the sprawling territory that would become Vologda Oblast in 1938 was known as the Vologda Governorate. Large Orthodox monasteries were erected to commemorate the wars fought from the fourteenth to the seventeenth centuries in the region, and these became the religious centres of the Russian North-West and outposts for the colonization of the Russian North and Siberia. The Vologda Orthodox Diocese was founded in 1589. By the end of the seventeenth century, it included more than 650 churches and around 60 monasteries and hermitages.[30] The war against religion waged by Soviet leadership had dramatic effects on the Russian Orthodox Church during the decades of Soviet rule. By the 1960s, there was not a single functioning monastery in the Vologda region and the network of Orthodox seminaries had been closed down.[31] In the 1970s, the number of Orthodox priests fell to a mere 23 across 17 parishes serving a population of almost 600,000 residents.[32] Those Orthodox churches that managed to continue functioning were located in the oblast's cities, and rural parishes were often left without a priest.[33] In this way, the Soviet state did everything it could to ensure that the Russian Orthodox Church lost its influence on the political, cultural, and social aspects of the country and the region. This did not mean, however, that the rural population of Vologda Oblast lost its connection with Orthodox tradition. The religiosity of the rural populace, as evidenced by the observance of church holidays and village customs, was linked during these years not to the work of the Russian Orthodox Church and the Orthodox priesthood but rather to the "legacy and remnants of the past," which reform ideologists claimed could be easily eradicated through education. The authorities did not see popular religiosity as a danger. As a result, atheistic instruction in Vologda rural schools seldom extended beyond a designated atheism section or a few talks about the negative effects of religion. The official reports of local authorities in the 1960s and '70s simply did not contain information regarding religious ceremonies, and thus state managers were not irritated by it. The state saw a danger in the existence of the Orthodox Church rather than in belief among the population.[34] Understood as a "vestige" of the pre-revolutionary past, Orthodox faith among villagers was expected to vanish on its own after the introduction of Soviet education. But as anthropologists have noted, these hopes were not completely realized, and former Vologda village residents continued to celebrate Orthodox holidays and bury their dead in accordance with Orthodox ritual into the 1970s and beyond.[35]

During the period analysed here, Vologda Oblast was one of the biggest, oldest, and most problematic agricultural regions in Russia.[36] In addition to challenges created by war, revolution, and collectivization, Vologda Oblast suffered from the Virgin Lands campaign (1954–64), the funds for which were extracted from territories in the Russian North.[37] As Liubov' Denisova observed, "the USSR as a whole reached the pre-war level of grain production in 1955, but the Non-Black Earth region did not do so until 1967."[38]

Population density was high in the southern parts of the country, while the European North, especially Vologda Oblast, which was considered part of the "Non-Black Earth region," was sparsely populated.[39] Urbanizing the latter region was difficult and economically unsound.[40] Eighty percent of Vologda Oblast's population centres were tiny villages in which the region's predominantly rural population lived until the 1970s.[41] They were an optimal type of settlement for a complicated forested landscape divvied up by a large number of rivers, lakes, and swamps. The plan to urbanize rural territories in the 1960s, however, did not take environmental specificity into account.[42] According to state logic, during fully developed socialism the rural population of the Vologda region was supposed to live in large, urban-type settlements. Although the process of these settlements' construction moved slowly, by the end of the 1960s, rural areas had seen the appearance of various types of settlements, each of which was valued differently by the regional government – some positively, while others were dismissed as inadequate.

As a result, the settlements that comprised these oblasts were divided between those that were rapidly changing, adopting the appearance of urban culture with multi-storey apartment houses, paved streets, playgrounds, and sports fields, and those that changed more slowly and looked much as they had decades prior. The latter type of settlement included the region's traditional thinly populated villages with wooden structures and residents who reproduced social relations and hierarchies characteristic of rural communities. These villages personified "old rurality," with its peasant "vestiges," beliefs, and hard peasant labour. Typically, peasant families lived in these villages for generations. It was these villages that become field study sites for ethnographers and linguists collecting local dialects and studying local traditional culture.

The urban-type settlements that formed as a result of the modernization of rural localities were a completely different type of settlement. These were transformed by newly created production enterprises and the development of transportation infrastructure. Life in urban-type settlements was structured according to principles that were largely alien to the countryside and that excluded traditional "old rural" practices like raising cattle on individual farms or public celebrations of traditional religious holidays.[43] Unlike in their villages, residents of these new settlements typically became migrants. These massive developments were meant to become the foundation for a "new socialist rurality," where production and life itself would be based on socialist progress rather than peasant world views.[44]

The region suffered under the state program to eliminate "unpromising" villages in the 1970s, and the agricultural economy developed more slowly there than in other regions of the country. The Soviet Union's brutal agricultural policies stimulated a mass outward migration of rural residents to cities. Nevertheless, Vologda Oblast remained a mostly rural region. Most people lived in small villages spaced far apart from each other. By 1967, Vologda Oblast was home to 15 cities, 11 urban-type settlements, and thousands of villages.[45] Its 25 districts each contained between 7 and 26 village soviets.[46] During the 1960s and '70s, Vologda's population was predominantly Russian and widely dispersed over a vast territory. The majority bred cattle for meat and dairy production.[47] Heavy industry had been introduced during the 1950s, and the Cherepovets Metallurgical Plant (known today as "Severstal") was built in the eponymous regional centre. The plant increased the proportion of urban residents, but the absolute numbers of the rural population remained relatively high.[48] By 1979, only 41 per cent of residents were rural, and the total population of the region was 530,400.[49]

My analysis focuses on three rural settlements located in Vologda Oblast. The history of these settlements was determined by various socialist development scenarios for rural territories in the twentieth century. By avoiding generalizations in favour of a detailed description of the organization of everyday life and living spaces in these settlements, I hope to illustrate how modernization played out differently in each place.

The first settlement covered a region containing sparsely populated villages that were under the jurisdiction of the Migachevo and Glazatovo Selsoviets in the Kirillovsky region of Vologda Oblast. Vorobyevo, Sosunovo, Ivitsy, Kabachino, Mys, Probudovo, Bykovo, Dom Popa, and Shuklino: this is how locals rhythmically list the names of the villages (although this is not a complete list for the area) that were part of the sovkhoz "Vorobyevsky." The famous colour photographs taken by Sergei Prokudin-Gorsky during his trip along the Mariinskaya Water System in 1907 illustrate the idyllic rural scenery of this locality. These were the villages that were founded on the right shore of the picturesque and navigable Sheksna River in the fourteenth and fifteenth centuries. Intensive government interference in this rural region led to mass migration and the abandonment of the territory in the twentieth century. This interference included the reorganization of farms into large sovkhozes, a policy of compulsorily resettling people whose villages were flooded during construction of the Volga–Baltic Waterway, and the beginning of Khrushchev's agrarian policies.

The second settlement is the urban-type settlement Maisky, which is located only eleven kilometres from Vologda Oblast's city centre in Vologodsky District. Maisky was the centre of the city sovkhoz "Fruit-Tree

Nursery," which was renamed "Maisky" to match with the settlement in 1974. Created in 1962 on the site of the tiny village of Barskaya, the sovkhoz was meant to be a model for new "Soviet rurality," with apartment-style panel homes, Soviet public institutions, bus access, a kindergarten, and a school. The population of Maisky consisted of migrants from other rural regions of the Russian Soviet Federal Socialist Republic (RSFSR) and Vologda Oblast. Maisky was the centre of a major farming enterprise that specialized in growing vegetables and fruit crops for the oblast centre, the city of Vologda. In the 1970s, the sovkhoz contained six production facilities with almost seven hundred workers.

The third settlement is the village of Molochnoe, the student city for VDI, and the site of the North-West Scientific Research Institute for Meadow Management and Dairy Farming, one of the most important scientific centres in north-western Russia. The appearance of Molochnoe was connected with the development of the oblast's dairy industry. It was considered an island of urban culture in a rural area and an example of a totally new approach to organizing a rural settlement. Throughout the course of its existence, it underwent urban development and provided a reproduced version of an urbanized lifestyle. This differentiated Molochnoe both from other newly built urban-type settlements and from the region's villages.

These three localities cannot be said to represent the vast and diverse scope of rural areas in Vologda Oblast. Nevertheless, they illustrate well the various means of subsistence and ways of organizing rural life during late socialism. It also should be noted that the majority of my research subjects are personally connected with these three settlements.

Sources

I use a combination of archival research and extensive oral history interviews. Many of the historical sources I have used for this book have never been published before and are brought into academic circulation now for the first time. I describe government policy in the realm of rural populations, school education, Komsomol work, and the training of the agricultural workforce on the basis of official documents (decrees, notes, informational documents, work reports). Considering the regional focus of my work, alongside my work in the Russian State Archive of Socio-Political History, I worked with two regional archives: the State Archive of Vologda Oblast and the Vologda Oblast Archive of New Political History, which was formerly the party archive. Reports from institutes working with young people followed specific guidelines and a form that was standard across the USSR, which significantly affected the information they contain.[50] These documents are opaque when it comes to outlining the actual functioning of the institutions they describe. To understand how basic Soviet institutions worked in a concrete way, I needed to see documentation describing life in specific rural settlements and talk with the people who had lived in these places.

The second level of my analysis is based on my interest in materials concerning the everyday life of rural youths living in the Maisky and Molochnoe settlements, as well as in the villages of the Migachevo Selsoviet. I was interested in the infrastructure of these places, in the details of their geographical position and their development. To reconstruct village life in Kirillovsky and Vologodsky Districts, I turned to materials from various executive committee commissions from the Migachevo and Worker-Peasant Selsoviets. I also made use of museums at the sovkhoz "Maisky" and the museum at VDI. Furthermore, I consulted a memory book containing the personal accounts of residents from the Molochnoe settlement. I was also interested in the yearly reports of rural schools located in these settlements. Of special interest to me were the documents prepared by the Commission for Minors' Affairs and the Commission for Youth Affairs, which were run by the Executive Committees of Kirillovsky and Vologodsky Districts. These documents shed light on how the geographical placement of settlements influenced the lives of their residents, their social composition, and their living spaces.

Lastly, in order to study individual reactions to the processes of modernization in rural areas I conducted biographical and collective interviews and worked with materials from personal archives. Altogether, I conducted thirty interviews over four years, during which I heard the stories of thirty-eight people. For the most part, these stories were delivered orally and recorded with the consent of the interviewees on a voice recorder using a face-to-face interview format at various locations across Vologda Oblast. However, there were some cases in which the partners of interviewees participated in the interviews. In one case, I conducted a group interview with five women. I met with some people multiple times, splitting each interview into two or three sessions.

In choosing my interviewees I relied on a few specific criteria. First, I chose from among people who had been born, socialized, or had lived for at least a few years in one of the three Vologda Oblast rural settlements I had focused on in my research. To be more specific, these were either villages that now belong to the Aleshinskoe rural settlement (but which had formerly belonged to the Migachevo, Zvozsky, Ivanoborsky, and Glazatovsky Selsoviets of Kirillovsky District), the Maisky settlement, or the Molochnoe settlement. Secondly, it was of principle importance that my interviewees had been children or adolescents during the 1960s and '70s, meaning most of them were born at the end of the 1940s or beginning of the 1950s. Only two of my interviewees were slightly older, one having been born in 1939, and the other in 1940. Lastly, I tried to maintain a gender-balanced sample, although, ultimately, I interviewed more women (twenty-five) than men (thirteen). The search for interviewees was conducted with the help of family, friends, and acquaintances, and it benefited from the snowball effect. Most of my interviewees currently reside in cities of the Russian North-West – Vologda, Cherepovets, or Saint Petersburg – with only a few having remained in rural localities, and even they had moved from villages to settlements.

Although I prepared questions in advance that focused on education, professional experience, and the specificities of day-to-day life in the 1960s and '70s, I preferred narrative interviews, which gave the participants the opportunity to choose the themes, chronology, and method of storytelling (monologue or question and answer) that were most comfortable for them.

Chapter Outline

This book consists of an introduction, nine chapters divided into four parts, and a conclusion. Part 1, "Being Rural in the USSR," is concerned with how the state and the population conceptualized rurality.

In chapter 1, "Ruralism in the State Discourse of Developed Socialism," I describe the formation of state discourse on rural localities and the rural population and how this discourse changed with the issuance of the Program for Building Communism at the Twenty-Second CPSU Congress in 1961. The program included the declaration of a policy to eliminate inequality between the city and the countryside. This policy changed official conceptions of rurality, without, however, eliminating inequality. At most, it veiled inequality and dressed it in new garb.

Chapter 2, "Staying Rural: Ex-Peasants and Identities," explores how individuals conceptualized inequality between urban and rural populations. It analyses interview narratives of everyday life in rural settings. These stories were profoundly informed, on the one hand, by the experience of life in the countryside and, on the other, by urban ideas about progress. I was interested in how the discursive construction of rurality in the Soviet context affected those who were raised and socialized in the countryside: How did rural people come to understand themselves when they had peasant roots but passed through the Soviet educational system?

Having explored in the first part what being "rural" entailed and how people interpreted inequality in the 1960s and '70s, I go on to investigate the chronology of young people's lives by examining the role of school, university studies, and sovkhoz VLKSM organization work. It is this chronology that structures subsequent chapters. Although many rural teenagers never finished school, joined the Komsomol, or enrolled in university, these structures were nevertheless the focus of youth policy in the countryside.

Part 2, "Rural Schools," is devoted to examining the role that rural schools played in socializing young people and in changing the nature of knowledge in the countryside. The new school curriculum supplanted and marginalized local knowledge while claiming to establish a new hierarchy of power in the rural world of Vologda villages.

In chapter 3, "The Colonization of Rural Knowledge Begins," I analyse the implementation of the 1958 school reforms in rural areas. In Vologda Oblast, this meant the closure of one-room elementary schools located within walking distance of peasant homes, and the creation of seven-year (later eight-year) schools and boarding schools. This reform made school the most important institution of youth socialization in rural areas.

In chapter 4, "Education Is Enlightenment, Ignorance Is Darkness," I talk about how the knowledge gained in rural schools facilitated the social mobility of young people by training them for non-agricultural jobs in the city. Young women in particular took advantage of this opportunity to avoid following in the footsteps of their mothers.

Chapter 5, "On the Margins of Vologda Villages: Poor-Performing and 'Mentally Deficient' Students," addresses the fate of "bad students" who did not see the point in formal education because they followed the behavioural patterns of their social class. Although avoiding school would not have led to their marginalization prior to 1958, afterwards, the refusal to go to school resulted in the ostracization of such pupils and their families. This chapter is based on materials from juvenile commissions, which assigned truant students medical diagnoses and sent them to special educational institutions.

Part 3, "Agrarian Institutes: 'High Modernity' in the Rural Outback," highlights how the new school curriculum and culture, created by urban intellectuals, changed social hierarchies in rural areas, placing young specialists and scholars at the top and undereducated peasants at the bottom.

Chapter 6, "Cadres for the Village," describes the history of the Vologda Dairy Institute as a critical agent of modernization in the Russian North. It fundamentally changed ideas about the development of dairy as well as the nature of peasant production in the region. Moreover, the university became an instrument of mass socialization among predominantly rural youth who were striving not so much for a specifically agricultural degree but any college diploma, which represented a ticket to the city for many young people.

Chapter 7, "Molochnoe: Urban Meets Rural," is devoted to the rural settlement of Molochnoe, where VDI was located. By focusing on housing and other patterns of life there, this chapter unpacks how local identities and hierarchies took shape in this college town and exacerbated inequalities between "town and gown."

Part 4, "The Rural Komsomol and the Reproduction of Inequality," shows how rural Komsomol organizations were held hostage by Soviet ideas of modernization. To spread urbanized values among rural youth, the Komsomol inflated and condemned the backwardness of the countryside.

Chapter 8, "Modernity's Conduit and Hostages of Backwardness," argues that the Komsomol, a product of urban culture, instilled the values of Soviet modernization and set new standards of life while also exacerbating inequality among the rural population. Guided by party leadership, the Komsomol fought (what the party considered) remnants of peasant life and sought to impose Bolshevik understandings of time, labour norms, gender roles, and social hierarchies. As a result, the rural population associated the Komsomol more closely with compulsory overtime labour duties than with an opportunity to improve the lives of young people. The resulting resistance to the Komsomol on state farms was often taken as another sign of peasant backwardness.

Chapter 9, "The Invisible Komsomol: Kolkhoz and Sovkhoz VLKSM Organizations," compares the Komsomol organizations of two state farms in Vologda Oblast. Although the interests of young people on state farms often aligned with Komsomol initiatives, youth participation in the organization was limited, as the Komsomol was generally thought to restrict youth freedom through its assault on rural life, rather than promising them opportunities for advancement. It would be schools, not the Komsomol, that brought young people into the modern and urban Bolshevik mindset.

PART ONE

Being Rural in the USSR

Chapter One

Ruralism in the State Discourse of Developed Socialism

What Is Rural?

"Niurka, ah Niurkh?" mocks city-dwelling Liudmila, played by Liubov' Gurchenko in the film *Love and Pigeons* (1985), in imitation of her rural rival: "Blech, the village!" This catchphrase, which became a "winged" (popular) expression in Russia, ironically plays upon the disdainful treatment of the rural population by those who lived in cities, and thus reflects a social reality well-known to every person born in the USSR: In Russia, in order to enjoy high social status, respect, and a promising future, one must be born in the city, and the closer to the centre, the better. Regardless of Soviet ideology, which issued assurances of equal opportunities for the country's various demographics, being born in the countryside in the USSR placed an ineradicable mark upon a person and condemned them to social, educational, and economic inequality. In the Soviet view of socialism, the urbanized city environment was taken to be normative, while villages and rural localities where conceptualized as vestiges (*perezhitki,* in Soviet parlance) of the backward past.[1]

If one were to ask the average person what exactly separates the countryside from the city, their answer would, more often than not, focus on the types of houses, the greater distances separating people, and the types of economic activity. Social research can extend this list to include specific types of rural communities, local knowledge, distinctive cultural practices, and rural identities.[2] Those especially knowledgeable in the topic might add that large distances influence the flow of rural time, distinguishing it from the urban, and that modern villages are shifting more and more from being the producers of goods to their consumers.[3] As Paul Cloke argued, the difficulty of conceptualizing "rurality" lies in the existence of a diversity of rural localities, the contrived nature of the boundaries separating them, and, despite urban stereotypes labelling the countryside as static and traditional, the fact that they are ever-changing, albeit in ways that are different from urban environments.[4]

Why, then, do researchers not simply reject this seemingly impractical analytical category altogether? As a rule, the answer lies in the global challenges facing humanity: Revolutions, the collapse of colonies, hunger, ecological problems, and migration tend to affect enormous masses of people, the majority of whom are involved in agricultural production. Researching these issues using "urban techniques" has proven impossible, since rural spaces, localities, and societies alter social theories to the point of unrecognizability. For this reason, rural research does not follow a standard methodology, although it tends to be highly empirical in nature, and is in high demand, as it has the potential to influence pressing political decisions – for example, those related to global food security.[5]

As Anna Martin Mathews has argued, researchers use the category of rurality to denote either a type of environment (i.e., ecologically) or a sociocultural category.[6] In the first case, the writing is focused on physical spaces, settlement types, and the specificities of infrastructure. In the second, the emphasis is placed on the social structure of rural communities, class divisions, culture, and identity. Sometimes these approaches intermingle and are superimposed onto one another, confusing the categories, as happened, Matthews's research shows, during an attempt to classify the elderly rural population of Canada. From her point of view, researchers working with the concept of rurality need to be aware how the concept is being constructed, by whom, and what types of categories are being considered. Who are the rural population? Those who were socialized in the countryside? Those who live there now? Those who consider themselves to be a part of that population? The representatives of various disciplines address this problem in different ways. Cultural geographers are prone to use formal criteria and boundaries: They define the city population as those who live in the city, and the rural population as those who live in the countryside. By contrast, anthropologists and sociologists prefer a more flexible approach that recognizes "rural culture" as a phenomenon shaped by people's identities, and therefore capable of existing in cities, just as aspects of urban culture can be found in the countryside. In this sense, rurality is not only a space, but an identity.

For a long time, both approaches – geographical and sociocultural – developed in parallel. In the mid-twentieth century, adherents of the sociological methods of Pitirim Sorokin in the United States studied rural landscapes, urbanization, and population mobility, while studies based on Marxist theory focused on economic and class structures.[7] It was precisely during these years that systemic studies of rural localities began to be produced almost simultaneously in Europe, the United States, and the USSR. A *Journal of Peasant Studies* was founded, and one of its idealogues, Teodor Shanin, opened the door into the world of the Russian peasantry.[8] Peasant studies was intended to enrich the Western "geographical" approach with the addition of Marxist theory while simultaneously introducing fresh currents of Western cultural theory into Soviet research, which had relied exclusively on economic analysis and the study of social relations. The resulting attempts to conceptualize social structure by studying "rurality" resulted in the appearance of "rural studies," which is currently divided into various sub-branches focusing on such subjects as demographic change, economic transformations, food systems and land, environment and resources, gender and rural society, social and economic inequality, social dynamics and institutional capacity, and power and governance.[9]

Thanks to this symbiosis of territorial principles and class theory, the concept of rurality itself was reworked on a global scale. The "geographers" began to take account of social conflict in the countryside, which they had earlier neglected, while those who worked on the basis of Marxist theory began to understand that class analysis alone could not reveal the full complexity of cultural and political relations or shed light on the interrelations between rural communities and local landscapes.

Conceptualizing Territory and Class Hierarchy

Urban and rural localities were analysed in the Soviet era with reference to ideas about class and progress. Marxism, which was fundamental to Soviet philosophical doctrine, cultivated an understanding of linearly progressing time and attributed a specific temporality to governmental transformations. This temporality was oriented towards technological progress, a planned economy, and the socialist future.[10] These ideas gave preference to urban society, which was tuned into global processes, rather than to local rural worlds, which were assumed to lie beyond such processes.[11]

In the first decades after the revolution, official Soviet discourse distinguished the urban from the rural not so much by the physical features of the landscape as by the class origin of the population who lived there. Subsequently, class origin determined whether that population was deemed capable of contributing to progress and building socialism. In the view of Soviet elites, the urban proletariat was more progressive than the rural peasantry.[12] Although the Soviet constitution adopted in 1936 replaced the concept of differentiated classes with a united "Soviet people," the class hierarchy created in the initial post-revolutionary years had already firmly taken root in Soviet culture and politics. Thus, the city, which was associated with modernization, was always viewed as the bulwark of socialism, while the village, where peasant farming practices and private property in the form of kolkhoz workers' individual plots of land were retained, was connected with backwardness.[13] Idealistic declarations of unity between city workers and rural peasants could not pull the wool over the eyes of the Soviet people, who understood as well in the 1930s as they would later, in the 1970s, that life in the city was easier, and to be a city resident more prestigious. As a result, concepts of Soviet modernity and socialist progress formed an enduring hierarchy in which peasants would never be equal to workers. And although the agricultural question was a constant feature of Russian politics starting with the abolishment of serfdom, it was viewed only in terms of the social relations of the peasantry working in rural regions.[14] Pressing debates were limited to addressing whether the peasantry could be viewed as a fully-fledged participant in progress, as was the view of the *narodniki* and Alexandr Chayanov, or whether, as Vladimir Lenin argued, the peasantry ought to be denied a unique subjectivity and thereby made "invisible" and disenfranchised within the broader society. (Lenin considered peasants to belong to either the proletariat or the bourgeoise, depending on the level of wealth they possessed.) The unequal social position of the peasants was cemented in their legal status, in social policy, in the passport system, in the method of distributing resources in the USSR, in language, and in ideas about behavioural norms. It is telling that, according to the 1918 and 1924 constitutions, the vote of a single city worker was equivalent to five peasant votes.[15]

Inequality between classes in Soviet society reinforced unequal conditions that had existed in various territories from before the time of Marx's theories.[16] In his research tracing the history of the Soviet passport, the anthropologist Albert Baiburin asserts that the "passportization" of the population of the USSR can be viewed as a process of bringing various social groups into the grand Soviet project to transform the country and the world – in other words, the project of Soviet modernity.[17] The choices the revolutionary government made concerning the country's various demographic categories reflect the new principles upon which the Bolsheviks "rebuilt" the country as a society of Soviet citizens: social background, revolutionary consciousness, and loyalty to the new government. If one follows Baiburin and looks at this process "geographically," then it becomes clear that the first people lucky enough to experience the new socialist world order were the residents of Moscow and Leningrad, who received passports in 1933.[18] Next came the proletariat of ten big cities that served as oblast and republic centres. Gradually, passports made their way to those who worked in industry or as builders at grandiose infrastructure projects on the country's periphery. The limit beyond which passports were no longer provided was set at 101 kilometres from an urban centre. This distance coincided with restrictions placed on those sentenced to internal exile under Soviet law, who were forbidden from settling within 100 kilometres of major cities. So familiar to Soviet dissidents and representatives of the "old classes," this line clearly demarcated the area within which socially transformative progress had taken place and, in the opinion of ideologues, had been successful. Outside of this boundary, progress was nowhere to be seen.

The gradual nature by which various territories and population demographics were brought into the Soviet modernization project can be easily explained by limited government resources and the existence of various non-Soviet ways of life within the USSR. Building a completely identical model for the future for everyone, despite the existence of a large variety of climates and cultural conditions, was beyond the power of even the most fervent revolutionaries. Nor was equality facilitated by the fact that the Bolsheviks' socialist ideals took modernized European industrial society as their model and completely disregarded the requests peasants directed at the government and agricultural scientists.[19] For a country with a predominately rural population, this modernist project would prove to be a challenge.

Prior to Khrushchev's reforms, the government's primary focus was on extracting resources from the countryside in order to build Soviet industry and cities. Consequently, programs to completely "Sovietize" the rural population were not undertaken.[20] Party and Komsomol organizations on sovkhozes and kolkhozes were expected first and foremost to fulfil production quotas rather than instil a Soviet mindset, although such a mindset was welcomed, of course. The collectivization of the 1930s, which destroyed an entire class of rural producers (the kulaks) and upended the basics of farming, was intended less to build socialism in rural areas than to simplify the process of extracting resources from countryside.[21] The peasantry, who were impoverished by this extraction, were not granted the social protections that were gradually introduced for people living in cities.[22] The timid attempts of kolkhoz workers to achieve fairness by sending letters to the government were met with an unwillingness on the part of the state to solve systemic problems.[23] As a result of this sort of treatment by the government, the socialist countryside looked as underdeveloped in the decades after the Second World War as it had in the first decades of Soviet rule. By the 1960s, the passportization project gradually began to reach residents of rural areas. It was finished only in 1974, when the last rural population demographic, ordinary kolkhoz workers, received the most important document in Soviet society. Only from that moment on was socialism as a society of Soviet citizens with a guaranteed right to public benefits truly put into practice, at least formally.

The Program for New Life

On 23 February 1963, the newspaper *Lenin's Banner*, the most important paper in Vologda Oblast's Kirillovsky District, received a new title; henceforth, it would be called *New Life*. Although the paper's editorial staff and political standpoint remained the same, the change in title was deeply symbolic. It reflected the government's intention to change life for the better for the rural population in the 1960s, to make it more modern.

The Program for Building Communism (also known as the "Third Party Platform"), adopted at the Twenty-Second Congress of the CPSU in October 1961, marks what is undoubtedly a landmark moment in the history of the USSR.[24] It made clear to the Soviet people what the socialist future would look like and elaborated the principles upon which it would be built. In his keynote address to the congress on 18 October, Khrushchev declared that "Communism … means that … in the realm of social relations the remnants of class distinctions will be liquidated, they will be united into a classless society of workers for communism, primarily there will a liquidation of differences between the city and the countryside."[25] To accomplish this, rural areas (understood as places with a large peasant population) needed to be drawn into projects aimed at building socialism. Peasants needed to become workers. Subsequently, the countryside became the forefront of Khrushchev's modernization project.[26] The intention was to create of a new Soviet rurality in which peasant life would be fundamentally restructured in agreement with socialist principles.[27] The project of socialist modernization undertaken during the 1950s and '60s had been based on the Marxist conception of the countryside as the rudiment of a new industrial world. It would thus be necessary to transform rural areas into urban ones in subsequent decades.

The project's underlying mission (to wage war against the vestiges of peasant life and the dark peasant past) presupposed a complete rejection of peasant ideas and the peasant world view that continued to guide the lives of rural producers. The agrarian reforms put forward by Nikita Khrushchev were based in a firm belief that rural backwardness was incompatible with socialism. Faith in progress (science, technology, the peaceful atom) was bound to transform backward rural life, to make it similar to the urban. The "new rurality," based on the rejection of individual farm plots and equal access to education and culture, was meant to replace the "old rurality," associated with the unequal position of the kolkhoz peasantry in comparison to workers and public servants.[28]

Attempts to create a new type of Soviet rural locality were seen at the 1954 Exhibition of Achievements of National Economy. The exhibitions showcased rural tea houses, rural clubhouses, buildings for selsoviet councils, and rural schools.[29] It was presumed that the rural population would react to these infrastructural changes by rejecting peasant traditions and becoming closely involved with socialism, no longer limiting their involvement to listening to radio broadcasts form Moscow and taking trips to big cities.

Beginning as early as the 1950s, Nikita Khrushchev had used urbanization policy to attempt to transform rural life. He advocated for the expansion of sovkhozes and the creation of agro-cities.[30] Whole villages had to be moved into agro-industrial centres or agro-cities, and kolkhoz workers had to be settled into new five-storey apartment buildings modelled on city apartments. Limits were introduced for individually farmed plots and individually owned livestock.[31]

Pragmatic choices about which rural settlements received resources for construction followed state logic about rational spending. Thus, it made sense to build schools, clubs, medical centres, shops, and libraries in large settlements rather than small villages because a greater number of people could therefore make use of them.[32] However, as Soviet geographers noted, while this logic proved successful in regions with favourable agricultural conditions or significant areas of virgin land, in Russia's northern and central regions the project found little support among the local population. This was because the program failed to take into account the specific needs of regions where sparse population distribution was necessitated by local landscapes.[33] Kolkhoz peasants did not understand why they should move their houses and agricultural structures to a single village, thereby destroying a system of ploughing and tilling that had been established over centuries. In a landscape where isolated agricultural plots were separated by forests and swamps, it was much easier for farmers to live near their fields in small, distributed villages of approximately ten houses than in a single large settlement located hours away from the farthest fields and separated from them by unnavigable roads. In reality, land that was cleared of pre-reform structures almost always became forested rather than put to agricultural use. Nevertheless, party policy was unshakable, and in Vologda Oblast as in the rest of the USSR new rural settlements began to appear in the 1960s. But in contrast with the restructuring of rural communities that had taken place in the Moscow region during the 1950s, the rural modernization program for

Vologda Oblast was characterized by the construction of new, standardized five-storey buildings rather than the relocation of peasant huts.[34] It was these new structures that were destined to become a socialist alternative to the traditional village. According to a 1974 directive from the CPSU Central Committee and the Council of Ministers of the USSR, "On Measures for the Further Development of Agriculture in the Non-Black Earth Zone of the RSFSR," the historical population distribution of the northern European region of the RSFSR was an obstacle for successful agricultural development in the region. Thus, all forces needed to be mustered to "transform towns and villages into built-up sovkhoz and kolkhoz settlements, realize the construction of agricultural and industrial sites in complexes with residential houses and sites of cultural-residential function, complete by the 1990s the relocation of residents from small inhabited localities to large settlements."[35]

Although intentions underlying the program of relocating village residents might have been honourable, the socio-economic effect was the complete opposite of what was expected.[36] The forced urbanization of the rural population led to increased migration and the loss of previously cultivated land.[37] Khrushchev's resignation, moreover, did not end the trends he had initiated; the state continued its program of relocating villages despite protest from below. As a result, in the opinion of historian Liubov' Denisova, the majority of rural residents left settlements for cities.[38] Nevertheless, oblast party committee efforts and the far-sightedness of individual sovkhoz leaders ensured that new urban-type settlements began to appear among the abandoned villages of the Vologda region. Ultimately, the oblast's territory was divided between areas associated with progress and those "unpromising" ones home to an aging population unwilling to move to the city or a kolkhoz settlement. Inequality became cemented in the various statuses rural territories were granted, and the future of individual settlements hinged on the plans of district and oblast leadership. Certain regions began to attract district and oblast investments. These regions saw the establishment of bus routes and airports and the construction of new schools, kindergartens, and stores. Even pontoon ferries were established for some settlements that relied on river crossings. Other settlements were doomed to isolation and could only be reached by unnavigable roads.

Rural settlement status also had a profound effect on goods distribution, the level of social support provided to the population, and the forms of cultural life available. As Sergei Vikulov wrote, new settlements resembled city blocks and created new types of relationships among those who moved in. Unlike villages where residents knew everyone in the community, urban-type settlements were comprised primarily of migrants, and were governed by sovkhoz leadership and the selsoviet administration in lieu of centuries-old traditions developed by a concrete community on a discrete territory and passed down by elders.[39] Governing bodies decided how streets and houses would be built, who would receive an apartment, and even the size vegetable garden allotments. The institutions that had regulated rural sociality in the past – comprised of neighbours, kin, elders – were relegated to a marginal role in the community.

An exemplary "new rural" settlement was the urban-type Maisky settlement. Maisky grew around the small village of Barskoe, situated eleven kilometres from the oblast's capital city, Vologda. Its agricultural centre was the sovkhoz "Fruit-Tree Nursery," which grew apples and vegetables to meet the needs of the big city and cultivated trees and bushes for the RSFSR's northern oblasts. In 1963, the sovkhoz, which spanned a total area of 2,055 square metres, boasted thirty-three panelled residential apartment blocks housing a population of four hundred. Additionally, the construction of three additional residential houses was underway.[40] The new settlement had electricity, gas, and telephone service, and was connected to the city's water and sewage systems. Active residential construction on the sovkhoz was carried out throughout the 1960s and '70s as more and more residential homes and buildings popped up. This drew a workforce for the sovkhoz as workers poured into Maisky from all over Vologda Oblast and even beyond its borders. Judging by the sovkhoz's worker migration statistics for the period 1975–77, nearly 100 people arrived in Maisky each year, although slightly fewer than that left annually. Thus, in 1975, 113 people arrived and 75 left; in 1976, 84 arrived and 87 left; and in 1977, 87 arrived and 92 left.[41] The 1977 sovkhoz passport[42] shows that from 1975 to 1977, most migrants came to Maisky from rural localities (85 out of 113 people in 1975; 68 out of 84 in 1976; and 69 out of 87 in 1977). These migrants came from within Vologda Oblast as well as from other oblasts. In 1975 more came from within Vologda Oblast than from without: 61 Vologda Oblast natives versus 52 who came from other regions. In 1976 the balance shifted to non-Vologda migrants: 38 people came from outside Vologda Oblast versus 28 from within the oblast.[43] Only around 20 locals who lived in the various settlements belonging to the local October and Peasant-Worker Selsoviets went to work on the sovkhoz between 1975 and 1977. This can be explained by the fact that the sovkhoz actively resettled labour reserves from the villages to Maisky. Consequently, those whose remained in the villages were predominately pensioners. Still, the tendency of people to leave rural localities was clear. Even an "advanced" settlement such as Maisky, as well as a successful farm near a big city such as "Fruit-Tree Nursery," were unable to stymie migration away from the countryside. At the same time, active residential construction and the opportunity of receiving an apartment were powerful stimuli for migration to the settlement from remote localities. Judging by a summary report written by the sovkhoz Komsomol secretary, the average age of workers and public servants on the sovkhoz in 1971 was thirty-two.[44]

The highway from Vologda to Kirillov neatly divided the settlement Maisky into two sections, thereby separating its residential and industrial areas. The former contained a school, a club, a post office, a store, and later a library, a medical clinic, a village administration building, the sovkhoz museum, and a sports complex with an indoor ice rink and swimming pool. Thus, although the byway leading to the settlement's residential homes remained unpaved for a long time to come, and the residents wore rubber boots nearly year-round, the settlement's structure, building types, green landscaped areas, indeed the entire conception behind its organization evinced the project designers' intentions: Maisky was a new type of rural settlement.

Maisky was akin to an urban micro-region and offered the population certain cultural opportunities that were characteristic of Soviet urbanology. It was a place where sports, education, and a rich "cultural life" with winter celebrations, Soviet holidays, and sovkhoz amateur performances were the foundation of a new rurality and proof that socialism could be built in a rural locale. At the same time, the seasonal character of agricultural production, the lower availability of goods compared to the city, and the "rural" habits of migrants moving into Maisky's apartments gave the settlement its distinctive local colour.

After counting off the achievements of Maisky's sovkhoz leadership for an hour, one of my interviewees suddenly added in a whisper that, for the most part, everything that happened in Maisky during the 1960s and '70s was done "for show" and could hardly be said to have been in the interests of the people living there. Many residents would have preferred to live in their own home, raise a cow, and work on their own farm rather than take part in sport and amateur performance. Indeed, a reversion to traditional peasant forms of life would eventually take place, beginning with perestroika. However, sovkhoz leaders, like their oblast and district party counterparts, viewed these practices as a return to the "vestiges" of peasant life that the Soviet government had so laboriously battled for the entirety of its existence.

While Khrushchev's new socialist project seemed more humane and considerably more focused on scientific and technical achievements than Stalin's before him, it was still based upon the idea that peasants, on account of their attachment to private property, were incapable of taking part in the building of socialism without the direction of the party. The policy of placing limits on privately owned plots of land was supposed to destroy the last bulwark of the old world in the countryside.[45] Ultimately, Khrushchev's envisioned modernity proved to be even more devastating for rural worlds and peasant culture than Stalin's had been. Khrushchev's project not only interfered in the rural economy in order to extract resources; it also uprooted the rural way of life with its characteristic temporality, particulars of everyday life, and values based in local knowledge.[46] Soviet historiography has named this process "depeasantization," the loss of rural people's connection to traditional means of agricultural production and their concomitant way of life.[47]

In hopes of building a classless society, Khrushchev replaced class with territory as the primary, determinative social construct: Rural localities needed to look like urban ones and be populated by sovkhoz workers instead of peasants. Brezhnev's later agrarian reforms, which created agro-holdings and further industrialized agricultural production, were a continuation of this logic and accelerated the depopulation and urbanization of rural areas.

Providing the benefits of socialism to the rural inhabitants of the USSR was a goal and a challenge for Soviet post-war leadership comparable with the Cold War in terms of the ideological resources expended upon it. Although some of Khrushchev's policies were reversed after he was no longer in power, his project to finish building socialism in the countryside remained in place throughout Brezhnev's regime – which is to say, until 1982.

Chapter Two

Staying Rural: Ex-Peasants and Identities

A Research Associate and Her Cow

I arranged to meet Valentina B. at my parent's apartment in the Moloch-noe settlement in July 2020. Ever since my parents became pensioners, they have taken annual summer trips to the countryside, where they rest at my father's native village in Vologda Oblast's Kirillovsky District. While they are gone, their city apartment stands deserted for three months, during which it gradually comes to exhibit small signs of abandonment. The cool kitchen in their panelled, five-storey building with windows facing to the north provided us with relief from the July heat and a space where we could work. Valentina was my mother's former colleague at the research institute in Molochnoe (the RSFSR North-West Scientific Research Institute for Meadow Management and Dairy Farming), and she agreed to my interview only after a great deal of convincing, and only out of a sense of indebtedness to my parents.

Born in 1948 in eastern Vologda Oblast, in the village Reshetnikovo, Kich-Gorodetsky District, Valentina had been the youngest member of a large family. Her mother had been a seamstress, and her father the head of one of the district committee departments. In 1950, her father died from tuberculosis, and her mother was forced to go to work on a kolkhoz in order to feed her five recently bereaved children. The family, who had previously enjoyed a privileged position on account of the father's party affiliation, suddenly found themselves on the verge of poverty without their breadwinner.[1] After finishing eight-year school in 1961, Valentina moved to the neighbouring district's central city, Veliky Ustyug, where she enrolled in Veliky Ustyug Agricultural Technical College. After three and a half years of study there, she received a work assignment in 1969 to the sovkhoz "Bereznyaki," located not far from Vologda, to serve as the brigadier of an agricultural brigade. She married at the sovkhoz, and after a period of time she and her husband moved back to her hometown in Kich-Gorodetsky District, where her mother still lived. In Kich-Gorodok, just a few kilometres from Reshetnikovo, she found work as a laboratory assistant at an agricultural procurement enterprise and enrolled to study part-time in the VDI Agronomics Faculty. After she had finished her institute studies, and her husband had finished his army service, the young family moved closer to Vologda, where Valentina had been offered a position as an agronomist at the Vologda "sorting field."[2] The job came with an apartment in a wooden panel-board home in the village Dulepovo, located a few kilometres from Molochnoe. Valentina's husband, after completing part-time studies at the Veliky Ustyug Agricultural Technical College, worked as a chauffeur at the research institute in Molochnoe before becoming the manager of the institute's garage. Her husband's employment at the institute allowed Valentina to find a position there as well, where she worked for the feed-production division arranging agreements with sovkhozes for seed sales. As one of the institute's staff, Valentina was able to move with her family to Molochnoe, where, in the early 1980s, the institute provided her with an apartment in a new multi-family brick house.

Moving into an urban-style apartment did not alter Valentina and her husband's peasant way of life. Even as residents of an urbanized settlement like Molochnoe, they continued to keep livestock. While living in Dulepovo, near Vologda, they bred sheep and earned good dividends selling wool. On the eve of the food crisis of the mid-1980s and 1990s, they purchased a cow and had a cowshed built for it in a neighbouring village.

The practice of working an urban profession while maintaining an individual peasant farm was not uncommon during late socialism or in the following decades. Moreover, as Valentina's experience exemplifies, it was perfectly possible to combine scientific work with traditional peasant practices such as haymaking and the daily feeding and milking of cattle.

Valentina's ambiguous position between urban and rural culture found expression in the way she constructed her identity while telling her life story. When she emphasized the unique and unusual aspects of village experience, she did so from the point of view of an urbanite. Detailing the main events in her biography (moves, marriage, and childbirth) she gave a detailed account of village existence in the oblast's eastern districts. She described special techniques for stowing hay, preparing rural meals, and weaving linen doormats. It was clear that Valentina's village past continued to carry a lot of value for her, and that by telling her stories she was able to signify her sense of belonging to the rural world.

At the same time, she chose topics that, from her point of view, most vividly illustrated the differences between rural and city life. In a sense, this made them reminiscent of stories collected on a folklore expedition. Valentina's knowledge allowed her to problematize her "rurality" because she constructed it from the point of view of an *urban* subject describing her rural past.

With the help of Valentina's interview, I began to understand how people living in the countryside perceived their rurality, how they remembered their rural past, and what role these factors played in constructing their modern identities.

In her research on the rural population of Canada, Anna Martin Matthews drew attention to the difficulties of classifying the population according to the criteria of urban and rural.[3] Without rejecting the existence of a "rural identity," she emphasized that rurality, instead of being an innate characteristic, is constructed under the influence of a variety of factors, including socialization, place of residency, and self-identification. This approach allows not only those currently living in the countryside to be considered rural, but also those who formerly lived in the countryside and retained their rural identity after moving away. I followed the same principles when I interviewed not only current but also former residents of Vologda Oblast's rural localities, with the goal of trying to understand how they conceptualized their own rurality.

At the core of my understanding of former Vologda villages, gleaned from the biographical stories of those who spent their childhood and adolescence there, and my method of representing them, is the idea that Soviet modernity, which developed in cities and urban-style settlements, came into conflict with rural conceptions of progress and development between the 1960s and the 1980s. Although the social structure of urban and rural communities in Vologda Oblast during late socialism was in fact a great deal more complicated than might be apparent from this text, I am purposefully simplifying the situation in order to present a clear argument: The extent to which interviewees viewed themselves as belonging to either a rural or urban cultural milieu had an influence on their identity and, consequently, on their memories of the past. In this chapter I review how two types of discourse, which I provisionally call "urban" and "rural," took root and interacted with each other in people's memories of the rural past.

In Soviet discourse, rural territories and the rural population were conceptualized through the lens of class structure and relegated to a peripheral position in the schema of socialist progress. The course that the Bolsheviks adopted in the first decades of Soviet rule, which emphasized the USSR's industrial development and granted social privileges to the urban proletariat, laid the foundation for long-lasting systemic inequality. In the view of Soviet leadership, rural territories were inferior to cities both because they housed fewer industrial enterprises and because the rural population were viewed as belonging to "suspicious" social groups, such as peasants and property owners. Khrushchev's campaign to merge the city and the countryside was intended to ameliorate this situation; instead of rurality being viewed as inimical to socialism, it came to represent underdevelopment. This shift played a key role in transforming rural identity in the USSR.

Describing their experiences of life in a rural locality, my interviewees relied on pre-existing Soviet hierarchies. Their stories about rural existence allowed them to interpret various forms of inequality through the most commonly accepted social categories in the USSR: categories that juxtaposed the city and the countryside. People were eager to make use of the opportunity to compare and evaluate their own lives with the lives of others, and they invested their stories with a sense of the injustice they had experienced. Discussions of this injustice, even it was often not a direct result of one's having grown up in a rural environment, were possible only through the lens of Soviet "rurality" during late socialism.

It is remarkable that, having experienced first-hand what it's like to grow up and live in the countryside, my subjects did not speak directly about class inequality in Soviet society, although they drew attention to the unequal distribution of goods, rural poverty, and the inaccessibility of certain opportunities available to city residents. At the same time, as historians Mikhail Beznin and Tatiana Dimoni have demonstrated, the stratification of rural communities between the 1960s and the 1980s was pronounced.[4] Soviet discourse in these decades, insofar as it viewed the inequality of urban and rural territories as one of "vestiges" of the past in the countryside, diverted the conversation away from the taboo topic of social conflict. As a result, those whom I talked to interpreted the inequality they experienced as surmountable; one simply had to migrate to the city. The fact that their experience of inequality did not cease after moving, however, did not play a significant role in their conceptualizations, because they continued to compare themselves to "their own" – that is, rural – communities. They compared themselves to those who remained in the village, and in that respect viewed their migration as a success. The outcome would be entirely different if they contrasted themselves with city people.

Genres and Discourses of Modernity for Conceptualizing the Rural Past

Writing about the nuances of interviewing residents of the rural Russian North-West, the anthropologist Ekaterina Melnikova noted that her interviews often hit a wall when she asked her interlocutors to talk about their lives.[5] This was not merely a reflection of the individual preferences and personal experiences of those being interviewed; it was above all an indication of a difference between urban and rural modes of communication. City dwellers are more likely to be comfortable with the urban habit of "talking about oneself." Among village residents, this behaviour remains unusual and uncharacteristic of popular communication. In rural communities, moreover, where everything happens "in the open" and "everybody knows one another," the telling of biographical stories is often considered unethical. My own rural grandmother called such stories "boasting and bragging," suggesting that biographical narratives are usually characterized by the listing of one's personal successes.

On this account, my intended genre of narrative biographical interview proved to be only partially successful. In place of an uninterrupted life story, I often received laconic answers. People typically felt more comfortable talking about the collective practices of their communities rather than their own lives. This left the figure of the speaker in the shadows, allowing the interviewee to speak about past experiences without drawing excessive attention to him- or herself.

This unwillingness or inability to talk about the past stems from several contributing factors. First, people who lived in villages and settlements often had little reason to create biographical narratives. Many never had the opportunity to write autobiographies or fill out biographical surveys. Second, with the exception of teachers and librarians, for whom literacy was part of their professional training, former kolkhoz workers often lacked the ability to clearly express themselves in writing. Analysing Soviet memoirs and autobiographies, the literary scholar Irina Paperno came to the conclusion that, in the process of creating biographical texts, people tended to copy pre-existing literary strategies of self-representation.[6] Reading artistic literature formed modern methods of self-expression and gave rise to new forms of conceptualizing self and community.[7] Mandatory schooling, introduced in the USSR in the 1960s, led to a situation in which the majority of the rural residents in the Vologda region were able to read and write. However, many former schoolchildren never had occasion to use literacy skills in their day-to-day lives. For this reason, "rural diaries" are extremely valuable and allow us to see how representatives of village culture make use of a modern instrument of self-expression.[8]

Soviet idealogues argued that peasants, having become literate, would thus gain the ability to express themselves as equals with city dwellers. For this reason, the state made massive efforts to create a cohort of rural writers capable of becoming the voice of the working peasantry. As a result, in the 1960s and '70s northern villages really did "gain a voice" through the works of the "village prose writers" (*pisateli-derevenshchiki*). "Village prose" was written by those who had grown up in the countryside and glorified the peasant way of life, albeit strictly within the confines of modern genres: essays, novels, narratives, and stories.

At the same time, although "village prose" itself constructed "rurality" in accordance with the laws of a literary text, in some aspects authors worked independently to reproduce their "rural view" of reality. As Kathleen Parthé has noted, "village prose writers" relied on rural temporality, idealizing a serene and stable past rather than focusing on the faith in progress demanded by socialist realism.[9] Additionally, even though such writers made villagers their protagonists, most of the readership for village prose came from the cities. The residents of Vologda villages themselves lived in a different, non-literary dimension, and their narratives and life stories were hardly in keeping with the depictions found in texts written by their famous neighbours. The residents' life stories had different plots and were built around different themes.[10] As anthropologists working in northern villages have noted, their culture contains an entire array of methods for passing down knowledge based not on texts, but on rituals and rites, physical techniques, and social connections. Artistic texts play a very mediated role in this culture, and are typically found in alternative mediums, such as folk songs about the village.[11] As a result, biographical interviews and life stories are still a new and unusual genre for residents of Vologda Oblast's rural localities.

My interviewees were also forced to grapple with various modes of temporality in understanding and describing rural experience and their own pasts. In contrast to the official "Soviet" understanding of time, residents of Vologda Oblast's rural villages possessed their own, alternative temporality.

In the rural communities of the Vologda region, temporality was understood through oral traditions and articulated through a culture of rituals.[12] Even when "experiencing the steady influence of book knowledge," Sergei Shtyrkov writes, in the village "the traditional practice of telling historical legends retains its features for a long time."[13] Margaret Paxson notes that stories about people who suffered under repression often featured forest spirits, called *leshii*, who took people away at night.[14] These and similar myths helped to keep local histories alive in collective memory into the 1990s without resorting to "urban" notions of time and progress.[15] Another important feature of "rural time" is the fact that peasant culture was oriented towards the past. Even in Russian "village prose," Kathleen Parthé has shown, the personal past, epitomized as childhood, was idealized and juxtaposed with the present.[16] As Paxson observes, the "golden age" of the village is connected with the past, even if villagers identify different events and eras with that ideal.[17] The spaces of rural memory include churchyards, cemeteries, temples, and other "holy places" associated with religious beliefs and rituals. Urbanized Soviet culture, by contrast, was oriented towards progress and the future.

Collectivization caused a decline in peasant farms and claimed millions of lives, but, as disruptive as it was, it did not alter the cyclical nature of "rural time." Cyclical time, with its seasonal rhythms, continued to govern human experience, rather than being subordinated to human will.[18] Until 1966, for example, the labour of collective farmers was still calculated in workdays, not in labour hours, as was the custom in cities.[19] This rural practice prevented an easy conversion from working hours into roubles when the time came to calculate workers' pay. Moreover, there was no concept of "free time" in rural areas.[20]

School lessons that became compulsory for all rural children after the launch of the universal education program were one way in which a new kind of knowledge – historical knowledge – was disseminated in the village. Before the school reforms, students in rural parts of Vologda Oblast did not study history as a subject, though teachers shared stories about the revolution and serfdom as part of the general curriculum. Rural children mainly learned about the past from these and other stories that circulated in the community.[21] However, the new standard curriculum, adopted in November 1966, made history a compulsory subject.[22] From the fourth grade on, students covered all stages of the country's development, from ancient times through the twentieth century. In the fifth grade, they studied the ancient world, in the sixth, the European Middle Ages. In grades 7, 8, and 9, Russian and Soviet history was the focus; the grade 7 curriculum concentrated on the eighteenth century, grade 8 on the nineteenth century, and grade 9 on the post-revolutionary period. This course of Russian history was repeated in grades 10 and 11. Primary schoolers had two history lessons per week, and secondary schoolers three to four per week. This was one-third of the time allocated for mathematics and the Russian language and about the same as the number of hours devoted to literature, physics, foreign languages, physical education, and labour. The schools taught rural children to historicize time, to conceive of it as linear, and to interpret their personal stories, those of their parents, and those of the places where they lived within Soviet context.

By involving children in local history, Soviet rituals, and anniversary commemorations, Soviet institutions gave young people alternative guidelines for understanding rural reality. Anniversary festivals required students to search for local heroes and reconceptualize local histories under the rubric of progress, thereby making rural students accomplices in the dissemination of Soviet notions of modernity and linear temporality. The local was valuable only insofar as it was part of this overarching narrative and shared its values. In addition, during anniversaries young people were introduced to a world outside the rural community – one that was attractive to them, regardless of whether they shared Soviet values.

As a result, former rural schoolchildren lived with both Soviet and rural modes of temporality and were able to easily switch between them according to their needs.

Also significant for rural biographical narratives was the disparity between the level of acceptance for modern values among those who live in rural communities and those who live in cities. An illustrative example is the story of Valentina B., who had a conflict with her school administration that led to her being expelled from the Pioneers. Valentina's expulsion was based on her unwillingness to participate in skiing competitions. Explaining her refusal to take part in these races, she cited her desire not to appear ridiculous (to be in public "with a red face"), something deeply important for an adolescent girl from a rural village, though it would hardly have crossed the minds of teachers striving for student success in sports or of urban girls her same age: "And so I said, 'Valentina Ivanovna, I won't go to the competitions.' And she said, 'How's that, you won't go? You must.' 'I won't go. I said I won't go.' And that was already, probably, in the seventh grade or so, at that point it was … it had already become … well, you're already growing up. And, well, imagine if I had gone – people run there [*mimics heavy breathing to illustrate*]. And that red face too. And how was I going to run like that? No, I won't go. It would be one thing if it was just us – but I won't go there … into the centre of Kich-Gorodok."[23] Ultimately, for a rural adolescent, participating in, and perhaps even winning, a skiing competition was less important than how she would be perceived by her acquaintances and neighbours.

This serves as an example of the way in which young people, although they were radically "modernized" by moving into cities, still carried remnants of their "unmodern" rural past with them for the rest of their lives.

The life stories of people who were socialized while living in the countryside differed not only by genre, but also in how people constructed their identities. Whereas modern discourses emphasized a person's national, state, and class identity, rural communities had their own structure: that of family, neighbours, and relationships with one's mother-in-law.[24] As Margaret Paxson wrote, residents of rural areas in Vologda Oblast in the 1990s had a strict sense of the line demarcating "our people," essentially those who had grown up in the surrounding area, and "others," which included everyone else.[25] They constructed their identify with a clear attachment to locality and territory. And although the boundaries of "our people" gradually expanded when the families of villagers moved to cities or other rural localities, local space, as conceptualized in traditional cultural categories, remained crucial to people's self-identification and views of reality.

Theorists of modernity view people's engagement with modern discourses as proof of a transition from the old to the new and from tradition to modernity.[26] And although various researchers attribute the appearance of modern discourses to various societal changes, they all agree on one point: The moment when people begin to use linguistic categories taken from new discourses to conceptualize reality indicates that a societal change has taken place. Perhaps the most thorough description of this was given by Michel Foucault in *The Archaeology of Knowledge*, in which he tied the production of any type of knowledge to political power.[27] In his view, changes in conceptual categories indicate a battle between different discourses and the creation of hierarchies in which, alongside the dominant discourse, there are "subjugated knowledges" – that is, knowledge belonging to an oppressed minority that is pushed out of the public space.[28] By belonging to rural communities in the epoch of mass urbanization, rural youth assumed the status of a vulnerable minority, and their knowledge was subjugated and marginalized accordingly.[29] In the opinion of Laura Olson and Svetlana Adonyeva, young people in rural northern villages gradually lost their connection with rural knowledge over the course of the twentieth century, interrupting traditions and leading to powerful changes in rural life.

Writing about how modernity changed Soviet reality, the anthropologist Serguei Oushakine, adopting a term originally coined by Marshall Berman, referred to "compensatory modernity."[30] Berman understood this to mean radical strategies for changing reality in the pursuit of progress.[31] Analysing the prose of Maxim Gorky, the ideas of Trofim Lysenko, and the pedagogical innovations of Anton Makarenko in the 1930s, Oushakine showed how some seemingly outdated discourses were replaced by new, radical ones tied to conceptions of modernity. Furthermore, the radical nature of these ideas was predicated on this notion of "compensatory modernity," the desire to quickly transform the present for the benefit of the future, even if there was a loss in quality or sense in the transformation taking place.[32] A similar modernity-based conceptual shift was described by Rebecca Friedman, who wrote about changes in residential building styles during the late imperial and early Soviet periods.[33] Former peasants and servants adjusted enthusiastically to changes in tastes, which were becoming more and more suited to social changes occurring within the country and the world as a whole. Anna Krylova linked the changes in post-war Soviet culture with the establishment of urbanized socialism and the accompanying rise of individualized practices of city life.[34] Thus, involvement in modernity demanded that its followers be ready to accept the new and reject the old.

The speed at which modern discourses spread throughout Soviet cities and rural localities differed from place to place, depending upon the infrastructure of knowledge in a given locale. In other words, when thinking about how modern rural subjects conceptualize their past, we can assume that they build their stories with the awareness that some of their values based in village experience have become outdated, while others have remained perfectly adaptable to a modern reconceptualization. And although this subjugated "rural" knowledge was placed lower in the knowledge hierarchy than urban and modern knowledge, its presence in the interview narratives nevertheless indicates that rural identity retained its significance.

Child Labour

In late-Soviet culture, descriptions of childhood and adolescence were often painted in nostalgic tones and based in descriptions of a "happy childhood" as conceptualized by Soviet idealogues soon after the revolution.[35] However, this gentle treatment of childhood was not specific to Soviet discourse. Both the idealization of childhood and childhood nostalgia are traits found in the majority of modern discourses dealing with the past.[36]

Another peculiarity of the normative Soviet view of childhood was that it was studied through the educational practices, games, and children's literature that were found, for the most part, in urban settings.[37] Again, this is in line with studies of childhood as they were conducted around the world. Cultural geographers, however, could offer a view of rural childhood from a spatial perspective, by way of comparative studies, and often through the eyes of the villagers themselves.[38] As a result, they were able not only to identify specific "rural practices," which were found all over the world, from Australia to Canada, but also the modern discourse that had formed around childhood and rurality. Thus, in a review prepared by a group of Australian childhood researchers, it was noted that the approaches used to study childhood in countries with developed economies differed from those used in countries with agrarian societies.[39] Projects studying geography and oral history have likewise demonstrated how space affects memory and people's construction of the past

Figure 2.1. A group of children from the village of Kabachino during a village holiday, Kabachino, Killovsky District, ca. 1953. Yuri V. is in the middle of the group, holding an accordion. Zinaida S. is to Yuri's left. Alexandr B. is on the far right.

Source: Photo from the family archive of Yuri V.

no less than education level or political views.[40] Moreover, how people talk about their past depends on which space (urban or rural) they associate themselves with, and which of them defines their modern identity.

Researchers of rural childhood have drawn attention to the fact that child labour is interpreted differently in modern and traditional cultures.[41] Most of the world's countries practise some form of agrarian economy, and child labour is understood in these places as common and necessary for the continued existence of rural life. Anthropologists have emphasized the ways in which child labour includes elements of play and allows children to create a sense of usefulness within the family, thereby affecting their status within the community. In the discourses of modern societies, however, child labour is not only condemned but punishable by law. International UN conventions ban the use of child labour.

In Soviet culture, views on child labour were, for a long time, ambivalent. On the one hand, Soviet ideologues condemned it, seeing it as the continuation of class exploitation. A ban on hard labour for Soviet children was thus considered a victory for socialism and was legally codified in certain labour documents. As Nadezhda Krupskaya explained, "Labour law has set clear limits: children younger than fourteen should not work for pay … children younger than sixteen should not work for more than four hours."[42] But on the other hand, these limits were primarily intended for children working in industrial production. Kolkhoz children, by contrast, took part in mandatory work from the age of twelve.[43] In addition, Soviet society fostered a cult of constructive labour in the name of socialism that called on Soviet children to take part in adult work. Makarenko's labour communes and the polytechnical school program introduced by Khrushchev testify to the fact that the government was in no rush to eliminate child labour.[44] Nonetheless, the fine line drawn by Soviet labour law was clear in establishing that child labour must not harm children or prevent them from studying.

A coloured insert in the fourth-grade textbook *Native Speech* displays two images by the artist V.S. Bayuskina, *Childhood Then* and *Childhood Now*.[45] The first depicts the exploitation of children for heavy labour in rural localities, while the second extols the virtues of a carefree and happy childhood. Healthy, well-dressed preschool- and kindergarten-aged children walk through a sunny garden accompanied by a nurse in a white hospital gown. Judging by the illustration, modern, urban childhood is associated with health and hygiene, while rural "pre-modern" childhood is characterized by poor sanitation and excessively heavy labour. It is also crucial to note that the introduction of general compulsory schooling in the countryside at the end of the 1950s was presented as an attempt to liberate rural children from peasant labour by giving them the opportunity to study.

Thus, by the 1960s child labour had come to be viewed within Soviet educational discourse not so much as an obligation but as a way of developing and working on oneself. As such it could be brought into alignment with the most important task of Soviet schoolchildren, studying and gaining knowledge.

In this contradictory context, memories of childhood labour in kolkhoz-worker households became complicated and emotionally charged for former rural schoolchildren. On the one hand, they did not see anything terribly wrong with the fact that they were required to help their families in a domestic setting; they understood such work was connected with family and peasant traditions. On the other hand, they expressed that this labour was often excessive and even traumatic.

Alexandr K. remembers the work he did in his childhood in the following way: "At home we had this sort of system: All the children had their own duties. Everyone knew that our father was not going to say things twice. If he said something, it had to be done. And there couldn't be any questions. Everyone, everyone knew. After school you would come home. One would do one thing, another something else, and a third person some third thing. I'm talking about a full yard of cattle, full of everything, rabbits, sheep, cows, calves. We had to give them all water, and everything was done by hand."[46]

For Alexandr, this domestic way of life seemed natural, just like the unquestioning authority of his father. He believed, moreover, that the physical demands required by the work the children performed ultimately proved beneficial for their health. He attributed his athletic successes as an adult to the work he did as a child. He said, "working in the fields from seven years old with that sort of handheld sickle – that is difficult, but it's all training for your core. For that reason, I stayed in shape. And I've maintained the same wight since childhood – seventy kilograms. Absolutely."[47] It is notable that Alexander K. used a modern discourse about the usefulness of physical exercise to justify the work he did in childhood.

Another interviewee justified child labour with a different type of argument based on work ethic as it was understood in the countryside. He emphasized that a good worker in the countryside was an authority figure, and that respect for one's hard work could be earned by a child. Thus, Yuri V. remembers that learning to mow with a sickle at a young age drew the attention of his neighbours and became a source of pride for him and his family: "So out we went to mow the lowland. And Aleksei was on his way from Mys for Ivitsy. He caught sight of me and said, 'Oh!' – we were with our father – 'And who is that with you?' 'Ah, it's that one … Oohy! What a helper you've got! He mows like a *muzhik*!'"[48]

A positive interpretation of childhood work is characteristic of rural social memory, but, at the same time, it clearly contradicts the judgmental, modern view of child labour as exploitation. My interviewees could describe the work as excessive, overly demanding, and even traumatic. For some of those I talked to, childhood labour was the defining characteristic of their rural childhood. As Yuri recalled, "in winter I had to work around the house, bringing in the firewood, the water, filling the oil lamps, cleaning the glass on the lamps … And when my mom had to go to the cowshed, I had to help clean it […] It would take about six buckets, and sometimes even more. Only it was difficult to carry them all the way, as they held seven litres; but somehow, we would get it done. Sometimes with mom. I remember once I asked her, 'And you can carry these, when they're so heavy?' It took everything I had to carry them, and I filled them up as much as I could so that I didn't have to run around as much. And she said, 'Of course, they're heavy.' But I understood that they weren't as heavy for her as for me. So that's how it was."[49]

It is clear from this recollection that Yuri understood that the demands placed on children could be excessive, even if they were often "natural" in a peasant context. There were various strategies for reconciling conceptions about the normality of work, characteristic of real social memory, with personal impressions of the excessiveness of the work. For example, an excessive work burden could be explained by extraordinary family circumstances and therefore viewed as an anomaly.

One of the women who refused to be interviewed explained that she did not want to return to painful childhood memories. She clarified that, for rural children, "there was no childhood, just work." She went on to explain that the reason for her refusal was the fact that her father had died young and her mother had been seriously ill. This meant that, along with typical domestic duties, the children had to engage in adult work as well. They even had to work in place of their mother on the kolkhoz under the *trudoden* system. In this woman's case, her mother's illness and her father's death exacerbated the already difficult position of rural children, a situation she experienced as traumatic. Somewhat similarly, Yuri explained the demands placed upon him as a child by the fact that he was an only child in a family where the father was a disabled veteran and unable to work on the kolkhoz. He said, "If the family had been a bit bigger, then the burden would have been more even."[50]

My interviewee Alexandr K. utilized modern discursive constructions when he compared his own childhood experience with that of his grandson, who was born and raised in a city. Alexandr told me, "They put a rake in my hands, I remember, when I was just five years old. I remember it very well. My mom taught me to rake, how to move around the hay correctly, and of course I held it wrong right from the start – I was a five-year-old kid. Now, Tyoma just runs around. He's already six. What would be the point of a rake?"[51]

With his rhetorical question, Alexandr was emphasizing the incongruous nature of a situation in which a six-year-old child is viewed as a serious helper on a farm. He compared himself and his grandchild to show how attitudes towards child labour had changed. In the first case, he recognized the necessity of his own childhood labour, but in the case of his grandson, he underscored that such labour would be out of place. It is worth noting that Alexandr's earlier statement justifying child labour as a physically strengthening experience that creates athletic people does not, in his mind, apply to his city-born grandson. In other words,

Alexandr simultaneously utilizes two logical frameworks. In the first, he uses the logic of a former peasant: He justifies labour, takes pride in it, and considers it useful. The second, that of an urban grandfather, allows him to criticize the same child labour, to consider it mostly useless, and to want something different for his grandson, even if work would potentially make him physically stronger.

In the case of child labour, the conflict between two different interpretations is clear. One of them accepts the "normalization" of child labour. According to this "rural" logic, people continue to hold on to the social norms of rural memory, what Aleida Assmann calls social class memory.[52] The other logical framework, by contrast, calls for judgment, and refers to modern, "urban" conceptions of child labour. In their statements, my subjects would use first one interpretation and then the other, depending upon which culture – urban or rural – they were associating themselves in a given moment.

The Rural Pastoral and Vologda Spaces

The aestheticization of nature and rural landscapes, as well as the recognition that living in a rural locality is healthy, are characteristic of a contrast between modern discourses on village life and the views of rural people themselves.[53] This is all the more true when speaking about rural childhood.[54] The European canon of Romanticism, formed at the beginning of the nineteenth century, set the tone for discourses about modernity.[55] Poets and writers idealized childhood spent in the arms of mother nature, where children learned by communicating with animals, could independently observe the changing of the seasons, and were protected from the "unhealthy" influence of urban culture. At the same time, it was precisely urban culture, industry, and production that were driving conceptions of modernity and progress.[56] Modern civilization saw nature as its property, tamed it, and used it to its own ends. The Marxist view of progress epitomized this approach.[57]

Soviet culture, as a result, was unprepared to address the question of how people should relate to nature.[58] On the one hand, socialist realism, dominant in the culture of the USSR in the 1930s, pitted man against nature, seeing nature as the "elemental beginning" that had to be tamed.[59] Nature was described as a force that could damage machinery, stop a workers' dormitory from being built, spoil harvests, or simply take a person's life. Seen through this framework, nature was something to be subdued.

On the other hand, the aesthetic education of rural schoolchildren was founded on the works of Russian and Soviet writers who described the beauty of unspoiled nature. These works were included in school literature curriculums and, it would seem, posed a challenge to the socialist imperative to tame nature.[60] Loving nature meant loving one's native land. "The birch or the rowan, the willows over the stream – familiar lands forever loved, you won't find them in a dream," goes one popular song written in 1955, expressing love and delight in place of a desire to overcome one's natural surroundings.

And yet, even many socialist realist novels contained descriptions of rural places that romanticized nature, and they could be unsparing in their descriptions of ample rivers, lakes, steppes, and fields. They used these descriptions to communicate the spiritual states of their characters and to help create a more realistic literature. The authors most dedicated to communicating a love of the nature of the region where one grew up, and of agricultural labour more generally, were the "village prose" writers.[61] They depicted pre-modern village life as a kingdom in which harmonious relations between man and nature reigned while describing contemporary villages of the 1970s with displeasure and bitterness. However, like the authors of other texts belonging to "high culture," they were more dependent on the discourses of modernization than were even the authors of industrial novels, in which a rational orientation towards nature aligns with peasant practicality. For the village prose writers, the abandoned Russian countryside was a lost paradise characterized by the peaceful coexistence of man and nature. Overgrown fields stirred more sympathy in them than rapidly changing rural localities, which were dealing with migrants, new technologies, and a lost past.

In 1960s and '70s, the "high culture" discourse of writers and political actors presumed that nature was not simply to be used but to be loved as well. In the text of a speech made by Stavropol Krai Komsomol Committee Secretary Vasiliy Kurilov and published in the magazine *Rural Youth* (*Sel'skaya molodezh'*) in 1972, this idea was made quite clear. In it he wrote, "speaking of the countryside, we often forget about the natural heritage that villages possess. Rivers, forest, steppes, lakes – in short, untrammelled nature – those bountiful surroundings have a colossal emotional factor. Preserving this, having a sense of responsibility for the beauty of a region, these qualities don't come about by themselves. They must be developed among young people. Doing so in the countryside is much easier."[62] In other words, the love of nature was not something inherent to people living in rural places. It had to be cultivated and encouraged, and was understood as part of a modern, urban, ecological discourse.

As a result, Soviet culture was shaped by two modern conceptions of nature: one that viewed nature as something that must be tamed, and another that conceived of it as a healthy influence for people developing aesthetic sensibilities. These ideas served as the basis for building the Pioneer camps where children were sent to the countryside on summer holidays and motivated city dwellers to purchase or build a dacha or otherwise spend their summers outside of the city.

In the social memory of the Russian countryside, nature played a completely different role. In the villages, nature was seen as the world in which man lives, one capable of feeding him or leaving him hungry, of curing sicknesses as well as inflicting damage.[63] Nature was something that demanded respect and required the observance of certain rules, but it was not something that inspired love or necessitated the expression of emotions.

In the interviews I collected, when people described their childhood or adolescence in the countryside they almost never talked about the beauty of the natural world. They valued physical places for different reasons. Tatiana K., for example,, describes her family moving in the following way: "The village was Nilovitsy. I don't remember it, how we left, because I was only three years old. I don't remember at all; I can't even picture it. But mom says that the village was good, big, that there were a lot of berries there, mushrooms […] She said, 'I didn't want to leave, but we had to because it flooded.'"[64] It is clear from Tatiana's story, based on her mother's memories, that the village was valued for its size and its access to resources – mushrooms and berries – and not, for example, for its view of the river or the lake, important criteria for a city dweller choosing a site to build a dacha.

Conceptions of rural space were constructed in a similar manner. What a city dweller might romanticize as "boundless space" for a rural resident often meant days of hard travel. As Yuri recalls, "it would happen that when you'd leave in the evening – we would be in the club – it was light out, warm, music would be playing, and you walk out and take a look at Ivitsy, at Kabachino. Dear mother above! And it was already evening, and the path had been washed out, and you had to get home alone. And you'd think, 'Well, that's it, I'm not coming back here again.' A week would pass, and you'd be out there again."[65]

In an interview with Tatiana, we discussed the difficulty of crossing the river: "Once, it's true … There was such a strong wind, and the boat wouldn't move, but we wanted to get home. And they said to us, 'Today the boat's not going to move,' because there was some type of storm or something. All of the children 'from beyond the river' – that's what they called us, 'beyond the river' children – they called us all into the dormitory. But we wanted to get home. So, we say to this Misha Zhizha, 'Uncle Misha, take us home!' He says, 'Kids, in this soup, it's not possible to sail, look at those waves!' And we say, 'Come on Uncle Misha! Come on let's go! We want to go home!' And we are all wailing. He goes, 'All right, let's go.' We sat down, I don't remember how many of us. A wave crashes and half the boat fills with water. And we used what we had – some sort of pull buoys, people had what they had – we were sitting just like this in the water. And we still had to get home, no matter."[66]

Conceptualizing (Non-)Modernity

The modernization of rural life in late socialism played a crucial role in the biographies of rural residents. When passports were issued to kolkhoz workers at the end of the 1960s and the early 1970s, followed shortly thereafter by the passportization of the entire rural population in the mid-1970s, it marked the end of an era of class predetermination and removed the barriers limiting where residents of Vologda Oblast's rural territories could live.[67] As a result, like most of the oblast's rural population, my interviewees chose to move out of the countryside, changing the social trajectory to which they had been assigned in keeping with their class and origin. In this sense, they were undoubtedly "modern subjects."

However, modernity is not only an "outer" but also an "inner" phenomenon. Whether a person believes him- or herself to be modern often proves crucial in determining a large array of that person's decisions. As such, the concept of "socially imagined modernity," introduced by Charles Taylor, is an important addition to our understanding of the modern person.[68]

During late socialism, the urban seemed far more modern than the rural, and this conception has remained strong up to the time I conducted these interviews. The capacious word *derevenshchina* (akin to "hick," and used as a derogatory term for someone living in a rural area, presumed to be rude and uncultured) had become a set feature of the language by the 1960s and '70s and reflected a social hierarchy in which Moscow and large industrial centres were considered crowning achievements surrounded by "unpromising villages." At that time, the more urbanized a place was, the more prestigious it was considered.

From the point of view of the village world, however, geographical origin did not play this cardinal role, although cities, as administrative, trade, and cultural centres, were traditionally considered to be important places because they contained markets, stores, administrative buildings and courts, and because they served as the seats of political power. There was no established hierarchical order in accordance with which one village was considered superior to another. When villages were split between promising (*perspectivnye*) and unpromising (*neperspektivnye*) during the years of "Khrushchev optimization," this did not result in a shift of opinion among the local population as to the relative prestige of a given village. They collectively viewed themselves as villagers, and, among those with a shared rural background, they were unashamed of their origin.

The idea of "non-modernity" arrived only when rural people collided with urban Soviet culture – in the form, say, of urbanite relatives who drove out to the countryside during summer vacation, or neighbours who brought with them not only food products inaccessible at the local village store but also the conviction that life in the cities was richer, more interesting, and fuller than village life, and that city dwellers, with whom they now self-identified, were more modern.

Rural children found themselves inside the Soviet educational hierarchy, where their abilities were considered lower than those of children from cities.[69] However, examples of discriminatory practices in school were by no means universally reported by my interviewees, and for various reasons. In some Vologda Oblast districts – as was the case in Kirillovsky District, for example – the social make-up of the population was more or less homogenous. The sense of differentiation between "cultural workers" and labourers was insignificant. The district was comprised of sovkhozes and timber production enterprises called *lespromkhozes*.[70] As a result, most schoolchildren came from families with very similar social backgrounds. Similarly, the schoolchildren at Goritsy Secondary School who continued to live at home (the *slobodskie* and *internatovskie* students) were not perceived as being starkly different than the children who lived "beyond the river," and who at times had to sleep in the dormitories. Although a former teacher at the school spoke about discriminatory practices against the students from "beyond the river," these students themselves never mentioned it, evidently because they did not experience it in a traumatic way. By contrast, social inequality was acutely felt and quite visible at the Molochnoe settlement near Vologda. Multiple interviewees mentioned that they had been objects of ridicule for the teachers and children who lived at the settlement.[71] They were laughed at for arriving late or missing class, often on account of poor road conditions, for the smell of their clothes, for their limited wardrobe, and because they had to wear rubber boots in order to navigate the muddy terrain. And although settlement and village children shared many of the same interests, the children who had to walk to school from outlying villages experienced acute vulnerability and incompatibility with their peers who lived in more developed settlements and had a more urbanized way of life.

A sense of inadequacy surrounding one's peasant origin and location in a rural locality could be caused by other factors too. Only someone who had come to understand the social hierarchy would be able to recognize the discrimination. Yuri V., for example, understood "rurality" as something retrograde and associated it with a lack of technological progress in the countryside. He remembers it in the following way: "I was born in the countryside – so, of course, I was already doomed to it. To the village – doomed. An example is right next to us. The horses, the cows, the domestic animals. [...] Probably, only at the age of fifteen, had something come into my head, the thought that in winter it was possible to drive cars. We only had tractors and the horses. And until that point I had just lived like that comfortably. But that was a discovery for me: Wait a minute, it would be possible by car. And that, I think, happened when I was already in the eighth grade, maybe even starting ninth grade. Something like that."[72] At another point during our interview, he explained to me how strange school singing lessons had seemed to him as a village child. In the village, people sang during processional holidays and on special occasions, so the idea that teachers were needed to instruct singing in a class setting seemed absurd. Luda M. interpreted urban cultural practices in a similar way. As a student at a rural school in the early 1960s she heard applause for the first time. When the audience began to clap after a student performance in the city of Belozersk, Luda felt so bewildered and scared that she hid in a wardrobe, mistaking the applause for a sign that the audience was displeased with the performance.[73] In yet another example, Yuri gave a no less colourful description of the enthusiasm among rural boys who learned that the technical school at Cherepovets was offering a plumbing specialization. The students at Goritsy school, who had no idea what being a plumber entailed, and who were at any rate completely unfamiliar with sewage and piping, believed that plumbing was a prestigious and modern profession: "Well now, this was all in eighth grade. And when eighth class ended, there were all these signs, well ... slogans. And we had all these kids running around, 'We're going to become plumbers – wow! Crazy salaries, dang, we'll have a uniform!' [*laughs*]. Plumbers."[74]

Discussing these situations, Yuri seems to be viewing himself through different lenses: He juxtaposes himself as a rural person (a schoolchild who delights at the prospect of becoming a plumber, is surprised by the possibility of driving a car in the winter, and is unwilling to sing in class) with himself as a city dweller, made wiser through the experience of life in an urban setting. The village teenager in Yuri's story appears laughable, simple, naive, and unmodern. The humour characteristic of his storytelling is evidence of the gulf separating him from his rural past, a past that he now views from the reflective standpoint of a city dweller.

Sergei, born in the village of Kryazhevo, in Ust-Kubensky District, remembered his rural past in terms of the schooling he received. Discussing schooling practices that were common at that time, Sergei noted that the director of the rural secondary school he attended employed corporal punishment. Notably, Sergei did not interpret this as strange. He told me the following: "This director, she was strict. She would call you up on the red rug. Right up to her. She was the sort ... Nowadays, you don't lay a hand on children. And she would buffet your ears and give you one right to the back of the neck. In her office there [...] For example, in seventh class we had to go for flax and carry the turnips, and the cows ... and we would [sneak] home, and then they would check. And the classroom teacher would go, 'So and so is not here.' And right down the list ... So, the curriculum director and school director would call you to their office, and you'd get a good crack [*laughs*]! Yes, she'd just wham you, she was that kind of director [...] Everyone was scared of her even. The whole school. She was strict. And she kept things in good order. No one smoked, no one drank, nothing. If you tried – oof! As soon as someone goes into the toilet, catches a whiff, even if it was a young man, straight to the director, and she, well ... [*laughs*] [...] Not like it is now, when they go straight to mom and dad to complain. They will even go to the police now. They didn't used to do that."[75]

Judging by the interview and the intonations Sergei used while telling his story, he did not consider the director's methods excessive or inappropriate in a pedagogical setting, nor did he criticize them. Moreover, he shared the director's first and last name with me, without worrying that this information could damage her reputation. Quite the opposite, in fact – he expressed his admiration for her organizational abilities. In some ways, the figure of the director in Sergei's narration has a lot in common with the parental figure within a traditional village power hierarchy. The two instances when Sergei made comparisons between the past and the present, he drew attention first to violence towards children (it used to be possible, now it is not) and then to the practice of filing complaints against children to the police (it used to be impossible, now it is possible). But Sergei is not quick to state his own opinion on the issue, as if he is weighing competing interpretations over the course of the conversation. From the standpoint of rural logic, which prizes order and discipline, the director's behaviour appears justified. However, physical punishment runs completely contrary to modern views on child rearing, and therefore it cannot be interpreted in a purely positive light. Sergei, seeing these discursive incompatibilities, decides against stating a clear conclusion and instead draws attention to the "gaps" in his interpretation of the situation so that the listener can make his or her own evaluation.

A final mode of storytelling about "rurality," apart from comparisons between the city and the countryside, came up in my interview with Vlad, who told me about village witchcraft. For Vlad, the presence of an otherworldly aspect in human life is natural and justified.[76] Remembering his childhood and adolescence in the countryside, he told me about a blacksmith who wielded power over the other local blacksmiths, as well as about witches who could help villagers find lost animals in the woods or cause crops to spoil when promises were broken. The stories Vlad told, citing himself as a witness, to illustrate the existence of conspiratorial witchcraft not only serve to support his argument, but also reveal his connection with village life. Maintaining village traditions by observing rituals (such as saying a curse upon seeing a witch) is natural for Vlad according to the rural framework that still defines his world view despite his having moved to the city.

In this chapter I tried to look at how cultural geography, and more specifically a person's sense of belonging to either a rural or an urban locality and class, influenced their evaluations and interpretations of their village past. When telling stories about their childhood, schooling, or everyday life, people communicated ideas that were, in large part, contingent either upon the environment in which they were socialized (the countryside) or upon the one in which they currently resided (a city or an urban-type settlement). As people who had grown up in the Vologda countryside, and who had accepted their "rurality" as a given in childhood, their judgments were foundationally influenced by the experience of adhering to contradictory discursive frameworks. Their stories were not only comprised of various memories, such as walking great distances to reach school or not having the time to complete their homework, but they also embodied various interpretive methods. This allowed them, in spite of modern beliefs, to see the labour they performed as children, and the position they occupied within their families, as something more than parental exploitation. Evaluations of child labour, nature, and modernity, as they are articulated within modern urban discourses, differ from the categorical understandings of rural residents. For people who lived in cities, and whose conceptions of rural places were formed in relation to their orientation towards progress, the village is associated with relaxation, nature, beautiful landscapes, and a backward way of life. For those who lived in rural localities, and who understood rural life through their personal experience of belonging to the rural world, "rurality" was conceptualized in completely different terms. People who grew up in the countryside associated "rurality" with child labour and domestic farms. Their relationship with the local environment was shaped by the necessity of harmonious coexistence with the natural world. Encountering discriminatory practices in school and feeling themselves to be "unmodern" in comparison with their urban peers was the result of a clash with Soviet modernity, where the city was considered highly valuable axiomatically.

When people moved into cities or urban-type settlements they gained a new identity and became city dwellers. They borrowed the values of urban modernity, with its cultural and consumerist practices and its educational and professional formations. However, people retained their sense of belonging to the rural world, and this allowed them to soften the consequences of the changes taking place around them. They perceived the "otherness" of the rural world and constructed it using a logical framework not totally identical with an urban framework.

Nevertheless, although people shared a common experience of life in the countryside, each individual evaluated it differently. Although a rural background likely created some preconceptions, it was no guarantee that, as adults, people would continue to describe their childhood and judge it from the position of a rural resident relying on the values of the peasant world. It is more accurate to say that these adults perceived the gaps and contradictions in their interpretations. They carried within themselves the intricacies of Soviet cultural geography.

PART TWO

Rural Schools

Chapter Three

The Colonization of Rural Knowledge Begins

Writing on the connection between power and knowledge in schooling, Michel Foucault asserted that "the entire system of education, which, at first glance appears to be created to disseminate knowledge ... is in fact created in order to preserve the power of a specific social class and exclude the instruments of power of any other social class."[1] In Foucault's view, although educational methods can vary significantly from country to country and from epoch to epoch, the fundamental purpose of schooling, to reproduce dominant knowledge, remains constant. Thus, schooling is always intimately connected with mechanisms for reproducing power and facilitates the domination of one type of knowledge over another.

Foucault's observation is as applicable to the Vologda countryside as it is to any other region in the world.[2] The Soviet school system was typical insofar as it inculcated people in ways that were beneficial to the state and justified its existence. Let us attempt, however, to ascertain precisely what type of knowledge was propagated in rural schools and whose interests it served.

In the view of Pierre Bourdieu and representatives of the "new sociological education" of the 1970s, the school systems of European countries and the United States functioned as a means of elite domination and legitimization, and concomitantly as an instrument of "symbolic violence against the working class."[3] In the USSR, the Soviet elite, as proclaimed representatives of working-class interests, functioned as a source of symbolic violence against other classes and groups. However, whereas Soviet cities could rely on a school system that was more or less established by the early twentieth century, the influence of educational institutions in rural localities was significantly weaker until the school reforms of the late 1950s and early 1960s, if only because schools in Vologda villages were primarily four-year primary schools, and attendance, despite the official implementation of general compulsory education, was non-mandatory.

Hardly all researchers, however, see rural school systems as a conduit of central power. It was not uncommon in certain jurisdictions for rural schools to advocate for the interests of local opposition groups in conflicts with the state. This was the case, for example, with schools in the Canadian province of Quebec between the 1930s and 1950s, when they refused to change the language of instruction from French to English and resisted the state's reform initiatives.[4] Nevertheless, these protests could not prevent communities from being pulled into global transformations. The unification of education and the implementation of stricter educational standards accompanied the nullification of the unique features of rural schools. Thus, problems presented by rural schools follow recognizable patterns on a global scale regardless of the specific rural region in which they are located.[5]

This chapter analyses Vologda Oblast's rural schools from multiple viewpoints. To begin, I analyse them as an important element of educational infrastructure with characteristic material features such as academic buildings, sports halls, and dormitories for pupils and teachers. The physical distribution of schools across the uneven and sparsely populated territory of Vologda Oblast created numerous problems, unconnected with the state's modernizing initiative. Additionally, I analyse the school system as a means of propagandizing a specific politics of education and social knowledge fundamentally different from the types of knowledge previously accepted by local communities in Vologda Oblast. Lastly, I consider the school system as an institution reproducing the class and social structures of Soviet society.

Rural Schools in the Soviet Education System

Researchers have long been interested in how educational programs and school systems provide insight into the histories of various national governments, shedding light on their political structures, their relationship to historical memory, and their impact on culture in general.[6] Soviet schooling was not unique in this respect and has been studied both within the USSR and beyond its borders for its role in the Soviet system and the means by which it reproduced its values.[7] Although the manner in which Soviet schooling was assessed by its proponents and detractors were diametrically opposed, especially during the Cold War years, both sides were united in focusing on its commitment to political ideology. The most recent studies have rejected this approach.[8] However, whereas sociologists studying education in Europe and the United States began in the 1960s to demonstrate the interdependence of school education and social and class structures, the Soviet academic tradition, while formally relying on Marxist conceptions of class, treated Soviet schools as "class-less," and thus neglected to analyse them as an institution for reproducing social inequality.[9] In my research, I show that rural geography and the predetermined class position of rural schoolchildren endowed rural schools with very unique features. As a result, geographical inequality intensified class inequality, which, in turn, influenced the status and life trajectories of rural youths.[10]

A nudge towards the development of a modern discussion of Soviet schools during late socialism was provided by Catriona Kelly's article "The School Waltz: Everyday Life in a Soviet School in the Post-Stalin Era."[11] Based on biographical interviews with former Soviet schoolchildren, Kelly offers a "collective portrait" of late-Soviet schools from the 1950s to the 1980s. Her primary focus were the rituals and practices comprising a "shared place" in the memories of those who had lived in the USSR during the post-war era. Kelly's conclusions cast doubt upon the effectiveness of indoctrination practices in Soviet schools, although she notes that these practices were ubiquitous, from the ways in which lessons were conducted to the relationships between students and teachers. In contrast, she argues that "many of the underpinnings of Soviet schooling are more closely concerned with the 'schooling' aspect than the 'Soviet' aspect."[12] The article begins by illustrating that Soviet schools, like other schools around the world, were institutions meant to educate the population and foster cultural values.[13] Although the state monopoly on education and the highly politicized nature of Soviet schools differentiated them from their analogues in other countries, a closer look reveals that these differences were not as great as has been assumed.[14]

Moreover, micro-histories of Soviet schools have shown that, despite the general conceptual framework of school education in the USSR, some schools differed from one another not only in terms of the quality of the teaching, the specialization, and the location, but also in terms of the atmosphere predominating in the classrooms.[15] In this sense, the metaphor of an island, which Pyotr Safronov, Maria Maiofis, and Ilya Kuklin used to describe the multiplicity and individuality of Soviet schools, is, in my view, very fitting.[16]

Prompted by Kelly's article, other scholars began to treat Soviet education as a topic whose implications reached beyond the USSR's political system.[17] Some authors drew attention to the continuities between Soviet schooling institutions and pre-revolutionary traditions and emphasized the important role Soviet schools played in processes of Soviet modernization. At the same time, they demonstrated that the opinions of former schoolchildren about the post-war Soviet educational system were based, as a rule, on urban compulsory schools with full-time attendance. This

Figure 3.1. Group of schoolchildren and teachers from Goritsy Eight-Year School on a field trip to Kirillo-Belozersky Monastery, located in Kirillov, Vologda Oblast, 1960. The banner's slogan reads, "Hello Tourists!" Yuri V. is in the centre of the top row, and Zinaida S. is to Youri's right.

Source: Photo from the family archive of Yuri V.

left the work of rural school institutions out of the picture, even though rural schools comprised an absolute majority of schools during that time. In Vologda Oblast, the number of urban schoolchildren caught up with the number of rural schoolchildren only in 1974, and even then, rural elementary schools remained the most common type of school institution.[18] Seen in this light, it turns out that what has traditionally been assumed among researchers to be the "typical" school experience was not so typical after all.

Another important question about Soviet schooling concerns whether and to what extent the system established during late socialism in the USSR addressed the social needs of Soviet society and opened opportunities for Soviet citizens.[19] In the early post-revolutionary years, providing equal opportunity meant limiting access to education for those considered part of the disenfranchised *lishenets* class (noblemen, the clergy, and the bourgeoisie) and the stimulation of education among those coming from the poorest classes (peasants and workers).[20] By contrast, in the post-war period inequality began to be associated with the places in which people lived and their access to education, rather than with their class origin or loyalty to the government. Thus, by the 1960s and '70s, universities would not admit those who lacked a school attestation. School program unification and the standardization of grading practices was understood during this period as a means of liquidating inequality.[21] This did not prevent the creation of urban schools with different types of programs. Their existence was not viewed as a threat to the egalitarian principle of Soviet schooling, even though it was no secret that the students of many of these schools were the children of the most privileged groups within Soviet society.

Khrushchev thought that unequal educational opportunities were produced not by barriers connected with the social origin of schoolchildren but by an insufficient number of schools and educational institutions in the countryside. To create a society of equal opportunity, he believed, it would be sufficient to expand the program of accessible education to those who were without it – namely, residents of the Soviet periphery and rural localities. In his view, all that was needed to ensure educational equality was to replace ungraded rural schools with "urban-type" schools that had a full educational curriculum encompassing an eight-year school program followed by secondary school up to the tenth grade. This logic formed the basis for school reforms and was reflected in school report documentation. Information about student academic performance started to be recorded in reports compiled by regional committees of public education in 1967, but a distinction between urban and rural schools was made starting only in 1973.[22] Before this time, descriptions of the education system in Vologda Oblast were made without taking into account school location, which allowed regional education commissions to report successes in the cities while ignoring problems in rural schools.[23]

Rather than promoting equal opportunity, the unwillingness to see disparities between urban and rural schooling served to exacerbate inequality. As the American sociologists Theodore Gerber and Michael Hout asserted after analysing Soviet census data, relatively equal access to education for young boys and girls was reached in late-socialist society at the same time that social inequality grew.[24] Even as the number of eight-year schools, secondary schools, and institutions of higher education grew in the 1960s and '70s, the "corridors of opportunity" presented after each consecutive level remained narrow, and the privileged layers of Soviet society grew larger and larger.[25] As a result, the social background of people in the USSR affected their careers and educational opportunities no less than was the case in countries of the "capitalist West."[26]

Soviet leadership's aspiration to provide the population of the USSR with equal access to education in the 1960s and '70s was accompanied by a number of measures aimed at improving the quality of teaching in rural schools and increasing the level of material support they received. In order to create modern schools in rural localities, an entire series of directives was issued from above. Thus, on 4 May 1971, a directive was issued by the Council of Ministers of the Soviet Union entitled "On Some Measures for Fortifying the Academic-Material Support for General Compulsory Schools in Rural Localities." This entailed an expansion of the boarding school system, improvements in the organization of transportation to school, enhanced school financing, and "the rational distribution of general compulsory schools." Rural schools began to be equipped with personnel and equipment according to the same criteria applied to urban schools, meaning the level of support depended on the size of the school and the extent to which it filled its classes. The more students in a class, the better it would be supplied with textbooks and equipment, and the better the work and life conditions of the teachers. In well-equipped schools there was enough work for physical education teachers, professional skills teachers, and other teachers outside of the primary subjects (mathematics, Russian language, and literature). In the countryside, however, where the population was constantly shrinking due to migration, schools often experienced a deficit of students. In 1973, the all-union directive was supplemented by another on 27 August from the Council of Ministers of the Soviet Union, as well a 23 September 23 directive from the Vologda Oblast CPSU Committee, "On Measures for the Further Improvement of Working Conditions in the Oblast's Rural Schools." The oblast-level directives, reiterating the aims of their all-union counterparts, called for an increase in schools' student capacities, in the number of boarding schools, and in the number of apartments for teachers; they strove to improve working conditions for rural teachers by restructuring the system of payment; and they introduced a management system for rural schools that cooperated with the labour collectives of local enterprises and urban Komsomol organizations.[27] The "Komsomol to the Rural School" campaign, announced at the Sixth Plenum of the VLKSM Central Committee in 1968, provided an opportunity to actualize the management system.[28] In other words, it attempted to draw local communities into the project of creating urban-like conditions for rural schools.

However, the Ministry of Education often viewed increasing oblast- and republic-level investments in rural schools as a senseless waste of funds because the number of schoolchildren in the country's rural oblasts was continually shrinking, which affected both student numbers and the distribution of teaching personnel. As Shutov, the director of the Vologda Oblast Committee of Public Education – or Oblono, as these committees were called – wrote, "in 1973 as compared to 1970, the first- to tenth-grade student population in rural general compulsory schools decreased from 134,300 to 112,800."[29] Ultimately, by trying to rationalize expenditures and support only the most vital schools that could boast robust class sizes, smaller schools were disbanded, which intensified the already serious problem of youth migration from rural districts.

As a result, reform initiatives in rural schools in the 1970s, in addition to aiming to improve student knowledge, also became part of the politics of personnel retention in villages. It was with this goal that rural schools in Vologda Oblast saw the reintroduction of professional training: school production brigades were formed, school lessons become professionally oriented, kolkhoz chairmen and sovkhoz directors gave speeches to students about the benefits of agricultural professions and called on them to stay and work on the farms where they were raised. As Udalova stated capaciously at the Vologda Oblast CPSU Committee plenum in 1973, "Our task is [to ensure] that kolkhozes and sovkhozes should work in cooperation with schools to provide a material basis for the organization of professional education for students, to engage the students in publicly beneficial labour, so that they receive a secondary education and can be retained to work in the village."[30] The idea of "retaining rural youths in the village," recognized as the primary task of rural schools in the 1970s, fundamentally contradicted the ideal of educational equality declared in official Soviet documents. The choice of professions and range of educational institutions available to rural youths in the 1960s and '70s was much narrower than that of their urban peers. Their educational possibilities were supposed to be realized strictly within the bounds of rural localities. As a result, inequality based on students' social origin did not disappear; it was instead reinterpreted through the terminology of cultural geography. Discrimination based on social origin became discrimination based on place of residence.

Yet another aspect of educational inequality that the Soviet school system attempted to liquidate in rural localities was gender inequality. Analysing the school system as an institution reproducing societal conceptions of gender, the sociologist Zhanna Chernova divided it into various historical stages. In the first years of Soviet rule, "the problems of the gendered socialization of children and adolescents ... were on the periphery of the educational process," and "the dominant element in education was shifted from the problem of sex differences to the unification of ideological convictions."[31] In her view, among the basic principles of Soviet schooling at this time were ideological engagement (the push to create a "new person"), democracy (the rejection of class and gender as criteria for educational access), totality (i.e., general educational for all children), and gender neutrality (a fundamental rejection of gender-segregated education).[32] The principles established in these years set the course for the gender politics of Soviet schools in proceeding eras. Although the sociologists Yelena Zdravomyslova and Anna Temkina argued that gender policy in the USSR changed multiple times, becoming either more traditionalistic or more oriented towards the reconceptualization of traditional gender roles, these changes tended sidestep rural schools.[33] These schools reacted to a significantly more limited extent to transformations in this sphere. For example, rural schools were totally untouched by the implementation of separate education for young boys and girls in Soviet cities between the 1930s and 1950s. They likewise avoided numerous experiments during the Khrushchev era: the establishment of closed boarding-type schools and the creation of specialized schools with intensive subject-specific curricula.[34] In primarily rural Vologda Oblast, such schools appeared only in the region's largest cities and district centres. And although industrial education, which accounted for the gendered life trajectories of schoolchildren, was introduced to rural schools beginning in the 1960s (girls were prepared for "female professions" such as milker or seamstress in place of "male professions" such as tractor operator, lathe operator, or electrician), school curricula primarily comprised gender-neutral general compulsory subjects. The general subjects at these schools, from literature to mathematics, were considered important for both sexes. Only the "additional" trade lessons and physical education, which became mandatory for village residents at the end of the 1960s, became exceptions to this trend. Trade lessons required young girls to learn to cook and sew, while young boys were taught carpentry and metalworking. Overall, however, as Gerber and Hout have argued, Soviet secondary school represented a very successful model of gender equality in education. The numbers of boys and girls finishing school corresponded to the sex proportions of the population at large, and young women had no less access to primary, secondary, or higher education than did young men.[35]

However, the gendered ideal of the "working mother," which reached rural regions in the 1960s and '70s, rendered the position of rural women highly precarious, even compared to city residents.[36] As Liubov' Denisova wrote, rural women not only had to balance work on the sovkhoz with work on their private plots, but they also carried the burden of cooking and caring for their relatives and family members. In the conditions of an underdeveloped social infrastructure characterized by a dearth of kindergartens, stores, laundromats, workshops, and social services, rural women found themselves in a difficult position.[37] Thus, many girls and women viewed the opportunity to receive equal education in school as a means of reassessing their vulnerable position in rural communities and a necessary condition for achieving a fairer distribution of gendered labour.

"Gen-Comp": General Compulsory Schooling

It is for good reason that sociologists who study education consider the establishment of general public education one of the most important milestones in the development of various national education systems.[38] Public schooling grants equal educational opportunities to groups and classes that had previously lacked access to education, and for that reason it became a symbol of the fight for social equality. It is thus unsurprising that demands for general education formed an important pillar of the Bolsheviks' program of social transformation and subsequently became an emblem of socialism.

According to Soviet statistics, despite the implementation of the seven-year "gen-comp" (*vseobuch*) curriculum in 1930, levels of education among the rural population remained low until the 1960s. All-union census data from 1959 offers the following portrait of Vologda Oblast: Only 1.5 per cent of the population had received higher education; 9 per cent had a specialized secondary education, unfinished higher education, or had attended a technical or professional college; 23 per cent had either finished or attended part of a seven-year educational program; 20 per cent had only a primary education; 20 per cent had either attended some primary schooling or learned to read outside of school; and 8 per cent were illiterate (the remaining 20 per cent of those surveyed were younger than nine years of age, and thus too young to be included among the previous categories).[39] In other words, nearly half of the population of Vologda Oblast had less than a secondary-level education at the start of the 1960s. Education reforms implemented at the end of the 1950s were intended above all to change this. The country that had launched a satellite and the first astronaut into space and created the "Peaceful Atom" nuclear program was simply obliged to end illiteracy. General compulsory schooling, followed by "secondary schooling," thus became one of the most important innovations of the 1960s and '70s. Although the government encouraged adult education, its primary focus was educating the younger generation.[40] Polytechnical schooling with a partial ten-year general compulsory secondary school curriculum became the educational standard, including in rural localities.[41]

Theoretically, since 1930 all Soviet children had been required to attend school starting at the age of seven. In practice, however, the percentage of children attending school in rural areas in the north-western RSFSR, a region that had been economically ravaged by collectivization and war, remained low. Even in cities, where the prospects for education looked better, the problem of "gen-comp" was felt very sharply.[42] In the first half of the 1960s, "gen-comp" was associated with a push to sit all Soviet children behind a school desk. This was achieved for the most part in Vologda Oblast by the middle of the decade. As the Oblono director, Shutov, wrote in 1964, "gen-comp has become a purely pedagogical issue and demands that measures be taken to improve the quality of student learning and by doing so liquidate the problem of [students] repeating years."[43]

Apart from its educational mission, "gen-comp" had one more priority. With the help of school reforms, leadership attempted to halt the mass exodus of young people from villages into cities. As the head of the Vologda Oblast Executive Committee's Department of Labour Resources, Podlepenkin, wrote in 1966, "[we need to] direct the attention of leadership to creating conditions for keeping school graduates on kolkhozes so that the number of workers stabilizes, and the available supply of labour resources improves."[44] In general, Podlepenkin's fears were justified. Judging by statistics from 1967, the rural population in Vologda Oblast had dropped from 1.3 million in 1939 to 459,000 in 1959; in other words, only around 35 per cent of the population remained. This decrease was due in large part to the migration of young people.[45] Thus, young people in the countryside were tasked with going to school and finding work in rural areas rather than seeking happiness in the cities.

The school reforms began with the signing of Khrushchev's education law in 1958, but the system founded on these educational institutions continued to exist even after his resignation in 1964. Although the experiment of combining general education with industrial production was broadly recognized to have been unsuccessful, the USSR saw the rise of a hybrid system of institutions for "secondary-level education" combining professional training with general education.[46] The secondary level of education linked the primary or basic level (from first to eighth grade) with higher university education.[47] In 1970, a law was passed concerning general secondary education that extended schooling by two years for most schoolchildren. Graduates from eight-year schools were now required to complete another two years of study in "schools for rural youths" or "working youths," as well as in technical and professional colleges, while schoolchildren in general compulsory educational programs were sent to upper (ninth- and tenth-year) grades.[48] After 1970, the compulsory educational program in the USSR spanned ten years and was aimed at children from seven to seventeen years of age. Additionally, schools for working youths and those for rural youths supplemented eight-year schools.[49]

Although gen-comp was considered an important tool for liquidating the differences between the city and the countryside, the conditions in which the program was realized in rural and urban localities differed. The issue was not only that cities were better supplied with teachers, buildings, and necessary educational infrastructure; the population distribution in Vologda Oblast created serious problems as well. The small size and remote locations of villages, far both from other villages and from regional centres, made it impossible to reform the educational system without urbanizing and restructuring the lives of people in rural localities.

Optimizing the School System

The most painful process for rural communities was school system optimization: In place of rural elementary schools, which had direct analogues among nineteenth-century zemstvo schools and parochial schools, came secondary schools and eight-year schools with specialized classrooms, teachers for single subjects, and a standardized system of assessing student performance.

When gen-comp was first implemented in Vologda Oblast in the 1960s, most of the region's schools were rural ungraded schools intended for grades 1–4. An example of this type of school was the primary school in Ivitsy, part of the kolkhoz "Red Banner" in Kirillovsky District. The school had been founded in 1915, and by the 1950s it was run in a single-storey wooden building with a floor area of 160 square metres: two classrooms (42 and 32 square metres, respectively), a small cloakroom, a corridor, and a teacher's room.[50] In the 1950s, it served schoolchildren from eight local villages. On account of the sparse population distribution, the number of pupils in rural schools was limited not by classroom capacity but by the distance between schools and the places where children lived. Walking 3–5 kilometres to school was often manageable, but when distances exceeded 7–10 kilometres it became a serious problem. It was precisely the long distances between villages that accounted for the existence of multiple primary schools on the territory of the sovkhoz "Vorobyevsky" prior to the 1970s.

In the 1950–1 school year, 51 schoolchildren attended the Ivitsy Primary School. In 1951–2, there were only 34.[51] In 1965, the number had dropped to a mere 15 children.[52] At that time, the same number of students attended the other two primary schools in the Migachevo Selsoviet (Migachevo and Volkhovskaya). Until the introduction of electricity in the 1960s, Ivitsy Primary School had been illuminated by kerosine lamps. There were seven stoves for heating the school, which were the responsibility of the selsoviet, and wood was provided by the kolkhoz. Until 1950, the school had a small farm building, most likely for the teacher's family as the teacher would have been expected to live near the school. The school possessed a 200-square-metre section of land.[53] In the 1950s and '60s, Nina Ivanovna, the school's teacher and director, lived with her family in her parents' home in the neighbouring village of Kabachino. Judging by inventory documentation from 1955, the school's property was comprised of 21 desks, 5 boards, and a few stools and buckets. The school library had 101 books. In 1952, a wall clock appeared in the school.[54] In the beginning of the 1960s, the kolkhoz "Red Banner" constructed a new school building, but within ten years Ivitsy Primary School was closed on account of low student numbers. The handful of local children attending primary school were once again forced to go to school across the river, in the village of Goritsy, and overcome a distance of many kilometres each day.[55]

Ungraded primary schools were subordinate to district educational committees but were funded by kolkhozes and selsoviets. In the beginning of the 1960s, these schools formed a "cluster unit" around the eight-year schools and secondary schools, where upper-class teachers provided methodological help to teachers of primary grades. In the Vorobyevo region, the centre of the cluster structure was the Goritsy Eight-Year School.[56] In addition to lessons, which were run for pupils of two grades simultaneously (the second and fourth or the first and third), the primary school at Ivitsy had lunchtimes. Children in the 1960s brought food from home while a school worker prepared tea. As Tatiana K. remembers it, "We had a family living at the school. They guarded the school. There was Auntie Zoya [...] We had a long break between classes. She would boil potatoes with the skins on and set up the samovar. Someone would bring cabbage from home, someone else would bring what they had. And there was a big table. We would sit around that table. We'd be gobbling up those potatoes with cabbage and we were so content, so happy. And then we'd get to drink our fill of tea from the samovar. Someone would bring jam from home. Well, parents would bring all sorts of things from home, and then Auntie Zoya would cook for us."[57]

Despite their seemingly archaic form of organizing the learning process, ungraded primary schools remained the optimal educational institutions for rural localities. In the absence of thoroughfares and the means to drive children to school, ungraded primary schools allowed for children to be taught without their parents being forced to move and without disrupting the routines of rural life. It seems evident that this is the reason such schools continued to exist in some rural regions until the mid-1980s, despite the stated objective of the Ministry of Education to liquidate them.

In Vologda Oblast, the policy of liquidating ungraded rural schools coincided with the policy of urbanization, and the government set about enthusiastically closing schools in "unpromising" villages. Out of the 99 schools in Kirillovsky District in the mid-1960s, 3 were secondary schools, 15 were eight-year schools, 5 were specialized schools, and 76 were primary schools.[58] In 1975–6, by contrast, there were only 40 schools, meaning the number of schools had decreased nearly by half.[59] Among those that remained, 5 were secondary schools, 9 were eight-year schools, and 26 were primary schools.

An aid program for the Non-Black Earth region was set up in the 1970s and slowed the wave of primary elementary school closures, although it did not fundamentally change the situation. Chernyshova, the deputy director of the Vologda Oblono, wrote, "closing even the most 'unpromising' school in a village is possible only in the case that school life in dormitory facilities is running smoothly, that timely transportation for students is guaranteed, and the parents are sure that their children have in fact been provided with conditions for successful study."[60] Her words of warning, admittedly, came too late: By that time the number of rural schoolchildren was fast depleting, and rural schools that had been built according to the standardized plan were already half empty.

Overall, the number of rural primary schools in Vologda Oblast decreased from 1,634 in the 1964–5 academic year to 866 in 1979–80 – that is, by 47 per cent.[61] The number of eight-year schools decreased by 36 per cent, or from 406 to 257, over the same period.[62] Concurrently, the number of high schools with a general compulsory program in rural localities grew from 14 to 122.[63]

The RSFSR's school reforms laid a heavy financial burden on the economies of rural regions, throwing their potential construction and continued functioning into doubt in places where kolkhozes and selsoviets did not have the means to rebuild schools, construct housing for teachers, and set up dormitories for children.[64] Even in relatively well-off villages (by Vologodsky District standards), the condition of rural schools was considered pitiful. The secretary of the Vologodsky District CPSU Committee, Verseov, spoke about this at the Second Plenum of the District Committee of the CPSU dedicated to questions of educational reform: "In order to reorganize schools in a normal and correct manner and

Figure 3.2. New building of the Barskaya Eight-Year School in settlement Maisky, Vologda region, 1971.

Source: Private collection of Alexandr Filin.

bring education into [people's] lives, we need to have material support for education. The region is unfavourable in this aspect. All the school buildings are old, unstandardized, and unequipped. Those primary schools that have grown into seven-year schools lack classrooms, Pioneer rooms, and sports facilities. In the Moseikovo, Pogorelovo, and Grigorevo schools, classes are conducted in two shifts. In most schools, classes are conducted in multiple buildings. Many of the school buildings need capital repairs."[65]

With the goal of improving the situation of rural schools in the country, the Soviet government passed a resolution in 1973, "Measures for the Further Improvement of Work in Rural General Compulsory Schools."[66] In accordance with the resolution, the central leadership increased spending on the construction of new rural schools, which were, from that moment forward, to be built primarily on government funds according to standardized plans with educational facilities, dormitories for students, and apartments for teachers. Moreover, the document required oblast and district leaders to provide free hot meals for schoolchildren living in the dormitories, equip school classrooms, and organize transportation between schools and economically weak farms that did not have the means to provide children with transportation independently.

More broadly, the document dictated the construction of a secondary school in every large sovkhoz and kolkhoz in the country.

Evidently, it was due to these efforts that secondary schools gradually became the new reality in the Vologda region. Although, in the words of Vologda Oblono Director Shutov, rural schools continued to have "a significantly poorer material base," new school buildings appeared in many of the oblast's sovkhozes and kolkhozes, and schooling conditions were noticeably improved.[67] As a result, in the 1975–6 school year, 89.4 per cent of schoolchildren in classes 1–10 in Vologda Oblast attended lessons during the first shift. In rural localities, this figure was even higher, at 99 per cent.[68]

The rebirth of rural schools is exemplified by Yermakovo school in Vologodsky District. Oblono Director Shutov wrote, "In the recent past this was the ungraded Shalygenskaya School with a poor material base and a whole number of difficult pedagogical problems. Today, it is one of the best schools in the oblast. The poultry farm 'Yermakovo' and comrade director P.N. Rosliakov built a standardized building for the school with a 596-student capacity. It … is equipped with qualified teachers who received higher education, works on the classroom system, and 98 per cent of the graduates from eighth grade go on to receive a secondary school education at various institutions. Many graduates stay on to work on the sovkhoz 'Spark' and the poultry farm."[69] The Oblono director did not hide the fact that the school's success was connected with the poultry farm's financial support. However, such generosity was by no means widespread among comparable schools. The Oblono director wrote in 1976 that 36 eight-year schools in the oblast had no physics classrooms, 140 had no chemistry classrooms, 56 had no biology classrooms, and 32 had no workshops.[70] He put it succinctly: "Clearly it behoves us to send visual aids and technological equipment primarily to rural schools, especially those in remote regions."[71]

School Dormitories at Rural Schools

School dormitories were intended to facilitate the realization of the gencomp curriculum in rural areas. The historian Maria Maiofis viewed dormitories as an institution "imposing serfdom upon Soviet children."[72] She argued that the creation of schools that required pupils' twenty-four-hour attendance both corresponded with Khrushchev's conception of the communist education of the individual in a collective and ensured that the government could assign pupils those professions that were the most valuable for the Soviet economy. Thus, children became prisoners of the state, which was free to determine their professional training and future work as it pleased. Boarding schools were created primarily in cities as "closed-type" experimental schools in line with pre-revolutionary educational institutions where children were raised and educated in isolation from their parents. Alongside these boarding schools, the 1960s also saw the widespread introduction of schools with attached living facilities in the form of paid dormitories for schoolchildren who lived in remote locations. The difference between boarding schools and schools with dormitories was, firstly, this issue of payment: Boarding schools were free, whereas dormitories came at a price. Secondly, students lived in dormitories not because of their parents' social problems, inability, or lack of willingness to raise them, but because of long distances separating their homes from school.

Admitting the fairness of Maiofis's argument about the inhumanity of the boarding school system for children who were stripped of their parents' care by the educational system, it is worth making a few points that, if they cannot justify the system, at least soften this researcher's verdict. First, in the 1963–4 school year, there were only ten boarding schools in Vologda Oblast district centres, and in 1969 the number had only climbed to thirteen.[73] That means that they made up a very small percentage of schools in the oblast. In the 1970s, they served as an alternative to orphanages, and children maintained contact with their parents to prevent social abandonment. Second, the absence of dormitories in rural schools threw into doubt the prospects of rural schoolchildren receiving even a basic education. Lastly, having children go to work or "into society" early, as was characteristic during the first half of the century, could hardly be considered more humane than organizing school dormitories for them.

Furthermore, the system of school dormitories was not an invention of the Khrushchev reforms. This practice was widespread in north-western Russia before the revolution.[74] It was implemented to address the problem of "large distances" and the chronic lack of navigable roads. It is not incidental that district educational committee documentation discusses building dormitory facilities in Vologda Oblast in tandem by with issues stemming from the need to transport children to schools.[75]

It is worth noting that Vologda Oblono Director Shutov saw the implementation of gen-comp in 1964 as a process of freeing rural children from agricultural work, which generally aligned with official rhetoric from that time.[76] He wrote, "In August, most schools held preliminary student fee collections; this … allowed us to identify cases of potential inability to pay, take early measures to offer material assistance, and free children from domestic work and work on kolkhozes and sovkhozes."[77]

Ensuring students made it to school and had access to school dormitory facilities, in the opinion of the Oblono director, saved them from toilsome agriculture labour. It is a separate issue that no one asked rural children themselves whether they wanted to be sent to school dormitories instead of fulfilling domestic duties.

Building and furnishing school dormitories required funds that neither kolkhozes, selsoviets, nor regional educational commissions had at their disposal. Vologda Oblono Director Shutov frequently wrote about insufficient school capacity in annual oblast school reports. In Vologda Oblast in the 1960s and '70s, there were 380 working school dormitory facilities, which typically housed less than half of the schools' student body.[78] The maximum number of dormitories was recorded in the 1966–7 school year, when 394 school dormitories functioned in the oblast and supported 25,450 schoolchildren. Of these dormitories, 15 were for primary schools, 283 were for eight-year schools, and 96 were for secondary schools.[79]

Even at those schools with dormitory facilities, living conditions were often unsatisfactory. The director of Pogorelovo School in Vologodsky District succinctly described the condition of his school's dormitory facility at the CPSU District Committee plenum in March 1961 in the following manner: "The dormitory is bad, the building is dilapidated, it could collapse."[80] The Vologda Oblono director noted in a 1966–7 report that in twelve out of fifteen dormitory facilities children had to share beds.[81] Only in 1975–6 could the head of the Regional Department of Public Education write in a report that "normal conditions have been created in most of the dormitories: They are all provided with soft and hard inventory, radio service, televisions, board game sets, newspapers, and magazines. Thrice-daily meals have been organized with funds from the budget and parent committees. Produce is provided by school plots and by kolkhozes and sovkhozes."[82]

Not all children were willing to move from home to stay in school dormitories. Quite the opposite, in many cases: My interviewees' personal recollections suggest that even those who had the opportunity to sleep in a dormitory often preferred to walk home, however long the distance. As Tatiana K. from Kabachino recalled, children from Migachevo and Zvosvky Selsoviets who were unable to cross the river by boat took a route nearly twenty kilometres long to get home.[83]

Sergei A., born into the family of a sovkhoz public servant in the village of Migachevo in 1954, had to live with other children from his village in the dormitory for the Goritsy Eight-Year School.[84] His village was located on the opposite riverbank more than five kilometres from the ferry service. So, when he finished four grades at the primary school in

Migachevo, he was taken to the dormitory at the eight-year school in Goritsy. In 1967, however, his father became the director of the Goritsy House for Disabled War Veterans, a dormitory for ex-soldiers, the elderly, and disabled people, and the selsoviet provided him with a home in Goritsy. Immediately afterwards, Sergei A. moved out of the dormitory to live with his father. They lived together for two years, setting off to Migachevo on the weekends. Sergei A. believes that his father went to work in Goritsy because he did not want to leave his son without parental supervision. As soon as Sergei finished school, his father changed his job and moved back to Migachevo. Unlike the idealogues of collective child rearing, he trusted neither the teachers nor the children's collective.

The Goritsy dormitory building was a two-storey wooden house located on the territory of the former Goritsky Voskresensky female monastery. Boys lived on the first storey of the house, while the second storey was reserved for girls. In the 1960s, the dormitory was intended for the twenty-four-hour habitation of around thirty children from the most remote villages of the Goritsy region. However, when conditions became unfavourable in spring and autumn, children from villages across the river stayed in the dormitory for one to two weeks while the river was uncrossable.[85] Typically, the dormitories were overseen by childminders, but in Goritsy the teachers took turns taking care of the facility. Children in the dormitory were given breakfast, lunch, and dinner. On the weekends, they went home to change clothes, have a bath, and see their loved ones.

Discussing his experience living in a school dormitory in the 1970s at one of the schools in Totemsky District, Sergei T. recalled that, although living conditions were not bad, he bore "a sense of missing home" during his school years.[86]

Transporting Schoolchildren and the Problem of Long Distances

The alternative to school dormitories was providing children with transportation to school from remote villages. A resolution of the Council of Ministers of the Soviet Union, passed on 26 August 1965, dictated that children living in rural locations more than three kilometres from a school were to be provided with free transportation to their place of study.[87] However, a decision made by central leadership was insufficient on its own. The swampy territory of Vologda Oblast, rich in streams, rivers, and lakes, was uncrossable by tractor or horse. Snowdrifts covered icy roads in winter and rendered travel by truck and bus impossible. In these conditions organizing transportation for schoolchildren was a major challenge.

Judging by the resolution, transportation to school was supposed to be organized by the farms where parents worked. But in practice, it became clear that kolkhozes and sovkhozes lacked the necessary technology and funds. Yearly school reports in Vologda Oblast contain records of some farms transporting students to school on tractors in the absence of cars or buses, which in many cases were not common until the 1980s.[88]

By 1972, in accordance with a resolution "For Measures for the Further Improvement of Work in Rural General Compulsory Schools," educational committees began to allot buses for transporting children from some "economically weak" farms in the oblast. According to data from annual Vologda Oblast school reports, in 1973–4 kolkhozes and sovkhozes received fifteen buses.[89] In 1975–6, they received another ten.[90] However, in 1972–3 only 43 per cent of students took the bus to school, and in 1975–6 only 54.7 per cent did.[91] Moreover, the buses only ran twice weekly, bringing children to school dormitories at the beginning of the week and driving them home again on the weekend.

Although with time the situation began to improve in several districts in the oblast (for example, 85.4 per cent of schoolchildren were being driven to school in Vologodsky District by 1975), the long distances separating homes from schools remained a problem for rural schools throughout the entirety of the 1960s and '70s.[92]

The ability to organize transportation for schoolchildren was in large part dependent on the relationship between school directors and kolkhoz or sovkhoz directors. If the farm was economically viable, then the school lived well, receiving wood and construction materials from the sovkhoz, along with produce for the school cafeteria and dormitory. This was the case in 1975–6 on the kolkhoz "Lenin's Path," in Vytegorsky District, which "allocates meat to the Andogskaya Secondary School, the kolkhoz 'Onezhsky' allocates fish, the kolkhoz 'Bolshevik' allocates cabbage. The *lespromkhoz* at Bely Ruchey in the same district allocates 150 roubles for student meals. The kolkhozes 'Dawn' and 'Sunrise' in Kharovsky District allocate free meat and milk to the dormitories."[93] Admittedly, these conditions were far from ubiquitous, and schools often experienced difficulties receiving financing from selsoviets and farms. This state of affairs was discussed openly at district plenums. Thus, speaking at a CPSU district plenum, the deputy chair of the District Executive Committee, Podguzov, complained about the difficulty of obtaining assistance in building and repairing a school: "On the sovkhoz 'Dawn of Communism,' the party organization secretary says that these issues will be addressed, but we have no timber. We brought timber, but there are no carpenters. And so, we still haven't addressed anything to this day."[94]

In the 1970s, the responsibility of building and equipping schools in the oblast was fully transferred to educational committees. Farms, which had paid for the construction of schools and dormitories up to that point, began to receive compensation for the funds they had invested. Thus, the kolkhozes "World," "Motherland," and "Russia," in Babaevsky District, were among the farms lucky enough to receive government funds in compensation for the money they had spent on schools.[95]

Professional Training for Rural Schools

While organizing transportation to school for rural schoolchildren and constructing school dormitories looked like government attempts to address educational inequality – that is, to make school accessible to schoolchildren regardless of where they lived – the introduction of professional training in rural schools again harkens back to the idea of social and class predeterminism. Rural schools were charged not simply with spreading knowledge, but also with supplying the agricultural workforce.

The sociologist Larisa Shpakovskaya, in her analysis of the influence of the educational system on the formation of social groups in Soviet society, noted that, in the 1970s, Soviet education saw a "complete rejection of the use of social selection criteria within the framework of educational institutions."[96] She argued that, during these years, a meritocratic student selection system took hold in universities (that is, one based strictly on student ability as reflected in academic marks), and that secondary general compulsory schools were the primary channel for university enrolments.

However, the official declaration of "equality" in education benefited children from educated urban families first and foremost, because they had access to the best schools, preparatory courses, and tutors.[97] Soviet leadership was preparing rural children for a future in rural localities and orientated them towards work on sovkhozes and kolkhozes, although nominally they attempted to do so without lowering educational standards. Despite these efforts, rural students lagged significantly behind their urban counterparts in level of education, and in most cases rural students did not have the opportunity to study in the country's most prestigious universities. Moreover, the defining feature of education in rural schools in the 1970s was the re-emergence of professional schooling, which Nikita Khrushchev had actively supported since the 1950s. Whereas in urban schools, students learned to drive automobiles and operate factory machinery or sewing machines, in rural schools they were trained as tractor operators and taught the nuances of milking technology. Professional schooling in the 1970s was aimed at limiting rural youth migration and motivating students to remain on the kolkhozes and sovkhozes where they were raised. These goals were the impetus for the adoption of an entire series of all-union, republic-, and oblast-level documents that initiated special programs for teaching agricultural disciplines in Vologda Oblast schools. Among them was a 27 July 1970 directive from the Council of Ministers of the USSR, "On the Condition of Professional Training and Prof-Orientation in the Oblast's Schools," which called for class time that had previously been dedicated to elective courses to be reallocated for professional training.[98] On 22 October 1975, another Council of Ministers of directive was issued, "On the Condition of the Rural General Compulsory School Network in the RSFSR and Measures for the Perfection of the Organization of Education in Villages," emphasizing that secondary school was the primary opportunity for receiving an education in rural localities and thus "should be closely tied to ... the needs of the farms on whose territory it is located and called to aid in the task of educating young people in the village."[99] A final order, issued by the Ministry of Education of the RFSFR on 2 August 1979, "On Additional Measures for Retaining Personnel in Agricultural in the Non-Black Earth Region of the RSFSR," made direct recommendations that committees of public education and school administrations should make efforts to ensure rural schoolchildren stayed on kolkhozes to work after graduating from school, rather than leaving to continue their education in cities.[100]

The trend of professionalization in school education was codified in school laws from 1958 on and was intended to ensure that all schools in the country had their own specializations, oriented to the needs of local economies. As the head of the Vologodsky District Committee of Public Education emphasized at a teacher conference in 1965, "the main task of rural schools is to draw rural youths into socially useful labour, to equip them with knowledge of agricultural technology and the practical skills necessary in conditions of ever-intensifying agricultural production."[101] Therefore, in the first half of the 1960s, rural schools reported not only their pupils' academic performance to the District Committee of Public Education, but also milk yields and the number of kilograms collected at harvests. A 1961 report for the Goritsy Eight-Year School showed that schoolchildren had collected 8,705 kilograms of ashes and 7,774 kilograms of bird droppings, installed 170 birdhouses, collected 11.3 kilograms of birch buds, put on 7 concerts for the local population, prepared 188 cubic metres of firewood for heating the school, drove out 105 loads of manure on *subbotniks*, and raised 60 rabbits.[102]

However, the organizing of professional training in rural schools was immediately accompanied by numerous problems. First, it became clear that school biology teachers had different skills and abilities than agricultural specialists and were thus unable to run school farms. Moreover, as a speaker at the 1964 teachers' conference for Vologodsky District noted, "in summer the biology teachers go on vacation, and all work stops."[103] Secondly, the schools lacked equipment and workshops for adequate professional training. Thus, after Khrushchev stepped down in 1964, agricultural activity ceased to be viewed as an indicator of school success, and rural schools began to focus once again on teaching children core subjects of the school curriculum.

Although agricultural activity was de-emphasized in schools after 1964, this did not completely free schoolchildren from agricultural work. From 1942, the children of kolkhoz workers had been required to work fifty workdays a year on the kolkhoz where they were born.[104] The *trudoden* (workday) system, which granted kolkhoz workers guaranteed payment for their labour, ended only in 1966. Until that time, in addition to school, rural teenagers had tended kolkhoz herds, worked on farms, and taken part in harvest and sowing campaigns. Thus, Alexander K., who lived in the village of Kargach and studied at the Goritsy Eight-Year School, remembers caring for a kolkhoz horse during the 1960s: "For two years I had this stallion, Frisky. I transported silage with him. They prepared silage because they had almost one thousand heads of cattle. It was an enormous herd. So, there were about, maybe, twenty of us kids – boys. Everyone was given a horse. There weren't many cars, nor was their much machinery, though there was machinery, of course. They already used it. And we used horses. Interesting. Each [young man] was sure to care for his horse. By God, you couldn't let your horse go hungry or thirsty! How could you? That wasn't supposed to happen. Everyone would answer for it. Everything was serious."[105] Sometimes, however, kolkhozes gave schoolchildren certificates for school kolkhoz work, which could be used to free them from additional work on the kolkhoz where they lived.

Another important aspect of labour preparation in rural schools in the 1960s and '70s was professional training or providing schoolchildren with specialist skills. As the representative of the Vologodsky District Committee of Public Education confirmed in 1964, "preparing the workforce for agricultural production should be carried out primarily in rural secondary schools. Questions of creating the necessary base for schools, who to prepare and to what extent, should be the responsibility of kolkhozes, sovkhozes, and their leadership. Kolkhozes and sovkhozes should become customers at rural schools."[106]

While adolescent boys in rural schools were expected to become tractor operators, adolescent girls were expected to became professionals in animal husbandry and mechanical milking. However, even by the end of the 1970s many sovkhozes in Vologda Oblast lacked mechanical milking apparatuses. As the author of a report on professional training in Vologda Oblast complained in 1964, "To this day many kolkhozes that are training children to become animal husbandry mechanization specialists have not undergone any mechanization."[107] Even if the farms had the necessary machinery, attracting a school graduate was extremely difficult in light of the laborious nature of such work and its low status in the professional hierarchy.

Although Khrushchev's resignation and the change of professional education's status in Soviet schools slowed the professionalization of schools (for example, by repealing the draconian law requiring school graduates to work for two years in production before enrolling in university), it did not end it completely. A 1969 resolution of the Council of Ministers of the RSFSR, "On Teaching Senior School Students Automobile Engineering, Work on Tractors, Combines and Other Agricultural Machinery," as well as a 1970 resolution, "Measures to Further Increase the Preparation of Mechanics for Agriculture," legally formalized the idea of training milkers and tractor operators in schools. According to data from 1976, of Vologda Oblast's 214 secondary schools, 197 provided students with training for various professions, including tractor operator, motor-car driver, car mechanic, line worker, animal farmer, seamstress, lathe operator, weaver, and poultry farmer.[108] Training was provided for tractor and combine operation in 45 secondary schools in the oblast, automobile engineering was provided in 22, and 2 schools provided training in "the fundamentals of modern production." Overall, in 1967, of the 24,170 schoolchildren who went through professional training programs in school, 11,916 (or around half) went on to take up an agricultural profession.[109]

After Khrushchev's resignation, professional training was offered as an addition to the basic school program and at the discretion of school administrations. In a report on schools in Kirillovsky District for the 1969–70 school year, it was recorded that only three of the fifteen eight-year and secondary schools offered professional training for grades 5–8.[110]

Yet another aspect of the professionalization of rural schools in the 1960s and '70s was the creation of student production brigades. First appearing in Stavropol Krai in 1956–7, they were seen as the optimal organization for introducing students to agricultural labour and training them for related professions. The brigades were usually made up of students in the upper classes who worked for pay after lessons in the fields of a kolkhoz or sovkhoz near their school. Student labour brigades assisted kolkhozes during sowing and harvesting campaigns and helped with haymaking on sovkhozes during summer work camps. Despite the fact that leadership widely encouraged participation in student brigades, many rural schools never made the effort to form one. It was not uncommon for brigades to exist on paper only, and, where they did exist, instead of training cutting-edge agricultural mechanics, as had been the intention, brigade participants were often used as low-paid labour.[111] Shutov, head of the Vologda Oblono, wrote about this misapplication of student labour in a note in 1976: "It is not an uncommon occurrence that the year-long work of student production brigades ... is replaced by episodic manual labour cultivating plants and bringing in harvests."[112]

There were, admittedly, positive examples of school-sovkhoz cooperation. One of them is described in a 1977 school brigade report from the village of Novlenskoe, in Vologodsky District.[113] It describes how the student production brigade for the Novlenskoe school was a "school aid force for the sovkhoz ... There was no land assigned to the school, all the work was done by hand."[114] Then, in 1971, after an agreement had been concluded with the sovkhoz, the brigade was allocated a tractor and twenty hectares of land. Later, "when the party and government passed a resolution for the Non-Black Earth region, connections between the school and the sovkhoz began to grow stronger": Professional training for schoolchildren was organized on the sovkhoz. When the report was written in 1977, the brigade had three participants in grades 6–9, who were divided into eleven sections. The brigade's work was overseen by the brigade soviet, made up of the sovkhoz director, the school director, an agronomist, the school's head of professional training, and section leaders.[115] The brigade frequently worked on the fields, and the pay the schoolchildren received was spent on their salaries and funding school excursions and tourist trips. However, similar examples are extremely rare. Usually, kolkhozes were ready and willing to use pupils and teachers as unpaid agricultural workers, "paying" the schools by providing transportation for school trips, buying school equipment, and similar methods.[116]

As a result, although having schoolchildren harvest vegetables on neighbouring farms was a widespread practice in rural areas, and assembling birch bundles to feed the school rabbitry was a requirement for receiving a school completion certificate, overall, professional training in rural schools did not succeed in "solidifying" the numbers of students in agriculture or influencing their choice of profession.[117] In the 1963–4 school year, only 2,708 of the 22,479 graduates of eighth grade in Vologda Oblast (just 12 per cent) went to work on kolkhozes.[118] In 1975, only 1,468 of the 6,105 graduates from rural secondary schools went to work in agriculture; furthermore, this indicator, at about 24 per cent of rural secondary school graduates, appears to have been greatly exaggerated because it took into account not only those who worked on a sovkhoz or kolkhoz, but those who went to study an agriculture specialty at university or technical college, which did not guarantee that they would return to work in the countryside.[119] Additionally, the mechanical preparation provided to schoolchildren was inadequate and did not correspond to kolkhoz needs. Schoolchildren on farms were not trusted with new tractors, and directors generally preferred to hire tractor operators who had finished a year-long course at a technical college.[120] Difficulties also arose finding teachers for professional training. Few agronomists or animal husbandry specialists agreed to run courses for schoolchildren.

At the end of 1970s and the beginning of the 1980s, another attempt was made to require rural schools and schoolchildren to participate in agricultural production. Plans were "dropped" on schools specifying quantities of land to be cultivated and dictating the creation of school facilities for raising animals.

As Elena V., the director of Maisky Secondary School, recalls, this decision seemed pointless both to the school administration and to the farm directors on whose land the schools were located.[121] The director of the sovkhoz "Maisky," making a concession to the CPSU District Committee, built a shed for sheep on school property instead of the recommended hog pen. Ultimately, no sheep were brought to the school.[122] A different solution for bypassing a CPSU regional committee professional training directive was offered by the head of another Vologda farm. He suggested that the school administration pick out as many animals from the sovkhoz farms as would satisfy educational committees and label them "school" animals. The animals would continue to be fed and tended to as usual by the farms, but the school would be able to record in official reports that it had fulfilled its obligations.[123]

In conclusion, the push to professionalize rural schools and transform them into professional training centres returned like a boomerang in party directives throughout the 1960s and '70s. Meanwhile, neither school directors nor farm directors believed that the measures were effective. Nevertheless, the government believed that by developing these schools it would be able to reproduce a class of agricultural producers and convince schoolchildren to stay and work on sovkhozes and kolkhozes. With one hand the government separated children from agricultural production by increasing the intensity of school curriculums, building dormitories, and protecting children from domestic peasant labour; with the other it did everything it could to keep rural schoolchildren on the land, train them for agricultural professions, accustom them to peasant labour, and continue to see them as peasant kolkhoz workers.

The Pedagogical Workforce

Rural teachers, although they were the stewards of Soviet modernity, were not the most important experts in rural communities. Because prosperity in the countryside was dependent upon agricultural production – and a peasant's garden plot was independent of government control – the state could not successfully impose its ideas on peasants. The most valued experts in rural communities were successful farmers who possessed local knowledge. Their neighbours asked them for advice on questions such as when to start a season's farming work or how to build a log structure. These "wise" people could be heads of household or experienced women called *bolshukhi*, who aided with childbirth and performed rites of passage. There were also witch doctors and people with occult knowledge who were in charge of maintaining harmonious relations with natural forces and who could return a cow lost in the woods or remove a curse.[124] In other words, rural communities had their own experts. However, when the type of dominant knowledge changed, so did the status of rural teachers. In the government's view, teachers were the bearers of progressive knowledge, and thus it is not surprising that it was precisely rural teachers who often filled the ranks of various public committees and commissions. Teachers were required to work in election commissions and to lead residential committees and the juvenile delinquency branches of the local police in a volunteer capacity. In essence, any "public activity" initiative launched by the government was realized in rural localities by the work of teachers.

Reforming rural schools required a large number of pedagogical personnel. In order to improve teacher training, measures were taken to broaden the network of secondary and higher-level pedagogical institutions and to create "support schools," at which teachers would be regularly required to take courses to raise their qualifications and adopt cutting-edge practices. In Vologda Oblast in the 1960s and '70s, the Vologda and Cherepovets Pedagogical Institutes trained pedagogues specialized by subject. Teachers of primary grades received their education in pedagogical colleges in Vologda, Belozersk, Ustyuzhna, Sokol, and Veliky Ustyug. Although there were too many teachers in the cities, there was a severe shortage of them in the countryside.[125] It was not uncommon for a rural school to be without a math teacher or a Russian language teacher. In the 1960s, the role of primary school teacher was often filled by a recent secondary school graduate. Thus, Galina S. finished secondary school in 1975 in the Vologodsky District centre of Gryazovets and, after not having been accepted into the pedagogical institute, worked for a year as a primary school teacher in one of the district villages.[126]

The career of Antonina K., a teacher at the Goritsy Elementary School, began in a similar way. After finishing Kirillov Secondary School in 1959, she was sent almost immediately to work at Sautino Primary School.[127] Teachers with a diploma and specialized education were a great rarity in rural regions in the 1950s and even the 1960s.

After the introduction of new educational standards and changes to how subjects were taught at the beginning of the 1960s, the demand for qualified teachers grew substantially. From that time on, only those who had attended pedagogical institutes were able to teach the basic subjects in secondary and eight-year schools. However, many pedagogical institute graduates with a rare (for Vologda Oblast) degree were unprepared to move to the backcountry. Consequently, the demand for teachers in rural schools in the Vologda region was addressed in two ways: Graduates from pedagogical institutes and technical colleges were sent to rural locations on work assignments, and students from those same institutes were sent to the countryside to gain practical pedagogical experience during their studies. In 1975, for example, 435 graduates of the Vologda and Cherepovets Pedagogical Institutes were assigned to rural schools in the oblast (87 per cent of overall work assignments), as were 331 pedagogical college graduates (92 per cent).[128] Graduate work assignments were managed by district educational committees, who tried to consider the needs of schools while at least partially meeting the expectations of the teachers who were sent to remote locations. In practice, it was not always possible. At first, pedagogical graduates were sent to the most remote selsoviets, where the lack of teachers was felt most sharply. The graduates worked there on two-year contracts before attempting to move as quickly as possible to locations closer to district centres, freeing up remote positions for new graduates. Generally, district educational committees were receptive to such desires, offering teachers who had finished their minimum contracts in rural areas a new placement that satisfied their expectations or was located much closer to the city.

The life path of Galina S. – from the settlement Molochnoe, in Vologodsky District – came together in precisely that manner. In 1971, she graduated from the Philology Department of Vologda Pedagogical Institute. During her last year at the institute, she married a student in the Math and Physics Department, and they were sent together to one of the most remote selsoviets in the oblast. After finishing their two years, the couple submitted a request to the Gryazovets District Committee of Public Education in hopes of each securing positions – her as a Russian language and literature teacher, and him as a math and physics teacher – in Galina's place of birth, the city of Gryazovets. However, the Gryazovets District Committee of Public Education turned down their application.

As a result, they sent their documents to the Vologodsky District Committee of Public Education and, to their great surprise, found that it was ready to assign the young couple to the dynamic and fast-developing urban-type settlement of Kurkino, located just thirty kilometres from the oblast centre. After moving to Kurkino, Galina S. almost immediately became the director of the newly built secondary school. They next moved to the settlement of Molochnoe at the beginning of the 1980s, where they received an apartment and Galina became the head of educational work and Russian language and literature in School No. 6, in the city of Vologda. Her husband worked for a time as the secretary of the party organization for the RSFSR North-West Scientific Research Institute for Meadow Management and Dairy Farming before going to work as a prorector at the Vologda Pedagogical Institute.

According to official data from the 1970s, up to 10 per cent of teachers in the North-West moved out of rural districts each year.[129] In fact, the numbers were much higher. According to statistics presented by the head of the Vologodsky District Committee of Public Education, from 1972 to 1975 there were 75 teachers with higher degrees sent to Velikoustyugsky District in Vologda Oblast, while 61 teachers left over the same period. In Nikolsky District, 101 teachers were sent in and 82 left. In Kich-Gorodetsky District, 63 were sent in and 59 left. In Vashkinsky District, 28 were sent in and 26 left.[130] The "slippage of pedagogical personnel" was an urgent problem for rural schools. As the director of the Pogorelovo School in Vologodsky District lamented in 1961 while explaining the causes of teachers moving out, "there are no apartments, teachers are forced to live in different villages, village stores are poorly supplied. There is no water in Pogorelovo."[131]

Thus, although the most popular profession among the rural intelligentsia was constantly being filled by new representatives, efforts at rotation failed to put an end to teacher personnel shortages in rural schools. The lack of benefits and privileges for rural teachers, along with worse working conditions for teachers in rural locations as compared with city schools, went unaddressed by the government for a long time. Only with the passage of laws meant to help rural schools in the 1970s did rural teachers begin to receive government attention in the form of salary bonuses, deferment from army service for men, and guaranteed housing provided by the District Committee of Public Education.

Effects of Schools Reforms

The school education reforms that began in rural regions in 1958 and continued throughout the 1960s and '70s reflected various Soviet modernization and development strategies; the actual conditions within the school system would determine the future of various regions of the country and the socialist project as a whole. However, these various modernization scenarios and the national policies that accompanied them changed too rapidly. Rural schools did not have time to restructure themselves and fulfil government initiatives. As a result, schools were simultaneously tasked with keeping their personnel in the countryside (and reproducing a class of agricultural producers) while at the same time encouraging students to receive advanced qualifications in cities. In reality, what typically played out in the Vologda region was that schoolchildren received secondary education in rural schools and then left the communities where they had been raised forever.

Unlike in the city, where the professionalization of schools was seen as the essential feature of Khrushchev's reforms, in rural areas of the Vologda region the essence of the reforms was the organization of general compulsory education: sitting rural children behind school desks and explaining to rural residents the value of the knowledge that schools brought. Making education accessible to all children in the countryside was part of Khrushchev's very ambitious plan to transform rural localities and create a new rurality. Rural youths, without needing to move to the city, were able to receive a diploma and professional skills that were important in the context of modernizing agriculture. However, reformers did not take into account the fact that schools in Vologda Oblast needed to be reopened as much as they needed to be reformed. Until the oblast had enough educational institutions to serve all eligible schoolchildren, it was extremely difficult to "professionalize" them. Ultimately, the push to professionalize schools had come to a halt by the end of the 1960s, before it had even begun in many places. By the 1970s, when more secondary and eight-year schools appeared in the oblast, there was no one to teach; the number of rural schoolchildren had dramatically decreased, and those who remained were required to continue their studies in accordance with the secondary-level general compulsory program.

When it became clear in the mid-1970s that young people who received their education in cities were not planning on returning to rural regions, the government made another attempt to transform rural schools into a bastion of sovkhoz worker training. The advent of school production brigades, conferences for graduates from rural schools, visible work placements of Komsomol members in villages, the emphasis on professionally oriented schooling, and, finally, requiring graduates from rural schools to work for a year on sovkhozes before enrolling in universities were all undertaken as part of a government strategy to limit the exodus of young people and address the reality of a vanishing workforce.

Enthusiastically attempting to build global socialism in the country-side, Soviet leaders in the 1960s and '70s believed that unifying the school program in cities and rural localities would lead to equal educational opportunities for schoolchildren. However, the spare population distribution across Vologda Oblast, coupled with the nuances of agricultural production, with its uneven seasonal work burden, created myriad problems for educational institutions. Many rural schools closed in response to decreasing student numbers. However, those schools that withstood the test of time and were located in "promising" (from the government's point of view) settlements grew increasingly similar to city schools in the 1970s, with standardized buildings, curriculums, and school rituals that were common throughout the entire USSR.

Improving school education in rural localities inevitably played a role in effecting structural change in rural communities. More and more often, the children of the kolkhoz peasantry used their education to move into other social classes or to migrate. Meanwhile, the disparities between cities and the countryside remained; providing young people with an urban-style education and downplaying the value of local knowledge, villages saw their futures move with new graduates to the cities.

Although structural changes to the school system took place fairly slowly, the very fact that primary school education was replaced by secondary schooling had a major impact on rural communities. Schools, by becoming the centre of youth policy in the countryside, were turned into an instrument for imposing modern values and a spatio-temporal framework that for the rural Vologda region were entirely new.

In capitalist countries, educational institutions in rural regions were dependent on markets, and researchers tended to use market relations to explain the purpose of education. In this way, Michael Corbett, writing about rural young people in Canada and Australia, has argued that the leaders of these countries were simultaneously interested in keeping young people in the countryside and providing them with an education that would allow them, if need be, to find work in the city:

> The discursive framing of rural youth is of a precariously connected population necessary for economic growth and development in rural areas. Rural youth are simultaneously encouraged and blamed as they are chided to aspire higher. This aspirational discourse encourages rural youth to transform themselves into credentialed, skilled neoliberal subjects, which we argue, has implicit spatial and mobility implications for them. In this discourse, they must be educated/educable, flexible, and deployable to wherever they are needed by capital. But they are also encouraged to stay

loyal, local, and help rebuild struggling communities, a task often linked to engineering their own entrepreneurial futures.[132]

I hope to show that the discursive strategies for conceptualizing rural youth were exceedingly similar in the USSR. By following the state's modernized conceptions about the development of rural territories, the population was simply obliged to integrate into the so-called global city of progress.

Chapter Four

Education Is Enlightenment, Ignorance Is Darkness

Education as a Social Resource

Apart from a few studies on rural education explaining the persistence of "vestiges" of peasant life as a product of under-financing, little has been written about the structural issues underlying educational inequality in the USSR during the late Soviet period.[1] Yet it is precisely the infrastructural specificities of schools in rural and urbans areas that scholarly literature addressing educational inequality tends to view as foundational.[2] Indeed, schooling in rural localities often lags behind urban education chiefly on account of the limitations imposed by such schools' remote locations.[3] Moreover, it is true the world over that rural schools tend to be smaller than urban schools, a fact reflected in the level of financing they receive. The countryside often suffers from a lack of pedagogical personnel, and schoolchildren may need to overcome great distances to reach school from their homes.[4] In this sense, the USSR was no different than other countries.

However, another dimension of inequality in rural education relates to schoolchildren's social position.[5] In the second half of the 1960s, researchers specializing in the sociology of education actively discussed the impact of social class on the school system. The general consensus was that class inequality within a society leads to inequality in schools, and that schools in turn reproduce class relations more actively than other institutions. As Collins argues, the reproduction of class occurs on the basis of three processes: preserving the structure of labour relations (social demand for a given profession), imposing the culture of dominant groups onto society at large, and, lastly, through the use of language.[6] Academics have shown that the class origin of students and their parents not only influenced educational possibilities, but limited them as well.[7] Annette Lareau has argued that some students will perform better than others and be more motivated to study even when all are provided with equal opportunities and mandatory universal education.[8] These differences are tied more closely to the attitude towards education within a student's family than to their individual abilities. Social groups reproduce certain attitudinal patterns related to education in their environment. As a result, the middle class is prepared to invest time and money into education, while the working class does so to a much lesser degree.[9]

In socialist societies, where domestic policy was focused above all on the task of building communism, there was no private property, and class status was determined differently than it was in the West.[10] Moreover, as Sheila Fitzpatrick asserts, post-revolutionary Russian society is better described in terms of social estates than socio-economic classes.[11] And although in the second half of the twentieth century social groups formed in the USSR, Europe, and North America that resembled each other in terms of interests, status, means of income, and so on, this was not the primary factor in school system transformation.[12] In contrast to liberal societies, in the USSR the state had a monopoly on education, and it was therefore the state, and not the market or the academy, that played a decisive role in shaping Soviet schools and universities.[13] However, this did not alter the disciplinary function or socially predetermined nature of the school system. The Soviet school system, like its Western counterparts, reproduced the social structures of Soviet society by preparing the rural population to form the peasantry and the urban population to fill the need for workers and intelligentsia. In other words, the educational system discriminated against one group and privileged another.[14]

However, the twentieth century saw major shifts in Soviet policy on rural schooling. Policies such as the push to eradicate class differences and dissolve the borders separating the city from the countryside, along with processes of modernization in the 1960s and '70s, led to the abandonment of the earlier post-revolutionary emphasis on eliminating educational inequality and the mechanisms of social reproduction. Beginning in the 1960s, the primary task of Soviet schools became the mass preparation of a qualified workforce. This shift in emphasis did not fully eliminate discrimination based on social origin, but it made steps in this direction.

Although official discourse began to group rural youths together with Soviet youths in general, this did not erase the real consequences of class origin.[15] Young people in rural areas in the 1960s and '70s were, for the most part, the children of the kolkhoz peasantry, and were thus subjected to the restrictions imposed upon that class. Until 1966, these young people worked alongside adults in the *trudoden* system, helped their parents meet yearly agricultural product taxes, and carried out necessary duties on the kolkhoz.[16] That rural youths in fact formed a distinct class is illustrated by the fact that within Soviet historiography they were studied in the context of peasant history, albeit in its most progressive guise. In the 1960s and '70s, in the heyday of Soviet "rural sociology," entire chapters in research works were dedicated to young people in rural areas.[17] Sociologists and ethnologists in those years wrote optimistically about the growing popularity of Soviet values and urban practices in rural areas. Indeed, they saw the young people themselves as becoming increasingly similar to their urban counterparts.[18]

However, if one is to look at other sources, such as at ethnographic and folklore-study expeditions to the Russian North, or at interviews, a more nuanced picture is revealed.[19] The talented photographer and teacher Yuri Garev, who photographed his fellow villagers in Vozhgora between 1968 and 1978, captured images of village residents who engaged in haymaking just as their ancestors had a century earlier, and who still buried their dead according to Orthodox customs.[20] Young people who lived in villages were now better educated than their parents and sported hairstyles and clothing inspired by urban fashions. Nevertheless, they differed from their urban counterparts not only because they knew how to do certain types of work, or because they had access to local knowledge, but also because they enjoyed significantly fewer government resources than those raised in urban environments. They moved to cities in an attempt to rid themselves of the stigma of their social background, which limited their ability to pursue a better life.[21] The anthropologists Svetlana Adonyeva and Lara Olson, who research rural women in the Russian North, argue that a dramatic break from rural tradition occurred in many families precisely during the mid-twentieth century – a time when the younger generations in the countryside began to orient their conceptions of home economy and agricultural management, as well as the organization of daily life and family structure, towards modern urban values rather than the bearers of tradition (local elders).[22]

In the 1960s, the introduction of mandatory general education for all rural children alongside the active propagandizing of scientific knowledge through lectures, the introduction of radio, film screenings at local clubs, and eventually television disseminated a different type of knowledge in the countryside, one that was circulating in the modern, global world.

In the USSR, the availability of educational opportunities for people who had previously been members of exploited classes was considered one of the greatest accomplishments of the Soviet government, on equal footing with providing education to women.[23] This opinion, however, was not shared by everyone. In the 1990s, the American sociologists Theodore Gerber and Michael Hout, in their analysis of statistical data collected by Soviet censuses, concluded that the Soviet educational system, with its three tiers of primary, secondary, and higher education, actually increased social inequality in the USSR.[24] They showed that the educational level attained by a student's parents, as well as the parent's professions and place of residency, to a large extent determined their level of access to higher education.[25] They asserted that a student's social background proved to be of great importance for moving from one tier of education to the next, and that students from privileged urban classes (the intelligentsia and those whose parents held administrative or leadership positions) found themselves in a more advantageous position than those from less privileged classes, such as workers and peasants. Thus, Gerber and Hout assert, Khrushchev's stated policy of equalizing cities and the countryside notwithstanding, it was more difficult for the children of peasants and workers to attain admission to universities and institutes of higher education in the 1960s and '70s than it was in the pre-reform 1930s.

In this chapter, I demonstrate, on the basis of Vologda Oblast annual school reports, that the drive for academic success among schoolchildren in the 1960 and '70s took on an additional dimension in rural contexts. High marks at school guaranteed the student social mobility and the opportunity to migrate to the city, which tacitly granted them a privileged position. This corresponds, generally, to global trends.[26] For example, it has been shown that poor farmers in nineteenth-century Quebec preferred to invest in educating their children rather than land because they perceived that the future of their region would be linked to industrialization and an increased demand for technical expertise.[27]

In the USSR, certain class advantages did not apply to the entire class of Soviet administrators, but only to those who worked in cities. The children of kolkhoz and sovkhoz directors, for example, often had no desire to inherit their parents' positions and instead preferred to live in the city, even in far less comfortable conditions. At the same time, because they had access to more resources, representatives of these members of the rural population strove to provide their children with the best available education and the opportunity to move to the city. Although there were undoubtedly some rural parents who wanted their children to inherit their professions and activities, the greater part of the Soviet rural administrative elite and intelligentsia worked to send their children to the city, where urban life, unlike that found in rural areas, corresponded with their conceptions of modernity.[28] However, whereas sovkhoz directors could provide their children with administrative and financial help (through kolkhoz stipends, for example), the rural intelligentsia had to rely on their knowledge and ability to convince their children of the value of education.. Taking this into account, it is unsurprising that the best-performing students in rural schools were often the children of teachers.[29]

Thus, rural youth experienced a twofold discrimination. On the one hand, because they were peasants and their future was tied to the countryside, rural schoolchildren had fewer chances to master the highest-paid and most prestigious professions in the USSR or to receive a higher education. On the other hand, mandatory schooling in and of itself presented a challenge to previously existing systems of local, rural knowledge based in experience. This meant that rural schoolchildren had to compete with better-educated city dwellers while also navigating a system of knowledge whose "rules," so to speak, were opaque to them. The benefits of local knowledge, which people had enjoyed in the past, were no longer applicable to the creation of modern, urbanized communities in the 1960s and '70s. This double discrimination, ultimately, determined the relationship of rural youths to schooling: While one portion of the youth population actively used education to change their social status and move to urban areas, the other chose resistance and rejected schooling altogether. In both cases, their relationship towards study served as an indicator of the place these rural schoolchildren would occupy in the socialist future.

Rural Biographies

Yuri V. was born in the village of Probudovo, in Zvozsky Selsoviet, Kirillovsky District, Vologda Oblast, on 20 April 1949.[30] After the village was flooded in 1953, his family moved to the village of Kabachino, in the neighbouring selsoviet. Yuri V.'s mother worked as a calf tender on the kolkhoz "Red Banner." His father had been seriously wounded in the leg during the war, rendering him unable to work; he received a small pension from the District Executive Committee and occupied himself by going around to houses in the vicinity and repairing shoes. Yuri was his family's the only child after his younger brother died in infancy. As was standard in the area, they lived in their own wooden home and kept a cow, a calf, and sheep. Yuri's parents had received a primary education and were not party members.

At the age of seven, Yuri began attending the ungraded primary school in Ivisty and afterwards continued his studies at Goritsy Eight-Year School, located on the opposite side of the Sheksna Reservoir. At the Goritsy school, he was accepted, along with most of his peers, first into the Pioneers and then into the Komsomol. After graduating from the eight-year school in 1961, he went on with four of his classmates to study in the upper grades at Kirillov Secondary School.

There was no space available for him in the school dormitories while he was studying in the district. So, each day, Yuri would return home on foot, covering a distance of more than five kilometres while studying in Goritsy and ten kilometres while studying in Kirillov.

Yuri was not a star pupil; he often received 4s (on a scale of 1–5) in his school reports and daily journals, and even a few 3s every quarter, although he was well liked by the teachers on account of his good behaviour and learning abilities. In 1964 he submitted documents to the Vologda Dairy Institute along with three other graduates from Kirillov Secondary School. After passing his exams, he became a student in the VDI Agricultural Mechanization Department. It was then, after presenting his acceptance notice to the Migachevo Selsoviet, that he received a passport and moved to the VDI "student city," the settlement Molochnoe. After the first, decisive semester, Yuri was the only 1964 graduate of Kirillov Secondary School to continue his studies at the institute.

Tatiana K. from Kabachino, the village neighbouring Yuri's, was ten years his junior. She had been born in the village of Nilovitsy, in Nilovitsky Selsoviet, Kirillovsky District, in 1958.[31] In 1961, Tatiana's family was resettled because the territory where the village was located was to be flooded, and her parents bought a house in Kabachino. Tatiana's father, a party member, worked first as an electrician and then as a forester. Her mother was a milker who worked first on the kolkhoz "Red Banner" and then on the sovkhoz "Vorobyevsky" following the unification of the two kolkhozes. Tatiana was the third of the family's four children. Like Yuri, she started her schooling at the ungraded primary school in Ivitsy in 1965 and went on to study at the eight-year school in Goritsy. During her school years, Tatiana was a dutiful student and became the school Komsomol organization secretary. Like Yuri, Tatiana did not stay at the dormitory and slept there only when the road conditions were poor in spring and fall. After graduating from the eight-year school in Goritsy, Tatiana enrolled in Professional College No. 12, part of the Vologda Linen Processing Plant, and graduated in 1973. She became a weaver and continued to work in Vologda. Then, in 1977, family circumstances obliged her to return to her parents in the countryside, where she became a lab technician for the sovkhoz "Vorobyevsky" and measured the fat content of milk produced on the farms. After a year she moved in with her relatives in Moldova and began working at the baby food plant in Tiraspol. At the beginning of the 1980s, she returned to her parents before moving once again, this time to Cherepovets. From that time on, Tatiana would live in

Cherepovets, working in the metallurgical plant and driving out to visit her parents in the village to help with haymaking.

Both Tatiana and Yuri left the countryside to receive an education. Although Tatiana's educational institution of choice was less prestigious than Yuri's, she chose to study in the oblast's city centre and picked a profession connected with an "urban" industry.

Sergei T. was born in 1967 in eastern Vologda Oblast, in the village of Nikolskoe, Totemsky District, the birthplace of the Vologda poet Nikolai Rubstov.[32] Like many of his rural peers, he changed schools three times over the course of his studies. First, he went to an ungraded primary school, located three kilometres from the village where he was born. Then he joined an "eight-year." Finally, he attended Nikolskoe Secondary School. From the age of ten, Sergei lived in school dormitories. He was a *khoroshist* (lit. "good-ist," one who studies in the "good" grade range of 4s and 5s) and always earned high marks. After receiving his school diploma in 1984, Sergei enrolled in the History Department of the Vologda Pedagogical Institute (VPI) and participated actively in the school's union life. Union activity became Sergei's primary occupation after graduating from VPI.

The choice to migrate from village to city in search of education was common among rural youths.[33] According to statistics from a 1967 report on youth migration in Vologda Oblast, young people were the largest segment of the population moving out of the more than one hundred kolkhozes in the oblast: "Among those moving out, 44 per cent are between 16 and 19 years old, 17 per cent are between 20 and 25 years old, 10 per cent are between 26 and 30 years old."[34] Evidently, the age of the remaining 10 per cent is unknown. Young people made up 81 per cent of the total number of migrants.

Nevertheless, during the 1960s secondary school "gen-comp" had yet to be implemented, which indicates that education was not the primary cause of migration. In 1967, 63 per cent of young people moved to the city for work after finishing seventh and eighth grades.[35] In the 1970s, however, the number of schoolchildren who chose to continue their education grew significantly. Thus, in the 1963–4 school year, there were 4,624 pupils in the oblast studying in the ninth grade. This was approximately one-fifth of the 22,947 students studying in the eighth grade. In the 1964–5 school year, there were already 7,759 ninth-year students versus 25,546 eighth-year students.[36] That means almost one-third of the eighth-grade graduates continued their studies. In the 1968–9 school year, the official push for general education boosted the percentage of eighth-grade graduates who continued to the upper grades of secondary school or enrolled in specialized secondary-level educational institutions to 65.5 per cent.[37]

For an *otlichnik* (excellent student) or a *khoroshist* (good student), leaving the countryside by enrolling in an urban professional college was much simpler than for those students who just barely passed their school subjects. Enrolment in a technical college almost always came with a guaranteed place in the dormitories and a small stipend. Although the stipend was insufficient to support a student without any parental help, for many, moving into a technical college became the start of independent life.[38] As Iya V. recalls, after moving out of the village of Ivanovskoe to the Ustiuzhensk Agricultural Technical College at the age of fifteen, "We would cry. We wanted to go home. But that was the first year. After that it became easier. We grew up."[39]

Students in rural localities studied assiduously not only out of curiosity and scientific propensity, but because they were motivated by the desire for a better "urban" life.[40] As Yuri remembers, his parents often reminded him that he would stay in the countryside if he studied poorly.[41] Tatiana K.'s family also prepared her to move out of the village, and her mother, who had only a primary education, would check every day to ensure that the children had completed their homework.[42]

The motivations of teenagers who strove to successfully graduate from school and attain a profession seemed to align with the goals of school administrations. However, the options for rural *otlichniks* and *khoroshists* in Vologda Oblast to continue their studies and pursue the specialties that interested them was significantly limited in the 1960s and '70s in comparison with the opportunities presented to school graduates from the oblast capital and other city schools. Rural schools were unable to provide the level of knowledge and preparation required by the country's most prestigious universities, and the array of professions offered at geographically accessible professional and technical colleges were typically limited to the agricultural, pedagogical, and medical spheres.

Yuri and Sergei did not choose to pursue higher education in Vologda foreseeing themselves returning or spending long periods of time in the countryside, although they were trained, respectively, as a teacher and engineer, which were important professions in villages. By contrast, Yuri's VDI experience and the fact that his professors noted his academic abilities allowed him to become a graduate student at the Leningrad Institute of Agricultural Mechanization. Similarly, Sergei's diploma from VPI was a stepping stone to a successful career in a union organization in the oblast centre rather than in the village where he was born.

Tatiana K., like many of her peers, preferred to study in a vocational college associated with a city industrial enterprise rather than attend the upper grades of secondary school, as this would guarantee her a job in Vologda. Although Tatiana's choice was orientated more towards quickly establishing a profession and obtaining necessary financial independence than securing long-term career opportunities, her pragmatism also resulted in her coming to understand the importance of education.

As she remembers, "Mom really wanted me to go study to become a doctor. But to do that I would have to finish the tenth grade. I could go only after the tenth grade, and I would have had to go to Kirillov for the ninth and tenth grades. And at that time there was still the perception that Kirillov, that's the city. You needed to dress up at least somewhat accordingly. And how were we walking around here? We didn't have winter boots – just *valenki* with galoshes. It was embarrassing to walk to school in *valenki* with galoshes. We didn't have a proper winter coat either, just a quilted jacket or some shabby old coat. And at that age – fifteen, sixteen years old – you already wanted to wear something ... to buy clothes, that's all. And so, I didn't go. I went to Vologda to a professional college. I thought, after a year of studying there, I'll be able to dress up."[43]

Characteristically, graduates from rural eight-year schools located in places significantly more developed and closer to urban locations, such as the Maisky settlement in Vologodsky District, also strove to attain "urban" professions or higher education. Judging from a 1975–6 work report on Maisky Eight-Year School, out of the 57 school graduates, 24 continued to the ninth grade, 10 enrolled in technical colleges with a three-year program of study, 2 enrolled in medical professional colleges, 1 enrolled in a jurisprudential technical college, 10 enrolled in city vocational colleges with a secondary-level curriculum, 5 enrolled in rural vocational colleges, and 1 enrolled in a Suvorov school.[44] The fate of the remaining 5 students was not mentioned in the report. Probably, they found work or moved to another region. Graduates of Ogarkovo Eight-Year School in Vologodsky District had similar preferences. Of the 87 eighth-grade graduates in the 1975–6 school year, 55 continued their secondary school education, 8 enrolled in technical colleges, 13 enrolled in city vocational colleges with a secondary-level curriculum, and 10 enrolled in rural vocational colleges. The plans of the remaining student were unknown.[45]

The demand for secondary and higher education was much greater in city schools than in rural schools. In industrialized Cherepovets in the 1968–9 school year, 89.3 per cent of the students finishing eighth grade continued their education. Meanwhile, in rural Velikoustyugsky, Ustyuzhensky, and Kichmengsko-Gorodetsky Districts, only 31–36 per cent did so.[46] Thus, education was a means of attaining a qualitative change in social status in Soviet society. Although the passports of rural school graduates still showed "kolkhoz worker" on the line denoting origin, by enrolling at universities and technical colleges, rural youths joined the social group "students," a step to becoming either public servants (intelligentsia) or workers. Receiving an education was guaranteed to raise a person's social position even if that person lived in a rural locality. Moreover, institutions of secondary and higher education were usually located in cities or large settlements. Thus, along with the benefits of changing their social affiliation, rural youths were able to legally migrate and receive a city residence permit, albeit temporarily. In this way, rural youths were able to address the problem of territorial inequality: Education gave them the chance to leave less developed rural districts and move to more developed ones.

The Hierarchy of Rural Schools

Despite a unified school curriculum, Soviet schools differed from one another significantly.[47] The Soviet elite studied in certain schools while the representatives of the "working class" and the "working peasantry" studied in others.[48] The inequality established in the 1930s become ever-more visible in the post-war period.[49]

The best schools in Vologda Oblast in the 1960s and '70s, those that offered the most comprehensive course of study (most importantly, English-language instruction), were located in the region's biggest cities, Vologda and Cherepovets. Thus, the former Aleksandrovskoe Realschule became Vologda School No. 1 after the revolution and conducted several subjects in English.[50] The Cherepovets Mariinskaya Women's Gymnasium became the Maxim Gorky Model School No. 1.[51] These schools prepared their graduates for enrolment in institutions of higher education in the oblast centre, as well as in Moscow and Leningrad. Pre-revolutionary educational establishments in district centres were also transformed into schools, but there were not enough of them to provide for all those wishing to study. New schools began to be built alongside older ones in the 1960s. These new schools, unlike the old institutions, had not only to bring together pedagogical personnel but also to obtain school supplies, of which there was a sharp deficit.

Graduates from rural "eight-years" did not usually go on to study at the best schools in Vologda Oblast's cities. Two crucial reasons contributing to this were, first, the practice of selecting students during the early stages of their education and, second, a lack of dormitory facilities to house the students. Nevertheless, some schoolchildren from rural localities did continue their studies in city schools, admittedly only when they lived in nearby villages. Thus, in Vologda Oblast in 1976, 10 per cent (1,416 people) of the total number of eighth-year graduates from rural schools went on to study in city schools.[52]

In the 1970s, graduates of Maisky Eight-Year School in Vologodsky District usually continued their studies either at School No. 6 in Vologda, located in VDI's Molochnoe student city settlement, or at School No. 27, on Klubova Street in Vologda proper. Both schools were considered city schools, and they were about equally distant from Maisky. The choice of school depended on the future plans of the student. If they planned on enrolling in VDI, then they would go to school in Molochnoe. If not, they preferred to go to Vologda.

After the privileged schools came regular city secondary schools, district centre secondary schools, schools located in military cities, and those created by railroad departments, such as School No. 39 in Vologda, created in 1905. These schools, unlike rural secondary schools lost in the backwoods, quickly received new buildings and equipment; they also rarely suffered from a lack of teachers, and their graduates were more willing to continue their education. For example, in the 1963–4 school year, the school in the city of Kirillov, one of the district centres of Vologda Oblast, graduated 60 students from the eleventh grade.[53] Of those, 33 enrolled in an institute of higher education, 6 went to specialized secondary educational establishments, 1 attended professional courses, 4 enlisted in the army, and 16 found employment. The high percentage of secondary school graduates from the district centre who enrolled in institutions of higher education can be explained not only by the high quality of the teaching, but also by student-selection practices in secondary schools for the 1963–4 school year. At that time, only the most motivated students were chosen to continue studying in the upper grades. The systemic change that led to universal admittance into the upper grades came during the late 1960s and early 1970s.

City schools and district centre schools were able to address personnel issues more easily as well. Teachers were more willing to take assignments in cities and railroad stations with a regular train service than in remote localities that were difficult to reach.[54] Schools connected to a governmental department often supported the teachers of "their" schools by providing them with access to department medical clinics and sanatoriums, which made these educational institutions even more attractive.[55] In a slightly advantaged position were schools located in "military cities" – that is, in places where military units were stationed. Remembering her experience being educated in such schools in various regions of the USSR during the 1960s, Tatiana S. emphasized that, while the quality of the teaching varied in different military cities, there was a universal emphasis on the strict observation of school rituals. These rituals included the wearing of required school uniforms, teachers' focus on disciple, and the practice of mandatory school "line" assemblies (so named because the attending children stood in rows).[56]

Fedotovo Secondary School was located at a military post approximately thirty kilometres from Vologda. Although it was considered a rural school, in many aspects it resembled the oblast's urban schools. The teaching faculty changed less often than in other schools because most of the teachers were the wives of officers. Military patronage enhanced the quality of military-patriotic events. During the 1971 school year, the student body had the best exam results in the district among graduating classes: 66.2 per cent of those who passed earned a mark of 4 or 5, and three graduates finished school with gold medals.[57] Judging by the school report from 1976, students from nearby villages were transported to the school either by bus and or in a specially equipped car.[58] The school had its own feldsher and dentist. There were two groups with an extended day (seventy people), eleven elective courses, clubs for ship and airplane modelling, a Club for International Friendship, and a Komsomol club called "Prometheus."[59] Professional training was provided in electrical engineering for military lighting installations (in contrast to the professional training provided in the Novlenskoe and Kurkino Secondary Schools in Vologodsky District, which prepared tractor operators). The school had nine active sport sections, and the hockey and volleyball teams became the champions of Vologodsky District more than once.[60]

The final and lowest rung on the ladder of school prestige were rural eight-year and secondary general compulsory educational institutions located in remote regions of the oblast, along with specialized schools. Housed in the buildings of former primary schools or churches, they received school supplies and equipment later than other schools. Often, these schools had very uneven student bodies, and, instead of full classes divided by age group, struggled to enrol a single class of children born the same year. In the 1960s and '70s, these schools were typically unattractive for teachers, and for years they "scraped by" only because the district public education authority assigned them trainees from pedagogical colleges and institutes. Glukharevo Eight-Year School, located on the kolkhoz "Vorobyevsky" in Glazatovsky Selsoviet, Kirillovsky District, is as an example of this type of school. In the 1966–7 school year, it served seven local villages, had a dormitory capable of hosting thirty-five students, and had five teachers, four of whom had already received pedagogical education, while the other was studying part-time at a pedagogical institute.[61] Built on an old ungraded primary school and funded by the kolkhoz "Battle" and later the sovkhoz "Vorobyevsky," the school was located in a wooden building heated by a stove and lacked sports facilities and a cafeteria. The school had five classrooms that together covered two hundred square metres.[62] One of the buildings served as a school workshop and, judging by the documentation, was equipped with lathes and drill presses to be used by classes of young boys. The girls had at their disposal a single sewing machine for the whole school. "Educational work" at the school in Glukharevo in 1966 included daily political education conducted by the teachers, various after-class excursions, as well as local studies (*kraevedenie*). One report mentions how students collected information about the history of the kolkhoz "Battle" in preparation for the fiftieth anniversary of the Soviet state.[63] Additionally, teachers organized birthday celebrations and festive evenings for the children. With this in mind, it is remarkable that in 1966, eighteen schoolchildren from the school were taken on an excursion to Moscow paid for by the gen-comp school fund.[64]

Ten years later, in the 1977 school year, there were only thirty-three students studying in Glukharevo Eight-Year School. Of these, most were in the eighth grade (eighteen), and both the first and second grades had only three students.[65] The school's technical equipment in 1977 consisted of a television and a narrow-film movie projector. The school library contained a thousand books, primarily textbooks.[66] The school was still housed in the old, stove-heated building. The Glukharevo school closed in the 1990s with the completion of the school optimization system.

The quality of schooling in rural localities depended not only on the location of schools but also on the relationships between sovkhoz and school administrations. In the settlement Maisky, the sovkhoz director held significant sway over school life. His decisions determined whether teachers received apartments in the settlement's new buildings, whether the school cafeteria received fresh fruit, berries, and meat, and whether rural athletes received a stadium. In response to the attention the sovkhoz paid to school affairs, schoolchildren and teachers helped by planting stock, bringing in the harvest, and sorting vegetables in the storehouse, all without pay. The Maisky student body and pedagogical collective provided this type of service for at least two weeks every year.[67]

Considering the limited number of schools in the oblast and the extremely long distances between each one, parents living in rural localities in most cases had no say over which school their children attended. Yuri ended up in the district's best school because the distance from Kabachino to Kirillov was less than the distance to Glukharevo. As it was, he still had to cover ten kilometres each day to reach school, travelling by foot, skis, or bicycle, depending on the time of year.

The most far-seeing parents sometimes changed their entire family's place of residence in the hopes of transferring their children closer to a "good" school. The family of Yuri's friend Aleksander B., whose mother worked as a teacher at the ungraded primary school in Ivitsy, moved from the village of Kabachino to Cherepovets to give their children an urban education.[68] Elena V.'s family, from Sokolsky District in Vologda Oblast, also moved several times. Elena V.'s father, a CPSU member and a kolkhoz chairperson, used the District Committee to move for work multiple times and took his family with him. However, with each new move, he tried to obtain a position located closer to the district centre in hopes that his children would finish their schooling there. As a result, having gone through her "eight-year" schooling in the remote country-side, Elena V. had her upper grades in an urban secondary school in the city of Sokol. This allowed her to enrol in the Sokol Pedagogical Professional College and later in the Vologda Pedagogical Institute.

"Cultural Leisure" for Rural Schoolchildren

In his research on free time in Russian culture, Stephen Lovell shows that leisure, as a cultural concept, took root in Russian and Soviet culture only with great difficultly.[69] Lovell writes, "From the very beginning, the Soviet 'new man' was supposed to include among his sterling qualities the ability to use time effectively and rationally. This would have obvious benefits for the productivity of labour ... yet it would also emancipate Soviet people from the wage slavery of the past. In view of this, free time became an important index of the success of the Soviet social transformation."[70] However, Soviet leaders could not ignore the fact that "Soviet promises of super-efficient industrial revolution" diverged from reality, and that the population was preoccupied with survival, entailing a blurring of the line between work and leisure. As a result, "one section of the population again had higher incomes and a wider range of opportunities to intensively and variously make use of its free time, while the other section lacked them."[71] The urban population, involved in Soviet transformations as a privileged group, found itself in an advantageous position compared to the rural population, who even in the mid-twentieth century had extremely limited time to spend on leisure.

Work on kolkhozes was followed by work on domestic plots, and, due to specific labour rhythms, that work was often irregular. As a milker from the sovkhoz "Russia," in Moscow Oblast, remarked at a meeting of agricultural *peredoviks* (state-of-the-art representatives) on the topic "Life for Young People in the Village" on 23 May 1968, "In the summertime people work without weekends. It's the same on the farm. Our day is disrupted ... Take our work: We milk three times a day. We don't have time to go to the club, let alone have conditions for studying. I finished eight grades and after that there's has been no way for me to study. We start to milk at eight in the morning and finish between ten and eleven o'clock."[72] The introduction of limited work hours and the division of work time from leisure in Vologodsky villages would occur only in the late 1960s with the abolishment of the *trudoden* system (1966) and the introduction of the sovkhoz system, which extended to the kolkhoz peasantry the privileges enjoyed by the working class: the right to an eight-hour workday, union benefits, weekends, and time off. Before this, leisure, understood as type of non-work activity, encompassed a very limited number of occasions and events. As R.V. Rykvina wrote, describing the way of life among the rural population in the 1960s and '70s, "there are groups of the population who do not experience a deficit of cultural benefits, and, in contrast, there are those who do not make use of what the village today can offer ... Elderly people in the village older than fifty and especially those older than sixty make practically no use of mass-cultural opportunities."[73] The author locates the reason for this in the dying out of traditional forms of leisure in the countryside, such as church holidays and customary peasant evening meetups called *posidelki*, as well as in the fact that "some forms of individual recreation that are widespread in cities (for example, collecting and amateur photography) are only weakly developed in the countryside."[74]

Rural children and young people were expected from a young age to shoulder the work responsibilities typical of village residents and therefore gained an understanding of free time through school. Teachers were the ones who explained how free time should be spent: on public works and cultural leisure. In the 1960s and '70s, schools gradually "won over" rural students' after-school time from traditional peasant domestic routines. Schoolchildren who lived in school dormitories or urban-type settlements usually did have free time, but most children from remote rural regions spent their after-school hours working and traversing the road between school and home. Yuri remembers that he had no time to read after his domestic duties, and so he read books while walking home.[75]

In terms of "cultural leisure," which was propagandized during those years, the school in Goritsy had a singing circle, a "DIY crafts" circle, a drama circle, a literature circle, and a Russian language circle.[76] The proximity to the House for Disabled War Veterans, the sole government institution that was not under the care of the kolkhoz workers but was instead funded through district and regional budgets, had a "civilizing" effect on the residents of the villages and surrounding area. The Goritsy House for Disabled War Veterans regularly showed films and had a wind orchestra and an active club. As a result, children from Goritsy preferred the cultural initiatives of this club to "extra-curricular work."[77] It was there that, if they desired, they could learn to play instruments, sing in the choir, or attend the film-mechanics circle.

Figure 4.1. Skating rink in Maisky settlement, 1973.

Source: Private collection of Alexandr Filin.

Thanks to the physical education teacher V.D. Ninilin, the Goritsy school had six working sports sections in the 1960s: skiing, shooting, track and field, tennis, volleyball, and football.[78] One student, Nadezhda V., from the village of Kabachino, who showed promise in cross-country skiing competitions as a student, tied her future profession with sports. After graduating from the Goritsy "eight-year" she enrolled in one of the technical colleges for construction in Leningrad that was putting together a "sports curriculum." Later she became a children's trainer. Aleksander K., from the village of Kargach, also attended a school skiing section.[79]

Generally, sport, as opposed to other types of school "extra-curricular activity," found adherents fairly easily among rural youth. Rural schoolchildren of the 1960s and '70s took ball games (football, volleyball, basketball) that they learned during physical education class in school and played them alongside traditional village games such as *lapta*. Handmade skis and chess sets became the first sports equipment in Yuri V.'s family.[80]

Organizing summer work camps and leisure camps for rural schoolchildren became obligatory for school administrations in the 1960s and '70s as a means of overseeing children's behaviour over the holidays. Unlike military sports camps, those that were part of the "Komsomol active," and Pioneer camps, "labour and leisure" camps entailed not only leisure but work in the fields of sovkhozes and kolkhozes. Thus, working in the Yermakovo Secondary School camp "Youth," schoolchildren sorted 3 million eggs, transported 150,000 heads of poultry, and prepared 150 tons of vitamin flour. The leisure aspect consisted of trips to the regional drama theatre, recreational evenings, hikes, Spartakiads, concerts, and meetings with front-line soldiers and veterans.[81]

In the labour and leisure camp for the school in Goritsy, which was organized in the 1960s, the participants were mostly young people from the settlement, including those who arrived in summer to their family dachas, rather than the schoolchildren who came from "beyond the river."[82] Adolescents from the villages were typically occupied during the summer helping their parents with haymaking. Yuri V. remembers feeling acute envy towards the children who came to the countryside from the city in summer, when, instead of swimming in the river and having fun, he had to spend his entire holidays working with his parents to prepare hay.[83] This was also why Yuri was unable to attend student construction brigades over the summer holidays.

In contrast to their counterparts in Goritsy, the students of Maisky Eight-Year School were enthusiastic about the leisure opportunities offered at the Pioneer camp "Builder," which was organized by the sovkhoz. Adolescents from Maisky did not work in the hay fields because the population of the settlement, though they held a certain number of domestic livestock (mostly pigs, chickens, and sheep), did not have to worry about feeding large animals. Instead, feed could be bought on the sovkhoz.[84] After Khrushchev's policies aimed at limiting domestic livestock on individual plots and a de facto ban on holding cows in urban-type settlements, the residents of Maisky did not keep cattle. As a result, the children of sovkhoz workers had a lot of time for recreational activities. The camp for the sovkhoz "Maisky" was located on the shore of the River Toshnya, not far from the settlement. It ran during all three summer shifts.

The number of children enrolled in school camps and labour-oriented summer camps grew throughout the Vologda region throughout the 1960s and '70s. In the summer of 1965, approximately 25,000 schoolchildren attended 102 Pioneer camps outside of cities. At the same time, 5 sports and wellness camps were organized for upper-year students by the sports societies "Labour," "Harvest," "Spartak," the regional sports school, and the regional Komsomol camp. Additionally, there were 9 tourist camps (*turbaza*) in the oblast's cities. Komsomol youth camps and labour and leisure camps, "where the manageable productive labour of students is combined with various interesting activities and character-building leisure," were created in all rural secondary schools.[85] Judging by one report, in the 1968–9 school year, 115,000 schoolchildren

(47 per cent) were involved in organized summer recreation, including tourist camps and playground groups put together by housing management offices.[86] In the 1979–80 school year, there were 262 labour and leisure camps working in the oblast, encompassing 10,715 people.

The Soviet sociologist of education Fridrich Filippov distinguished between the Soviet educational system and the educational systems of capitalist countries by arguing that, whereas the latter reproduced class inequality, the Soviet system liquidated it.[87] The primary task of the educational system in a mature socialist society was understood to be overcoming the vestiges of class distinctions. In the Soviet view, then, rural schools in the 1960s and '70s were understood not as an institute reproducing a class identity and the values of a given social group, but as a part of the general Soviet educational system. The school was conceptualized as outside of the class system and capable of offering identical curriculums in the city and in the countryside. Schoolchildren in villages and settlements memorized the same poems and solved the same mathematics problems as children in cities. And although the school system did not guarantee that students would master the school program as thoroughly in the countryside as in the best schools in oblast centres, the similarity in school programs allowed the most motivated rural children to enrol in institutes, technical colleges, and universities after graduation, albeit within the oblast. At the same time, creating analogous school curriculums could not mask the colossal differences between the educational opportunities afforded students at rural schools and those at urban schools. These discrepancies included disparities in teacher staffing, the availability of equipment and buildings, as well as the possession of sports facilities and equipment. Soviet leadership admitted these discrepancies only in 1974, when it initiated an aid program for rural schools that required oblast funds to be sent to remote educational institutions as a priority.

Nevertheless, rural adolescents made ample use of the opportunity to study and raise their social status within rural localities, leveraging continued study as an opportunity to move out of the countryside. Even given this situation, however, the remote locations of schools, lower levels of funding, a lack of teachers, and the exacting pragmatism of the government, which tried to influence the professional choices of graduates, proved to be obstacles to educational equality. The best students scoring 5s in rural schools lagged behind their urban counterparts not only in terms of their level of knowledge, but also in their access to it. The obligation to help their parents with haymaking, the long roads they traversed to school, shortages of textbooks and equipment, and, finally, a lack of connections when enrolling in higher education and funds on which to live at dormitories kept rural *otlichniks* and *khoroshists* from entering the most prestigious universities. As a result, the most realistic opportunity to receive an education for the majority of rural youths came in the form of professional and technical colleges with short training periods and ensured employment.

Chapter Five

On the Margins of Vologda Villages: Poor-Performing and "Mentally Deficient" Students

The Story of Gena S., or Why Rural Schoolchildren Did Not Want to Go to School

In Soviet discourse, the government regarded the academic success of rural students and their participation in Komsomol and Pioneer organizations as indicative of progressive changes to rural communities. By contrast, unwillingness to study, entering family life immediately after school, and/or avoiding government social initiatives were interpreted by the state not only as rejections of progress, but as dangerous developments in Soviet society. The government condemned such behaviour, and in certain cases deemed it socially dangerous. As a result, it could provoke disciplinary action, such as compulsory school placement, punishments for absenteeism, fines, and even a referral to a prison-type school. These measures, admittedly, were far from universally effective, and the rural population continued to reproduce practices that it considered correct and acceptable according to its own standards, independently of the government's stance.

Gennady ("Gena") S. was born in 1954 into a family of public servants who had worked in inland river navigation before settling in the village of Mys, in Kirillovsky District, Vologda Oblast. Gena's parents were of peasant origin and had been raised in nearby villages. They gave up their work in navigation to provide an education to their children (three sons, of which Gennady was the youngest). In 1961, Gena started first grade at the four-year ungraded primary school in Ivitsy and finished his studies there in 1965. He decided not to continue his education and refused to enrol in Goritsy Eight-Year School, located across the Sheksna Reservoir from Mys. Gena went on to spend his life in villages in Migachevo and Zvozsky Selsoviets, where he worked as an odd-jobber for the sovkhoz "Vorobyevsky." After the sovkhoz went bankrupt at the beginning of the 1990s, Gena had no official work appointment. He was not called to the army for medical reasons. He was unmarried, had no children, and spent his whole life living with his mother, who, until the mid-1990s, kept a cow, a calf, and sheep. Accordingly, along with his primary work on the sovkhoz, Gena tended their household plot, growing vegetables and preparing firewood and hay for the winter. He never returned to school. He was the last permanent resident of Kabachino, and, after his death in 2015, the village was completely deserted, coming back to life only in the warm months with the arrival of dacha vacationers who had permanently moved from the countryside to the city.

Gena S.'s life story was not unique in rural localities during the 1960s and '70s. Every year, commissions for minors' affairs removed dozens of students from schools in the oblast's various districts. For example, during the first half of 1974, the Vologodsky District commission removed ten students who failed to graduate from eighth grade and who were unwilling to pursue their studies further.[1] Among them was Yuri E., a seventh-grade student from Svetliakovskaya Eight-Year School. In 1976, he left school and enrolled in tractor operator courses independently.[2] Nikolai V., a student from the village of Dubrovskoe, left Zaonikievskaya Secondary School during the eighth grade. A commission arranged for his employment on the kolkhoz "Red Star."[3] Anatoly R., a sixth-grade student from the settlement Maisky, left school in 1974 and was employed on the sovkhoz "Maisky."[4] Another student who counted on being removed from school was Vladmir K., a tenth-grade student from the settlement Yermakovo, in Vologodsky District, who attended only twenty-nine of ninety-five days of school in 1976.[5] When a commission questioned him about his absences, he replied that he preferred working to studying.

The same was true in Kirillovsky District, where students also regularly left school without graduating. For example, a 1964–5 report on the condition of school education in the district reported that 4 students left Petrovskoe Secondary School in September 1964 alone. Another left the school in Charozero, and both the Goritsy and Nikolsky Torzhok schools lost 2 students.[6] In 1972, 8 students were removed from schools in Kirillovsky District.[7] According to the Vologda Oblast Statistics Department, altogether in 1965 there were 1,586 teenagers younger than eighteen and without an eight-year education who began employment at various enterprises in the oblast. Of these, 802 went to work on sovkhozes.[8]

Even though the number of rural youths in the oblast who did not finish or left school early in the 1960s and '70s was less than the number of students who successfully completed the eight-year school program, the cases of Gena S. and other adolescents who abandoned school illustrate a significant phenomenon of late-Soviet village life. In particular, they show that many rural children did not build their lives around receiving an education and did not consider education a necessity for rural life.

In the view of Michel Foucault, formal education functions as an instrument of oppression and a tool for imposing dominant knowledge.[9] Thus, it comes as no surprise that the history of national systems of education is full of stories of resistance to schools or school reforms by certain social groups. Although scholarship usually connects the opposition potential of school protests with groups struggling for their national language or with the forced Christianization of Indigenous peoples (in Canada, for example, where this has been recognized as a genocide), resistance to schooling is not limited to these contexts.[10] Furthermore, since the 1960s pedagogical research addressing conflicts and opposition among various participants in the educational process has analysed these issues through the lens of sociological "resistance theory."[11]

It was interest in the "quiet protest" of students (and their parents) who were unwilling to accept academic standards as definitive and vital life strategies, and the connection between these processes and the concept of social class, that laid the foundation for the theoretical discussion around Paul Willis's study of working-class teenagers in Britain.[12] The historian of education Kirill Maslinsky argued that, from the point of view of this theory, school protests could take on very different forms: "Tardiness, unfinished homework, inattention and chatter in class, various pranks on the teacher (a tack on a chair, a board coated in wax, a rat thrown into a briefcase), anecdotes about school, indecent and mocking alterations of the school curriculum – these and many other widely recognizable features of everyday school life can be interpreted as forms of quotidian resistance among schoolchildren."[13] This is not to mention absenteeism. However, whereas Soviet pedagogy interpreted all of these phenomena according to the criteria of individual behaviour and deviation,[14] Paul Willis and his proponents demonstrated that there are social factors underlying people's relationship to education.[15]

The state, personified by the school administration and the teachers, unwillingly found itself on the front line of this social conflict. The system of student monitoring in schools was created to minimize the possibility of protest.[16] Thus, on the eve of the implementation of "gen-comp" in the 1960s, a whole system of public and state institutes was created to provide supervision over schoolchildren.[17] Pedagogical soviets, commissions for minors' affairs, parents' committees, and the teachers themselves were responsible not only for students' academic success, but also for monitoring whether they attended school and were integrated into the state's educational system.[18] As a result, keeping schoolchildren in rural classrooms became just as important as providing them with new knowledge.

Of course, it was not only in rural localities that children left school and exhibited apathy in their studies; city schools had their truants and low performers too. In the countryside, however, "typical" school problems occurred against the background of a much more complex conflict between traditional village life and government-imposed modernization. Rural students who failed their classes, like the underperforming students in Paul Willis's study of working-class teenagers in Britain, were the prisoners of social stereotypes that hindered their integration into a rapidly modernizing society.[19] Conceptions of the future based in class consciousness or social consciousness often contradicted the scenarios of modernization that the government prepared for young people. British teenagers from the outskirts of cities were not eager to use education for social mobility because they believed that the stable existence of factories would provide employment for multiple generations of workers. In the same way, poor-performing rural students in the Vologda region had no doubt that working the land and having knowledge of local life would provide them with the tools they needed to lead prosperous lives.

Gena S.'s decision to terminate his studies was in keeping with traditional peasant conceptions from the North-West, which viewed school knowledge in terms of its applicability to peasant labour.[20] Knowing how to read, write, and count was considered a sufficient skill set for life in the village. Moreover, for a long time lacking a school education did not prevent rural children and teenagers from moving to the city to work as nannies and domestic servants or to find employment at industrial enterprises.[21] Indeed, many of Gena's fellow villagers from the older generation had already left the countryside. However, the situation changed in the 1960s. The newest developments of the "gen-comp" program, initiated by the school reforms of 1957, made moving to the city problematic for uneducated rural youths. Soviet children were now required to attend school rather than work for hire. It also became problematic for employers to hire a teenager at an enterprise. The Veliky Ustyug Commission for Minors' Affairs *Work Report on Adolescent Employment and Education* describes a situation in which, for the 562 vacancies reserved for young people at urban enterprises, administrations turned down candidates in 50 cases.[22] Explaining the refusals, enterprises cited a lack of necessary resources such as professional training courses, skilled mentors to monitor them, etc. As a result, while families continued to send their children to live with relatives in cities, it was now to study rather than to work. This was the case for Galina K., from the village of Kargach, who moved to

Leningrad to live with her elder brother's family as soon as she became old enough to attend school.[23]

Meanwhile, for those who preferred to remain in the countryside and tie their future with traditional rural activities, mastering the eight-year school program often seemed excessive. This perception was intensified by the fact that it was often necessary for adolescents to move to attend school. Work on farms, in the forest, and in the fields frequently remained unautomated during the 1960s and '70s, which meant there was still a reliance on traditional skills and abilities passed on from one generation to the next.[24] Despite this, in the logic of state modernizers true knowledge could only be provided by government educational institutions: Only they could prepare literate tractor and combine operators, animal husbandry specialists, and milkers for modern agro-farms. And even though the quality of specialized-subject teaching turned out to be insufficient for preparing students to work as sovkhoz mechanics, leadership still considered this type of education to be more reliable than knowledge acquired through experience outside of school.[25] As the head of the Ministry of Agriculture's Chief Directorate for Educational Institutions, V.F. Krasota, stated at a meeting of Komsomol committee secretaries from agricultural institutions of higher education in 1967, "Over the past fifty years our country has seen striking changes in agriculture. There has been unhindered growth in the level of mechanization of all processes, technologies have changed, each year the portion of manual labour has decreased, and this process continues quite intensively ... All of this entails new, higher demands for organizing and overseeing agricultural production, as well as for quality specialist training ... Their role is growing on kolkhozes and sovkhozes."[26] Although the speaker embellished the state of agricultural education in the country fairly heavily here, the main point – that rural youths must study in order to operate machinery and organize agriculture – was articulated clearly in the speech and understood to be an immutable truth.

The push to teach the village to live "according to science" was not exclusive to Soviet leadership. As James Scott has shown, attempts to rationalize agriculture were made in many countries, including pre-revolutionary Russia.[27] In the USSR, however, this campaign reached its widest and most ambitious extent.

An active idealogue of the compulsory introduction of science into agriculture was Nikita Khrushchev, who directly linked the growth of harvest and milk yields in the USSR with new land management techniques, the introduction of novel crop cultures (most famously corn), new technologies, and the rationalization of agricultural production.[28] It is emblematic that the Virgin Lands campaign and subduing the "hungry steppe," both ways of throwing down the gauntlet to nature and demonstrating technological mastery, became the calling card for his agricultural reforms.[29] The push for land development, chemical development, and mechanization in the 1970s were proposed as a solution to ingrained problems in Non-Black Earth region agriculture and were the logical outcome of Khrushchev's programs. Subsequently, the policy of introducing science into agriculture was realized in several ways – namely, the appearance of a greater number of agricultural educational institutions throughout the country, a campaign to replace "practitioners" with "specialists," increased capital investments in mechanizing production, and the creation of a district-level agricultural management system to provide aid to kolkhoz and sovkhoz leadership. The consequences of these policies for Vologda region villages were not only increased numbers of tractors on the kolkhoz fields and the introduction of crop rotation on sovkhozes that were growing at excessive rates, but also the appearance of new rural hierarchies in which the "practitioners," who until then had been in charge of cultivating harvests, found themselves in a less privileged position compared to newly arrived "specialists" with state-recognized degrees.[30]

The government's disregard for traditional village agricultural methods also resulted in the policy of liquidating individual peasant land allotments.[31] Khrushchev's reformers were not deterred by the fact that these tiny plots, hitherto granted to kolkhoz workers, had been crucial to fulfilling the party's agricultural production quotas since the 1950s.[32] Working on individual plots, Vologda region kolkhoz workers brought in greater harvests and produced more milk than on the scientifically organized kolkhozes and sovkhozes. However, reformers saw peasant land allotments as competition for kolkhoz production and as an unfortunate development of private ownership in the countryside. As a result, Soviet leaders' faith in science and their conviction that it would open new horizons for agriculture became the foundation of political policy in Soviet villages. Educational reforms were a direct continuation of this policy. Those rural teenagers who refused to attend school and preferred local techniques and skills were automatically assigned to the margins of progress. In the 1960s and '70s, their ability to perform heavy peasant labour began to be valued less than their ability to complete school assignments. Although rural youths continued to master basic agricultural labour skills from a young age (without this, families would not have been able to survive in the countryside), they no longer considered this knowledge to be of critical importance for their futures.

Theoretically, young people who did not wish to study should not have been subject to sharp antipathy from sovkhoz and district leadership.

Many kolkhoz leaders understood that, alongside young specialists, farms needed workers to milk the cows and bring the sovkhoz herd out to pasture. The rural population was growing older, and the number of young people fit to work was becoming smaller and smaller.[33] However, leaders did not have real mechanisms for stopping youth migration from the countryside. Moreover, gen-comp programs, which were closely monitored by central leadership, stimulated migration. District leaders were obligated to do everything in their power to make young people study, even if it contradicted the desires of young people themselves, their families, and the kolkhoz leadership. As a result, after not finishing school, Gena S. was viewed by the government not as a bearer of traditional culture who should be involved in developing the locality, but as a marginal person on the fringes of rurality who symbolized the dead-end trajectories of those unconnected with educational processes in the countryside.

Teachers' Social Obligations: The Battle Against *Dvoechniks* and "Grade Repeaters"

Evgenii K. was born into a single-parent family on 21 December 1950, in the village of Sosunovo, Migachevo Selsoviet, Kirillovsky District.[34] His mother raised him alone and worked, like the majority of village residents, on a kolkhoz farm. When he turned seven years old, Evgenii was enrolled in a small rural primary school in Ivitsy located several kilometres' walking distance from home, a trek he made alongside other local schoolchildren. After first grade, Evgenii was held back a year. The impetus for this decision was provided by the teacher, who had requested that Evgenii's mother hold him back a year in order to balance the number of students, as there were significantly fewer in the first grade at that time than there were in the second. His academic performance was not a factor, and from the beginning he had received average marks. In other words, the decision was purely technical. Although the delay did not affect Evgenii's overall academic trajectory – he finished elementary school, then secondary school in Goritsy, completed a specialist program for tractor operators at the Belozersk Agricultural College, served in the army, returned to the sovkhoz, and finally left for Leningrad – it is extremely important to note the influence rural teachers could have on the extent, and time frame, of a child's schooling. An extra year spent in school held rural students back from independence and self-sufficiency.

A ban on removing children from school due to academic underperformance or bad behaviour, not strictly enforced in prior years, became general school policy in the 1960s and '70s. School administrations and committees of public education began to receive harsh penalties for student removals. The fact that Gena S. was in a transitional phase (having finished primary school but not yet having started eight-year school) saved him from the procedures typically accompanying deviations from the typical academic progression. Usually, a student could leave school only after passing through all the stages of the "fall of man": heart-to-heart and disciplinary conversations with the teacher, curriculum director, and school director; a meeting with the student's parents at the school; discussions of the student's behaviour at class and pedagogical meetings; and the final, decisive meeting of the Commission for Minors' Affairs, which would determine the student's fate.[35] This difficult, multi-step process was supposed to show students the error of their chosen path.

In response to the ban on removing children from school, teachers began to make children repeat years more often. "Year repeating" (*vtorogodnichestvo*), a system in which a child was prevented from progressing to the next grade if they had not attended enough classes or had not passed some or other subject, began to flourish. Thus, in a Vologda Oblast school report for 1971–2, 8.3 per cent of those finishing eighth grade were graduating late, and 4,236 children were repeating a class.[36] In Vologodsky District, 125 of the 9,790 pupils were "year repeaters"; in Kirillovsky District, 68 of the 5,289 students were repeating a year of the school program.[37]

The reason for this increase in "year repeating" in rural schools, apart from the general broadening of school studies, was the fact that new demands on educational programs were constantly being made while the conditions for meeting these demands simply did not exist in rural localities. For example, the introduction of the "classroom principle" to rural localities in the 1970s was predicated on the assumption that schools would have separate facilities for each school subject being taught: Specially equipped classrooms for chemistry, physics, and biology were supposed to have inventories of instruments and appliances – from microscopes and student lab sets to apparatuses for showing popular scientific films. However, rural "eight-years" did not have enough buildings.[38] The construction of new standard-model schools was slow and concentrated in cities and district centres, where the number of students was greater in comparison with rural secondary schools.

Several of the oblast's schools lacked teachers for basic subjects. There were instances in which math lessons were not held for periods of up to two years due to lack of teachers, as was the case for some classes at the Larionovo and Zaonikievskaya Eight-Year Schools in Vologodsky District during the 1963–4 school year.[39] Rural secondary and eight-year schools in the 1960s experienced problems not only with facilities and teachers but also due to a lack of books and course materials for teaching new curriculums, as well as with a shortage of basic materials for running the school, like lightbulbs. The Vologodsky District distribution order for 1965 allocated a mere six hundred lightbulbs to the district's eleven secondary and eight-year schools.[40] In such conditions, the only way to address year repeating was by lowering educational standards, which was a widespread phenomenon.

Both the removal of children from general compulsory schools and the practice of having them repeat a year of studies were perceived as the consequences of defective teaching. Teachers who worked without grade repeaters were lauded at meetings and described in reports as heroes of pedagogical labour.[41] Schools without repeating students were touted as models in front of the district's school directors.

The natural outcome of encouraging teachers who had no grade repeaters or students who fell behind was that teachers artificially inflated students' grades. According to the recollections of rural schoolteachers, the practice of "pulling" weak students up to the 3s – the grade necessary for receiving their school attestation – was commonplace. In one case, a student from the school in Kurkino who had failed eighth-grade chemistry multiple times passed the subject in the 1970 by correctly identifying Mendeleev in a portrait.[42] Extended-day groups, introduced to schools on a large scale in the 1960s and '70s, were designed to solve this problem. Teachers who led them ensured that students completed their homework, meaning they monitored the children in their after-school time as well as during school hours.

The history of Maisky Eight-Year School's battle for student performance is quite illustrative. A work report from 1975 tells the story of Leonid Z., a student in the sixth grade. He attended an extended-day group because his "parents were illiterate and could not ensure he passed."[43] Leonid was "attached" to a strong student, who attended the extended-day group with him and "reported difficulties to the teacher [and] worked through difficult questions together with him."[44] Additionally, Leonid's performance was discussed at a meeting of the Police Juvenile Department (Detskaya Komnata). As a result of all these efforts, he managed to pass his yearly exams and progressed to the seventh grade.[45] In another case, Seriozha F., who was falling behind in his studies and skipping "extended-day," was summoned along with his family to the police juvenile department. There, they threatened to change his mother's job as a civil servant on the sovkhoz "Maisky" so that she would "better look after her son."[46] The result of this meeting, the report notes, was that the young man stopped skipping his lessons and began to perform better. Ultimately, he passed his yearly tests and went on to the next grade. Another *dvoechnik*,[47] who arrived at the Maisky school in 1965, become subject to the influence of the school's student assembly, "where Pioneers themselves strictly inquired about Sasha I.'s absences and grades. Sasha gave his word that he would get his act together, and [he] held it."[48]

The Maisky school was located in an urban-style settlement close to a city. Meanwhile, other schools located in villages or on sovkhozes had a much harder time addressing year repeaters. The inspector for the Oblast Committee of Public Education, after examining secondary and eight-year schools in Kirillovsky District in 1972, wrote that "the schools have accumulated a significant number of sixteen- to seventeen-year-old students who are behind, requiring constant attention from school leadership and teachers. Thus, in Kuzino Eight-Year School there are 15 such students; Charozero and Petrovskoe secondary schools each have 6, in Kirillov Secondary School there are 5, in Kovarzino there are 7."[49] The inspector noted that schools had a "very low progression rate." In the Kuzino school only 50 per cent of the students finished eighth grade on schedule. The remaining children repeated a grade for two to three years. In the Glukharevo and Kotetskaya Eight-Year Schools the "progression percentage" was 66.6 per cent, while in Charozero Secondary School it was 47 per cent.[50] The statistics recorded in the report also illustrated that passing rates in rural schools were lower than in cities, as was with student motivation.

Aside from essentially pedagogical methods for addressing year repeating, there existed more radical measures. The 1960s saw the implementation of a system of specialized schools for children who were unable to fit into the general compulsory program. Poor grades came to be understood not only as the result of a student's living and schooling conditions, or of a teacher's level of experience, but as a reflection of the child's mental aptitude as well.

The Politics of Forced Modernization

Leaving school in the 1960s and '70s was not all that simple, especially if the student lived not live in a backcountry region of Kirillovsky District but in an urban-type settlement in Vologodsky District, where passing rates were monitored by commissions for minors' affairs.[51]

When a young person's case was reviewed by a commission, it was recognition that the efforts undertaken by the school's pedagogical staff had proven insufficient and that the involvement of authorities was needed to set the student on the correct path. A mark denoting that a student had been called to a district commission was grounds to have him or her put under police monitoring. Looking at the cases reviewed by the Vologodsky District commission throughout the 1960s and '70s, one can conclude that the majority of them were related to "gen-comp" – in other words, to removing a teenager from school and finding them employment. In the 1970s, with the appearance of specialized schools where school administrations could send children (and in doing so bypass commissions for minors' affairs) the number of such cases reviewed by commissions fell, to be replaced primarily juvenile delinquents. Thus, of the 113 cases reviewed in 1969 by the Vologodsky District Executive Committee's Commission For Minors' Affairs, 52 were related to missing school. In 1970, 26 out of 66 cases were related to schooling; in 1971, the equivalent figure was 35 out of 98, and in 1972 it was just 36 of 86.[52]

A district commission for minors' affairs was the only authority that could "free" a young person from the obligation of attending school and send them to work. It was not permitted for a minor to find employment independently without first finishing school or a professional college. For example, after reviewing the materials of Sergei M., a student of Specialized Professional Technical College No. 2 who lived in a brick factory settlement and had independently found work in Vologda Transportation Branch No. 1117, the commission required him to return to college.[53] In another case, the commission, while inspecting working conditions at the poultry factory "Vologodskaya," located in the settlement Gribkovo in Vologodsky District, made it a point to remind factory leadership that employing minors (eight-year school graduates) without notifying the district commission was a serious infraction on the part of the factory administration.[54]

The fact that the cases of teenagers who skipped grades or did not want to continue their studies were reviewed alongside those of teenagers who committed crimes is telling: From the government's point of view, both sets of teenagers diverged from the norm. They needed to be monitored by parents, teachers, and work collectives. Social policy research has shown that the deviant behaviour of children was conceptualized as criminal and medically diagnosable.[55] Moreover, the tendency to criminalize adolescent behaviour, although it grew more lax in the late Soviet period, remained an important facet of social policy in the USSR.[56] It is not incidental that the so-called Zabota-76 operation, initiated by the Ministry of the Interior alongside regional and district Komsomol committees and commissions for minors' affairs as a preventative measure against child and adolescent crime, began by compiling a list of all the schoolchildren who were not attending school.[57] Children who had left school, irrespective of whatever individual reasons might lie behind their choices, were nevertheless viewed as the source of the district's criminogenic situation. The persistent demand made by party and government institutions to commissions for minors' affairs to keep a list of children and adolescents "unreached" by study lasted throughout the entirety of the 1960s and '70s.

District commission case reviews were usually initiated by school administrations, police organs, or the representatives of public organizations such as publicly run police juvenile departments. When a child stopped studying in school this instantly raised the suspicions of the administration and placed the child in a high-risk group. For teachers, it was a signal that the child had "lost their way," that they might come from a troubled single-parent family or that they had become involved with the wrong group of people.[58] This logic was embraced primarily by teachers located in urban-type settlements; teachers in schools located far from district centres tended to be more patient when students missed class because they knew rural schoolchildren could face severe frosts, flooding, seasonal work on sovkhozes, or, as happened in Vologda Oblast in the 1960s, not having shoes to walk to school in.[59] People's Education Committees understood the seriousness of these issues, and, along with other novel changes introduced in the 1958 reforms, all rural schools received a "gen-comp fund," which distributed money to buy clothing and shoes for impoverished students.[60] For example, the gen-comp fund for the Goritsy Eight-Year School distributed eight pairs of felt boots to schoolchildren in 1968.[61]

For many young people who were chronically absent from school and systematically kept in the same class year after year, disparagingly called *pererostki* (lit. "overgrownagers" in a play on the word "teenager") by teachers, a work assignment was a long-awaited event, freeing them of the unpleasant obligation of studying in a class with much younger children. However, removal from school was viewed by teachers as a radical measure.[62] It was much more common that, after reviewing a student's case, fines were imposed on the parents and warnings issued for the student. Thus, the parents of Aleksandr A., a seventh-grade student from the Maisky settlement, were fined twenty roubles for their son's absences. They also received a warning that, in the case of another teacher complaint, Aleksandr would be sent to a medical commission and transferred to a specialized training school.[63] It is worth noting that the commission had no doubt that Aleksandr would receive the diagnosis necessary to authorize transferring him to a "specialized" school (*spets-shkola*) or training school (*spets-uchilishche*).

Transferring a negligent student from a general compulsory school to a correctional school, a school for working youths, a gen-comp consulting point, or somewhere else where they could complete their education, proved to be an effective solution. Young people who found themselves standing before the commission in Maisky could be sent, depending on their age, to a special agricultural training college in the village of Kubenskoe or enrolled in the settlement's school for working youths. This was fate of Olga M., who dropped out of Urban Professional Technical College No. 29 in Vologda and was subsequently employed at the settlement Maisky, where she became an officially registered resident and was required to attend ninth grade at a school for working youths.[64] In cases where there was no school for working youths in the vicinity, a teenager would be required to return to the school they had left. For example, the resolution for the case of Yuri E., who left school to take tractor operating courses, included an order to finish those courses and receive a tractor operating licence, but also required that he return to school and complete his education afterwards.[65] Leaving school before finishing eighth grade was simply not permitted.

There were few "evening schools" or schools for working youths in the rural localities of Vologda Oblast. Those that existed were usually located in district centres, which were extremely difficult to reach for residents of remote selsoviets. Therefore, hopes that young people who had dropped out of school would be able to finish their education were unfounded, although students who left were persistently enrolled in school "consulting points," which were meant to provide education to anyone who desired it.[66]

However, the most unpleasant decision a commission could take was to send young people to a so-called specialized school run by the Ministry of Education. These establishments were more reminiscent of prison colonies than schools and, evidently, were preserved in the Soviet education system from the 1930s, when the country's leadership subscribed to the idea that problematic youth needed to be punished rather than reformed.[67] These were closed schools for children with behavioural deviations. The teenagers who were sent to them had broken the law multiple times but who, on account of their age or insufficient evidence of a crime, could not be sent to youth detention centres. The biography of Lev R., a sixth-grade student from Boarding School No. 2 in Vologda who was sent to a specialized school by the Ministry of Education in April 1976, can shed light on how a rural adolescent could find himself in such an institution.

From the biographical information recorded in documents from that period, we learn that Lev was born on 22 May 1963, and that, until he was sent to the boarding school, he had lived with his parents in one of the peat-processing settlements in Turundaevsky Selsoviet, Vologodsky

District.[68] According to the documents, Lev's father "often drank and was rowdy, for which he had been brought before the law," and was being treated at Velikoustyuzhsky Medical-Labour Centre. His mother was also neglectful, and Lev often lived with his grandfather. He began to roam the streets in third grade and to smoke in fourth. Lev's behaviour was discussed multiple times at the boarding school's class and administrative meetings. On 13 December 1976, his behaviour was reviewed by a commission for minors' affairs after he was caught stealing vegetables from a dacha. As a result, Lev's parents were fined ten roubles and the boy himself was given a strict warning. On 1 April 1976, Lev was once again called before the commission on account of his vagrancy. Afterwards, the commission sent him to be assessed by a psychiatrist. The third meeting, held on 16 April, proved to be decisive. The result was that Lev was sent to a specialized closed-type school run by the RFSFR's Ministry of Education.[69] The decisive factor was that Lev had stood before the commission three times, and although his crimes were not severe – the issues under discussion were vagrancy and vegetable theft – the punishment, being sent to a specialized school, points to the radical nature of the measures the government undertook to counter not only those who rejected education but also those who disregarded the warnings of government organs.

Rural schoolchildren, well known in city secondary and eight-year schools for their tardiness and untidy appearance, were often marginalized by teachers and school administrations. According to a teacher from the school in Goritsy, Kirillovsky District, rural children, unlike those who lived near the school and did not need to live in the school dormitories (*slobodskie* and *internatovskie*), usually had their own class for each age group and were considered the most problematic.[70] Classes assembled from graduates of the Goritsy "bush-like" network of ungraded schools were viewed by teachers as a source of year repeaters, *dvoechniks*, and grade skippers.[71] Although, according to the memories of the teacher herself, the academic performance of these classes was no lower than that of others of the same age group, there was a persistent perception in the school that the "village kids" were the worst students.

A similar practice of segregating children from rural schools by grades was observed in other schools in the oblast. In the secondary school in the settlement Molochnoe, the children from the villages surrounding the student city were put into grade "C," while those who were the children of professors and instructors at VDI or of the public servants of various scientific institutions were usually enrolled in grades "A" and "B."

Secondary school teachers did not expect meaningful achievements from rural schoolchildren because they viewed them not only as schoolchildren but also as "carriers of peasant consciousness," ready at any moment to quit their schooling and shirk their academic duties. School dormitories and extended-day groups, created to establish better study conditions and increase monitoring of student performance, cut the tie between rural students and their peasant lifestyle. Now children were supposed to think about homework rather than domestic work. Any attempts by rural schoolchildren to avoid the system of mandatory modernization imposed on them by the ten-year school program were impeded whenever it was possible.

Dvoechniks in Kirillovsky villages and those in newly formed Vologda Oblast settlements were two completely different groups of young people. In the first case, they were adolescents who preferred being good peasants to poor students; in the second, they lived in furnished apartments in a new type of rural settlement and were free from having to work on the farm. In this way, they resembled urban *dvoechniks*. Their motives for quitting school were quite different: troubled families, protest against teaching methods, a boring school routine, and all of the other issues that have been described widely in literature on troubled youths.[72] Nevertheless, for district commissions of minors' affairs, as for many of the schoolteachers and administrators, differences in students' motives were not clear. They "punished" juvenile delinquents who stole motorcycles and engaged in hooliganism at railroad stations just as they punished timid rural adolescents who simply had no desire to attend school or spend their time receiving an education that was irrelevant to them.

The "Mentally Deficient" and Instrumentalizing Diagnoses

In her book *Right to Be Helped,* Maria Cristina Galmarini-Kabala argues that in the USSR in the 1930s, as in Europe, the basic contours of social policy towards marginalized social groups was formed around three constituencies: disabled people, single mothers, and children whose behaviour was deemed deviant.[73] As was the case in European countries, those placed in the latter category were either criminalized or medicalized. These strategies were supplementary, sometimes competing and sometimes augmenting each other. Thus, in the early post-revolutionary years, unsupervised children were considered the product of a social illness and reform was preferred to punishment.[74] It was at that time that "defectology" and "pedology" arose and attempted to explain childhood behavioural deviation in terms of the social conditions in which children were raised. In the 1930s, governments tended to criminalize the behaviour of "disobedient youth."[75] Children who demonstrated asocial behaviour were isolated from society in closed-type schools and were considered irremediable. However, beginning in the 1940s, children with behavioural disorders began to receive medical diagnoses more and more often, which entailed treatment and more humane societal treatment.[76] In the years of the "battle against hooliganism," overlapping with the Khrushchev reforms, severe punishments alternated with attempts to adopt prophylactic measures.[77] As Galmarini-Kabala writes, "Using medicalizing discourse, childhood psychiatrists could diagnose children showing 'incorrect' behaviour as psychologically traumatized and physically weakened, move them to medical facilities and blame their psychological defects on environmental factors, all without openly criticizing the existing social order."[78] Galmarini-Kabala emphasizes that the "pathologizing label of 'psychologically ill' was the lesser evil when compared to the label 'delinquent' in an authoritarian society."[79]

This important observation, based on research on Soviet social policy from the 1930 to the 1950s, remained relevant in the late Soviet period. Given the trajectory of the spread of modern knowledge (first in the city, then in the countryside), it is unsurprising that academic conceptions of the medical basis of delinquency reached the backwoods of Vologda Oblast only after a long delay. Furthermore, the lack of secondary and eight-year schools in rural areas until the 1960s, along with the limited level of medical care available to the rural population in the first postwar decade, kept rural childhood deviation under the state's radar for a long time. Its major manifestation – rural social conflict – were usually viewed through the lens of criminal justice rather than in terms of a psychological disorder of the participants.[80] However, the introduction of "gen-comp" in the 1960s fundamentally changed the situation. Rural adolescents who found themselves in the classroom often did not turn out to be the most assiduous students. Moreover, conceptualizing student behaviour in terms of social determination was extremely problematic because it contradicted the idea of a classless, egalitarian communist school system. In these conditions, a medical basis for explaining poor results or a lack of motivation became very popular. By adopting the diagnoses of "feeble-mindedness" (*slaboumie*), teachers and school administrations were able to adopt "soft" measures for addressing delinquency. Thus, in lieu of prison sentences for juvenile delinquents, children could be transferred to special schools with looser curriculum requirements or, as a last resort, released from schooling and given a work assignment.

In order to send a student to a specialized school, to work, or to free them from their studies, more was needed than the willingness of a teacher and the student or the permission of the parents. A crucial requirement was a medical assessment by a psychiatrist stating that the student was incapable of handling the school program.[81] Freeing a healthy but unmotivated rural adolescent from school was seen as a de facto admission that committees of public education were not coping with their "gen-comp" responsibilities. For this reason, the practice of removing a child on the basis of a diagnosis of mental deficiency (*slaboumie* or *umstvennaya otstalost*) became widespread in the 1960s.

Medical examinations for adolescents were conducted by military commissariats as well as by medical institutions. The commissariats ran health inspections for conscripts and young men who were on the military register. Sometimes they would "meet [students] halfway" by diagnosing secondary school–age "adolescents" with mental deficiency, giving them a basis to leave school and begin work on a sovkhoz. It was characteristic that this diagnosis, recorded in adolescents' case files during commissions for minors' affairs, did not, in some cases, prevent military conscription. For example, one such commission held in 1974 allowed Valentine B., a seventeen-year-old sixth-grade student from Sychevo Eight-Year School, in Kipelovsky Selsoviet, Vologodsky District, to find employment on the sovkhoz "Kipelovsky," whence, upon reaching lawful age, he would be sent to serve in the army.[82] The same decision was made concerning Leonid P., a seventh-grade student of Maisky Eight-Year School, who in 1976 was ordered by a commission to "find employment after finishing seventh grade on the basis of a Revolutionary Military Commissariat decision authorizing study in a school for working youths."[83] In contrast, sometimes a military commissariat would reject schoolchildren permanently, and the diagnosis of "mental deficiency," which was handed to them by a military psychiatrist, followed them to the end of their lives, albeit freeing them from army service.

Thus, a school report for Vologodsky District recorded that, "as a result of the decrease in year repeating, the number of held-back students has declined in the district's schools. Whereas in the 1969–1970 schoolyear there were 418 [such] persons, in the 1970–1971 school year there were 311, and at the end of the 1971–1972 schoolyear there are only 125 held-back students."[84] The report made clear that it was from this pool of students that schoolchildren were sifted out and employed without having finished the eight-year program. In 1972, there were only nine such students in the entire district: "They have all been employed according to a decision of the commission for work with minors and the military commissariat after medical examinations at the psychiatric hospital in Kuvshinovo. According to the conclusion of the medical commission, they have been recognized as mentally deficient and removed from the military register."[85] In other words, according to the logic of the report's authors, only ill or mentally deficient students could leave school. Other reasons for removal from school were not acknowledged.

The popularity of the "mental deficiency" diagnoses for describing adolescent behaviour in the 1970s can be judged by the fact that in 1971 the chairman for commissions of minors' affairs in Vologodsky District, G.V. Tsvetkova, used the diagnosis to explain the growth of juvenile crime. She wrote, "a large percentage of the adolescents who have committed crimes are persons whom a medical psychiatrist has assessed to be mentally deficient."[86] This wording indicates that the diagnosis, given to specialized school students by medical commissions, had become widespread, and that crimes and offences committed by students at specialized schools made up a large percentage of offences in the district overall.[87] During her report to party leadership about mental deficiency among adolescents, Tsvetkova seems to have been shifting responsibility for the growth of crime in the district away from her colleagues and herself. Thus, it was not the educators or the workers at educational institutions who should be held guilty for increased criminality, but the students' mental deficiency, which was diagnosed by a specialist and used to explain behavioural deviation. As a result, responsibility for underperformance was placed on children and their diagnoses rather than on the teaching collective.

Many of the schools for "mentally deficient" children were used as alternatives to schools for rural and working youths in the 1960s and '70s. The "Standard Statute for Specialized General Compulsory Boarding Schools for Mentally Deficient Children" set out the standard protocols in the 1970s.[88] These schools differed from general compulsory schools in their simplified curriculum and the additional measures taken for teaching children with developmental differences. Schoolchildren at specialized schools had almost the same daily academic rhythm as children in general compulsory schools, with the difference that classes were shorter and that their life took place primarily within the bounds of boarding facilities. In the 1964–5 school year, there were several specialized schools in Vologda Oblast. These included the Sazonovo Boarding School for Children with Tuberculosis and 15 schools for children "with defects in mental and physical development," which together housed 2,109 students.[89] In the following school year (1965–6), there were two more specialized schools added, and the student population grew to 2,520.[90] Moreover, wrote the author of a school report, "this year the regional public education authority has taken additional measures to find children with physical and mental developmental defects and bring them into schools. In all the oblast's districts and cities medical-pedagogical commissions have been assembled, headed by the leadership of specialized schools, where the oblast's paediatric psychiatrists are brought to work."[91] In 1966–7, there were already 18 specialized schools, and the number of "spets-students" grew to 2,978. By the 1971–2 school year there were already 22 specialized schools, of which 12 were located in rural localities and 10 were in the oblast's cities. There were 3,508 children studying in them, including 1,442 studying in rural localities.[92] In 1978, of the 166,608 schoolchildren in Vologda Oblast, 3,287 were counted as "children with defects in mental and physical development." This meant that 0.5 per cent of the total number of students were studying in one of the then 21 specialized schools.[93] Of these, 1,115 lived in a rural locality.[94] With every passing year, the oblast's contingent of specialized schools grew, and more and more children were deemed to be suffering from mental deficiency.

Underperforming students in Vologodsky District were sent to the Zaonikievskaya Specialized Boarding School, which had been founded in 1964 and was located within the cells of the Vladimirskaya Zaonikiyeva Pustyn religious hermitage in the village of Novoe, by Lake Kubenskoe. Transferring a student from a general compulsory school to a specialized school did not always occur with voluntary agreement between teachers and parents. This was the case even in rural localities, where teachers were generally trusted, and their advice usually followed.

One such conflict is described in a letter sent to the Vologodsky District Committee of Public Education on 10 October 1965.[95] The department received the letter from the village of Vedrakovo, in Novlensky Selsoviet. It was written by Alexander Ivanovich R., a kolkhoz worker and father of five children. The letter discussed the transfer of his daughter, Angelina, to the Zaonikievskaya school, located fifteen kilometres from Vedrakovo. Angelina, in the opinion of her teacher at an ungraded primary school, was unable to handle the first-grade program, and, as her father wrote "she sent my daughter to a specialized school."[96] Alexander Ivanovich brought to the department's attention that the girl had been the youngest in her grade, and that the teacher had decided right away to "send her to a school for imbeciles," and therefore "did not give her any marks and neglected the first-grader."[97] After she was transferred to a specialized school, Angelina's grades improved, and she received 4s and 5s. But, as her father wrote obvious emotion, "the girl gets upset in school and cries. It hurts her that she can't study in a normal school and not in a specialized school."[98] In conclusion, the father requested that the department transfer his daughter back to a general compulsory school, insisting that "there won't be any problem if she must repeat the first class. She is a healthy child and has never suffered from illnesses or complications of any kind."[99] In making his case, Alexander Ivanovich pointed out some important circumstances. First, he mentioned a teacher's duty and reminded the department that teachers must try to teach all students, both those who perform well in class and those who do not. Secondly, he explained that his daughter "is not crazy, and only [children] with health problems are sent to specialized schools," such as "after paralysis or flu complications."[100] Finally, he expressed his disagreement with Angelina's living in a boarding facility far from her parents: "she still has not turned eight and she should be living and studying with her parents rather than shedding tears in a specialized school ... I will not allow her to live in captivity."[101]

An answer to the distressed father's letter was prepared by 30 October. The head of the Vologodsky District Committee of Public Education was not swayed by the letter's arguments. He wrote that Angelina was required to continue studying in Vologodsky Assisted School No. 2 in Novoe: "according to the assessment of a doctor she is unfit for study in a general school."[102] Furthermore, the head warned, if the child was not present in school by 1 November, Novlensky Selsoviet would send the letter's author to a commission for minors' affairs, where he "would answer for disrupting gen-comp."

From the point of view of the father's peasant logic, sending an eight-year-old child to study fifteen kilometres from home while there was a school in her own village was a senseless act. He neither believed in the medical diagnosis given to his daughter nor understood the true reason for the transfer. The arguments he offered reflected his beliefs about the purpose of teachers in rural schools and the role of family in bringing up children. Ultimately, he was against boarding schools and wanted rural teachers to continue to work with all local children. This logic, however, contradicted the Committee of Public Education's conceptions of modernization, according to which specialized schools were the best means of ensuring underperforming students complete "gen-comp." as the prospect of an eight-year-old child being separated from her parents did not appear tragic to them, and it was not entertained that such a circumstance might have a negative personal impact on the child. In this way, the unification of urban and rural educational programs and the creation of educational infrastructure in rural localities expanded educational possibilities for high-performing rural students but reproduced discriminatory practices for rural schoolchildren who did not wish to study.

The school reforms of 1958, in bringing about serious changes in the late-Soviet countryside, not only occasioned transformations in everyday life for rural children and young people but also played a key role in rethinking child labour and the role of children in the process of articulating rural knowledge and traditions. The push to link school

Figure 5.1. Yuri V. and village girls during the seasonal village holiday in Kabachino, July 1967.

Source: Photo from the family archive of Yuri V.

with production in Khrushchev's policies came at the cost of disrupting the reproduction of generational rural practices. Although at times the burden rural children were forced to shoulder increased (they experienced pressure from the school to study and from their parents to work), overall, they were gradually excluded from the cycle of agricultural production and became more and more involved in the cycle of urban modernity. In essence, the generation of rural children and teenagers who grew up in Vologda Oblast villages in the 1960 and '70s were the first rural generation liberated from the necessity of dedicating all their time to agricultural labour. Studying and receiving an education became the primary obligation of rural adolescents during this period.

The existence of a large number of underperforming students in rural localities who differed from their motivated peers on account of their unwillingness to walk many kilometres to school and receive school attestations indicates that not all members of rural communities in Vologda villages shared the state's conception of progress. For many rural residents "life on earth" did not require additional knowledge. Moreover, unlike high-performing rural students, the *dvoechniks* had no plans to move away. However, instead of supporting such students and encouraging them to work on farms, the government marginalized them, labelled them "mentally deficient," and sent them to study in specialized boarding schools. In doing so, they robbed kolkhozes of their last hope of retaining a workforce. Even those who remained on sovkhozes to work could not, relying on their work ethic or savvy alone, compete with the status of their educated colleagues.

At the same time, rural school reforms that aimed to draw as many rural youths as possible into the educational process ultimately had a positive effect on the fates of many people who moved to cities. School graduates who came from the unprivileged peasant population were given the chance to start urban careers. It is remarkable that not one of my interviewees regretted having moved out of the countryside. Thanks to school education, rural youths – like Soviet youth in general – became part of a global trend towards urbanization that allowed them to perceive themselves as modern.

"Female Anti-Modernity": School Pregnancies

The majority of cases reviewed by commissions of minors' affairs in Kirillovsky and Vologodsky Districts involved young or adolescent boys; girls' cases were reviewed far less often. This was true both for situations involving violations of public norms and rules and for those connected with "gen-comp." In comparison to boys, girls dropped out of school at much lower rates.

Rather than searching for an explanation for this phenomenon in the specific social behaviour of girls, who tend to show a greater inclination than boys to upholding social norms and discipline, it should be sought in the distribution of gender roles in rural regions of the Russian North-West during late socialism.[103] "Female" work in peasant communities was connected with the fields – planting, bringing in the harvest, and looking after domestic animals.[104] Such work was marked by the social rituals accompanying it, often indicating who would be required to fulfil the work.[105] At the same time, modernization in rural communities (which had begun long before the revolution), the poor post-war demographic situation, and the acute necessity of partaking in "male work" regardless of sex, led to a significant shift in the gender structures of the post-war Vologda countryside. Nonetheless, in the USSR in the 1960s and '70s, the state actively emphasized gender differences, encouraging people to integrate into pre-existing gender roles dependent upon their sex.[106] It is true that, in rural localities, the situation was complicated by the fact that gender roles were traditionally monitored not only by the state but by "elder women" and the older generation.[107] Moreover, on account of the war and mass migration to urban areas, the sex make-up of the countryside was in a state of imbalance. Soviet post-war society had a severe lack of men of age to become fathers, which had a direct effect on gender roles.[108] In the 1960s and '70s, the mechanization that had reached rural locations had, for the most part, replaced the most labour-intensive agricultural processes, which had until that point been done by men: ploughing, sowing, bringing in the harvest, and mowing grass was done with tractors.[109] Meanwhile, mechanization lagged behind in "less labour-intensive" processes, such as weeding, watering, milking, and cleaning cattle enclosures, jobs usually performed by women. As a result, with the introduction of mechanized agricultural production men, who had traditionally performed the heaviest forms of labour in the countryside, found themselves in a privileged position. Moreover, "male" labour had always been better paid in rural localities than the labour of women.[110]

The model for distributing gender roles in the USSR, which had become entrenched by the 1960s, and which presupposed that in the second half of the twentieth century women were responsible both for production-related and domestic duties (such as preparing meals, caring for domestic livestock, cleaning the house, and looking after children), made the position of women in rural localities especially difficult.[111] The situation was further exacerbated by a labour shortage in rural districts of the North-West, meaning that the load placed on a single agricultural worker was much greater than in southern regions, where the availability of labour was greater. This was reflected, in particular, in the fact that it was almost impossible to put together an afternoon shift for sovkhoz farms in Vologda Oblast, meaning that women milker personnel were made to work without leave or weekends.[112]

Obviously, this scenario did not satisfy young women, many of whom tried tirelessly to escape the fate of their mothers and tied their future to receiving education and migrating.[113] In an attempt to alter the situation of gender-divided labour in the countryside, reform idealogues tried to "sit young women on tractors." That is, they tried to introduce them to more modernized "male" professions. These campaigns of the mid-1970s, like those of the 1930s, were not met with much support among the female population, despite being widely propagandized. Thus, there was no mention of women machine operators, women technical college graduates, or women who had taken classes in tractor operation in the participant records for the 1974 "All-Union Showing of Technical Preparation and Professional Mastery" for rural youths in Kirillovsky District.[114] But even when young women mastered agricultural technology, as had tractor operator Tatiana Novozhilova on the sovkhoz "Hard

Worker" in Kirillovsky District, who presented at the Regional Congress for Rural School Graduates in Vologda Oblast in April 1977, this did not change the disproportionate gender distribution of young rural workers.[115] As Novozhilova stated during her presentation, "there are few girls left on the sovkhozes. Work in animal husbandry does not attract them."[116]

There were various measures that sovkhoz leadership took in hopes of "securing" young women for the village. The professional orientation of schools and school trips to farms not only failed to attract young women to animal husbandry – it actually had the reverse effect. As A.A. Zametalov, the director of the sovkhoz "Kipelovsky" stated, "Work on farms is still fully unmechanized. Therefore, young people do not stay. Last year, three young women expressed their desire to go into animal husbandry, but, after seeing with their own eyes the heavy labour of milkers, rejected those ambitions. There is a great lack of personnel. Last year five people were sent to study at technical colleges and institutions of higher education. But because we are undergoing construction, the trained personnel must be sent to other farms."[117]

The secretary of the Vologodsky VLSKM District Committee offered the following solutions to stop youth migration in a 1977 youth work inspection report for the sovkhoz "Novlensky": "accelerate the construction and launch of mechanized farms"; "create conditions for youth labour and leisure"; address the problem of weekends; build a dormitory for young people; "improve mass-political work and cultural services for the population"; and build a bathhouse in the settlement.[118] But "the most important point for securing young women," in the VLKSM district secretary's opinion, "should be expanding the service sector: a hairdresser, a seamstress shop, a knitting workshop, and, accordingly, the organization of hobby circles in school."[119] In other words, the report's author understood that "women's jobs" could not be restricted to fields and farms.

Often, the circumstance that did in fact keep a young woman from migrating to the city was pregnancy (and the early marriage and motherhood that often ensued). It was not uncommon among rural youths in Vologda Oblast in the 1960s for a seventeen-year-old girl to become pregnant. At that time, the average age of marriage for women in the RSFSR was between eighteen and twenty-one.[120] Thus, pregnancies among secondary school students who were one year younger than the "statistically average" age of rural brides was not especially exotic in this context, although school administrations perceived them as extreme events. As Svetlana Adonievna wrote, "in the pre-war years having a child out of wedlock, as well as [intimate] relations out of wedlock, was not considered shameful or a moral crime," and only "Soviet post-war morality viewed relations out of wedlock differently: a young Soviet woman who had sexual relations was considered to have lost her 'honor and dignity.'"[121]

Typically, cases of school-age pregnancies were reviewed at pedagogical meetings with the participation of the parents and the "delinquent" herself. In accordance with the USSR codex of family laws, the age of marriage was eighteen. However, in cases where a pregnancy was attested by a medical note and the permission of the parents had been granted, marriage could occur at an earlier age.[122] As a result, a scandal sometimes ended in marriage.

News of a student pregnancy could reach the school by various routes. In some cases, the schoolchild herself told the class leader, while in other cases the pregnancy was reported by the medical workers to whom she had turned for help.[123] News of a student pregnancy would initiate a teachers' meeting, where the causes of the pregnancy were discussed. The student's personal characteristics were noted and the circumstances surrounding the pregnancy explained. If it became known during the investigation that the pregnant girl had been subjected to "coercive lewd actions," the police would become involved and the girl would be allowed an abortion.[124] If the pregnancy in question resulted from willing involvement in sexual relations, discussion focused on the girl's plans and the intentions of the father and the girl's parents. Either way, school administrations were unceremonious in how they intruded into the student's affairs and exerted influence on her decisions. Schools were held responsible by government educational organs for students leaving school or not completing "gen-comp." Thus, pregnancies, alongside suicides, were among the least desirable incidents for a school administration.[125]

After a case had been reviewed at a teachers' meeting, it would be sent to a commission for minors' affairs, which would then free the girl from the responsibility to attend lessons. Admittedly, however, commissions sometimes required the young woman to continue her education in a school for working youths or a professional college. This was the recommendation, for example, handed down to Liubov' E., a tenth-grade student from School No. 22 in the city of Vologda, who resided in a village in Vologodsky District and had been released from her studies due to pregnancy. She received an assignment to work at a dormitory for the disabled and elderly and was required to attended classes at a school for working youths.[126] Another tenth-grade student, Galina G. from Yermakovo Secondary School, was likewise released from school on account of pregnancy and marriage and then sent to study at the agricultural professional college in Kubenskoe.[127]

Finding information on school pregnancy in archival sources is an extremely complicated task due to the secrecy with which the materials were handled. However, it is not difficult to presume that, with greater numbers of teenagers being drawn into school by gen-comp, and with the typical ages for school graduation having been raised from 15–16 to 17–18, such cases were not uncommon. Pregnancies were viewed as disciplinary and behavioural violations when they occurred among school students, whom Soviet discourse refused to view as sexually mature young people. Any case of a school pregnancy in the 1960 and '70s resonated with rural teachers and students and tended to remain in their memories.

In one interview, a teacher from Goritsy Eight-Year School described school pregnancies in the 1960s as the natural outcome of poor upbringing and troubled families. The two examples of school pregnancy she mentioned during the interview were caused, in the first case, by the rape of a stepfather and, in the second, by a student having to share a room with her brother. The primary motif of her account was the exceptionality and marginality of such incidents.[128] A less categorical evaluation of school pregnancy was given in an interview with a different teacher. She mentioned the story of a high-performing young woman at the school in Kurkino, Vologodsky District, who, despite having a child, finished her schooling and got married.[129]

It was not only teachers and school administrators who expressed negative views of pregnancies in rural schools. As Elena V. recalls, when one student became pregnant during ninth grade in the early 1970s at Sokol Secondary School, the girl's situation was discussed at a class meeting where her classmates publicly rebuked her and put her to shame: "And now I remember, they stood her at the front of the class and started [to tear into her] any way they could … And the way she looked, I even remembered her eyes, those big eyes, and the tears were falling and falling. And we flung ourselves at her like a pack of hounds. And the thought didn't come into anyone's head that it was like that. She didn't come to school the next day."[130]

Such public procedures, enforcing the idea that pregnancy was incompatible with the moral character of a Soviet schoolgirl, were meant to discipline female students and orient them towards receiving an education, a profession, or a degree rather than creating a family early. As a result, the public discussion of early pregnancies and marriages at Komsomol and school meetings and actively propagandized by schools contrasted with more tolerant attitudes in rural localities, where pregnancy and childbirth out of wedlock, although not welcomed, did not occasion punitive measures.

PART THREE

Agrarian Institutes: "High Modernity" in the Rural Outback

Chapter Six

Cadres for the Village

Higher Education: Knowledge and Diplomas

In Soviet studies the deep-rooted nature of the inequality between the city and the countryside has not traditionally been universally acknowledged. Instead, Soviet territorial inequality was conceptualized as the result of the lagging spread of knowledge and technology to rural areas. Soviet ideologues supposed that, in order to solve inequality, it would suffice to increase the number of educated people in the countryside. Reforms to secondary and higher education that were implemented during the Khrushchev years turned this view into policy. In the pre-war USSR, education was no less valued than someone's social background as a working peasant, as is illustrated clearly by the high status granted to the scientific intelligentsia in Soviet society.[1] In the 1950s, during the Khrushchev reform years, when policy aimed to professionalize education, schooling was divided into primary, secondary, and higher education. Gradually, the secondary level became necessary for obtaining a profession, while higher-level education was viewed as preparation for management personnel.[2]

The task of reproducing social class in Soviet society, which secured the privileges of certain groups of the population to the detriment of others, clashed with one of the fundamental challenges of modernization: the need to increase the stratum of educated people, while, hopefully, preserving their class background. This section of my study will address how the system of higher education, which was meant to produce elites, was adjusted for the rural economy and how provincial agricultural institutions of higher education impacted types of knowledge and social reality for residents of Vologda Oblast.

In 1966, Yuri V., a young man from the village of Kabachino, in Kirillovsky District, chose to receive his higher education at Vologda Dairy

Figure 6.1. Students of Vologda Dairy Institute at Dynamo Stadium in Vologda after watching a soccer match, 1968. Yuri V. is on the far right.

Source: Photo from the family archive of Yuri V.

Institute. This decision was determined by several factors, among which the level of school preparation he had received and the specializations on offer at VDI were especially important.

At the moment of Yuri's enrolment, VDI was composed of eight academic units and included, aside from the core units (those concentrating on milk technologies, agricultural machinery mechanization, agronomics, animal husbandry, veterinary, and economics), two special faculties: a part-time "mid-level technological" faculty and a faculty for raising the qualifications of agricultural and dairy industry workers.[3] Yuri chose the most "masculine" of these specializations, which was also one of the most prestigious – agricultural machine engineering.

In the years following VDI's founding in 1911, the institute was geared towards people who already worked in agriculture.[4] They came to Molochnoe to conduct scientific research or work in dairy production management. In the 1960 and '70s, however, a VDI education came to be valued more for the diploma it conferred than the specialist knowledge it provided. As A.P. Teremov, the chief of the Vologda Oblast Statistics Department, noted, of the 1,240 agronomists trained between 1970 and 1977 at VDI, 571 (46 per cent) had never worked in agriculture.[5] Among the graduates of the Animal Husbandry and Veterinary Faculties, only 758 (58 per cent) went to work on sovkhozes.[6] Out of the 1,450 engineers who graduated from the Agricultural Machine Mechanization Faculty, only 371 (27 per cent) worked in agriculture. The remaining 1,063 diploma-holding engineers found work at the oblast's construction or industrial enterprises.[7] Looking at the institute as a whole, more than a third of the students who received a specialized agricultural education at VDI never used it.

Several reasonable questions thus present themselves: Why pursue an institute education, and spend five years doing so, knowing in advance that the professional training will not be applicable to one's future profession? What made this behaviour rational? What does it reveal about the social order of the 1960s and '70s, and how does it reflect inequality between the city and the countryside?

It is with such questions in mind that I turn to the story of Vologda Oblast's oldest institution of higher education, Vologda Dairy Agricultural Institute (later renamed Vologda Dairy Institute and now called Vereshchagin Vologda Dairy Academy). In what follows, I focus on the role the institute played in the lives of rural youths from Vologda Oblast in the 1960s and '70s, what opportunities it opened for them, and what limitations it created.

Global studies of university education usually emphasize the connection between the reproduction of the elite and the formation of the middle class.[8] This research demonstrates that university education is, more than other forms of education, linked to the social reproduction of inequality.[9] A university education usually guarantees that the student will secure a high-paying profession and thus enter a higher income level, characteristic of the middle class or elite. In the USSR, however, a proclaimed classless society, the impetus for receiving a higher education was supposed to be the Soviet population's political awareness of the state's need for a highly qualified workforce.[10] Soviet universities were made free in the 1950s and were thus open to anyone who could pass the entrance exams.[11] However, "Soviet" motivations did not replace more global social tendencies. Thus, the educated classes of the USSR and the Soviet elite strove to secure a good education for their children to guarantee that they would retain their parents' social status. In other words, although the rhetoric surrounding higher education differed in the USSR from that of other countries, the reality of people's motivations was very similar.

However, attempts at analysing the class subtext of Soviet education run into a deeply ingrained problem: It is no simple task to conceptualize the class divisions that existed under socialism.[12] Socialist societies, despite being equipped with Marxist theory, cannot be fit into the procrustean bed of orthodox Marxism.[13] Nevertheless, this incongruence does not cast doubt upon the primary thesis of sociologists that the structure of higher education is influenced by class conceptions and their role as symbols of dominance,[14] or the related thesis that representatives of various classes and social groups express differing views on study and the importance of receiving an education.[15] For example, from the point of view of the Soviet elite, the kolkhoz peasantry had abandoned its personal property tendencies and had assumed the status of a rural proletariat. Consequently, rural students were not officially considered to have a distinct class background distinguishing them from their urban working-class counterparts, and their desire to raise their social status was viewed by the state as a natural social development. Conversely, there was a view that even after receiving an education, students from the countryside retained their peasant background and that therefore there was no need to worry about the "dissolution" of this class. Lastly, although the state considered it desirable for rural youths to receive agricultural specializations, it did not prevent them from enrolling in other institutions.

In the 1960s, however, inequality between the city and the countryside began to be associated with territoriality rather than social background, and the demand for agricultural specializations, which required relocating to the countryside, noticeably declined among city residents. Understanding that urban youths had no intention of working in rural localities, the country's leadership looked to the peasantry. It was representatives of this class who were supposed to form the local agricultural elite. As a result, agricultural schools of higher education became not only conduits of "urban" knowledge in the countryside but also a mechanism for producing the social structure of the rural population.

Given this context, government policy aimed at bringing rural youths into the higher education system constitutes a profound shift in the social structure of the USSR of the 1960s and '70s. The school reforms launched in 1958 to sit rural children at school desks were supposed to bear their first fruit in 1968 with the mass graduation of rural students from tenth class. These graduates would become candidates for higher and secondary-level education and subsequently the future management personnel of the agricultural sector. Thus, under Khrushchev, agricultural institutes were key objects of government attention. According to statistics cited by V.D. Krasota, the head of the Ministry of Agriculture's Chief Directorate for Educational Institutions, the number of higher education agricultural institutions in the USSR increased ninefold (from eleven to one hundred) over the period 1917–67.[16] Many of them appeared at the end of the 1950s and the beginning of the 1960s.

During these years, student dormitories were being constructed on a mass scale, providing rural students with a place to live during their studies. Unlike at other institutions of higher education, students at agricultural schools began to receive guaranteed stipends.[17] Judging, moreover, by presentations made at seminars and academic conferences, scientific-experimental farms tested new equipment and technologies, thus allowing at least some agronomists and animal husbandry specialists to keep pace with progress.[18]

Sociologists of education Isak Froumin and Oleg Leshukov classified Soviet institutions of higher education into several groups. Some were formed according to territorial principles, in response to the workforce demands of various regions. Others still were founded to meet the production needs of various ministries and were considered industrial institutions.[19] Additionally, the USSR fostered "flagship" universities oriented towards the production of academic knowledge. Ultimately, the education received at a given university was valued differently in accordance with its placement in the context of Soviet society. Among the various types of educational institutions, it was the universities that formed the national elite, and which have been the most studied by sociologists.[20] Nevertheless, although Soviet universities and institutes offered students a diverse body of specialized knowledge, they all shared one general characteristic: They offered students a specific social status, one that came with important privileges in Soviet society. In his research analysing the effects Soviet universities had on post-war Soviet society, Benjamin Tromly has argued that higher education became a necessary requirement for people who wished to raise their social status.[21] More generally, many researchers tie the birth of the "middle class" in the USSR in the 1960 and '70s with the rise of higher education.[22] Although, formally, there were only two classes in Soviet society, workers and peasants, in reality, students at technical colleges and other institutions of higher education joined an "intelligentsia" group, at least for a few years. Researchers of socialism have noted the importance of this group within society, its privileged influence on society and the state, and its power in all spheres, from production to agriculture.[23] For rural youths, alongside these benefits, having student status guaranteed an opportunity to move, at least temporarily, to the city, and to escape the class of the kolkhoz peasantry (at least formally), which, in Soviet society in the 1960 and '70s, was a significant rung up on the ladder of social mobility.

This change in status concerned both the type of labour they engaged in and the social privileges available to them. A very illustrative example of the privileges afforded to students can be seen in the fact that those who came from villages could receive a passport, while kolkhoz workers could not. Yuri V., for example, was given a passport in 1966 after presenting proof of his acceptance to VDI to the Migachevo Selsoviet. His mother, in contrast, who worked as a calf tender on the "Vorobyevsky" farm, received her passport only after kolkhozes were restructured in 1970.[24]

Thus, in contrast to universities in countries with liberal economies, higher education in the USSR was created not only with the goal of cultivating a national elite but was regarded as a tool for eliminating class inequality as well. Although receiving a higher education always came with additional difficulties for those leaving the countryside, the lucky ones who managed to gain admittance to an institute, even one with an agricultural focus, were given a ticket to professional advancement. This was the case for my interviewee Yuri, for example, when he enrolled in VDI.

Milk and Modernity: Vologda Dairy Institute

The Vologda Dairy Agricultural Institute (VDAI) was planned as a modern centre for scientific research capable of preparing students for work in the upper ranks of the milk industry and agricultural sector. One of the core ideas underlying its creation was the modernization of rural life; in this vision, milk was to serve as the link between the city and the countryside. Within the framework of this project, scientific experts were supposed to develop models for interacting with nature, society, and new technologies while creating flourishing rural economies and a developed dairy sector. In Russia, as was the case throughout the world, milk production was seen as a panacea to a myriad of social problems.

The entire cycle of dairy production was compressed into a single, unified complex (from the formation of dairy cow herds and the selective breeding of dairy cattle to the development of technologies for milk storage and the production of various milk-based dairy products). This was intended to showcase the benefits of a scientific approach to agricultural organization and to develop optimal forms of interaction between milk producers and the technologies that turned milk into a consumable good. The first VDAI graduates were seen not only as people with valuable knowledge pertaining to the dairy business but as potential reformers who could organize a new form of dairy production in Russia.

The development of the Russian dairy sector was closely tied to the peasant cooperative movement that was brutally smashed in the 1930s, and it has thus generally been ignored in later Soviet and Russian historiography.[25] Meanwhile, in American and European research, the development of the dairy business is widely recognized as an important chapter in the history of technology.[26] The "dairy revolution" in Europe and the United States occurred during the late ninetieth and early twentieth centuries in connection with an increasing demand for cow's milk among populations who used it in children's nutrition and as a replacement for breastmilk.[27] The first technologies in the sphere of milk processing included purification processes that increased its quality and methods for lengthening its storage life. Gradually, the production and processing of cow's milk would fundamentally change the food sectors of modern economies.[28] Milk powder and canned milk made milk a strategic product that could be stored for years and transported across great distances. By the beginning of the twentieth century, milk had become part of the daily diet of city residents and a product of the global market. In this way, it established a new relationship between the city and countryside.[29]

In Russian and Soviet history, milk also played a significant role in modernization. It should be noted that reports on milk yields made headlines in the post-war USSR and were viewed as indicators of Soviet prosperity and a symbol of modernized consumption. In the post-war period, as the historian Elena Kochetkova has written, "milk became a focus of both state policy and industrial development and part of official propaganda in the midst of Cold War rivalry."[30] Thus, it is unsurprising that Soviet cows became world record holders in milk yields on multiple occasions and that the number of milk factories increased from 200 in 1940 to 307 in 1960. By 1989, breed herd numbers and per capita milk consumption in the USSR surpassed that of the United States.[31]

In the 1960s and '70s, official strategies for optimizing agricultural production began to focus solely on technological progress rather than on creating effective forms of interaction between farms and dairy industry enterprises.[32] Among the scientists responsible for creating production models and organizing the "dairy cycle," agriculturalists turned into technocrats who worked on narrowly defined problems within the party-approved development plan. However, the same fate awaited Soviet engineers who lost control of the production process and were turned into easily replaceable cogs in the industrial machine.[33] Soviet higher education came to be characterized by the separation of study and research beginning in the 1920s.[34] However, higher education institutions that prepared their students for industrial careers retained some laboratories and could conduct scientific research within the walls of the university. Periodic changes to the status of VDI (at times it was considered a specialized dairy industry institute, at others an agricultural institute) had a serious impact on the institute's "agricultural section": the experimental livestock breeding farm, the machinery workshop, the student fields, and the milk factory. These sometimes belonged to VDI, while sometimes they were transferred to other farms.

The technocratic approach to the dairy business led to a division between production and processing. The experimental stations, milk factory, and breeding farms at VDI were divided into separate structures and detached from the dairy institute.[35] The dairy institute began to train students primarily for agricultural professions, retaining only a single faculty dedicated to dairy production. In return, rural youths were given a key role in the project of modernizing the countryside. They were the ones who were to become the next generation of agricultural experts.[36]

Evelina M. was born at a small railroad-stop settlement on the border of Udmurtia and Bashkiria in 1940.[37] For the past few generations, her family had lived in the Southern Urals. Her grandfather had received a university education in medicine, and her father graduated from Orenburg University and worked as a veterinarian. Evelina's family often moved from place to place, usually because her father received a work transfer, but at times in search of better living conditions. Her father was offered various respected positions in the food industry, but he worked for most of his life as a veterinary doctor for meat combines and poultry factories in the Urals, which allowed him to support his large family in conditions of chronic Soviet food deficits. In 1959, Evelina graduated from Chishmy Secondary School and, after an unsuccessful attempt to enrol in the Technical College of Stomatology in Ufa, went to work at the laboratory of the meat and dairy combine in Tuymazy, where her father served as head veterinary doctor. This would be the beginning of Evelina's career as a milk production technologist.

After she had been working for some time, the head of the laboratory suggested that Evelina apply to the Dairy Technology Faculty at VDI, where she had studied herself. In 1961, Evelina showed up for entry examinations at VDI with a work directive for the Tuymazy dairy combine in hand, which significantly simplified the acceptance process. During her studies there she met her future husband, who was then a student in the Agricultural Mechanization Faculty who had come to Molochnoe from a remote Vologda Oblast village. They married in 1963, while still students. When she graduated from VDI, the milk production technologist position at the Tuymazy combine had been filled, and Evelina was not required to return to Bashkiria. Additionally, her husband worked in the VDI garage, making them eligible to receive work assignments at the institute. As a result, Evelina was able to find employment as a laboratory assistant for the VDI Organic Chemistry Faculty. With the good favour of her research supervisor, she was then given a teaching post in the Mid-Level Technological Faculty, which she occupied until her retirement.

The fact that Evelina, who came from a well-off urban family, chose a specialization as a dairy production technologist shows how milk not only modernized production and education, but influenced the status of those who chose to connect their profession with it.

Despite all the repression and organizational changes to which VDI was subjected between the 1930 and the 1950s, the Technology Faculty remained one of the school's most prestigious. Some of the luminaries of the milk industry had taken part in its creation and invested enormous efforts into organizing a scientific centre and introducing scientifically rationalized production to Vologda Oblast. As a result, Vologda became the meeting place for the inaugural Congress of Dairy Industry Workers in 1924. The faculty's teaching staff made headlines in influential all-union and international journals for the dairy business during the early twentieth century and actively collaborated with the leading scientific centres.[38]

On the eve of the repression of the 1930s, this collaboration led to layoffs and even a temporary suspension of its operation as an educational institution.[39] In 1937–8, nearly half of the VDI teaching staff was fired for having connections with the professors of the Petrovskaya Agricultural Academy in Moscow (since 1923 known as the K.A. Timiryazev Agricultural Academy), where Alexander Chayanov and Nikolai Kondratiev worked.[40] The new faculties created as a result (those focusing on agronomics, zootechnics, and veterinary medicine), as well as the new emphasis on agriculture generally, rather than strictly dairy-related research, propagandized collectivization and did all they could to remove the cooperative inclinations of those working in the dairy industry.[41] A new wave of interest in the Dairy Product Technologies Faculty came only in the post-war period, when milk became a tool for touting the pre-eminence of socialism over capitalism in the USSR's competition with the United States.[42] As a result, the Technologics Faculty at VDI was not only allowed to continue functioning, but its student recruitments were in fact enlarged, while the dairy herd in Molochnoe was restored and a new scientific-experimental factory was opened.

Dairy industry students were distinct from their peers in other academic units on account of their mainly "urban" social background and because the academic demands placed upon them were higher. Thus, only half of the group of students who enrolled in the Technologies Faculty with Evelina M. completed their studies.[43] Many of the students were simply incapable of mastering the difficult curriculum, which required a strong grasp of organic chemistry, a subject rarely taught in Vologda Oblast rural school programs.

The geographical distribution of VDI graduates is also worth noting. In the 1960s and '70s, the institute continued to prepare engineer-technologists to meet the needs of the dairy industry across the USSR. Additionally, it prepared agricultural machine operators, agronomists, animal husbandry specialists, veterinarians, and economists for the northern oblasts of the Russian Non-Black Earth region (Karelia, Komi ASSR, Arkhangelsk Oblast, Murmansk Oblast, and Vologda Oblast). Thus, in accordance with a 1965 plan from the Ministry of Agriculture, only 4 of the 87 graduates of the Technologies Faculty were assigned to work in Vologda Oblast; of the 63 graduates of the Zootechnics Faculty, half remained in the Vologda region while the other half were sent to neighbouring oblasts; of the students in the Dairy Production Technologies Faculty who graduated from VDI after three years (mid-level technological), 15 remained in the oblast while 80 were sent to other regions.[44] Only the Agricultural Mechanization Faculty, created in 1950 to train engineers, sent all of its graduates to work at enterprises located within the oblast.

The privileged position of dairy production technologists at VDI in comparison with the institute's "agricultural" specializations demonstrates one of the key facets of inequality in the 1960s and '70s. The ubiquitous Soviet trend of supporting industrial production while chronically under-financing agriculture was reflected even in the distribution of funding within a single institute. As a result, the Technologies Faculty at VDI not only had the best-trained professors, but it also had better funding than the faculties specializing in the preparation of agricultural specialists. This inequality was further facilitated by the fact that most of the faculty's students were supported financially by their future enterprise employers. Thus, in 1964–5, eighty students in the VDI Technologies Faculty were funded by enterprises, while only seventeen of the students in the Agricultural Faculties were "kolkhoz stipend" recipients.[45]

In contrast, a report prepared after a 1960 inspection of VDI describes a whole spectrum of problems in the teaching of agricultural disciplines. One of the crucial concerns was that staff were ill-prepared to teach: "the majority of teachers ... do not have specialist training, which would give them the right to teach in institutions of higher education, [and] therefore the subject material is partially unqualified." Furthermore, some of the instructors – as was the case for the head of the Metal Technologies Faculty, for example – worked in research institutions in Moscow and were at VDI only for rare visits.[46] Another problem concerned "poorly equipped laboratories," where a lack of student work stations and "mock-ups of distinct tractor components and units ... ma[de] it significantly more difficult to study their assembly."[47] Moreover, students who studied agricultural specializations did not have the opportunity to test new types of agricultural machinery that the institute did not have at its disposal. Lessons at VDI throughout the 1960s and '70s were conducted in two, and sometimes three, shifts. The lack of a qualitative improvement in the equipment at agricultural institutes during the Khrushchev years appears to have been connected to the increasing numbers of students. Money had to be spent on opening more and more educational facilities, rather than on re-equipping the old ones.

In this context, the VDI technologies laboratories were comparatively well-equipped. The faculty was the face of VDI; it was where dissertations were defended, and where professors authored books to be used across the Soviet Union. In fact, histories of Molochnoe almost always mention the faculty's professors, who were, furthermore, sometimes featured in newsreel reports.

Thus, even within the framework of a single institution, one section of the student body ended up in a more favourable position than the others. The underlying reason for this was that the various disciplines offered at VDI were accorded different statuses. The public demand for agricultural specialists proved to be less than the demand for technologists, which was reflected, consequently, in the student population recruited by VDI.

University for Rural People: Komsomol Recruitments and Kolkhoz Stipends

One of the acute problems facing agricultural institutes in the USSR was the comparatively low number of enrolments from among the kolkhoz peasantry in comparison with other social groups.[48] The causes lay not only in the quality of school teaching, but in the weaker economic position of the families of rural schoolchildren, who struggled to provide for their schooling and life away from home. Additionally, the peasantry often distrusted the knowledge offered by agricultural institutes. As a result, the rural population was much less motivated to pursue a higher education oriented towards obtaining future managerial posts. As Theodore Gerber and Michael Hout have noted, higher education in the USSR in the 1960 and '70s was received primarily by children whose parents had themselves been university or institute graduates. These findings are backed by an analysis of the composition of student populations in Soviet institutions of higher education.[49]

VDI was no exception: As the oldest institution of higher education in Vologda Oblast, until 1960 it had been attended primarily by city residents seeking a higher education. As VDI Komsomol Committee Secretary Valiuzhenich complained at the 1960 regional VLKSM plenum, "A situation is forming in which institutions of higher education are attended primarily by urban youths. This year for the first time the Komsomol District Committees in conjunction with enterprises had the opportunity to send cutting-edge agricultural workers and producers to study, but, however, there was no turnout."[50] Indeed, such measure did not fundamentally change the demographic situation at universities, and during 1960–1 academic year VDI once again enrolled a majority of its students from cities.

Only by the 1964–5 academic year were 300 of the 415 students accepted for full-time, first-year studies from rural localities. They comprised 64.8 per cent of enrolments (although, judging from the documentation, it appears the report's authors counted small, urbanized district centres as rural localities).[51]

The influx of rural youths into the student population is accounted for by the increase in the number of student acceptances at VDI, the introduction of measures for supporting students from rural localities, and the opening of other institutions of higher education in the oblast (thus lowering competition for VDI diplomas among city residents). Despite these efforts, however, rural students did not obtain an absolute majority among student populations in the 1970s. The ever-increasing complexity of organizational systems in rural communities, where peasant kolkhoz workers now lived alongside a rural "intelligentsia" that was greatly invested in securing education for their children, meant that higher education remained difficult to access for the children of rank-and-file kolkhoz workers. In the 1960s and '70s, children of kolkhoz workers competed for university spots not only against city dwellers but also against the children of the educated section of the rural population. Among the latter were the children of teachers, sovkhoz managers, and specialists who had a different set of opportunities than did rank-and-file kolkhoz workers.

In an attempt to stimulate rural student enrolments, VDI constructed new buildings throughout this period. Practically all of the institute's faculties received their own academic structures during those years, along with comfortable dormitories with centralized water and sewage systems. Furthermore, the VDI administration took unprecedented recruitment measures to increase the number of rural students, including Komsomol recruitments and kolkhoz stipends.

Kolkhoz stipends were given to students by a sovkhoz or kolkhoz with the stipulation that the student would return to work on the farm after graduation. Students with these scholarships were more likely to be accepted into institutes than those who enrolled in the general pool, although stipend candidates, like all other students, were still required to pass entrance examinations. Before 1967, kolkhoz stipends were available for any young man or woman given the approval of kolkhoz leadership. After a decree by the Council of Ministers of the USSR on 25 August 1967, new rules were established: From then on, kolkhoz stipends would be available only to those who agreed to work on a sovkhoz for at a least a year following their graduation from school.[52] Yuri V. made use of the opportunity to receive a "kolkhoz stipend" during his fourth year of studies, when he was determining his future place of employment. Over the holidays, he came to an agreement with the director of the sovkhoz "Vorobyevsky" that the sovkhoz administration would employ him as an engineer following the completion of his studies.[53] This allowed Yuri simultaneously to avoid an obligatory assignment to the "backwoods" and increase his stipend, henceforth to be paid by the sovkhoz, from thirty to thirty-five roubles a month.

In theory, the intended recipients of kolkhoz stipends were kolkhoz workers from families economically involved in agriculture. In practice, however, this rule was far from universally observed. Often, kolkhozes provided scholarships to the children of chairmen or civil servants whose work was totally unrelated to the farm. Data from an inspection of sixty-six sovkhozes and thirty-three kolkhozes in Vologda Oblast conducted by the regional Financial Department in July 1970 uncovered ten cases in which the parents of students sent on scholarship did not work in agriculture. In one case, the sovkhoz "Red North" sent V.I. Burako, whose father worked as an inspector in the Personnel Department of Veliky Ustyug Agricultural Technical College, to study at VDI. In another case, the sovkhoz "Onward," in Ustyuzhensky District, sent a student named Lebedeva to study at Leningrad Agricultural Institute. Her parents were permanent residents of the city of Ustyuzhna, where her mother worked as a nurse and her father worked at a public services combine.[54] It was not uncommon for farm directors to allocate kolkhoz scholarships to their children. For example, the director of a farm in Nyuksensky District sent his daughter to study at the Leningrad Agricultural with an increased stipend immediately after she finished school.[55] Consequently, access to higher education in rural communities was uneven, just as government conceptions about the ideal social origin of an agricultural institute student varied.

In addition to kolkhoz scholarships, "Komsomol recruitments" were used as a means of stimulating rural youth enrolments in agricultural institutes in the 1960s. This was a system in which district Komsomol committees could recommend rural students to institutes for enrolment consideration without competition and obligate farms to fund their studies. The lack of teachers in rural schools, for example, was addressed with this mechanism. In a decree prepared by the minister of higher and secondary education, the minister of education, and the secretary of the VLKSM Central Committee on 30 June 1969, it was declared that Komsomol central committees in the USSR, along with people's education organs, would be required to recommend ten thousand of the "most talented young workers, kolkhoz workers and rural school graduates well disposed to work at schools" for rural pedagogical posts over the next two years.[56] However, it was kolkhozes that were responsible for funding their studies. Ultimately, this system achieved only partial success in stimulating rural students to seek higher education. In 1970, the Vologda and Cherepovets Pedagogical Institutes offered thirty spots reserved for rural students with a professional referral.[57]

Komsomol recruitments were also used at VDI. At one of the regional party plenums, Valiuzhenich, the secretary of the institute's Komsomol organization, described the first Komsomol recruitment of full-time students that took place in 1960 and allowed prior part-time students and rural school graduates to become full-time VDI students.[58]

However, encouraging enrolments in institutions of higher education did not automatically resolve student difficulties securing funding for five years of study. After exam sessions, it was often rural students who were expelled for underperformance. Thus, of the four graduates from Kirillov Secondary School who were admitted to VDI together with Yuri V., three were expelled after failing to pass the first round of examinations.[59]

In addition, students were required to pass all their subjects to continue receiving their stipend, which, in any case, often fell below the level of a living wage. For this reason, Yuri, an assiduous student, received money transfers for ten roubles from his parents throughout all five years of his studies to supplement his thirty-five-rouble stipend. This allowed him to eat in the cafeteria each day, use the bathhouse and laundromat, and go home on the holidays.[60] Students who did not receive financial assistance from their parents and who had come from afar were unlikely to have the means to finish their studies even if they persevered through the difficulties of enrolment. Thus, Kapitalina K., from Kirillovsky District, was unable to follow in the footsteps of her elder brother, who went to study at Leningrad Technological Institute; her kolkhoz-worker parents did not have the means to support two students in Leningrad. Kapitalina was thus forced to limit herself to studying at Molochnoe, where her parents visited every month and brought vegetables to her dormitory so that she had enough to eat.[61]

Ultimately, the motivations underlying student enrolment in agricultural institutes in the 1960s and '70s were numerous and at times unconnected with the desire to obtain an agricultural profession. For students who came from families in the intelligentsia or *nomenklatura* (bureaucratic elite), enrolment often merely indicated a student's desire to maintain a privileged social status, while for the children of kolkhoz workers the motivation could be connected with moving up in the social hierarchy.

Policies meant to draw rural school graduates into institutions of higher education were unable to guarantee equal opportunities for city and rural residents. Rural adolescents were offered spots, for the most part, in schools with an agricultural focus. This meant that, in fact, they were offered only a small subset of the opportunities available to young people in cities, who had clear advantages in determining their future.

The Formation of the VDI Student Body

Because VDI was not listed among the most prestigious institutions of higher education in the country, its graduates rarely occupied leadership positions in the capital regions. They were, however, in high demand in the Russian North-West. In Vologda Oblast, the number of general agricultural personnel training lagged significantly behind that of the Soviet Union as a whole. Whereas the number of diploma-holding agricultural specialists in Vologda Oblast increased from 1940 to 1962 by 2.5 times, in the USSR overall, this figure had grown by a factor of 8.5.[62] Outside of the relevant VDI faculties (the Faculties of Agricultural Machine Operation, Agronomy, Animal Husbandry, and then the Veterinary and Economics Faculties opened at a later date) the oblast's agricultural specialists in the 1960s and '70s were trained by the "Hydromelioration" Faculty of the Vologda Polytechnic Institute.[63] An additional five agricultural technical colleges working in the oblast offered students agricultural specializations and a secondary-level diploma. At the start of the 1978–9 school year, there were 7,719 students studying for an agricultural specialization, comprising 17.8 per cent of the oblast's higher education and technical college students.[64] It should be noted that this calculation does not consider professional-technical schools (*proftechuchilishche* or *gorodskoe proftechuchilishche*), of which there were ten in the oblast graduating up to 2,000 agricultural workers annually.[65]

For rural youths in Vologda Oblast, enrolling in an agricultural school, technical college, or VDI was a comparatively accessible route to receiving a diploma. Nevertheless, securing acceptance could be extremely difficult. As Yuri V. recalls, the year he applied to the Mechanization Faculty at VDI, there were nine times more applications than there were spots available.[66] The high level of competition was spurred not only by demand for engineering specialists and higher education in general in

Vologda Oblast, but also by the fact that the application pool that year consisted of two student groups finishing two different school programs (both those graduating from ten-year programs and those who had completed an additional year in accordance with schooling reforms). A year earlier, in 1965, the acceptance commission at VDI had reviewed 623 applications and accepted 420 students, meaning there were less than two applicants for each seat.[67] Party organization demands to increase the number of students accepted from the oblast's secondary schools without lowering the quality of the education, and while maintaining high passing rates, placed a heavy burden on the VDI administration. The solution offered was paid preparatory courses, which the institute began to conduct annually.[68] By the time that Yuri was applying to VDI, tuition payments had already been cancelled, but the VDI exams in 1965 covered four subjects: chemistry, physics, Russian language, and mathematics.

Vologda Oblast residents were not the only people who came to VDI to study; the student body included enrolments from other regions as well. In 1965, for example, a little more than half of the student body (56.2 per cent) came from the Vologda region, with the other 43.8 per cent having moved for their studies.[69] On the one hand, interest in VDI among non-locals was linked to the institute's dairy focus, and the faculty that prepared dairy technologists was constantly in high demand. On the other hand, VDI was attractive because it offered relatively underprepared students the chance to receive a higher education when acceptance into more prestigious universities in capital cities was unobtainable. As Secretary Antropov of the Komsomol organization for the Kazan Agricultural Institute complained, "the most-prepared graduates from rural secondary schools leave the villages for technical institutes, they go to medical institutes or to universities," thus leaving agricultural institutes with less favourable candidates.[70] A final factor stimulating enrolment in VDI was that there were no agricultural institutes in the northern oblasts bordering Vologda Oblast. Moreover, VDI was being outfitted with an entire scientific-educational infrastructure that included, alongside VDI itself, a research institute, experimental farms, and laboratories.

As was the case with the school system, Soviet higher education positioned itself as gender-neutral. Curriculums were not oriented towards the sex of the students. Moreover, statistically, it was no less common for women to enter Soviet institutions of higher educations than for men, which allowed Gerber and Hout to describe the successes of Soviet higher education in pushing gender equality and James Scott to write about the success of educational modernization in the USSR as a whole.[71] Statistics from Vologda Oblast confirm the general trend. The compilation *Agriculture in Vologda Oblast*, prepared by the Vologda Oblast Statistics Department, indicates that, in the 1966, women made up 68.8 per cent (44,012 individuals) of those with higher or secondary specialized education in the oblast.[72] Moreover, of its 18,061 diploma-holding graduates, 11,353 were women, comprising 62.8 per cent of the oblast's "specialists."[73] This was, generally, a little higher than the average in the USSR, where women nonetheless were in the process of steadily gaining ground among highly qualified professions.[74] Although having a higher education did not guarantee a young woman a leadership position in the workforce, many preferred to invest their time in receiving an education than creating a family or running the household.

Judging by personal accounts, in the 1960s and '70s the Technologies Faculty and the Economics Faculty were considered the "women's faculties" at VDI. The female groups were only rarely "diluted" by young men. As Kapitalina K. recalls, among the few young men in the Economics Faculty, many had disabilities and were likely sent to the institute on kolkhoz referrals after completing specialized schooling.[75] By contrast, the Mechanization Faculty, which prepared engineers, was primarily male. Nevertheless, there were young women who studied mechanics.[76] Although they may have been outnumbered at a ratio of one or two to one hundred by young men, there were no formal sex barriers to entering the engineering profession at VDI. The distribution of the sexes among the faculties was determined not so much by state regulation as by student conceptions of the nature of labour distribution within Soviet society.

Assignments to the Village

Social inequality was felt sharply among agricultural institute graduates who were required to take on work assignments. City dwellers were typically unenthusiastic about moving to the countryside, and, because they were registered in cities and had places of residence there, they could quickly find work in the city and ignore their work assignments by changing professions. As a result, only some students were affected by post-graduation work assignments, and, generally, it was graduates who had come from kolkhozes and sovkhozes who were sent to rural localities after their studies.

By the end of the 1950s, the issue of sending specialist graduates to work in rural localities had become an extremely tense one, and university administrations had to make great efforts and resort to various schemes in order to ensure students went to work in accordance with their specialization. For example, until 1966, there was a special procedure for issuing diplomas to graduates of educational institutions that had an agricultural focus.[77] Following the completion of their courses, graduates were required to work for a year in agricultural production before receiving their diploma. After this measure was done away with, institute administrations could only appeal to the consciences of their former students. It was with this aim that V.D. Krasota, head of the Ministry of Agriculture's Chief Directorate for Educational Institutions, proclaimed from the platform of an all-union conference that "Young university graduates ought to have a sense of responsibility before the Motherland and go to work when they are directed by an assignment committee."[78] Similarly, the School Department instructor for the Vologda CPSU Regional Committee, V. Kichigina, cuttingly remarked in a report that the rector and VDI party committee "are not bothered that ice cream is sold in a kiosk next to the institute by Ivanovskaya, a 1962 graduate of the Animal Husbandry Faculty."[79] The author was understandably distressed that Ivanovskaya, a qualified young specialist, preferred selling ice cream to working as a head animal husbandry specialist in a rural locality. She blamed the VDI rector for his seeming inability to exert an influence on her decision.

The problems faced when attempting to assign graduates to rural localities were discussed at the highest levels. Judging by a 1967 report written by Krasota, 123 of the 249 diploma-holding graduates of the Georgian Agricultural Institute did not show up at their assigned posts. The same was true of 105 of the 464 graduates from the Kazan Agricultural Institute. Overall, Krasota's statistics indicate that 9 per cent of graduates ignored their work directives during the 1963–5 period.[80] VDI faced a similar problem in the 1970s. Although many of its graduates showed up at work in accordance with their directives, approximately 20 per cent of them left before completing the agreed-upon term of work.[81]

Refusing a work assignment in the 1960s and '70s could entail various unpleasant consequences for a graduating student. If the situation could not be resolved by mutual agreement (that is, if the student could not convince the administration of the prospective sovkhoz or enterprise employer that he or she was not the best candidate for the post, leading to the latter "releasing" the graduate) then the case would be reviewed by a court. The proceedings would be initiated by the kolkhoz or sovkhoz that had been left without a specialist. Evelina M. recalled such a case within the Technologies Faculty: "A young woman had been assigned to work at Tarnoga, but she did not want to [go there]. And she was then bothered by the court for a fairly long time." Ultimately, she was forced to go to work, but, in time, "she [...] somehow got out of there anyway."[82] Nevertheless, legal scenarios were rare for VDI. Usually, graduates and sovkhoz administrations strove to resolve issues without conflict. It was more common that, after driving out to a work assignment, young people would seize upon any small opportunity to leave the countryside and find work in the city. Thus, Yuri V. worked for a year as the chief engineer for the sovkhoz "Vorobyevsky" before being called into the army. During his service, the chief engineer position at VDI was given to another of the institute's graduates, allowing Yuri to leave village life with a clean conscience and no need to sign a new agreement with the sovkhoz.

Graduates who did end up in the countryside often found more lucrative professions because a higher education, regardless of specialization, opened numerous career opportunities in rural localities. According to the Vologda Oblast Statistics Department, 237 of the 1,240 diploma-holding agronomists who graduated from VDI between 1970 and 1977 secured work in rural district administrations. Approximately as many veterinarians and animal husbandry specialists ended up with district-level administrative posts within the oblast.[83]

VDI graduates who were wary of being "assigned" to posts on sovkhozes and kolkhozes had good reason for their uneasiness. At the end of the 1950s, with reforms that brought the transfer of machine tractor stations to kolkhozes and sovkhozes, engineers, agronomists, veterinarians, and animal husbandry specialists lost their public servant (*sluzhashchie*) status. Unlike kolkhoz workers, public servants had been granted passports, a guaranteed pension, a stable salary, and weekends and vacation days throughout the 1950s. The loss of these privileges during Khrushchev's agrarian reforms quickly created a mass migration of specialists from the countryside. According to the statistics of Mikhail Beznin and Tatiana Dimoni, in 1956 alone more than 13,000 animal husbandry specialists and agronomists resigned from their posts at kolkhozes across the USSR, which comprised 23 per cent of the workforce. In 1957, this figure rose to 25 per cent.[84]

This situation was corrected in the 1960s. Diploma-holding specialists not only saw these earlier rights reinstated; they also gained new ones, such as the right to be provided with housing, the right to access loans to build a house, and additional income payments.[85] In the 1970s, VDI graduates were in high demand among farm directors. Requests for graduate assignments came from oblast-level and krai-level headquarters across the USSR. Moreover, sovkhozes were offering comfortable conditions. In the 1970s, almost all farms provided young specialists with housing (an apartment or, less commonly, a room), and their salaries were greater than an average city salary. The salaries listed for engineers, agronomists, veterinarians, and animal husbandry specialists in 1971 usually began at around 120 roubles per month or more, while dairy production technologists with city assignments, for example, could expect around 90 to 100 roubles per month.[86] The only caveat to these offers was that young people would have to move to remote rural localities, a condition many considered unacceptable by the 1970s.

Matching graduates to vacancies was the task of institute administrations. The latter received offers from personnel departments and agricultural headquarters across Vologda Oblast and the greater USSR. A vacancy description would contain the name of the enterprise, the position, the salary, and noted whether living accommodations were provided. Evidently, these indicators were considered sufficient for forming an idea of the workplace. Vacancies in Vologodsky and Cherepovetsky Districts were always more coveted than those in the oblast's eastern regions, which were far from the big cities, although conditions at the latter could be more favourable. Typically, the first choice of work assignments was given to high-performing students. As a result, the chances of being sent to the "back of beyond" were higher for those who demonstrated weak academic performance. Some graduates, like Yuri V., chose to return to the kolkhoz where they were raised. To make that happen, clever students could keep a request from a district agricultural headquarters or enterprise at hand until it was time for their post-graduation work assignment. For example, in 1972 the kolkhoz "Soviet Russia," in Sheksninsky District, made a personal request for VDI Economics Faculty graduate Kuliganova.[87] Similarly, another graduate of the Economics Faculty, Sashnikova, had a 160-rouble salary waiting for her on the sovkhoz "Corners."[88]

A small proportion of high-performing students received recommendations from VDI professors for work assignments as laboratory assistants and junior research associates within the institute itself. However, they had to agree to rent accommodations, which was extremely difficult on the very modest institute salary.[89] For Yuri V., an opportunity to work at VDI opened up after he graduated when he decided to leave the sovkhoz where he had begun work in 1970. The offer to move back to Molochnoe came from a former classmate who had been accepted as a full-time graduate student in Leningrad and was preparing to move out, leaving Yuri both his room in a dormitory and his position as a junior research associate in the Mechanization Faculty. A colleague's recommendation and an interview proved sufficient, and Yuri, by then with a family of his own, moved from the Kirillovsky countryside to Molochnoe in 1974, where he was given a position among the VDI teaching staff. It turned out that, if one had the right friends, "a research assignment" post-VDI in the 1970s could be attained without a village residency registration.

The informal *blat* system, in which personal connections provided professional or financial advancement, was as present in VDI education as it was in other sections of Soviet society.[90]

Graduates of the Agricultural Mechanisation Faculty in 1971 were offered chief engineer vacancies on sovkhozes and kolkhozes across Vologda Oblast.[91] They were provided with housing and promised salaries ranging from 120 to 170 roubles, depending on the sovkhoz's location. In 1971, thirty graduates were additionally able to choose from positions on farms in Kaliningrad Oblast.[92] In the same year, Agronomy Faculty graduates were invited to work as chief agronomists on farms located for the most part in Arkhangelsk and Vologda Oblasts. Additionally, a few graduates, if they so desired, could become teachers at the agricultural technical college in Ustyuzhna.[93] The graduates of the Animal Husbandry Faculty in 1970 awaited careers as chief animal husbandry specialists on Vologda Oblast sovkhozes, as well as in Ukraine, where they worked on the sovkhozes "Kirovsky" in Chernigov Oblast, "Olevskaya' in Zhytomyr Oblast, and on the Kalinin Artemonovsky stud farm in Donetsk Oblast.[94] The job descriptions for these posts offered better conditions than those in Vologda Oblast sovkhozes; the salary was higher and the candidates were offered furnished accommodations. However, one could only learn about actual work conditions after arriving on site. In this sense, work assignments always had a lottery aspect to them, both for the employer and the specialist.

VDI and the Propaganda of Progress

Elucidating the complexities of the term "Soviet intelligentsia," Benjamin Tromly has argued that, although the Soviet intelligentsia shared some continuity with the intelligentsia of the Russian Empire, it operated on a different set of ideological presuppositions.[95] Although serving the people remained a core motivation, the Soviet intelligentsia was characterized by subdivisions denoting class origin and labour specialization.[96] It is likely that among the various subsections of the intelligentsia – practitioners of the liberal arts, engineers, and teachers – the agricultural intelligentsia was viewed with the greatest degree of scepticism. In the 1950s and '60s, the rural intelligentsia held professional positions as teachers and cultural workers. But how can one socially conceptualize those who, although they attained a higher education, found employment in agricultural production and had their origins in the flesh and blood of the working peasantry? Ilya Gerasimov has drawn attention to this tension by attempting to categorize and analyse groups of rural specialists during the period spanning 1905 to 1930. He asserts that a unique social group was formed at the beginning of the twentieth century that henceforth could not be assigned solely to the intelligentsia or the peasantry.[97] In the 1960s and '70s, the ambivalent position of young specialists in rural localities remained just as palpable.

Although Soviet analysts had no unified conception of the rural intelligentsia, they nonetheless agreed that rural specialists had an obligation to hold progressive views.[98] Whether or not to consider them as truly belonging to the intelligentsia depended on specific contexts and situations.[99] Furthermore, the logistical need to assign this group of people to a distinct category disappeared in the 1970s, when the position of the kolkhoz population improved significantly with the abolishment of the *trudoden* system, the introduction of pensions for old age, social security, salary raises, and other improvements to quality of life. In the 1960s and '70s, the two primary social categories in villages were agricultural workers (*rabochie*) and public servants (*sluzhashchie*). Agricultural workers were comprised of the former kolkhoz peasantry, while public servants were those who worked in farm management, including specialists arriving on work assignments.

Regardless of whether a young specialist was called a public servant or a member of the intelligentsia, he or she was viewed as a conduit of progressive views and as a pillar of the political system. Therefore, as was the case at all the country's institutions of higher education, the teachers, employees, and students at Vologda Dairy Institute were regularly enlisted to fulfil party and Komsomol objectives, including spreading scientific knowledge and political education, the main components of the Soviet conception of progress.

In the USSR, in addition to specialist disciplines, there was a whole range of theoretical subjects that were not directly connected to a student's chosen profession. In fact, only about half of the subjects taught at agricultural technical institutes in the 1960s and '70s had a direct relationship to student specializations; the remainder of the courses were meant to broaden their world view by acquainting them with Marxist philosophy, CPSU history, world art and cultural history, and other primarily social disciplines. This universal, "unspecialized" knowledge was required at all institutions of higher education regardless of their specialization profiles and was valued very highly because it gave academic knowledge in the USSR its genuine character and legitimacy. It allowed specialized scientific undertakings and the achievements of academics to be conceptualized as part of a unified system of knowledge based in Marxism-Leninism and confirming the existence of socialism.[100]

Although by the 1960s Marxism was no longer used to explain linguistic knowledge or genetics, as it had been in the Stalin era, it was

Figure 6.2. School Street (Shkolnaya ulitsa) in Molochnoe, ca. 1968. On the left, with the space-age decoration, is the new building for the Faculty of Agricultural Machinery Mechanization at Vologda Dairy Institute. In the background, to the left, is Molochnoe High School, while two apartment blocks sit off to the right.

Source: Photo from the Centre for Museum Work for the Vologda Molochnoe Dairy Institute and Vologda Butter.

still an active form of dominant discourse at the core of every field. Thus, references to the works of Marx, Engels, and Lenin were required in any academic text, and courses in CPSU history and the fundamentals of political economy were studied both by humanities students and engineers.

The same courses on Marxism-Leninism were required in all institutions of higher education, and the course selection was invariable. This provided students with a "universal" basis of knowledge, a fact that was highly valued in a context where different regions of the country were developing at an unequal pace. In essence, education (considered outside concrete specializations or institutes) was universally valued in the USSR for its ability to serve as a "safety net" and regulate the labour market within the framework of a planned economy. As Isak Froumin and Oleg Leshukov have argued, Soviet higher education was a "highly state-regulated system, with weak authority by academics and university leaders, with little influence by markets; indeed, within a command economy, the state determined the market. All universities were 'cogs in the central-government machine.'"[101]

Although in the 1960s and '70s an agricultural specialist could end up working as the director of a theatre, and a medical graduate might become a district leader, both were considered suitable candidates by the government because they had the "mark of quality," the necessary political preparation, which was considered more important for management positions than whatever narrow specialization a person may have studied at an institute. Thus, former VDI student Anatoly Ivanovich Valiuzhenich began his career with the institute's Komsomol organization. During his studies he became the VDI Komsomol secretary and, after graduation, the secretary of the Vologda VLKSM City Committee. Then, from 1964 to 1970, he worked as the director of the sovkhoz "Nikolotorzhsky," in Kirillovsky District. In time, he became first secretary of the CPSU District Committee. Finally, from 1984 to 1993, he worked as department chief for one of the CPSU regional committee departments and as deputy chairman of the regional Executive Committee.[102] Anatoly's career path serves as an example of how an institute's Komsomol organization could serve as the starting point for a party career.

From the 1950s, VDI had a working branch of the all-union "Knowledge" (Znanie) society, which in 1969 had 241 members who gave public lectures[103] and wrote articles for oblast- and district-level newspapers.[104] Usually it was VDI teachers who delivered lectures to the more intellectual city audiences as well as at party and Soviet institutions. Students typically propagandized their knowledge and read lectures to less sophisticated audiences: workers and public servants at kolkhozes and sovkhozes. These lectures took place during professional training and on regular trips "to the potato fields." In a VDI Komsomol student work report from 1960, 102 agitators were listed among the student body, and they were all recorded as having worked with the population of Molochnoe and neighbouring villages.[105] It was also noted that at meetings between agitators and the local population, topics for discussion included "red calendar dates, current events, and elections." As the report's authors noted, discussions usually went smoothly. However, there were some difficult moments. For instance, student agitators proved unprepared for the topic "The Relationship of the Soviet Government and Religion." Although agitators were trained by the VDI party organization, training attendance was, according to the report, "typically unimpressive, approximately 30 per cent."[106]

Lecture propaganda was also an important part of student construction brigade work in rural localities. Admittedly, it is difficult to ascertain the extent to which students and teachers took this work seriously. In a report on the condition of educational work at VDI for the 1964–5 academic year, it was noted that "public work practices are developing

Figure 6.3. Students of VDI who were participating in the "Pobeda" motocross, 1975.

Source: Photo from the Centre for Museum Work for the Vologda Molochnoe Dairy Institute and Vologda Butter.

weakly among students: The public works faculty is not functioning this year; the young-lecturer school created under the auspices of the Marxism-Leninism Department fell apart after conducting a few lessons; it proved impossible to organize a film-mechanics circle"; and, generally speaking, the students' public activity overall was "reduced to amateur arts performances and agitational work among the local population during training trips," which, additionally, were not checked.[107] The performative character of the educational events put on at VDI was recognized, apparently, by the organs monitoring the institute as well as the students.[108]

Yuri V. gained "public work" experience outside of the institute's walls, on the sovkhoz "Vorobyevsky," where he was raised and where he returned after graduating from VDI in 1970. Recalling that time, he remembered how the CPSU District Committee assigned him to present a lecture on the economic theory of socialism. Ultimately, it proved to be unengaging for his listeners, who were comprised of sovkhoz tractor operators and party organization members. He decided not to waste his time and never again read a lecture to the kolkhoz.[109] Nevertheless, whenever district leadership visited the farm, they asked if Yuri was conducting educational work for the workers and public servants. Each time they received the same answer about the single lesson he had conducted. After once again hearing this unencouraging bit of information, the Kirillovsky CPSU District Committee secretary asked whether Yuri was a party member. Having received a negative answer, he dropped his line of questioning. Not having a party ticket saved Yuri from being reprimanded for breaching party discipline, party organs' most powerful instrument of leverage in those years.

In the 1970s, a non-party young specialist was less vulnerable than a party member because he could not be disciplined by being made to maintain "the party line." District committees had little leverage against a person outside of the party system. Political education and Komsomol work at VDI were the responsibility of the institute's party organization, the CPSU Political Economy Department, state security organs, and the institute's Komsomol organization. Unlike the period spanning the 1930s through the 1950s, when the pursuit of "Trotskyists" and "rootless cosmopolitans" led to tumultuous party shake-ups, in the 1960s and '70s the institute's party organization was more likely to discuss academic plans and student performance. It worked on solving production-related issues and decided which colleagues would be sent to party conferences.[110]

Judging by department reports from these later decades, VDI offered its students approximately the same list of events as other educational institutions: It conducted political education, lectures, and discussions; organized excursions to theatres, museums, and hikes to Lenin excursion points; and hosted film showings on "ideological topics."[111] The most politicized VDI departments were those of Scientific Atheism and Socialist Political Economy. Unlike other departments, which were tied to students' future professions, teachers in these departments were responsible for ideological work, the fulfilment of party directives, and the quality of "ideological" events. Thus, a department report for the 1970–1 academic year announced that scientific conferences dedicated to the one hundred fiftieth birthday of Friedrich Engels had been conducted in all VDI faculties, that the department instructors had organized excursions for first- and second-course students to the Mary Ulyanova Museum House in Raskopino (2 excursions), to the Mary Ulyanova Memorial Museum House in Vologda (6 excursions), to monuments dedicated to revolutionary history (10 excursions), and to the local history museum. Overall, 28 trips were organized. The report also noted that the department had shown students the films *Liberation* and *Red Square* in their office space, and that they had organized various thematic exhibitions on Komsomol work and Leninist heritage.[112] There was nothing particularly new about the ideological events conducted at VDI, and they were mentioned in annual reports throughout the 1960s and '70s. At the same time, rural students who were recognized for their Komsomol work at VDI had a good chance of continuing their Komsomol and party work in the future.

The Public Professions Faculty

More than political literacy or Komsomol membership was needed in order for VDI students to become the standard-bearers of progressive views in rural localities. Although forming students' cultural world view was on every institution of higher education's agenda, it became something of a mission in agricultural institutes. A VDI graduate who was sent to the countryside was supposed to be a conduit of modernity. It was with this goal in mind that public professions faculties (*facultet obshchestvennikh professiy*) were opened in agricultural institutes and pedagogical colleges across the USSR. As V.F. Krasota, head of the Ministry of Agriculture's Chief Directorate for Educational Institutions, announced in 1967, "no specialist in any profession should stand on the sidelines in the battle to raise the population's cultural level; he should be our permanent cultural representative in the village."[113] This seemed all the more pertinent when that figure was an agricultural specialist.

Public professions faculties gave students an opportunity to gain a second "public" specialization, in areas that were in demand in rural localities, in addition to their primary agricultural specialization. There was a sharp deficit of club workers, librarians, and sports organizers in the countryside, and public professions faculties were meant to address this issue. The USSR's first such faculty was opened in 1958 at the Krasnoyarsk Agricultural Institute, where students could receive a specialization in bayan playing, choreography, or dramatic or vocal arts leadership.[114] The idea of organizing these faculties was so popular within the Ministry of Agriculture that by 1967 there were already sixty-seven of them operating in more than one hundred schools.[115] At the same time, the fact that public professions faculties did not receive special funding created numerous problems for university administrations.

The VDI Public Professions Faculty was opened and closed multiple times. In 1960, it was mentioned by VDI Secretary Valyuzhenich at a Komsomol plenum.[116] But by the 1964–5 school year it was described in an educational work report as having been disbanded.[117] The faculty was also mentioned in a letter written by VDI Rector Viktorin Slivko, who explained its closure on the basis that VDI lacked the necessary funds and that it was impossible to find part-time, hourly-wage lecturers who were prepared to drive to Molochnoe from Vologda.[118] The rector went on to write that there was no one capable of training ballerina-veterinarians, bayan player–agronomists, and referee-engineers. It is interesting that Slivko did not mention the institute's Komsomol as a potential organizing body for the faculty, even though in 1960 it was the institute's VLKSM organization that had led the public professions initiative and had even reported to the Vologda CPSU Regional Committee on the new career specializations offered at VDI ("sport sector specialist" and "public librarian").[119] Clearly, the pragmatically minded rector did not wish to take on extra responsibilities.

Nevertheless, the Public Professions Faculty was revived once again in the mid-1970s. It included a Marxism-Leninism school, a journalism branch, a theatre group, a cinema group, a ballroom dancing branch, a choreography branch, a librarians' branch, a choir signing branch, and a branch for preparing sports instructors and referees.[120] It is difficult to say how popular the Department of Social Professions was among students, but there is evidence that it played a cardinal role in the life trajectory of at least one student. According to Nikolai Uvarov, a journalist for the regional newspaper *Red North*, his interest in the journalistic profession was sparked by his participation in launching the institute's limited-circulation newspaper *For the Cadres*, as well as his attendance at the institute's Public Professions Faculty classes in 1974.[121]

During the periods when the Public Professions Faculty was defunct, the institute's Komsomol and departmental leadership created amateur circles, sports sections, and various interest groups such as a student club, a student scientific society, and an editorial board to helm *For the Cadres*. In the 1960–1 academic year, students put on an amateur arts performance for the first and second courses. Additionally, departmental teams organized student concerts in rural clubs and associated kolkhozes, cultural trips to the oblast theatre, a Q&A session, and a waltz.[122] There were also institute interest circles, which functioned on a permanent basis, such as the wind instrument circle, the stage performance circle, and the choreography circle. However, as Timirkhanova, the student chief of mass-cultural work, lamented, "only some small part of the students participate, [while] the others do nothing. All that is organized on Saturdays and Sundays are dances."[123]

It is rather difficult to ascertain how popular these activities were among students. Yuri V. recalled that during his student years he did not participate in student life at the institute, apart from attending sport competitions. In fact, he avoided Komsomol meetings and did not sign up for sections or circles. The only leisure activities that interested him were dances and ice skating in the winter.[124] In contrast, Kapitolina K., who studied in the economics department over the same years as Yuri, led a flourishing student life. As a group leader, she was busy all the time, whether with putting on a concert or organizing tourist trips and excursions. The young women in her group participated in competitions, attended dances, and attended every showing at the local cinema, World.[125]

Evidently, students were free to choose the lifestyle they found the most fitting, as was reflected in their varying relationships to the opportunities on offer at VDI. And although this was not directly connected with the activities of the Public Professions Faculty, the types of opportunities the department offered were, generally, closely related to the interests of the student body (even if many would have preferred to watch films more in keeping with the tastes of contemporary youth than about Lenin).[126] Moreover, on account of the closed nature of the Russian Federal Security Service archives and the inaccessibility of VDI party meeting materials, it is extremely difficult to come to a conclusion about the presence of political opposition groups. Interview materials are of no more help in the matter. Those who agreed to interviews spoke about the lack of political discussion among the student body during their studies. However, modern studies of Soviet youth culture have shown that opposition circles were not a rare phenomenon at either urban universities or provincial institutes.[127] Thus, the lack of testimony about a counterculture and political activism among VDI students should not be taken as proof that neither existed, although it is reasonable to assume that in an institute where the majority of students came from rural localities, the oppositional potential of the student body would be expressed differently than in the dissident milieu of universities in major cities.

VDI Construction Brigades

Vladimir P. was born into a family of VDI teachers in 1954. His father, who had served at the front, was the secretary of the institute's party organization in the 1960s, and his mother taught foreign languages at VDI.[128] After finishing ten grades at Vologda School No. 6, in Molochnoe, he enrolled in the Agricultural Machine Mechanization Department, where he went on to study with honours. Vladimir had joined the VLKSM while still a schoolchild, and he became an active member of the institute's Komsomol organization after being accepted to VDI. As was the case for many children of VDI teachers, he remained in Molochnoe after graduation, began graduate studies, and then went on to lead one of the institute's laboratories. At the same time, he served as head of the VDI Komsomol organization. Discussing his work in this role, Vladimir emphasized that the most important achievement and the main task of the VDI Komsomol in the 1960s and '70s was its participation in the construction brigade (*stroiotriad*) movement.

The VDI Komsomol organization was one of the oldest in Vologda Oblast and had 1,614 members in the 1964–5 academic year.[129] That number grew in the 1970s as more students came to the institute from schools (most of whom were already Komsomol members). An increase in the number of Komsomol members, however, did not indicate an increase in the quality of Komsomol activity, which was noted on multiple occasions by VLKSM Regional Committee inspections. V. Kichina, the instructor for the school branch of the Vologda CPSU Regional Committee, wrote, "one doesn't feel that initiative, that flame, among department Komsomol groups, [and] Komsomol meetings are reduced to discussions of behaviour, academic performance, and attendance, all of which is conducted in a formal manner. Therefore, one finds Komsomol member students who do not question why they study, why they live."[130]

It is probable that had VDI not become involved in the construction brigade movement, many of the institute's students would not have noticed the existence of the institute's Komsomol at all. As in many Soviet structures, almost all Komsomol work was done by members of the VLKSM Bureau, which, in essence, was a sort of limited-access club.[131] Membership in student brigades, in contrast, organized by the VDI Komsomol, constituted a memorable experience in the lives of many former students. VDI's participation in student construction brigades conformed to contemporary popular trends.[132] The Komsomol provided this economically opaque project its legal and ideologically approved status.[133]

Unlike *subbotniks* and unpaid work within the framework of professional training, which was focused on bringing in harvests on the school farms and associated kolkhozes and sovkhozes, construction brigades offered students the opportunity to earn money. Moreover, unlike the professions offered by the Public Professions Faculty (such as bayan player and librarian), students who became temporary builders, intercity rail conductors, and excavator operators could earn money over the summer. This was a big incentive, seeing as the VDI stipends had always been small, amounting to approximately thirty to thirty-five roubles a month in the 1960s.[134] Furthermore, over the course of their studies, students in construction brigades received a second specialization that was in demand in the urban labour market, whether as a builder, a fitter, a concrete layer, or an excavator operator. A few students in the construction brigade movement even managed to secure offers for full-time work by the end of the building season when circumstances proved favourable. Not incidentally, construction brigades at VDI were organized by the Agricultural Mechanisation Faculty, which trained engineers, and whose graduates were most likely to find employment in industry or construction, rather than on sovkhozes and kolkhozes.[135]

Party and Komsomol leaders in Vologda Oblast and at VDI viewed the development of the construction brigade movement as a continuation of communist *subbotniks* and as an opportunity to use student labour to address pressing agricultural issues. V.F. Sakharov, commander of the regional student construction brigade, informed the Vologda CPSU Regional Committee of the benefits the student movement was bringing the oblast's economy. He wrote that the Energy-72 brigades, which had worked for Vologda Mechanization Column No. 19 in 1972, had completed a volume of construction and installation work equivalent to 797,000 roubles, which was 19 per cent of the column's annual plan.[136] Another example mentioned was the construction of a compressor station in the village of Rostilovo, in Gryazovetsky District, where "[thanks to] student efforts, a volume of work equal to 423,000 roubles was completed, which was 43 per cent of the third-quarter management plan and 66 per cent of the compressor station plan."[137]

In 1967, the oblast's first construction brigade was created under the auspices of the Vologda VLKSM Regional Committee. Its members were a group of VDI students who worked to introduce electricity to villages and settlements throughout the oblast.[138] In the following year, the first VDI Komsomol construction brigade was organized by the institute's Komsomol organization. It had 24 members, half of whom were young women, and was sent to work on agricultural land-development projects within the oblast. Two years later, in 1970, the institute's construction brigade could already boast 265 student members.[139] During these years, VDI organized the first construction brigade to work beyond the oblast's boundaries: 50 VDI students were sent to build a farm in Krasnodar Krai. Although students from various departments participated in the movement, the organizational backbone was usually formed by students of the Mechanization Department. In 1979, for example, 120 of the 395 institute's construction brigade members were first- and third-course Mechanization Department students.[140] Beginning in 1975, institute construction brigades began to use VDI equipment, such as tractors and combines. Before this they had provided only manpower.

Recalling their participation in the VDI construction movement, former participants described brigades as having a certain level of autonomy within the overall leadership structure. Members were able to choose the brigade's name, its command and commissar, and they were often in charge of distributing salaries among themselves. Brigade names that sounded romantic in the 1960s and '70s, such as Arolit, Flame, Diana, Nadezhda, Orbit, and Seeker, added colour to the various construction headquarters' abbreviations.

Often, construction brigades were tasked with low-paid, labour-intensive work that was barely connected to their members' professional specialization. For example, Valintina Ganicheva, who participated in a VDI construction brigade in 1969–70, recalled, "the first year we worked in Sheksninsky District. The brigade was divided into groups of twenty. We lived in small trailers and cooked our meals on a field kitchen. Generally, we did heavy physical labour related to turfing irrigation canals. The girls cut up twenty- to forty-centimetre turf sheets, loaded them on wagons, wheeled them to the canals, and lined the canals with the sheets. The guys worked on fortifying the canal beds: they lined the beds with hedging and panelled them with boards."[141] Essentially, young agronomists were doing the jobs of agricultural workers.

The labour sites where construction brigades were employed varied, as did the level of compensation members received. Stanislav Rusetsky, a 1977–8 VDI construction brigade member, recalled how "the first year we went to build a livestock complex in the village of Charozero, in Kirill-ovsky District. They housed us in the school's sports hall. First, we worked on the church building, mended the roof, repaired the walls, so that the farm could use it for grain storage. Then we installed a conveyor for manure transport. We knew that we had to look for another place to work. It turned out that they earned the most here, in Molochnoe. The following year we found work on the settlement's sovkhoz, where they tasked us with building a two-storey house. We lived in the dormitories and ate in the cafeteria. We calculated the cost of the work, and it turned out that every person would get six hundred roubles. That was good money in those days."[142]

In addition to the salary, students could receive incentives from the VLKSM Regional Committee and the institute Komsomol organization. Winners of construction brigade socialist competitions were awarded not only with certificates and VLKSM trophies, but were also often given vacation trips, especially to the VDI tourist base in Krasnodar Krai. In 1977, six student winners of construction brigade socialist competitions were given certificates by the VLKSM Central Committee and sent on a trip to Czechoslovakia.[143] For their outstanding work replacing the floors on the Molochnoe student farms during the 1977–8 academic year, the Veterinary Faculty's construction brigade was awarded with a trip to a resort on the Black Sea.[144]

According to N.A. Kuznetsova, a 1979 zonal student brigade partici-pant from VDI, the student construction brigade would start to form in March, when brigade recruitment announcements were made. He recalled that "specialists from the trust 'Vologda Agricultural Construction' would drive into Molochnoe to read lectures, and we learned the nuts and bolts of working professions."[145] He went on to describe how students signed work contracts for a specific volume of labour.

On account of the construction brigade system, the academic year was typically pushed back a month, to start in October rather than September. According to Yuri Viktorovich Lukinsky, the institute's VLKSM organization secretary and a teacher in the Mechanization Department, in the 1970s the institute tended to manage brigade specializations along faculty lines: Students from the Technologies Faculty typically formed conductor brigades to work on railways, while students from faculties linked to agricultural production (the Agronomics, Veterinary, Animal Husbandry, and Agricultural Production Mechanization Faculties) usually worked on tasks such as building farms, introducing electricity, and installing equipment.[146]

Participation in the institute construction brigade movement created an interesting precedent for VDI students from rural areas. A portion of the student population with kolkhoz-worker parents were unable to take part in the construction movement during the summer. Yuri V., for example, though he wished to join his faculty colleagues, was prevented from doing so by the necessity of helping with summer haymaking at home. In a family of three people, including a disabled father and a kolkhoz-worker mother, Yuri's help preparing hay for domestic livestock was indispensable. As a result, Yuri was unable to participate in construction brigades.

However, many students from rural localities found themselves in a more favourable position and were able to spend a month or two of the summer holidays far from home. Many found themselves working in rural areas in a completely new capacity, as visiting students from the city, viewed by VDI leadership and by the inviting party as a progressive, modernizing force in the countryside. These students not only built new facilities – they also organized lectures, put on concerts, held competitions for local youths, and, generally speaking, found themselves popularizing a new, modern lifestyle. Fashionable haircuts and workwear visually emphasized the difference between students and the local population, and the general lifestyle and pastimes of the students, which included dances, songs around the campfire, and radio music, created the sense of belonging to a different, urban culture. Arriving at a village as part of a construction brigade, yesterday's rural school students stepped into their new role as conduits of modernity.

Ultimately, the system of higher agricultural education that existed in the 1960s and '70s was in large part intended to train students in

Vologda Oblast for management roles in the agricultural sector. The measures that the administration introduced to engage rural youths, such as conducting preparatory courses, building dormitories, introducing kolkhoz stipends, and Komsomol recruitments, were aimed at increasing the number of agricultural specialists. In reality, however, the institute was unable to cope with the task at hand, and deficits of agricultural personnel lasted throughout the entirety of the late socialist period. According to the Vologda Statistics Department, on 1 April 1978, 42 per cent of Vologda Oblast kolkhoz leadership and specialist personnel had no higher or specialized education, with the figure being 32 per cent on sovkhozes.[147] The root of this problem was not that students strove to work outside their specialization; rather, rural young people did not perceive returning to work on the sovkhozes where they were raised as offering the best life trajectory. Often, receiving an education at VDI was viewed as a means of moving into the city. And although a year or two working in a rural locality was often the price to pay, ultimately, a diploma allowed VDI graduates to find better opportunities to apply their knowledge, even if these were not directly connected with their specialist training.

At the same time, a VDI education increased professional and career opportunities for former students. It allowed them to occupy positions and build careers in cities as well as in rural localities. Furthermore, unlike other agricultural institutes, which often carried less prestige, VDI maintained a degree of authority both because it was the oldest institution of higher education in the oblast and because of its dairy specialization. The institute infrastructure created for the dairy sector – including the dairy factory, the specialized breeding farms, and the research institute – allowed students not only to become VDI agronomists and animal husbandry specialists but also to continue their studies at the graduate level and find work at the RSFSR North-West Scientific Research Institute for Meadow Management and Dairy Farming. As a rule, the majority of teaching careers at VDI were connected in some way or another with having graduated from VDI. In other words, the backbone of academic faculty that had been created by the developing dairy industry allowed VDI to maintain a reputation as a well-known and relatively prestigious educational institution in the Russian North-West. In addition to preparing personnel to serve in Vologda villages, it also produced a rare thing indeed: dairy production technologists. As a result, VDI brought a large number of urban students to study in Molochnoe, which undoubtedly played a role in creating the special urbanized atmosphere that prevailed on the campus. This was something of which few other Soviet institutes could boast.

Chapter Seven

Molochnoe: Urban Meets Rural

Rural, Not Peasant

Cultural and social space in the settlement Molochnoe was formed under the strong influence of ideas about the modernization of Soviet agriculture. The appearance of a scientific, technological, and educational centre in the Vologda backwoods became a social experiment in which people with very different group and class backgrounds lived side by side: the peasantry (as representatives of "former classes"), scientists, workers, and students. The hierarchy into which they were organized is clearly imprinted on the settlement's architecture and structures.

Although, as a result of propaganda about new Soviet values, public spaces, whether stadiums or cultural parks, became symbols of new conceptions about social order, residential homes and the organization of everyday life clearly indicated how disparate the social environments that formed in the settlement were from one another. The status afforded to VDI's professorial and teaching staff remained high throughout the settlement's existence, and was attested to by the numerous institute buildings, which occupied the most prestigious spaces in the settlement, as well as by the privileges granted this group in residential and social policy. At the same time, the appearance of other "elite" housing in Molochnoe, intended for non-institute *nomenklatura*, shows that another class of Soviet managers was gaining significance: the heads of various social services, as the people who were in charge of food goods distribution and infrastructure within the settlement.

Urbanization in Molochnoe went hand in hand with the Sovietization of life. Soviet rituals, whether May Day demonstrations or flower-laying ceremonies at the base of an obelisk in honour of fallen soldiers, sports celebrations or theatrical performances, formed public demand for new facilities from the settlement administration and institute leadership: a student club, sports halls, a movie theatre, playgrounds. Nevertheless, the agricultural focus of the institute, which presumed that students would gain experience working in the fields and in laboratories, on farms and in plant nurseries, raised the value of attaining agricultural experience. As a result, the ties between agricultural science and agricultural production remained an important element of settlement society. Visiting farms and nurseries and working in the scientific-experimental fields was as important a part of student life as participation in sports sections or going to dances and films.

Despite all the changes that took place in Molochnoe over the decades of its existence, the students and the institute's professorial-teaching staff remained the most notable group; they set the tone for the settlement's public and cultural life. Due to the constant influx of VDI students, youth subculture did as much as the area's urban attributes to give the Molochnoe locality its unique atmosphere. Student study and leisure activities gave life its unique rhythm, drawing residents into the changes taking place both as observers and participants. Moving to Molochnoe, rural students acquired new practices from the settlement: participating in sports, attending the movie theatre and going to the cafeteria, learning to use the laundromat. The settlement's physical layout, which needed to meet student and academic demands, seemed to codify the value of belonging to and identifying with this group. Concurrently, other identities, held by people who had grown up in Molochnoe or had moved there at various stages of their careers as workers, also found their place. Former peasants kept domestic livestock in the settlement "sheds," which in no way impeded the ability of some of them to work in the research institute.[1] Molochnoe was a place with many identities in the 1960s and '70s, but it was the student or academic communities that proved to be the most prestigious and that reaped the most benefits.

The Milk-and-Honey Shores of Rural Modernity

Whereas in school, rural youths were introduced to socialism as a phenomenon existing in places far from their native villages, in the 1960s and '70s, life in the Molochnoe settlement, the site of Vologda Dairy Institute, served as proof that socialism could exist in rural localities. For many rural school graduates who moved to the settlement, Molochnoe exemplified a scientifically organized space, one saturated with ideas about modernized agricultural production, and modernized rural life in general. Despite the settlement's being located in a rural locality seventeen kilometres from Vologda, it was long considered the most progressive place in the oblast and had the largest percentage of degree holders among its population, up to half of which was comprised of students.[2]

Figure 7.1. View of the settlement Molochnoe, ca. 1969. In the foreground are old wooden dormitories belonging to VDI on Student Street (Studencheskaya ulitsa), as well as VDI employee housing. In the background are new residential buildings, various VDI faculties, a student canteen, and a hospital.

Source: Photo from the Center for Museum Work on the history of the Vologda Dairy Institute and Vologda butter.

Kapitolina K. moved to Molochnoe from the village of Kogach, in Kirillovsky District, in 1966 in order to begin her studies in the VDI Economics Faculty.[3] As the daughter of a kolkhoz worker mother and a selsoviet chairman father, she, like most village children, attended three schools at three different locations: a primary, an eight-year, and a secondary school. On the advice of her parents, Kapitolina had originally applied to study mathematics and physics at a pedagogical institute, but, unable to pass the entrance examination, she was sent by the Kirillovsky Educational Committee to work in one of the district clubs. It was there that Kapitolina learned about the economics faculty opening at VDI. The competition was fierce, but Kapitolina proved successful. In 1996, she joined the faculty's first ever group of students and moved to Molochnoe, where she would stay for the rest of her life and go on to teach for the faculty.

For Kapitolina, as someone moving out of the countryside, the settlement provided a comfortable lifestyle in comparison with the villages where she had previously lived. Recalling the experience, she noted, "It was a very quiet, peaceful settlement. Young people all around. It was very beautiful, very."[4] The settlement's charm, however, was not appreciated by all the institute students. Evelina M.'s first impressions of the settlement after moving from the Bashkirian city of Tuymazy were utterly different. For city-born Evalina, the settlement seemed unremarkable, less cared-for and less comfortable than the cities she had seen in the Ural region. Evelina remembered her shock at the disorder in the student dormitories and dirty public spaces: "You can't imagine – there would be a layer of sunflower seed shells this thick on the floor – ten centimetres, at least … Of course, I was a little taken aback. Sure, there was plenty of garbage in Tuymazy too, but not that much. In public spaces especially."[5] Clearly, students' experience growing up in urban or rural localities influenced their perception of the settlement.

Adopting the pre-revolutionary government's initiative to develop the region's dairy industry, the Soviet *nomenklatura* took over control of the dairy institute and framed itself as a progressive force capable of leading Vologda Oblast to new, modernized heights. Although the "high modernism" of the founders eventually resulted in a worker settlement with standardized two-, three-, and five-storey apartment buildings and dormitories, an element of its grand conception was forever stamped onto the village's appearance by the contour of the institute's main building, Molochnoe's primary architectural achievement and the centrepiece of most photograph and film representations of the settlement.

In landscape characterized by traditional villages and manors built for the Russian nobility, constructing a settlement specially designed for scientific experimentation and training dairy specialists seemed revolutionary to its founders, thanks to whose efforts an institution of higher education was appearing in the Vologda backwoods. Admittedly, the approach was not specific to a Russian or Soviet context; the oldest agricultural institutions in Europe were also created with architectural flourishes emphasizing their missionary conception.[6]

And yet, the character of the architecture, as well as the social relations that arose among those who settled the area at various times, gave Molochnoe a unique atmosphere. Without understanding this, it would be very difficult to explain the changes with took place among the student population there during the 1960–70 period. How and what did they learn living in this place? What opportunities did the settlement offer and what kinds of identities did it give rise to?

Progressive Socialist Space

In his research, Henri Lefebvre suggested that space be viewed not as a scene upon which social action occurs, but as an active participant in social processes.[7] Lefebvre defined space according to three levels: physical, mental, and social. Streets, houses, people, relationships, events – all of them, in his view, comprise a unified social phenomenon, one that evolves over time. He believed that being in a space created in people a sense of belonging to that space and influenced the formation of their identity, as well as arguing that space itself influenced their social relations. Accordingly, being located in a space is no less important for people's self-definition than their social status.

The social aspects of residential spaces have been described by the anthropologist Arjun Appadurai, who drew attention to the boundaries of social environments.[8] He understood these boundaries in a social rather than a geographical sense, as illustrating the various actors that create these spaces. In his opinion, the existence of boundaries and implicit neighbour categories comprise an important source of knowledge about local communities. Various rites and rituals – holidays, naming customs, etc. – mark locality and make it visible, first and foremost, to residents themselves. He emphasized that "locality is ephemeral if intensive and regular work is not done to produce and support its materiality."[9]

The social dimension of space was also addressed by Pierre Bourdieu, for whom space is the symbolic reflection of the cultural and social imperatives that define life for a given culture.[10] Describing the traditional home of a Moroccan peasant, Bourdieu saw coded ideas about the distribution of gender roles and power.[11] The term "habitus," which he introduced into the lexicon to describe the habits, skills, dispositions, and ways of thinking that together comprise inherited sociality, is helpful for viewing space in terms of social and class relationships.

Conceptualizing space as a locality defined by its boundaries, actors, history, and materiality was not new to the second half of the twentieth century, although it was at that time that it became a central research focus. The architectural innovations of Le Corbusier and the urban planning of Frank Llyod Wright were based upon ideas of inevitable social construction in which architectural form and urban planning were said to reflect a pre-existing or future social order. It is unsurprising that Soviet architects, principal theoreticians of "high modernism," were the most consistent in bringing these ideas to life.

In the USSR, urban localities were the priority site for revolutionary change. As Alexandra Kasatkina noted, "In the projects of so-called 'high modernism,' city space was assigned a special role: the city was called up to form a new type of person and a new sociality."[12] In 1924, Moisei Ginzburg wrote in his book *Style and Epoch* that "New organisms of industrial and engineering structures, more sensitive and closer to the noise of life, should ... help form a new system for architecturally organizing space. Forming a new way of life for modern man will be the starting point for these endeavours, a concrete example of which will be industrial and engineering structures – the cutting-edge outposts of the modern form."[13] And although new technologies were often inaccessible to Soviet architects who dreamed of modern cities, social experimentation, as El Lisitsky has argued, took their place: "The projects are intended for an equal playing field and are based on these cities being intended for a society in which there are no longer classes."[14] And slightly earlier: "The city will absorb nature into itself; with the help of industrialization it will introduce the countryside to a higher level of cultural."[15]

Alongside those who advocated for Soviet cities as a home for a classless community, in the first decades of Soviet rule there were some who believed in creating socialist spaces on the basis of rural settlements. Until the peasantry was granted the ability to express its opinions and have a say in defining its interests (privileges it was deprived of beginning with collectivization), the types of houses and settlements they lived in were decided for them. This was reflected in the *désurbanisme* projects of the 1920 and '30s, where cramped urbanity was juxtaposed with "spacious rurality" and industrial production with agriculture.[16] Among such projects was Mikhail Okhitovkich's attempt at "margining the city and the countryside" by building band-shaped settlements with individual houses along highways.[17] Another project, conceived by Alexander Chayanov and described in his book *The Travels of My Brother Alexei into the Country of Peasant Utopia*, advocated for the even distribution of individual farms alternating with public spaces. The Moscow of the future, in the resulting vision, would look like a giant village drowning in a sea of green.[18]

All of these projects were involved in reorganizing daily life, but unlike in cities, in the *désurbanisme*-based settlements of the future, houses and structures would be more broadly distributed across space and integrated with the natural landscape. This meant that personal vegetable gardens were as important an element of planning as public institutions. Even the concept of the garden city,[19] which was extremely popular in the first decades of Soviet rule, relied on blurring the boundaries between urban and rural spaces, creating a place where the city dweller could enjoy natural landscapes and urban infrastructure simultaneously.[20]

Gradually, socialist spaces began to be associated primarily with urban culture, and urbanism became a sign of modernity. This is clearly reflected in Nikita Khrushchev's advocacy of the urbanization of rural settlements, which became the basis of a major campaign to transform rural territories. However, as Neil Melvin wrote, "although the general principles that were to guide rural development had been accepted, there were neither sufficient individual plans for rural buildings, settlements and agricultural areas, nor the construction capacity to implement any plans that might be produced. As a result, in the early 1960s, the Soviet Union was still far from being in a position to fully implement the new rural planning ideas."[21] It was only in the 1970s that the USSR began to use *selstroi* and inter-kolkhoz cooperation to work on construction projects in rural localities. However, even these projects were limited to large rural settlements. Small, "unpromising" villages and farmsteads were supposed to disappear from the map under socialism, just like individual peasant farms and land allotments (considered unpromising in the global economy). Urban-type settlements became the personification of social progress in Vologda Oblast's rural spaces.

Molochnoe, which had been built over the course of decades, was a clear example of a progressive and rapidly developing rural settlement. Its houses, parks, and public spaces were viewed by officials as instruments of modernity just as capable of spreading an awareness of progress in rural localities as a VDI education. Social space in the settlement, and the hierarchies entrenched within it, provided newly arrived students with discipline and informed their behaviour no less than the intellectual activity they partook in within the institute's walls.

Access to this space also created a colossal difference between two fundamental segments of the student population in the 1960s and '70s: full-time, in-person students and part-time, long-distance students. The full-time form, also called "day studies," involved daily class attendance at the institute, life in a dormitory, and participation in university and settlement affairs. This created specific residential environments and a student routine. The part-time students, who came to Molochnoe only during examination sessions, were not given the same opportunity. For this reason, Ministry of Agriculture representative V.F. Krasota, addressing the Komsomol active for agricultural institutes in 1967, called upon those present to increase the number of students studying in the university's full-time division, citing the increased effectiveness of this format.[22]

Before the 1960s there had been no part-time students at VDI. The situation changed when Khrushchev ordered a mass preparation of agricultural specialists, and by the 1964–5 academic year, the five faculties that offered an education through the part-time division had amassed a greater student population than those in the full-time division: the institute had 1,963 "part-timers" and 1,345 students studying full-time.[23] Admittedly, the attrition rate among part-time students was much higher than among full-time attendees. Of the 265 VDI graduates in 1962, only 45 were part-time students.[24]

The material environment of the settlement reflected not only the modernizing conception of its founders, but also significant differences in the lives of its various inhabitants. It was an environment that revealed inequality and fortified it in its structures. The types and quality of the residential structures, the dachas and stores, the location of roads and sidewalks within the settlement – all of this made it clear that one category of residents had more rights to the space than others. The settlement's material environment normalized pre-existing inequality, while simultaneously bearing witness to its reconceptualization.

The History of the Molochnoe Settlement

In the view of the apologists of "high modernism," the Molochnoe settlement arose on a totally undeveloped track of land, from scratch.[25] As James Scott wrote, narratives of modernity require that the starting point be a territory free from all influence and cultural interference.[26] The high modern required an empty space, such as a locality atop the steep banks of the Vologda River, dozens of kilometres from the oblast centre. And although local historians in the 1990s determined that the construction site was chosen for its proximity to the dairy factory owned by the Bowmans, a Danish family,[27] which was famous at that time for its rapid butter production and could offer students practical work experience, the creators of Soviet documentary films produced for the fifty-year anniversary of VDI began their account of the settlement's history with the founding of VDAI, rather than the factory.[28]

The life stories and scientific achievements of those who had worked at VDI comprised an important chapter in the local narrative concerning the settlement's past and present. The local press wrote primarily about those who worked at the institute, publishing reviews of the institute's history or covering notable residents through anniversary announcements or obituaries. In this sense, Molochnoe is comparable with famous Soviet *naukograd* science cities, whose discursive construction was based on technology and modernity.[29] It is also quite notable that, for residents of Molochnoe, the "progressive place" discourse was an important part of their self-identity. In the 1990s, the local VDI newspaper, *For the Cadres* – a standard title for an agricultural institute – was renamed *Academic City* (*Akademgorodok*), drawing an analogy with the Novosibirsk region of the same name.

The journalist Giorgi Dudchenko, in his book *Molochnoe: A Scientists' Settlement*, describes the ideology upon which VDI was built and includes stories of many notable figures from the institute's history, including founding professor Avetis Airapetovich Kalantar, professor Yakov Ilyich Khavenson, and candidate of agricultural sciences Margarita Yakovlevna Rubtsova, each advocates of breeding hybrid cattle; Olga Gennadievna

Kotova, a docent of the Dairy Technologies Faculty and specialist in Vologda butter production; and Lydia Vasilievna and Nikolai Mikhailovich Chekulaev, specialists in milk conservation and teachers for the Technologies Faculty.[30] The names and biographies of the founders of the dairy institute adorn the pages of the publication dedicated to celebrating VDI's one-hundred-year anniversary and play a central part in the institute's museum expositions.[31] The professors and teachers at VDI were the face of "the settlement for scientists of the dairy business."

This can further be explained by the fact that, unlike other institutions of higher education in Vologda Oblast, the students and professors at VDI lived in close quarters, creating a clearly visible group of the most privileged residents, those for whom the institute was built and who were considered the settlement's future. In reality, however, there were not only professors, teachers, and students living in Molochnoe; there were others too, although their stories have often been overlooked. Despite falling into the "invisible" categories of modern discourse, the presence of these unprivileged groups was felt in the life of the settlement, often in definitive ways. The existence of the dairy institute and experimental stations, the scientific-experimental factory, and the breeding stock herds on the experimental farms – all of this all had an influence on the settlement's cultural and social landscape. Molochnoe was a space where various identities met and lived in close proximity, even if only the academic segment of the population retained untrammelled authority.

Judging by the first brochures dedicated to the construction of the dairy institute, its buildings, dormitories, laboratories, cow pens, and residential houses all belonged to the scientific centre under construction and were built more or less simultaneously. Describing VDI in 1919, almost eight years after the decision had been made to construct the settlement, the institute's prorector, Professor Georgiy Inikhov, asserted that "at the present moment the following have been built and occupied: the main building with the butter production factory and experimental stockyard, seven residential houses, an accident ward and quarantining barrack, an electric station with a bathhouse and laundry facility, the building housing the dairy farming school with apartments for teachers, two biofiltration facilities, two workers' barracks, a fire station and an inventory storage facility, a barn for storing grain, a horse stable with a carriage house, two storage houses for root vegetables and a number of small constructions."[32] Inikhov continued:

Due to wartime conditions and insufficient credit the following have remained unfinished: the women's dormitory building, the pigpen. Construction of the following has not been started: a stockyard with a two-hundred-head capacity, an auditorium, and scientific laboratories, a threshing house, and a storage facility for hay. In accordance with an additional project from 1918, construction has begun on two stone residential houses for junior public servants, along with one wooden house. Until the construction of the stockyard is complete, one of the old yards has been temporarily refurbished and a manure storage facility set up. In 1916–17, earthworks were conducted on a large scale in accordance with plans for creating plots of land between buildings and paved roads were lain.[33]

The architects and engineers who led the construction of the institute and developed the blueprints for the buildings automatically took into account the social hierarchies that existed at that time. The houses in Molochnoe thus varied in quality, with the best reserved for the professors and fitted with plumbing, running water, front and back stairs, mansards, and servants' quarters. They were located close to the institute's main building, which had previously been used for holding classes and housing students. Humbler, corridor-type houses with private two- or three-room apartments were built for institute personnel. Finally, there were the barracks. Built for the workers, these were communal structures without amenities and equipped with bunks. Dividing the potential residents into groups (the professorial and teaching staff at the institute, the personnel for the dairy factory and laboratories, students, and, finally, the workers building the settlement) seemed utterly natural to the architects.

Efforts to build the most comfortable housing possible for professors reflected the pragmatic interests of institute leadership: Building lower-quality apartments would have rendered the already challenging task of "retaining personnel" even more difficult. During the first years of the institute's operation, it was difficult to find scientific specialists in the dairy field who would agree to move to a settlement in the process of construction. The housing for students and attendees of the dairy institute, although it was humbler than the professorial housing, still afforded a high degree of privacy and isolation. The architects took into consideration that the first attendees of the institute would be people who had already received an education.[34] The workers themselves were viewed by those in charge as temporary residents, and therefore only temporary barracks were built for them. The privileged status of the first residents and the "professorial houses" remained for years to come.

In terms of beautification and amenities, Molochnoe in the 1960s and '70s was in a better position than many rural localities. This was in large part thanks to the fact that, for much of its history, Molochnoe was under direct administrative subordination to Vologda and essentially considered an urban region. The benefits of belonging to an urban local-ity were reflected in better educational opportunities, medical care, and the availability of goods compared to rural regions. Nevertheless, becom-ing part of the city was a gradual process, and the seventeen kilome-tres separating the settlement from Vologda often created a whole host of problems. In 1934, the Vologda City Soviet first discussed granting Molochnoe worker settlement status, which would include the territory around the institute itself (known as Andreevsko-Fominsky area) and the villages that contained VDI's former institute farms (made indepen-dent during the reforms of the 1930s). As a result, Molochnoe housed 2,220 sovkhoz workers, for the most part in the thirty-one villages most closely located to the settlement, and 1,642 institute employees. In 1948, Molochnoe's status as a worker settlement was officially approved. At the time, the settlement was the centre of the Worker-Peasant Selsoviet, which included the villages in the area around the institute where the institute's experimental farms and fields were located. The settlement's connections with surrounding villages remained firm. It is worth add-ing here, in drawing the discussion of administrative subordination to a conclusion, that the final change to the status of the settlement occurred in the 1990s, when Molochnoe was removed from city subordination and put under the management of Vologodsky District. The status was changed in response to changes in land prices, which had decreased and become attractive for purchase and sale. As a result, on the level of administrative recognition Molochnoe went from being a settlement (*posyolok*) to a large village (*selo*) and was transferred to district level gov-ernment administration. This, however, had little effect on the function-ing of the majority of settlement institutions, which remained under the control of the city as they had been before. The duality of Molochnoe's administrative status – being at once an urban and a rural locality – made it politically flexible and allowed residents to make use of its location.

"Scientists" and "the Proletariat"

Perhaps the most striking social contrast within the settlement was the entrenched inequality between people in some way associated with the institute and those who were deprived of this privilege. The division of Molochnoe's population into "scientists" (*nauchniki*) and everyone else – workers and public servants, those employed in servicing the insti-tute's factory, nurseries, experimental farms, construction workers – was part of the local lexicon even in the pre-war era. The term *nauchniki* can be heard in stories told by settlement residents to this day.[35] The term's appearance in local speech is indicative of the special place reserved for this group of people in the social environment of Molochnoe during the Soviet era.

Attempts by the revolutionary government to change the settlement hierarchy by making the proletariat (workers in the institute's garage and dairy factory, students from worker and peasant backgrounds) the privileged class among other groups were generally unsuccessful. A system in which academic workers possessed the greatest privileges existed in the settlement throughout Soviet rule, although some of the apartments designated for professors were compressed and even replanned at the end of the 1920s. Yet even in the 1930s, at the height of the campaigns against specialists and the temporary subordination of the institute to the sovkhoz, the professorial and teaching staff received special treatment. The professors who were fired during the campaigns were simply replaced with new professors, trained by the institute and with a proletarian background.

Originally, the teachers and personnel at the institute were easy to recognize by their class origin, level of education, and the affluence they enjoyed. In photographs from that time, preserved in the VDI institute museum, one finds solid-looking men with frock coats, smart dress shirts, and ties. The city clothes of the ladies, with their fashionable dresses and hats, struck a clear contrast with the handkerchiefs and scarves characteristic of female worker and peasant dress. The noblemen and *raznochintsy* who viewed studying agriculture as a means of serving the people stood out sharply among Vologda region's overwhelming peasant population.

The post-war period saw the outward differences between the professorial staff and the general population become far less stark. Clothes had become tattered over years of war and made the intelligentsia hard to recognize by such outward identifiers. Moreover, the new generation of professorial staff came from proletarian backgrounds and had the experience of going through *rabfak* (a Soviet institution that prepared working-class people for higher education). In their comportment and lifestyle, they were closer to workers than noblemen and differed from the first VDI professors, who had received their education abroad or in the capitals.

Institute worker accommodations were scant in those years but nevertheless remained better than those of the institute's other residents. Even in the 1950s, institute teachers retained the right to shop in an exclusive store. According to A.G. Titov, "the 'scientist store' sold everything from jewellery to bread, which was not delivered daily and which people formed an enormous line to get."[36] The limits placed on food distribution to teachers and institute personnel may not have exceeded work allowance cards, but food goods were given out with greater regularity.[37]

Unlike other population segments in the settlement, starting in the 1930s the children of institute workers had the opportunity to attend kindergarten, an extremely valuable privilege at a time when there was an acute lack of children's institutions. The institute kindergarten was originally organized in the apartment of one of the "institute" houses on Schmidt Street.[38] In response to the increasing number of children enrolling in the 1950s, it was moved to a small space on Lenin Street that was later made into a musical school.[39] In 1967, VDI constructed a new, standardized building for the kindergarten with a six-group capacity. Its design was intended for a warmer climate, as is indicated by the glass verandas at the ends of the building, which freeze up during harsh Vologda winters. The institute was forced to build a coal-fuelled heating room for the building in order to heat the air inside to around eighteen or nineteen degrees Celsius.

The kindergarten built next to Molochnoe for the children of sovkhoz workers was housed in a wooden building in the village of Fominskoe. Later, kindergartens were established in other villages, where sovkhoz workers and public servants lived in compact residential areas. In the 1960s and '70s, it was much simpler to enrol a child in one of these kindergartens than it was in the institute kindergarten. As a result, the children of migrants moving to Molochnoe often attended kindergartens in neighbouring villages such as Ilyinskoe, Marfino, or Fominskoe.[40] Nevertheless, for a long time the existing kindergartens were unable to accommodate the number of children. This led to high demand for hired nannies and older women willing to look after children.

The privileges of professors and teachers were also visible during the formation of school classes at the settlement school, Vologda City School No. 6. The teaching personnel and the quality of the teaching were expected to meet exceptional standards. "Institute children" were put into separate classes taught by the most experienced teachers, and the demands for academic success placed on both the teachers and the students were higher.[41] Secondary School No. 6 was in good standing with the City Education Committee. In the 1969–70 academic year it had three buildings (one for primary grades, another for grades 4–11, and an old wooden school building that had been converted into a dormitory and a Pioneer house). There were 58 teachers and 1,149 students, 330 of whom lived farther than three kilometres from school.[42] The school had a buffet and a cafeteria, student workshops with stations for wood- and metalworking, sewing machines, a library, an after-school group, two sport's halls, a scientific-experimental land plot, and thirty-one school classrooms with specially equipped rooms for physics, chemistry, and biology. The school in Molochnoe was better equipped than schools in the oblast's other rural districts. The fact that the students who studied there were the children of VDI professors played no small role in this.

In the 1960s, settlement children could freely move from house to house without remaining strictly within the bounds of their own social circles, but the ways in which they were raised differed from family to family. Children of VDI professors and teachers often chose academic careers. Nikolai, son of V.A. Krylov, the head of the institute's Energy Department from 1941 to 1953, enrolled in the Mathematics Faculty at Moscow State University after finishing school. In 1966, he defended a candidate's dissertation and in 1973 a doctoral dissertation. After a period of teaching at Moscow, he moved to the United States in the 1990s, where he continued his work at the University of Minnesota.[43] Lev, son of the Ostroumovs, who both taught at VDI and lived at 3 Schmidt Street, graduated from VDI in 1957. After his master's studies and a period of working at scientific institutions in Moscow, he moved to Kemerovo, where he later became a professor and headed the Food Industry Department at the Kemerovo Technical Institute.[44] One of the sons of the Skvortsovs, another pair of VDI teachers, who lived at 6 Student Street, became the deputy for USSR Minister of Education V.P. Yelyutin.[45] Although it appeared as if the children of professors were provided with the same educational opportunities as the children of workers and sovkhoz public servants, they were much more likely to reach the pinnacles of their respective fields.

The anthropologist Annette Lareau explained this phenomenon with reference to differing modes of child raising.[46] Comparing the attitudes towards education of the students and parents of two American schools, one located in a "rich suburb" and the other in a "poor" industrial centre of Richmond, Virginia, Lareau came to the conclusion that, assuming identical educational curriculums, it was precisely family situations and predetermined class background that helped some, primarily middle-class students achieve greater success that other children from working families.[47] As the Molochnoe experiment has shown, social and class differences were just as tangible under late socialism as in the United States. In some families, children were raised in a way that motivated them to receive a higher education. This was fuelled by the idea that children needed to be highly developed, whereas the sovkhoz-worker parents were more likely to stress "natural development" and the solving of pragmatic issues such as attaining a profession and financial independence as early as possible.

Before the war, there was no stable bus access between Vologda and the Molochnoe settlement. According to A.A. Makarova, a teacher in the settlement, a truck used for public transportation appeared only in the

1940s, and the first small bus was introduced in the 1950s, offering trips to Vologda twice daily.[48] The car and the bus were primarily intended for transporting dairy institute workers. Other residents could use the transport only if there was space remaining, and their tickets cost twice as much as those of institute workers.[49]

The creation of an oblast experimental station in Molochnoe in 1921, intended to introduce science into agricultural production, facilitated the creation of another scientific centre in the settlement. In 1930, the experimental station was expanded into the Northern Scientific Research Institute of Dairy Farming, which would operate under the leadership of A.S. Yemelyanov, member and correspondent for the Lenin All-Union Academy of Agricultural Sciences, for the next forty-three years. In 1956, the local livestock experimental station was combined with the state plant-breeding station. Ultimately, in 1968 all of these structures were combined into the RSFSR North-West Scientific Research Institute for Meadow Management and Dairy Farming.[50] The employees of the oblast station lived in Molochnoe, as did many of the future laboratory researchers and workers of the scientific research institute. In the 1960s and '70s, VDI teachers often held positions at the research institute. "Spillover" from one of the scientific institutions into the other was a common feature of settlement academic careers.

Unlike the professorial-teaching staff at VDI, who were a privileged minority in Molochnoe, the other residents did not form a unified group. Workers and public servants laboured at various enterprises and had various professions and social origins. Although it was thanks to these groups that the Molochnoe became a rather large settlement by oblast standards from an early stage of its development, they were not represented by a workers' union or a party organization. Thanks to the settlement's large population, by the 1930s it already had a public bath-house, a post office, and its first medical institution – the "cholera barrack," which later became a feldshers' station and then a city hospital with inpatient and outpatient services.[51]

In all likelihood, the attempt by Vologda communists in the 1930s to deprive VDI of its status as an educational institution and transfer its buildings and laboratories to the sovkhoz "Molochnoe" was based on the government's desire to rid the settlement of institute privileges and "proletarianize" VDI. The experiment was short-lived, and within two years the institute had its rights as an institution of higher education restored and Vologda diary industry specialists were able to keep their right to a higher education.

Ultimately, there were not very many working-class people with a specialized education in the settlement, and those who were there tended to work in the institute's workshops and garages or at the dairy factory. The majority of workers were former peasants who have moved to Molochnoe from nearby villages and worked on the sovkhoz or the VDI scientific-experimental farm. A personal story of this type of migration was recounted by E.A. Litvin:

> In 1934 Grandpa Vitaliy and Grandma Marusya built their nest – the first generation of Odentsov-Kurenkovs to move to Molochnoe from Shadrino, a middle-of-nowhere village in Norobovsky Selsoviet. They fled the repressions after being sent to a timber enterprise. My great grandfather, Mikhail Pavlovich Kurenkov, a father of eight children, churchwarden, and kolkhoz chairman, was arrested in January 1938 as a kulak and saboteur and shot in July 1938 ... After his execution, the siblings, covering twenty square metres [the size of their small apartment], made their way here; they all found a home, everyone got help finding work, one would find a husband, and another would find a wife. So, the whole bunch of Kurenkovs found a second little homeland in Molochnoe.[52]

The majority of the "non-scientific" population worked either at the dairy factory, which achieved economic independence from the institute at the beginning of the 1930s, or on the scientific-experimental Molochnoe State Breeding Farm. Originally, the dairy factory and experimental farm workers did not enjoy special privileges, but with time the situation changed, especially after the breeding farm drew oblast-level party attention because of its achievements. It should be noted that for the leadership of Vologda Oblast, which was separated administratively from Northern Krai in 1938, having a scientific centre of union-wide importance was a crucial way of demonstrating their own work achievements. Therefore, many initiatives originating at the station or institute found support among oblast-level communists. Working in close cooperation with the agricultural experimental station under the leadership of animal husbandry specialists, scientists at Molochnoe State Breeding Farm developed breeding herds and produced cows with the best milk yields in the country. The record-breaking milk cow "Vena" became an object of all-union pride in 1940, with an 82.4-litre milk yield in a single day.[53] In 1956, a brochure was dedicated to the event.[54]

As has been discussed, the settlement space was formed in large part to reflect the benefits the student body and the professorial-teaching staff enjoyed, unlike Molochnoe's other residents. Dissatisfaction with this state of affairs became apparent when settlement residents waited in long lines and talked among themselves in communal kitchens. In its own way, social conflict became visible in fights between local youths (for the most part from nearby villages) and students who were characterized as non-local "others."[55] Although fights were not as big as they were in the 1960s, and far less frequent than in earlier decades, isolated conflicts were recorded even at later times.[56]

The Academic Elite: Institute and "Professorial" Housing

The clearest example of social inequality among the settlement population concerned residential housing. Appolinaria Alexandrovna Makarova, who moved to Molochnoe in 1942 after graduating from the Vologda Pedagogical Institute to work in the school, remembered that "the settlement was not small and was densely populated. I counted twenty-nine residential buildings and seventeen public buildings serving the population, five streets [...] The professorial housing and the [institute] employee housing were at the beginning of Schmidt Street, and the housing for employees of the experimental station and sovkhoz was at the end of the street; there were dormitories on Student Street; and on Proletariat Street there was housing for sovkhoz and factory workers."[57] The pre-war housing hierarchy lasted until major construction projects took place in the settlement in the 1980s.

There was an acute lack of housing and indoor space in the settlement. The deficit was addressed in various ways over the years: The old housing stock could be rebuilt and compressed, houses and structures could be moved from other places, or new housing could be built. Residential and institute construction came in waves. After a boom in the 1910s, when the foundations were laid for most of the institute's buildings, construction gave way to stagnation caused by the Civil War and the resulting large-scale devastation. During the Second World War, a large evacuation hospital was moved into the settlement, and the demand for residential housing grew sharply. Settlement infrastructure was pushed to its limits during the war years, and restoring housing services in the post-war period proved to be very difficult. The Khrushchev reforms brought about another stage of construction. Two two-storey residential buildings, the first to be erected in the settlement since the war, were constructed out of slag concrete. Built by prisoners of war in 1952, they became the start of a new street, which would be called Lenin Street.[58] At the end of the 1950s and the beginning of the 1960s, almost all of VDI's five faculties had their own building. In those years, the first three-storey brick student dormitory was built, along with a club building and a sports hall. Boiler rooms provided central heating, adding a new level of comfort to residential buildings and a new secondary school, also constructed of brick.

Throughout the period, new residential buildings stood alongside old ones, the latter gradually falling into disrepair but still experiencing a steady influx of newcomers. These new arrivals were moving to Molochnoe from other cities and nearby villages and taking the rooms and apartments of those lucky enough to have received orders for new, comfortable apartments in the settlement's first *khrushchevki*.[59] In the 1970s, the settlement added new blocks built by VDI and other enterprises – the dairy factory, Molochnoe State Breeding Farm, the RSFSR North-West Scientific Research Institute for Meadow Management and Dairy Farming in Molochnoe, and various trade organizations. The settlement's centralized plumbing system and running water were installed in the 1960s to replace the autonomous system that had fallen into utter disrepair during the war. In 1976, the first "cooperative house" was established, where people could buy apartments for money.[60] During this time, the growth of residential construction in the settlement barely kept up with the ever-increasing population, which peaked in the mid-1980s. In 1959, the settlement had 4,396 permanent residents;[61] by 1970, that number had increased to 6,019.[62] In 1979, there were 6,656 residents, not including the students, who numbered up to 4,000.[63]

Originally, teachers' families were settled in three houses on Schmidt Street. After the revolution, slogans about social equality and the destruction of class privileges led to a redistribution of residential space. Apartments in the three "professorial houses" were compressed, transforming the spacious interiors to make room for the families of public servants and institute workers who had previously lived in worse conditions. Main entrances were boarded up and then turned into living spaces. In 1939 a new two-storey, eight-apartment brick house was built for institute employees at 8 Student Street. Later, in 1952, two more institute housing structures were built on the same street. Like the "professorial houses" on Schmidt Street, apartments in these buildings were spacious, featuring high ceilings and equipped with toilets and bathrooms. The first post-war "elite" housing structure was the deluxe twelve-apartment building at 1 Soviet Street, where the settlement's highest-status families lived. Among the residents was V.V. Slivko, rector of VDI, D.B. Popov, director of the dairy factory, N.N. Rozov, the VDI prorector for academic work, P.V. Mordvintsev, the docent for the Organization Department (who later went to work for the oblast's CPSU committee apparatus), P.A. Polovinkin, the head of the Political Economics Department, A.G. Elin, the VDI science prorector, and G.N. Drozd, a professor of economics at the institute.[64]

The original and oldest houses in the settlement were not connected to the centralized heating system, so even professors' houses could have woodstoves and sheds with firewood and logs. The houses constructed in the 1950s were built with plumbing and running water, but only cold water came from the taps, and a wood-fuelled "titan" stove in the bathroom was needed to heat water. In the 1950s, a few Molochnoe houses ("Petrovksy" and "Sivkovsky" on Soviet Street), were built with coal heaters; these regulated the temperatures of two or three buildings at once. The central boiler at Molochnoe was built concurrently with the dormitories on Schmidt Street at the end of the 1950s.

According to former neighbours, many of the residents in the institute housing were those who moved into the settlement and had formerly lived in cities. V.S. Kuznetsova recalled that apartment 3 at 6 Student Street was occupied in the 1960s by the family of Raxil Iosifovna Mitilman, who had moved from Petrozavodsk on the eve of the war. The adjacent apartment was occupied by the Rossikhins, teachers in the Non-Organic Chemistry Department who had moved from Arkhangelsk.[65] Another apartment in the building housed Abram Lvovich Marshak from Leningrad. The family of Antsifirov, the head of the Agronomics Faculty, had moved to VDI from Kazan.[66] Remembering the building's atmosphere in the 1950s and '60s, V.S. Kuznetsova wrote about regular visits from institute professors and teachers: "These honourable people, when I greeted them, always kissed my hand, which quite embarrassed me. During lunch, they often had very interesting conversations, but spoke simply, respectfully; it was fun. I felt that these were not merely the Antsifrovs' acquaintances, but their friends, highly educated friends, well-mannered, interesting, and cultured, with whom it was pleasant to talk."[67] Describing everyday life in the building, the memoirist noted that the residents always ate in the dining room, as "there could be no mention of eating in the kitchen." The head of one of the Agronomics Faculty departments, V.P. Usov, was responsible for keeping the courtyard in order. He hung up a schedule for clearing snow, and if the duty went neglected, he "would never tell the person off, but [instead] write a note and pin it to their apartment door. This way he calmed the indignance of certain residents."[68]

Another memoirist, E.V. Britvina, described the intelligentsia who lived in the "institute housing" and dwelt on the leisure and recreation of the children who lived there. Sledding and snowball fights were among the forms of recreation most common among settlement residents. Concerts and other performances were organized in institute employee housing: "I remember how we staged impromptu mini-plays, recited poems, danced, and I played clumsily on the violin. And our neighbours, who supported all of our endeavours, clapped enthusiastically for each of us!"[69] M.M. Kazanskaya, the daughter of one of VDI's first rectors, who lived at 3 Schmidt Street, also mentions home concerts put on by children: "In our third house we sometimes put on concerts for the parents: We read poems by Pushkin, Nekrasov, Marshak, Svetlov, sang the songs that played on the radio and those that we heard on record performed by Kozin. We danced 'the apple' and the *plyasovaya* [folk dance]."[70]

The interiors of professors' apartments were also remarkable. Describing a visit to the Glagolevs, who taught at the dairy institute, one memoirist wrote, "I was always stuck by their decor – an old German mirror in an intricate frame stretched from the ceiling to the floor. There were long bookshelves, pre-war German leather armchairs and a sofa, sideboards with antique dishes, the table with its paperweight and ancient inkwell."[71] Remembering the childhood she spent in Molochnoe, Tatiana Berman, the niece of VDI teachers, recalled that their apartment contained the collected classic works of Russian and foreign writers. Sofia Leonidovna, Berman's aunt, knew three foreign languages and regularly received microfilms with new literature from the Lenin Library in Moscow.[72] Describing her visits to the Berman's apartment, O.A. Plastinina added, "Holidays were held in due form, from the table, set according to proper etiquette, to the prizes, dress-up performances, competitions, etc. ... The woman of the house was known for preparing dishes that were slightly unusual for the North and Vologda Oblast traditions."[73]

Residents of the "institute housing" took a fancy to gardening, and small plots in the courtyards contained plants that were exotic for the northern climate. N.A. Seregicheva (Yanina), who spent her childhood at 1 Schmidt Street, recalled, "there were many flowers around the house, planted by the residents. The phloxes and surprisingly colourful gladioluses were especially beautiful. No one ever touched the flowers. Acacias grew along the fence."[74] There was *Tropaeolum* growing on the terrace and in the garden of 3 Schmidt Street.[75]

Memoir descriptions of neighbourhood recreation usually revolved around sports. As O.V. Okhrimenko, head of "gen-comp" at the Molochnoe institute, remarked, the technologies teacher V.A. Krylov was the tennis champion of Ivanovo Oblast. After moving to Molochnoe at the end of the 1930s, he became the tennis team captain at Molochnoe and initiated the construction of the settlement's tennis court. He organized table tennis, *lapta*,[76] and *gorodki*[77] sections and played a role in developing motorsports.[78] Other residents of the institute housing described additional hobbies, such as woodcarving and the playing of musical instruments.[79]

Another exceptional aspect of life in the institute housing was summer visits by relatives from various cities across the USSR. Molochnoe was considered an excellent location for spending the summer holidays, a place where the charms of being "in nature" were coupled with urban infrastructure. Rector V.V. Slivko, for example, often received visits from his granddaughter Irina. Evgeniy G., before moving to Molochnoe, was a regular guest at the home of his stepfather, who taught at VDI.[80] But for those who had moved from villages to live permanently in the settlement, Molochnoe was an urban locality. Their children were sent to their grandparents in Vologda region's villages to help with haymaking during the summer holidays.

"Petrovsky": Housing for the Soviet Elite

The privileges of teachers who lived in institute housing depended upon the dairy institute's building apartments and houses to attract valuable employees. With time, different organizations began to build houses in Molochnoe, and the settlement soviet contributed to this process. The settlement soviet did not have its own funds to allocate for residential construction, but it always had the right to demand a small part of the living space from builders in order to distribute it to teachers, medical workers, and other residents unaffiliated with the organization heading the construction. Practically every residential building in Molochnoe belonged to some institution, which was often reflected in the nicknames given to them: conversations about Molochnoe included mention of the "professorial," "factory," and "sovkhoz" housing. Sometimes, however, houses were given names based on their unusual construction, for their impressive size or height, as was the case with the "hundred-apartment" or "nine-storey" house.

In addition to institutional housing, Molochnoe had residential buildings named in honour of its famous residents: "Petrovsky" in honour of V.D. Petrov, head of the city food trade organization; "Slivkovsky," in honour of VDI Rector V.V. Slivko; and the "Vakhrushevsky" building, named in honour of settlement soviet Chairman M.K. Vakhrushev.

These elite "named" housing structures were built in the post-war period, and not always by VDI. Their appearance in the settlement symbolized the rise of new hierarchy. From that point on, the most comfortable and spacious apartments were no longer reserved for famous professors at the dairy institute, as in the beginning of the century; instead, there were given to those who occupied important positions in the settlement hierarchy, often having no connection to VDI. In other words, "Petrovsky," "Slikovsky," and "Vakhrushevsky" were housing structures for the *nomenklatura*, and the apartments there were for the settlement's highest-status residents. The "Petrovksy" building was especially notable. Built in 1958 on the site of the former settlement market, this

Figure 7.2. "Petrovsky" house in Molochnoe, 1967.

Source: Photo from the Center for Museum Work on the history of the Vologda Dairy Institute and the Vologda butter.

twenty-four-apartment, three-storey building with a store and a warehouse was constructed under the guidance of D.V. Petrov, director of the city food trade organization.[81] The apartments in it were given to representatives of trade and the food industry (headed by Petrov himself), but not only to them; it also included such figures as settlement store directors, the head of the settlement bathhouse, the head doctor of the settlement hospital, the chief of VDI's administrative services, and the director of the secondary school. The house had its own coal-fuelled heating room, so the residents had no need for woodstoves, and there was a bomb shelter in the basement.

It is likely that the appearance of the "Petrovsky" building, along with that of the best store in the region – also named "Petrovsky" – was connected to the settlement's proximity to the "Obkom dachas,"[82] where oblast-level party leadership went on vacation. Indeed, it was in the "Petrovsky" store that oblast leadership bought goods during their countryside retreats.[83] In the 1960s and '70s the store's inventory was especially remarkable. Even on the eve of deficits, whose effects touched nearly all Vologda region rural settlements, "Petrovsky" sold various delicacies. As some residents explained, these were unsold oblast party leadership rations.[84] In the opinion of some former residents, "The variety was greater than in the city. This is how he [Petrov] immortalized the house and the store."[85]

Iya V., who moved to Molochnoe in 1974, told me in her interview that she had been struck by the black caviar sold at "Petrovsky." She also recalled that the store regularly sold various types of butter, albeit in exchange for coupons, offered ice cream, and had chocolate delivered.[86] Not all settlement residents had access to these deficit goods, however. As Evgeniy G. recalled, there was a segment of settlement society who had significantly more privileges than the rest: "But, you see, again there were these … insiders.[87] So, everyone knew him [his stepfather, science prorector at VDI], and in any store – 'For you, we might be all out, but we have some for him.' Like that. It happened, of course. By the way, I remember, the black caviar – yes, it was there. In the 'Petrovsky' store there was a barrel of black caviar."[88]

The settlement's comparatively better food options were also a result of its proximity to the dairy factory, which, as a scientific-experimental institution, was under the management of the Ministry of Agriculture rather than the Ministry of the Food Industry, meaning it was not subject to strict norms regulating the technical characteristics of its products. As a result, the milk, sour cream, butter, and cottage cheese produced at Molochnoe in the 1960s and '70s were of a significantly higher quality than those produced at factories required to standardize fat content in accordance with new "Khrushchev" state standards. Even residents of Vologda often drove to Molochnoe to buy groceries, causing overcrowding and lines.

In addition to its store, the "Petrov" building was known for its square. Olga and Elena Makarova, who grew up there, remembered, "No other courtyard had one like it. There was a big flower bed in the middle, and there were four enormous benches around it – like wooden couches with curved backrests. Besides that, there were all sorts of bushes and trees, where some of the children would 'build nests,' shelters of branches. There was also table tennis in the square, people played ping-pong. There were a lot of children. In the summer we would organize a camp. We'd raise the flag in the morning and lower it in the evening."[89]

In the 1960s and '70s, the *nomenklatura*'s "Petrovsky" was a place of friendly, neighbourly relations where residents celebrated Soviet holidays. As Galina Guseva explained, "On holidays we formed into columns to go to the demonstration with flags and banners. After the demonstration we would meet up back in the courtyard. It was a lot of fun – songs, dances. There was an accordion player living in the house too."[90] The former residents of the house remember how people watched television together in the entranceways, how neighbours baked pies and pancakes for each other, how people hosted friends and neighbours.

Like at the institute housing, "Petrovsky" had an outdoor children's culture. Unlike in the professors' housing, however, where collective practices were limited to cleaning shared spaces and organizing birthday celebrations for the children, "Petrovsky" residents were more integrated into a communal lifestyle. Moreover, the habits of the school director, who was in charge of organizing recreational activities for the building's children, likely played a role in the more "Soviet" aspects of life for the children "Petrovsky" residents. All the same, even the daughter of VDI Rector M.M. Kazansky, who lived on Schmidt Street, remembered playing "Young Pioneers" in the 1940s.[91] The urbanization of the settlement occurred in parallel with its "Sovietization."

The old "little-terem house" for schoolteachers, the "chemlab house," the first "hundred-apartment" house with a playground, the houses for workers at the dormitory for disabled veterans, the housing for postal workers – each of these residencies had their own courtyards, squares, and neighbourhood histories. They were all united by a shared urban courtyard culture where children spent their free time together and by access to luxuries of which many of their rural peers could only dream.

Sovkhoz Housing and Its Inhabitants

Class differences among residents were also reflected in the organization of daily life. Sovkhoz housing had completely different habits than the *nomenklatura*'s "Petrovsky" house or the intelligentsia's "professorial" housing. Indeed, people who lived there had a different level of education and a different social position.

The administration and specialists of the sovkhoz "Molochnoe," which raised breeding stock and was located in close proximity to the settlement, were for the most part educated people. Many scientific careers at the research institute began with practical work or lab work on the sovkhoz. For example, Evgeniy G., who graduated from the VDI Zoology Faculty and later became a VDI prorector, started his career running a twelve-hundred-head cow farm for a few years in the Dawn of Communism settlement.[92] Sovkhoz specialists were among the first to receive housing with amenities, but many of them lived in significantly worse conditions than those in the settlement, as the sovkhoz, unlike the institute, did not have adequate resources for residential construction.

The sovkhoz housing, unlike the institute housing, was not located in the centre of the settlement; rather, it was built close to the sovkhoz production facilities – cow yards, nurseries, garages, and repair workshops. The primary structures of Molochnoe State Breeding Farm were its headquarters, club building, kindergarten, and "sovkhoz housing." These buildings were located in the region of the old Bumanov

Figure 7.3. View of the "drunk village" in Molochnoe, ca. 1967.

Source: Photo from the Center for Museum Work on the history of the Vologda Dairy Institute and the Vologda butter.

and Fominskoe manorial territories. It was in Fominskoe that the first wooden building for the dairy farm had been built, near the location of the two-storey brick building for the lower school of dairy farming built in the 1910s.[93] During the division of VDI property in the 1930s, almost all of the Fominskoe structures, where most of the experimental farm's workers spent their lives, were transferred to Molochnoe State Breeding Farm. At the end of the 1970s, a new building was erected for the scientific-experimental dairy factory not far from the former manor.

Another segment of the sovkhoz's housing stock was located on Proletarian Street, in low-comfort housing that lacked running water and had communal kitchens, woodstove heating, and unequipped lavatories. Eventually, in the 1970s and '80s, the sovkhoz began to build five-storey *khrushchevki,* urban-style apartments for distinguished milkers, animal husbandry specialists, and drivers who had formerly lived in the surrounding villages. In the early 1980s, distinguished agricultural workers were moved into a panel house at 6 Park Street: I.N. Serkova, a milker who received the Order of Lenin three times and the Hero of Labour star once; B.A. Baskova, who worked on the breeding farm; A.P. Krasilnikov, a driver at Gosplemzavod Molochnoe; and the veterinarian feldsher Z.S. Lebedeva, among others.[94]

Two more sovkhoz residential buildings were located at the edge of Molochnoe in the village of Agafonovo. Around ten private worker's houses were located in what was known as the "drunk village." Liubov' Beliaeva discussed the etymology of the village's name: "It's possible that breaking the norm of building houses in a straight line during street construction became the basis for calling this part of Molochnoe the 'drunken village.'"[95] There was, however, another possible explanation: "Unlike the central part of Molochnoe, where, for the most part, Vologda Dairy Institute employees lived (we called them 'scientists' [*nauchniki*] in our circle), these were streets where simple labourers lived: builders, drivers, who loved to spend their free time with a cup of wine or vodka."[96] Olga Martinovich also touched on the issue of drunkenness among sovkhoz workers, and called her neighbour "Vasya-Cuckoo" because, "when he was drunk, hardly anyone could understand what he was saying."[97]

Judging by interview accounts, the families of peasants turned sovkhoz workers often had a large number of children. S.A. and T.A. Shishigin, for example, remembered the Sergeev family, who lived in a former institute house at 16 Schmidt Street that had been transferred to Molochnoe State Breeding Farm. Sergei Sergeevich was an avid hunter and dog breeder: "Only thanks to his hunting did he manage to feed his ten children. They had five boys and five girls. A lot of the neighbours bought the game he caught."[98] Unlike the family environment at the teacher's housing, the children of sovkhoz workers took an active part in housework and had duties connected to caring for livestock and vegetable gardens. The family of L.D. Belyaeva kept a cow, sheep, chickens, and geese, so the children spent a lot of time preparing hay. They were also responsible for making purchases at local stores.[99] E.A. Litvina, who lived on Soviet Street in the 1960s, recalled, "I helped my parents with everything: collecting mushrooms in the woods, berries, fishing; it was the children's task, providing for the family for winter."[100]

Because pre-war houses in the settlement were heated by woodstoves, and many of them lacked running water and plumbing, the residents chopped their own wood, carried water in and out, and cleaned communal facilities. That such tasks were not mentioned in the recollections of those who lived in the institute housing provides indirect evidence that these tasks were likely performed by hired help rather than family members. Thus, Yuri V.'s neighbour in Kabachino, Valentina B., moved to Molochnoe in the early 1950s to work as a nanny.[101] The Chekulaevs, professors at VDI, lived with both a nanny and a household helper.[102]

Food preparation and consumption practices also differed greatly by social class. In the institute housing, people ate in dining rooms rather than kitchens. Sovkhoz houses had simpler rituals and foods. G.U.

Tsaregorodtseva (Povshednaya), who lived at 13 Schmidt Street in the 1970s, recalled that "every family had its own table in the kitchen. In the evenings, when everyone was cooking food, it seemed really good in the kitchen. Everything was very simple, uncomplicated. The neighbours all knew who ate what in the morning and evening."[103] Describing the interiors of the houses, Tsaregorodtseva (Povshednaya) mentioned metal tubs hanging in the corridor where clothes were washed. Sovkhoz housing residents, likely to save money, forwent the laundromat service offered in the settlement.

The Chuglovs, who had moved out of a village, had a diet comprised of what they grew in their vegetable garden: "The stove produced very delicious food. I'll never forget stewed soup on the stove, rice kasha with skim, baked milk (even if it wasn't from Aunt Kisa in Ilyinskoe, and just from the store in a triangle packet), braised duck from papa's hunts with gentle, soft meat. And baked mushrooms retain their charming taste for a whole year (salted *ryzhik* mushrooms last only half a year). That was our family's secret dish for holidays and everyday life."[104] It is worth reflection that the Chuglovs bought milk from the store in order to cook their village kashas, which, on the one hand, represented a deviation from the traditional recipe, and, on the other, shows that modern practices (in this case buying milk from a store instead of getting it from a cow) were gradually taking root in peasant families who were originally less orientated towards change.

Like in peasant huts, stoves in the sovkhoz housing were used for heating, cooking, and preparing food for the winter. As Y.L. Zyuzina, who lived at 16 Schmidt Street, remembered, "Apart from the Russian stove, each household had a little kerosene-fuelled stove in the communal kitchen, a kerosine-gas stove or an oil stove. The [Russian] stove was used to bake pies, smoke fresh fish, and dry mushrooms for the winter. People usually prepared firewood for heating in nearby forests, but technical college workers (the dairy production technical college was transferred from Sokol and became the mid-level technologies faculty at VDI) transported it to the sovkhoz housing for free – seven cubic metres per family."[105]

Among the occupations of people who settled in the sovkhoz housing, two traditional Vologda region crafts were represented: weaving and lace-making. Alexandra Dmitrievna Sloeva lived in one of the apartments at 10 Podlesnaya Street after moving to Molochnoe from the village of Molbishche, in Vologodsky District. Her husband, Alexsei Ivanovich, worked as a sovkhoz driver. "Grandma Shura wove Vologda lace," her granddaughter, who would visit her at Poldlesnsaya, told me. "Her lace was even sent to international expositions. In the lacc museum in Vologda there's a big lace panel, woven by the Vologda lace makers artel; well, one of the elements was woven by my Grandma Shura. I am very thankful to my grandmother for teaching me this technique."[106] Apart from being able to weave lace, Alexandra Dmitrievna could sew, and therefore she "sewed up the whole family, from underwear to cotton winter hats."[107] It is important to note that Molochnoe had a working seamstress workshop since the 1950s with full-time cutters, and that the residents had the option of having their clothes sown by a professional.[108] However, the practical approach of this rural woman attests that the need for sewn clothing was easily met at home, as had been the case in the village.

According to Alexander A., children at the sovkhoz houses in the 1960s were often christened. He described the practice in the following way: "They were christened wholesale, probably, about ten people, kids of various ages [...] A priest would be invited. I remember it like this: Young, so, with black hair, a beard all neat and spade-style, he had no silver hairs. The font that he brought would be this big one, you see, like that. So ... And now there all these kids of various ages. They were christened. Without any special problems – no police, no machine guns came running up. It's another thing that, well, officially, let's say, this wasn't really advertised."[109]

At first glance, the way of life in private sovkhoz houses and apartments might seem to differ little from the lifestyle of peasants living far from the cities, but this is only partially true. Thanks to Molochnoe's "urban" infrastructure, elements of a new way of life (such as buying milk in packets for stove-cooked kasha or the use of a public bathhouse instead of a personal one) simplified housekeeping and became the new reality for fresh arrivals to the settlement.[110]

Ultimately, residential construction in the Molochnoe settlement testifies to the ways in various members of its population were assigned to different rungs of the social ladder. Inequities were tangible in the location of residencies, levels of material support, access to deficit goods, and access to education. The courtyard culture that existed around most settlement homes, the communal nature of the apartments, and the practice of buying food at stores show that settlement residents, for the most part, engaged in urban everyday practices, although the denizens of the private sector (the "drunk village" and the sovkhoz houses in Agafonovo, Famoinskoe, and Ilyinskoe) preserved attributes of rural life and held on to the practice of holding cows.

By the 1970s, the social markers determining class origin in the settlement had changed somewhat. At that time, Molochnoe abolished the practice of differentiating levels of access to goods, and all of the residents were able to shop at the same stores. Many settlement structures also lost their original ties with the specific institutions that had built them. Residents were able to improve their living conditions by moving out of old, less-sophisticated homes into five-storey *khrushchovki* buildings where there were bigger apartments and the social composition of the neighbours was mixed. This led to a shift in the status attached to certain structures. The "professorial housing," which was falling into disrepair by the 1970s, no longer housed professors, and instead housed young couples waiting for a spot to open in one of the newly built residences for "non-local" pensioners who had moved to Molochnoe. Thus, in 1977, Yuri V. drove his parents from their Kirillovsky village to a room on Schmidt Street. His father, a disabled war veteran, was put into the queue for housing, and after a few years received a one-room apartment in a sovkhoz house at 6 Park Street. In 1978, Yuri's family was allowed to move from a "professorial" building to a separate *polutorka* (a type of expanded one-room apartment) in an old brick house at 8 Professor Emelyanov Street on account of his job as a young specialist at the research institute. Having lived in a communal apartment for only three years, Yuri considered himself very lucky to have been able to move so early one.

PART FOUR

The Rural Komsomol and the Reproduction of Inequality

Chapter Eight

Modernity's Conduit and Hostages of Backwardness

A Discussion of Soviet Youth

I spoke with Ludmila S. in the kitchen of her two-room apartment on a summer day in 2021.[1] Ludmila is a strong woman with a loud voice and a straight gaze who is used to taking the lead and making decisions. Her life story reveals that she did not develop these qualities by chance. She is a single mother who raised a daughter during the years of perestroika and the economic and political crises of the 1990s. She is also a candidate of sciences in agriculture, a member of the CPSU, and the former secretary of the Komsomol organization at the North-West Scientific Research Institute for Meadow Management and Dairy Farming.

Ludmila was born in 1954 in the village of Lukino, in Vologda Oblast's Chagodoshchensky District. She and her older brother were raised by their grandmother, who was a kolkhoz worker. Like many children in rural areas, Ludmila studied at multiple schools: First, an elementary school, and then a middle school, in the village of Izboishchi. During high school, she studied in Sazonovo, in Chagodoshchensky District, located more than twenty kilometres from Lukino.

While still at school, Ludmila entered the Komsomol and was chosen to be the secretary of the Komsomol organisation. After graduation, the VLKSM District Committee wrote a recommendation on her behalf to the Department of Law at Leningrad State University. On the eve of her examinations, however, Ludmila came down with laryngitis and lost her voice. As a result, she applied in 1971 to the Department of Zoology at the Vologda Dairy Institute. It was easier to gain acceptance into that particular department than others, and, for a strong student like Ludmila, passing the entrance exams did not prove to be very difficult.

Although Ludmila did not occupy any significant Komsomol positions during her time at VDI, she entered the CPSU during her third year.

This led to her being invited to a scientific research institute immediately after graduation, where she was promptly offered a secretary position in the Komsomol organization.

Upon reciting her life story, Ludmila begins by listing the most important milestones of her biography: "Little Octobrist, Pioneer, then the Komsomol, then the party." She concludes, "I don't regret it. It gave me a lot."[2] This sequence of political affiliations, so familiar to anyone who lived in the Soviet Union, forms a strong contrast with the traditional life trajectory of rural women, in which marriage and childbirth were the essential motifs around which the straightforward march of human existence revolved. Looking at Ludmila's biography, one gets the sense that it was Komsomol and party work that transformed a young, rural teenage girl, skilled in the art of haymaking, into an independent and confident woman scientist. But is it true that joining the rural Komsomol always paved the way to a successful career in Soviet society?

Whereas young people in the West were commonly associated with rule breaking and consumerism in the popular imagination, in Soviet discourse, youth were seen as important contributors to revolutionary progress.[3] In fact, the creation of the VLKSM in 1918 was intended to harness and give direction to young people's enthusiasm.[4]

The primary work of the rural Komsomol reflected the party's vision for rural areas and its understanding of the role of young people in the project of building socialism. The rural Komsomol was tasked with raising a new generation of rural youth who would be capable of bringing about a scientific and technical revolution in the countryside. As the first secretary of the Cherepovets VLKSM District Committee stated at a conference of rural school graduates in 1977, "By expanding the network of general technical schools and courses, VLKSM sovkhoz committees are solving a fundamental issue [by] creating a suitable replacement for the peasantry. They are striving to see that every young person living in a village has a mechanical specialization, that they can operate a tractor, a combine harvester, an automobile, and other machinery."[5] Regardless of the class into which they were born, educated Komsomol members who were able to operate machinery were seen as a "suitable replacement" for the peasantry, rather than as peasants themselves.

Consequently, one of the most important tasks assigned to rural VLKSM organizations, and rural youth in general, was to increase the Komsomol's influence in the countryside and to educate the Komsomol's members. Graduates of schools, vocational colleges, technical colleges, and institutes were seen as the new face of the modernized Vologda countryside. Notably, the inequalities that the rural population faced in their daily lives were directly reflected in the inferior performance of their Komsomol organizations, which occupied the least privileged position in the Komsomol hierarchy.

In some ways, the Komsomol was not unique among the various mass youth organizations of the twentieth century. Like its counterparts in many countries around the world, it was created to promote certain values. The Komsomol's values were atheistic and oriented towards socialism, but, like other youth organizations, its purpose was to set the political agenda for young people.[6] There are, however, some factors that set the VLKSM apart from other youth organizations around the world, including the Komsomol's integration with state political organs; its complex, many-levelled system of management; and its access to significant government resources and power (which placed increased responsibility on Komsomol organizations).[7]

In terms of its organizational structure, the VLKSM resembled a state institution rather than a community organization. It was modelled on the structure of the CPSU (Communist Party of the Soviet Union), although, in the 1960s and '70s, it had more limited functions, a smaller budget, and a lower level of compulsory membership. As in the CPSU, there were those who worked "professionally" in the Komsomol and those who contributed as "amateurs." The work of the former group was paid, and they could occupy positions in the Komsomol even if they were beyond the age limit for Komsomol membership. The work of the latter group was voluntary and relied on enthusiasts and organizers (typically secretaries and bureau members of VLKSM organizations). In the 1960s and '70s, boys and girls usually entered the Komsomol at fourteen or fifteen years of age and left either after having moved on to party work or upon reaching the age of twenty-eight. Occasionally, members were expelled for misconduct, which was regarded as a punishment and as a blot upon a person's record.

The role of the Komsomol in Soviet society is a central focus of those who study youth organizations in the USSR. Alexei Yurchak, who dedicated his research in large part to analysing Komsomol organizations in the late socialist period, divides Komsomol activities into two categories[8]. The first category, "pure pro forma," pertains to official activity. This activity was governed by strict meeting protocols and was written up in the reports of Komsomol organizations. The other category, "work with meaning," pertains to those activities that Yurchak considered to be truly beneficial for young people.[9] Yurchak asserts that youth participation in the Komsomol during late socialism had a performative character, which included parroting the views of authorities. As such, membership in the Komsomol did not define the interests of youth or prevent the development of a distinct youth culture in the USSR. At times, the Komsomol even created a space that was very attractive for young people. For example, the Leningrad Rock Club existed legally under the auspices of the Leningrad District Committee of the VLKSM, despite the fact that the bands and musicians who comprised its membership were far from, and often opposed to, Soviet and Komsomol ideology.

Similar conclusions have been reached by other researchers of post-war Soviet youth culture. Thus, Gleb Tsipursky, Juliane Fürst, and Hilary Pilkington have emphasized the notion that Komsomol initiatives played an important role in cultural politics during the first post-war decades.[10] This was especially noticeable during the period of the Thaw, when Komsomol management was reformed and initiatives "from the bottom up" became more prominent. In those years, the Komsomol organized the opening of clubs and youth cafes. In fact, it was the Komsomol that hosted youth, jazz, student, and bard song festivals, set up youth tours along tourist routes, and organized hikes and competitions.[11] According to this view, although the Komsomol suffered from being overly regimented throughout the entirety of its existence, it reflected the aspirations of the youth as best it could.

Other researchers have assessed the Komsomol's work with youth more sceptically. They emphasize the Komsomol's efforts to suppress youth initiatives and replace them with official doctrine, especially in late Soviet times. Such arguments are founded upon the premise that the Komsomol was primarily a bureaucratic structure too dependent on CPSU decisions to reflect the interests of young people. For example, the research of Sergei Zhuk on youth subculture in late-Soviet Dnepropetrovsk draws attention to the harsh juxtaposition between young people oriented towards Western music and Western values, on the one hand, and Komsomol activists, on the other.[12] He suggests that the rise of alternative youth subcultures in the USSR (starting with the *stilyagi*[13] and ending with rock fans), taken in conjunction with the falling popularity of the Komsomol among students in the 1970s and '80s, attests to Soviet ideology's having lost the battle for the youth. Western values proved more appealing to young people than Soviet values, which were seen as old-fashioned and propagandistic.

Researchers of opposition sentiments among young people in the USSR generally agree that the Komsomol was an important organization even for dissident Soviet youth.[14] Dmitry Kozlov studies unofficial youth groups in north-western Russia in the post-war period, with a special focus on these groups' participation in dissident movements. He asserts that Komsomol ideology was unable to prevent the development of opposition attitudes, even when those attitudes were expressed in the form of protest.[15] In fact, Komsomol slogans became a tool with which young people made demands for their rights and interests vis-à-vis adults.[16]

Despite the association between youth and urban life in the historiography, it was rural youth moving into cities who first sparked scholarly interest in young people. According to Pilkington, it was the rise of hooliganism among rural youth who had migrated to cities that led researchers to assign young people characteristics traditionally associated with being young.[17] Cultural geographers show that rural youth experience higher rates of unemployment during the process of modernization. Their vulnerability in the labour market is the result of discrepancies in rural and urban technologies, as well as the lower level of education generally attained by rural youth compared to their urban counterparts.[18]

Soviet sociological scholarship has typically focused on the unique issues with which rural Soviet youth were faced. Thus, Soviet "rural sociology" has closely examined the connections between changes in rural life for young people and phenomena such as the birth of the rural intelligentsia and the kolkhoz peasantry.[19]

Although the flight of young people from rural areas was a problem for rural producers around the globe in the twentieth century, Soviet leadership viewed migration to cities not only as a problem, but as an inevitable social development. Accordingly, Soviet leadership's views on rural migration always contained a certain level of self-contradiction. Exhortatory speeches about increasing Komsomol membership in the agricultural sector were periodically given in district committees, oblast committees, and the VLKSM Central Committee. Special programs to "retain personnel" were implemented in villages. Nevertheless, the Komsomol was generally unable to prevent migration. In fact, it often stimulated the flight of young people by preaching the ideals of the Soviet urban modernization project and by instilling faith in global socialism's ability to create new opportunities in cities.

Komsomol Mobilization

Aleksandr B.'s story begins in the village of Kabachino, in Vologda Oblast's Kirillovsky District, in 1950. His family, which consisted of his father (the captain of a small inland navigation vessel), his mother (an elementary school teacher), and his elder (by a year) sister, lived in the countryside until his mother hatched a plan with her colleague to move into the city. Selling their property in the village, the teachers bought part of a run-down house in Cherepovets, the district centre. They moved in with their families, knowing that residents of buildings under demolition would be provided with new accommodation: either another house or an apartment in a new development. In fact, they did not have to live in crowded conditions for long. Soon after they had moved in, the old house was demolished, and the enterprising schoolteachers and their families were given apartments in the city.

Aleksandr and his sister were accepted into the Cherepovets Komsomol. After finishing eighth grade, Aleksandr went to study at a professional-technical college. Not finishing his studies there, he immediately enrolled in evening classes at the Cherepovets Polytechnic Institute and went to work in a factory. At that time, work was underway in Cherepovets to build new workshops for the metallurgical plant. Aleksandr was assigned to work at the plant's steel-rolling shop, where he remained until being called to the army in 1970. While at the factory, Aleksandr joined the party. He recalls, "people thought, if you had gone to the institute and planned on taking a management role, then join the party."[20]

After serving in the army, he returned to Cherepovets, got married, and had children. After a few years, however, he was called to the army a second time. It turned out that there was a shortage of workers at the Cherepovets chemical plant, which was then under construction. The secretary of the CPSU Vologda Oblast Committee, Anatoly Drygin, had decided to mobilize young party members from the metallurgical plant by calling them to the army for a second time; they were meant to form the core staff of the new construction project and oversee the work. As a result, young party members and professionals, such as Aleksandr, were sent as political deputies to construction projects at the chemical plant. Thus, a highly qualified metallurgical engineer reverted to being a soldier for two years. Being called to the army for a second time was not common in the USSR during peacetime, and the call had a much more compulsory character than a Komsomol mobilization. Those who were brought to work in this way were often far from satisfied. As Aleksandr remembers, "It's called violence against the individual. The first time in the army, I'm telling you, is like a vacation. But a second time, it's despicable."[21]

One aspect of the Soviet Komsomol that made it attractive to the government was its ability to quickly mobilize its members. Raised on Soviet values and not yet weighed down with the responsibility of providing for a family, Komsomol members were seen as the ideal instrument for solving the country's most pressing socio-economic problems. While most Komsomol projects were related to infrastructure or heavy industry, they also had a role in rural agriculture.[22] For example, district committees recruited young people to work on Komsomol construction projects, sent Komsomol members to work or study in the most in-demand sectors of the economy, organized work brigades, managed enterprises and schools, and put out "Komsomol appeals" in newspapers.[23] The VLKSM Vologda Oblast Committee's "Harvest 75" and "Harvest 76" initiatives sent students to bring in the harvest from kolkhoz fields in Vologda Oblast.[24] Campaigns such as "Labour Watch" and "Komsomol for Rural School" sent Komsomol members to address important issues in the realm of education.

Estimating the overall volume of work carried out through Komsomol mobilizations is extremely difficult, but we can nonetheless say that their economic effect was significant, and they were often relied upon during the period of late socialism. As a result, the government's efforts to draw as many boys and girls into the Komsomol as possible can be viewed as a pragmatic economic decision.

Komsomol mobilizations were nevertheless ineffective at addressing personnel shortages in livestock farming. In a report outlining the failures of Vologda's VLKSM District and City Committees for the year 1960, it was documented that only five out of twenty district committees had fulfilled their quotas for sending young people to work in livestock farming.[25] Young people did not want to work on farms, and the Komsomol was powerless to change that. As the years passed, the situation grew more dire. In 1977, the secretary of the Kirillovsky VLKSM District Committee remarked, "Only the rare individual goes to work in livestock farming after graduating from school. Every year the District Committee fails to fulfill its plan for agricultural production mobilization."[26]

"Komsomol" status was most often given to infrastructural projects, such as bridges and roads, as well as to heavy industrial enterprises, which were considered the personification of progress and modernization in Soviet discourse. It was not a coincidence that Soviet agitprop in the 1960s and '70s adopted the practice of sending work brigades directly from Komsomol conventions to the sites of grandiose socialist construction projects. In this way, the country's leadership showed young people where their energies ought to be directed, and which projects were given top priority.

In 1963, thirty-four projects were designated as Komsomol or "shock" (high-priority) construction projects in Vologda Oblast. The shock projects included a cold rolling shop, a blast furnace, a coking plant, a coke-pitch shop, a medium section mill at the Cherepovets Metallurgical Plant, a refrigerator for the Vologda Meat Plant, and logging roads.[27] The biggest projects in the oblast were the Volga–Baltic Waterway (1959–64), various projects at the Cherepovets Metallurgical Plant, and construction of the "Northern Lights" natural gas pipeline system, which followed a Ukhta–Kotlas–Cherepovets–Leningrad route (1967–9).[28]

Technology and scientific knowledge played an important role in the Soviet post-war project to build socialism. Development in these fields was seen as a panacea against economic problems. Consequently, the rural Komsomol took responsibility for mechanizing production. It ran inspections of levels of technological mastery among workers and introduced innovative methods for running farms. In fact, the majority of rural Komsomol campaigns during the late socialist period were focused on achieving these goals. For example, the "General Mechanical Instruction" campaign was intended to teach all young people how to work with various types of agricultural machines.[29] The "Komsomol Searchlight" campaign monitored the use of technologies during working hours. The "Best Young Innovator" competition was created in order to introduce new technologies into agricultural production.[30]

After the Seventeenth VLSKM Congress, held 23–27 April 1974, rural construction projects and land development in the Non-Black Earth region were given "all-union shock project" status.[31] This marked the beginning of a party and Komsomol initiative to "retain agricultural personnel." The Komsomol was charged with increasing the number of young people in rural areas.[32] Additionally, Komsomol organizations in the north-western oblasts were asked to "draw young people into the battle for an advanced culture of land cultivation and animal husbandry, to implement scientific achievements and cutting-edge practices [in agriculture], to build modern livestock farms and 'welfare projects,'[33] and to develop land."[34]

Starting around this time, Komsomol leadership began to give out "Komsomol passes"[35] entitling their bearers to work at the region's kolkhozes and sovkhozes, rather than to work construction at the Cherepovets metallurgical plant.[36] A report from the Kirillovsky VLKSM District Committee indicates that, in 1975, only 24 Komsomol members were sent to all-union shock projects. A total of 44 members were mobilized for local shock projects: 4 were sent to work in the food industry, 12 were sent into retail and public catering, 6 into domestic services, 17 to vocational schools, and 1 into livestock farming.[37] Additionally, only 1 person responded to the "public call to action" to work on the Baikal–Amur Mainline in 1975, while 43 went to work on the oblast's land development and rural construction projects.[38] The remaining Komsomol members chose their fate as they saw fit, rather than follow the "directives" of Komsomol organizations.

Progress vs. "Vestiges" of the Past

In the European discourse on modernization, country life was exoticized.[39] From the point of view of the elites who championed modernization, rural life seemed backward and was assumed to lag behind the urban.[40] Unlike in the majority of western European countries and America, however, where the process of urbanization had started earlier,

Russia remained an agrarian society until the middle of the twentieth century. For this reason, even though the revolutionary transformative processes envisioned by the Bolsheviks began in cities, it was necessary that they be realized in rural areas. The rural Komsomol was called upon to help make that happen.

Placed at the forefront of global changes and reflecting the revolutionary aesthetic, the Komsomol was expected to personify everything that was new and progressive about the Soviet project. Consequently, cultural activism was an essential part of the Komsomol's mission. Isabel Tirado, in her description of the rural Komsomol's work in the 1920s, emphasizes that, although the older generation had mixed reactions to some Komsomol initiatives (especially the anti-religious campaigns of the 1920s), the younger generation generally reacted positively to VLKSM programs.[41] The VLSKM inspired young people from villages with hopes for new and broader possibilities.

Party members from cities, however, were unsettled by the fervour with which young people from the countryside joined the Komsomol. The rural Komsomol was viewed as the embodiment of rural peasant life. The position of rural organizations within the Komsomol power hierarchy was predetermined by this distrust. The VLKSM was always intended to be an "urban" organization comprised of young workers, soldiers, and students who would go on to fill the party ranks.[42] Therefore, debate over the character, structure, and leadership of the VLKSM was directly connected with the question of whether residents of rural areas, with their "petty-owner peasant philosophy," should be allowed to assume positions of power. Many Soviet leaders doubted that rural Komsomol activists were capable of "following the party line" while presiding over VLKSM councils and organizations. On the eve of Lenin's New Economic Policy, party leadership feared that peasant majority opinion, if given representation in rural VLKSM cells, would drown out the more progressive but less numerous urban organizations in a "peasant sea."[43] Isabel Tirado argues that the separation of urban and rural Komsomol organizations was officially nullified in 1928 to prevent the "rural" from dominating the "urban." This organizational shift was intended to mask the fact that the social base was disproportionately rural.[44]

As a result, the rural Komsomol was assigned a very definite role in the first decades of Soviet rule. It was meant to propagandize Soviet values in the countryside and carry out Bolshevik politics while at the same time functioning strictly within the agenda developed by urban party organizations. The Komsomol was meant to function as a mentor and educator in rural areas, not as a representative political organ for young people from villages to be managed by rural residents themselves.

Distrust of rural Komsomol members' class background, suspicions concerning their peasant sympathies, and the conviction that they were politically uneducated created inequality within Komsomol organizations from their inception. Industrial enterprise Komsomol cells became the most authoritative, while village organizations were seen as the last link in the chain. Although the adoption of the so-called Stalin Constitution in 1936 supposedly established equality between all classes within Soviet society, this did not get rid of the perception that the rural Komsomol was overly dependent on the backward peasantry. For this reason, it became common practice to send Komsomol members and communists from the cities to work in rural areas. City Komsomol organizations presided over their rural counterparts. The urban was considered by default to be more progressive than the rural.

The work of the Komsomol in rural areas, such as in the villages of Vologodsky District, was made significantly more difficult by the fact that local communities in the middle of the twentieth century held their own views about the role of young people in society. These views often contradicted those espoused by the Komsomol. Rural communities saw themselves as a united whole composed of relatives, neighbours, and fellow villagers of all generations, with leadership roles being assumed by male heads of households.[45] In this system of values, youth was less prized than maturity or "adulthood," which one reached upon entering into marriage. Marriage was viewed as the life event at which a person attained self-sufficiency, the independence to make their own decisions, and the right to manage property.

In Soviet discourse during the second half of the twentieth century, there was a certain level of "youthism," based in perceptions of young people as being "not yet fully developed" and immature. This resulted in some discriminatory practices (one of the most visible being that children under the age of sixteen were not allowed at film screenings). There was also, however, an acceptance that young people should be granted certain rights and opportunities.[46] Offering an alternative to the rural system of values, which granted young people rights only after they had entered marriage, the Komsomol provided young people with the opportunity to prove themselves from the moment they entered the organization at the age of fourteen. In fact, they were often granted this opportunity without being required to demonstrate any special merit. In a further deviation from rural society, Komsomol members held on to their transitional "teenage" status for a longer period of time. In party and Komsomol documentation, Komsomol members were almost never referred to by their full names or by their first name and patronymic. Instead, they were usually addressed in shortened, informal versions of their names: Petya instead of Pyotr, Lyosha instead of Alexey, Nadia instead of Nadezhda, etc. The practice of rarely addressing Komsomol members by their patronymic was a way of emphasizing that they had not yet reached adulthood.

The Soviet conception of young people as a specific social group with special rights and duties was viewed by rural communities in the 1960s as a serious challenge to their way of life. In the process of creating a family, Komsomol members were faced with a decision: Should they remain "young" Komsomol members until the age of twenty-seven, or should they become responsible "adult" members of their families after marriage at twenty to twenty-five years of age?

Komsomol members who joined the VLKSM as schoolchildren often found that their Komsomol duties became burdensome after they got married and had children. This is attested to, for example, by Secretary Subbotin of the Vologda Oblast VLSKM Committee, who complained that "it is still a common practice to exclude young fathers and mothers from the Komsomol for breaking away from the Komsomol and non-attendance at meetings. We should think about how to organize work with these people and take their circumstances into account in the Komsomol."[47] In another instance, one of the members of the VLKSM District Committee for the sovkhoz "Vorobyevsky" asked in 1971 that she be excluded from the Komsomol because her husband had forbidden her to attend meetings.[48] She argued that marriage and childbirth were not compatible with Komsomol work, which required a large amount of free time.

Moreover, the Komsomol's cultural agenda in the countryside was different than in the cities. Whereas the battle for the minds and spirits of young people in cities was waged against "the pernicious influence of the West," the rural VLKSM found itself battling peasant superstitions and religiosity. Thus, while discussing the Kirillovsky District Komsomol, members of the VLKSM Oblast Committee observed that "the situation is unfavourable in the district as concerns addressing economic problems and educating the youth": Socialist obligations are not being fulfilled, personnel are moving away, "only two farms are striving for the distinction of earning 'communist' status, and only four people work on them," cases of drunkenness and hooliganism are on the rise, and around sixty-six religious holidays are celebrated in the district, at "which [time] young people do not work for two to three days."[49]

The reforms of the VLKSM that took place in the 1960s were undertaken in the context of de-Stalinization and the democratization of Komsomol management. These reforms had a definite influence on rural Komsomol organizations. This period saw the introduction of more choice for Komsomol members. "Political departments"[50] were disbanded, marking the end of compulsory Komsomol assignments to various "difficult assignments" (such as kolkhozes).[51] The delegation of certain management functions to local communities, which Khrushchev had announced as part of his reforms, resulted in staff reductions among paid Komsomol workers and the restructuring of the VLKSM management apparatus. Thus, in Vologda Oblast in 1963, the number of paid Komsomol positions was reduced from 203 to 175.[52] At the same time, 116 non-staff departments populated by unpaid workers were created.[53] The rural Komsomol was reorganized along "territorial-production" principles, meaning that all the Komsomol organizations in a given district were restructured to answer directly to their local VLKSM District Committee.[54] An important outcome of this restructuring was that VLKSM organizations for schools, vocational colleges, and technical colleges began to appear alongside sovkhoz and kolkhoz VLKSM organizations. Overall, the rural Komsomol became more diversified in the 1960s, as did the tasks that were asked of it.

Low Numbers in Rural Komsomol Organizations

Luda M. was born in 1946 in one of the hamlets of Belozersky District, in Vologda Oblast. Her father was a rural communist, a former front-line soldier, and a disabled veteran. Her mother was a worker on a collective farm. Due to the concussive injuries and wounds Luda's father sustained as a soldier, he was unable to work as a kolkhoz tractor operator in accordance with his pre-war training. In order to support his family, he was retrained as an accountant. This large family with seven children lived in extreme poverty and was supported primarily by the money that Luda's mother earned on the kolkhoz. Luda graduated from Artiushino Eight-year School in in 1961 and enrolled in the Ustiuzhensk Agricultural Technical College, where she studied animal husbandry. She had been a Komsomol member during her school years and, looking back on this period of her life, she recalled the VLKSM initiation process. Unlike her initiation into the Pioneers, which had taken place in school and was not particularly ceremonious, her Komsomol initiation was held in front of the district committee in Belozersk: "They gave us questions, and we shook – we were so scared."[55] Her participation in the Komsomol continued during her studies at the college, where she and the other young women in her group took part in Komsomol-organized volunteer work. After graduating from her technical college, she received a work assignment on a remote sovkhoz in Cherepovetsky District. As she recounts, a Komsomol organization already existed on the farm when she arrived.

However, as the new Komsomol member on the sovkhoz and a young specialist, she was placed in charge of almost all of the public Komsomol initiatives, including providing social services for elderly kolkhoz workers. As she recalls it, "Over there … we held meetings … At that time it was still … in fashion – well, I am saying 'in fashion'; now they would say it was 'trending' – to help the elderly. We would go and help old women stack firewood. It's a lot of work to do that in the countryside: With that firewood you would have to saw it, chop it, lay it out, dry it, and then move it somewhere in a shed. At that time … they would dig vegetable beds for the grannies, but that's what strong young men would do. And we would help those who were really all alone … to clean up the hut before the holidays."[56] Luda recalled that people typically requested help cleaning their homes on the eve of religious holidays, which were widely celebrated in the village. Although party leadership discouraged Komsomol members from organizing public works on the eve of Orthodox Easter or Christmas, the issue was never escalated above rhetoric. Ultimately, the temptation of adding another *subbotnik* to Komsomol work reports proved stronger than the fear of appearing to be enabling the church. Moreover, it is unlikely that the village public service "trend" was started by a VLKSM District Committee initiative. Before the appearance of the Komsomol, the Vologda countryside had a centuries-old tradition of peasant *pomochi*, a practice in which village members helped their neighbours in need who were struggling to finish work on time or on their own.[57] It is unsurprising that Luda M. interpreted this peasant tradition as Komsomol "public work" and recorded it in VLKSM work reports.

Luda worked as an animal husbandry specialist on the sovkhoz "Worker" for almost ten years. She was married there and gave birth to two children. At first, her life as a young specialist was extremely unorganized. When she moved to the village, it became clear that there was no available housing, and she was forced to rent a corner in a village hut where she shared a bed with another young specialist assigned to the farm. Housing troubles in rural areas often spurred young specialists to leave or get married. Married kolkhoz workers had the advantage in rural regions with housing shortages.

In the 1970s, Luda divorced her husband and moved to the village of Raskopino, on the outskirts of Vologda, after answering an advertisement for an animal husbandry specialist position in the newspaper. She began working on the farms of the Molochnoe State Breeding Plant and received an urban-type apartment in a panel home in the Molochnoe settlement, where she lives to this day.

Even when the mass enrolment of Soviet schoolchildren into the Komsomol was in full swing in the 1960s and '70s, the number of

Komsomol members in sovkhoz and kolkhoz VLKSM organizations steadily declined. Schoolchildren were not eager to establish careers in agriculture, and the population of sovkhozes and kolkhozes was growing older. Additionally, Komsomol personnel were rotating very quickly. District committees were hardly able to make the acquaintance of the young men and women who were assigned to work as secretaries in rural areas before they left. In 1962, the average length of time that a Komsomol secretary held their position in Vologda Oblast was no more than a year and a half.[58] By 1969, the oblast had a total of 1,012 Komsomol cells with less than twenty members in each.[59] This was a mere 47.7 per cent of the original number of organizations in the oblast.

According to data presented by the Vologda Oblast Committee to the VLKSM Central Committee on 1 January 1963, 18.5 per cent of the oblast's Komsomol organizations were considered to have "low numbers." By 1 January 1966, that statistic had risen to 26.9 per cent, and by 1 January 1969, it had reached 32.4 per cent.[60] The size of Komsomol organizations did not increase even when farms were merged together and the total number of sovkhoz workers went up. The driving factor for this was the migration of rural youths to the cities. The following statistics illustrate the depletion of the rural population in Vologda Oblast. In 1939, 1,311,700 people (82 per cent of the oblast's population) lived in rural areas.[61] By 1969, the number of people living in rural areas had decreased to 696,300 (53.2 per cent). Every year, the rural population dropped by roughly 5,000 people. In 1959, around 132,800 people between the ages of sixteen and twenty-nine (14.5 per cent of the total rural population) lived in rural areas in the Vologda region. In 1969, only 92,000 people (12.9 per cent of the rural population) fell into this age group.[62] The decrease in the population of rural youths led to a decrease in the membership of Komsomol organizations. Over the ten years between 1959 and 1969, the proportion of VLKSM members who were in kolkhoz and sovkhoz organizations dropped from 20.8 per cent to 6 per cent. At the same time, the proportion of VLKSM members in school organizations grew from 26.7 per cent to 50.1 per cent.[63] The magnitude of the "influx" of schoolchildren can be gauged from the following figures: In Vologda Oblast over the course of 1962 and 1963, the VLKSM accepted 3,431 workers, 1,468 kolkhoz workers, and 29,140 schoolchildren into its ranks.[64] In 1969, half of Vologda Oblast's rural Komsomol members were in organizations tied to educational institutions, and only an insignificant number were in sovkhoz organizations.

Vologda newspapers had been reporting on low membership numbers in rural Komsomol organizations since the 1940s. In 1947, the journalist Neverov wrote a story for *The Red North* regional newspaper about

Komsomol members in Vologda Oblast's Ustyuzhensky District.[65] In the story, the kolkhoz "Old-Young" is described as having only 3 Komsomol members, although there are more than 20 young people in the village. In reality, there were only 74 Komsomol organizations for the district's 200 kolkhozes in 1947, and 47 of these organizations had a mere 3 to 5 members.

There were various reasons for low membership in rural Komsomol organizations. In the 1920s and '30s, the government feared an influx of rural Komsomol activists and thus strove to limit rural Komsomol numbers. By the 1940s, Komsomol membership offered benefits such as a career in the city and guaranteed access to positions of power within the community. In the 1960s, everything changed. The youth no longer wished to remain in rural areas and no longer saw a benefit to joining VLKSM organizations.

While conceding that urbanization and the movement of the rural population into cities were natural developments, the authors of numerous memos, informational documents, and reports from the rural regions of north-western Russia expressed their concern about these phenomena. They saw that migration carried direct consequences not only for Komsomol membership counts, but for rural economies too. In 1967, First Secretary V. Kukushkin of the Vologda Oblast VLKSM Committee wrote the following to V.T. Duvakin: "The intensive departure of young people from villages is a cause for worry … We need to come up with concrete measures to keep young people in the countryside."[66] Similar sentiments were expressed by the secretary of the Pskov Oblast Committee, who stressed that without young people, rural areas had no future.[67]

The VLKSM Central Committee's Department for Rural Youth picked up on the anxieties of regional leadership. Department workers organized inspections, called meetings, and launched investigations to determine the cause of mass migration from rural regions. Ultimately, they could not find an effective means of preventing it. Personnel retention programs were similarly ineffective and undertook measures that were in general overdue. These included the introduction of professional programs to rural schools, the creation of professional-technical colleges in rural areas, "kolkhoz stipends" for rural youth, postponement of army service for graduates of rural vocational colleges, and even efforts to drastically improve the conditions of life and work for young people in rural areas.[68]

Nevertheless, the decline of the sovkhoz Komsomol was more than compensated for by the growth of school Komsomol organizations. This latter development seemed to guarantee that young people would be drawn into Komsomol work through schools even in the absence of a strong sovkhoz Komsomol. In this view, the Komsomol's fundamental mission to educate the younger generation was still being accomplished, albeit through a new channel. Moreover, under the supervision of "adults" (school administrations), the Komsomol was functioning even better than it had on sovkhozes, where the Komsomol had to provide for itself. Even within active party organizations, kolkhozes and sovkhozes discussed the Komsomol at most once a year.[69]

Party leadership and the VLKSM viewed low membership numbers in sovkhoz Komsomols as a natural stage in the development of rural areas. At the same time, by discussing low Komsomol membership numbers, they attempted to publicly evaluate the future of Russian villages in the North-West. However, by the time the issue of migration from rural areas came to be considered of union-wide importance at the end of the 1970s and aide programs for the Non-Black Earth region were implemented in 1973, the rural portion of Vologda Oblast was practically without young people.

The Komsomol and Non-Union Youth

The exodus of young people was only one of the problems facing the rural Komsomol. Another important factor contributing to the rural Komsomol's low membership numbers during the late socialist period was the fact that rural youth did not see significant benefits from entering into the organization's ranks. Consequently, they were in no rush to become members.

Lacking Komsomol documentation (called a "Komsomol ticket") had almost no effect on the life trajectory of young people in rural areas. Alexandr T. was born in 1955 in the village of Kargach, Migachevo Selsoviet, Kirillovsky District. He recalls how his father, who had fought on the front in the Second World War and then taken over leadership of the kolkhoz "Red Banner" after the war, refused to give up the kolkhoz's cattle for meat in the 1950s. He was subsequently expelled from the party, removed from his leadership position, and, on top of it all, imprisoned for embezzlement. After living through these difficulties and having become disillusioned with the political trajectory of the CPSU, he forbade his children to join the Komsomol. As a result, Alexandr and his siblings never became members.[70]

The fact that Alexandr did not have a Komsomol ticket did not negatively affect his life course. After graduating from Ivitsy Elementary School, Goritsy Middle School, and then Kirillov High School, he enrolled in a technical college in Cherepovets. Upon graduating, he was called to the army. Then he worked as a welder on one of the oblast's

Komsomol projects, the Northern Lights gas pipeline. Later, he took part in opening the Cherepovets Chemical Plant. Alexandr had played sports actively since school. Everywhere he went he received positive feedback and, alongside it, invitations to join Komsomol organizations. Following his father's advice, he declined each time. In his own words, Alexandr explained his ability to sidestep membership in the Komsomol as follows: "So, how did I manage to get out of joining the Komsomol the first time? I was the youngest in the class ... and they accepted members up until the birthday of Vladimir Ilyich [Lenin]. I wasn't yet fourteen, so that was it [...] Then, when I was in secondary school they would say, 'What's this? Why aren't you a Komsomol member yet?' I would answer, 'I'm not worthy of it, I have a 3[71] in this or that subject.' And they would sort of leave me alone. Basically, that was it. I made it through. I never became a Komsomol member at school."[72]

He did not become a Komsomol member in the army either, or when he worked on Komsomol construction projects; in each case he was able to find a reason to avoid joining. It is true, however, that his lack of membership did not free him from taking part in VLKSM initiatives, such as *subbotniki*, which were required of all young workers regardless of the fact that the initiatives were attributed to the Komsomol. Ultimately, Aleksander was not forced onto the sidelines because he was not a VLKSM member, nor did this interfere with his career.

Although Komsomol membership was not a prerequisite for entering working professions, the Komsomol did play an important role for those who wished to receive higher education in the 1970s. For Rimma F., a graduate of Novokemsky High School, in Belozersky District, not being a member of the Komsomol prevented her from being accepted into medical school.[73] Without a Komsomol ticket, her excellent grades were insufficient to grant her a spot at the Leningrad Medical Institute. Although this did not stop her from eventually becoming a doctor, her path into the profession turned out to be much more difficult than for her peers who were Komsomol members. For this reason, young people who wished to receive higher education actively joined the Komsomol. Those who were not enthusiastic about continuing their education, or who were focused on starting a career, often saw no benefit.

This state of affairs is illustrated very clearly by the VLKSM membership statistics of two districts in Vologda Oblast. In the second half of 1975, out of the 6,850 people aged fourteen to thirty in Kirillovsky District, 2,908 (42.4 per cent) were members of the Komsomol.[74] In 1972 in Vologodsky District, 4,745 (81 per cent) of people in the same age range were Komsomol members.[75] The discrepancy in membership numbers is attributable to the much higher number of educational institutions in

Vologodsky District. Young people in that area generally strove to study at one of the educational institutions in the district's titular city, Vologda.

Although VLKSM membership was always considered a sign of loyalty to the government and was associated with an entire set of respectable personal qualities, rural Komsomol members during the 1960s and '70s were often indistinguishable from "non-union youth" (those not belonging to the Komsomol). As Kirillov's prosecutor, A.O. Ganichev, eloquently stated at the Kirillovsky VLKSM District Committee plenum, "[the Komsomol youth] take part in mass drinking parties," and misbehave just like "non-union youth."[76] The same point was made at party meetings of the kolkhoz "Battle," convened by the Glazatovsky Village Council. At a meeting on 4 January 1967, members discussed an incident in which young people from the village of Glukharevo had stolen vodka from a store.[77] The communist who gave the speech at the meeting reproached the sovkhoz's Komsomol organization not only for failing to prevent the crime in the first place, but also because its members had allegedly taken part in it (claiming that, "after the theft, they drank the vodka together").

Iya V., secretary of the Komsomol organization on the sovkhoz "Vorobyevsky," recalls that young people on the sovkhoz were friendly with one another without distinguishing between Komsomol members and non-members.[78] In recreational settings, rural youths were on equal footing. It would seem that a clear distinction between union and "non-union" youth existed only in the minds of Soviet leadership, who were tasked with increasing membership in the former group and decreasing the numbers of the latter.

The "non-union" youth were viewed by party organs as a potential source of disciplinary infractions. The Komsomol, by contrast, was on good terms with the party. In fact, the Komsomol was considered responsible not only for the behaviour of VLKSM members, but for all those involved in a given collective organization. This gave sovkhoz administrations additional leverage over the Komsomol.[79] Moreover, Komsomol members, like party members, were expected to be the best workers in a given organization, and for this reason more was asked of them. As one of the communists on the kolkhoz "Battle" stated at a party meeting in 1968, "There are no communists working in livestock farming. The party has no influence."[80] Therefore, it had no additional leverage with which to apply pressure on workers. The push to draw all Soviet youths into VLKSM organizations resulted in both an easing of Komsomol entrance requirements and the development of new ways of filtering out suitable party candidates from the organization.

It is worth noting that Vologda Oblast's district party committees carried out almost the same work with non-union youth as they did with the

Komsomol. Indeed, Komsomol and non-Komsomol youth often worked on the same projects.[81]

Unlike party initiatives, Komsomol initiatives were not strictly compulsory for the organization's members; neither the party nor the VLKSM leadership in the regional district had any illusions about this. Thus, even though the city and district Komsomol organizations in Veliky Ustyug were ostensibly held responsible for the increase in youth crime and homelessness by an Oblast Committee investigation, the recommendations published by the region's communists did not list the Komsomol as the "main actor."

The Komsomol was involved in helping various political state and party entities. Some VLKSM work was coordinated with administrative organizations (for example, creating a Komsomol brigade to monitor a dance). Other work was done in conjunction with the executive committee (supervising minors). Lastly, the Komsomol worked with trade unions, schools, and cultural institutions (organizing hobby clubs and sports groups, putting on concerts, etc.).

The Komsomol was not, however, considered the primary organization responsible for the behaviour of young people in the city.[82] The means that the Komsomol had to discipline its members, such as discussing misbehaviour at Komsomol meetings or leveraging the import of its recommendations in determining whether a student was accepted into higher education, were often insufficient to "correct" a Komsomol member's behaviour without the intervention of "adult" government organs. In rural areas, the futility of Komsomol disciplinary measures was felt even more strongly than in the cities.

Youth Migration and the Rural Komsomol

Before the reforms of the Thaw, the Komsomol in Vologda villages was primarily focused on helping party organizations with production-related issues. The top priority for Komsomol members in the post-war period had been fulfilling quotas for the "agriculture tax,"[83] socialist obligations, and socialist competitions. Komsomol district plenums issued a flurry of reports on Komsomol shock initiatives on kolkhozes. These initiatives offered not only pennants and prizes, but also more unusual rewards. The award for the "best milkmaid" was a bucket passed from one winner to the next. Another reward was free tickets to rural recreational clubs.[84] In the first decades after the war, the rural Komsomol was more likely to discuss farm economies than "Komsomol work" as such. The "backward" kolkhoz was not seen as a suitable place for a good VLKSM committee, just as it was not seen as fit for a good party cell. No matter how many concerts a Komsomol committee had put on in rural clubs, no matter how many youth debates it had organized, if the sovkhoz did not fulfil its work plan, the sovkhoz Komsomol was considered weak and inadequate. The economic standing of the farm where the Komsomol organization existed determined how successful the Komsomol was judged to be.

After the reforms of Nikita Khrushchev in the 1960s, when villages were drawn into the project to create a "new rurality," Komsomol initiatives were no longer exclusively limited to improving production. Gone were the days when oblast committees considered labour figures to be the sole criterion on which a Komsomol organization could be evaluated; suddenly, young people were expected to prove themselves in other spheres of public life. Thus, on 16 March 1961, leaders at the Vologda Oblast VLKSM Bureau recommended that "it be considered wrong when the title 'Communist Labour Collective' is bestowed on the basis of labour figures alone, not taking into account to what extent the organization's members implement progressive principles at work and at their residences."[85] Starting in the mid-1960s, sovkhoz Komsomol organizations began to be assessed along different, more varied criteria. Organizational, cultural, athletic, and educational work with youth started to be taken into consideration. The knot binding the Komsomol to the economy became much looser.

Official discussion of rural youth was also a prerogative of the party organizations that were responsible for a given sovkhoz. As a rule, the opinions of Komsomol members differed from those of party members. In their meeting protocols, communists from rural regions wrote about the inactivity of the rural Komsomol at the same time that Komsomol documents recorded high levels of activity.[86] The discrepancies in these reports can be explained by their intended recipients. VLKSM village committees answered to VLKSM district committees, while party organizations answered to CPSU district committees. The VLKSM reports were intended to showcase Komsomol accomplishments and plans to VLKSM district committees. Party members used kolkhoz youth as a scapegoat on whom they could pin the blame for various negative developments on sovkhozes and kolkhozes. Both sets of reports were intended to emphasize the fact that Komsomol organizations were still functioning on sovkhozes, even if membership in them had an exclusively nominal character.

It is worth noting that there was almost no discussion of youth migration at kolkhoz party or Komsomol meetings, despite the fact that migration was one of the most important issues in youth politics in the 1960s and '70s. For some kolkhozes, such as "Maisky," where there were plenty of workers, youth flight was not a pressing issue; new housing was constantly being built in the village, and young workers and specialists

Figure 8.1. A group of machine operators on the sovkhoz "Maisky," 1970.

Source: Private collection of Alexandr Filin.

willingly went to work on the kolkhoz. But the sovkhoz "Vorobyevsky," which steadily lost its young people over the course of the 1960s and '70s, experienced increasingly disruptive personnel issues with each passing year. In light of this situation, the lack of discussion surrounding this problem at meetings seems unusual.

In all likelihood, rural communists and Komsomol members avoided discussing youth migration publicly because they found themselves in a delicate situation. On the one hand, party members were supposed to follow the party line and speak out against young people leaving the village. On the other, the Komsomol members who wanted to leave often included the party members' own children. The desire to leave was widespread among village residents, regardless of whether or not they belonged to the party or the Komsomol.[87] Party members were left with two options, then: either "not notice" youth migration, or speak out very carefully, keeping in mind how important the subject was to village communities.

Despite the lack of public discussions about migration on the level of Komsomol and party meetings, local party organizations and the Komsomol did have some means to apply pressure on young people planning to leave their villages. First, they could exert influence over kolkhoz and sovkhoz referrals to institutions of higher education, which were one of a limited number of ways a young person could legally leave the kolkhoz. Secondly, party organization members could entice young people to stay after finishing school with offers provided by the farm establishment. These offers could be promises to build new houses and apartments, or to provide high-paying work. This is what the communist Kropachev put forward at a party meeting for the kolkhoz "Banner" on 6 April 1966. He advocated "keeping graduates working in the kolkhoz where they grew up."[88] Thirdly, party organizations could forbid party members themselves from leaving a village. Party members who wished to leave a kolkhoz could have their case reviewed and face harsh disciplinary measures.

In 1963, the Vozhegodskiy Rural Production Party Committee reviewed just such case. Popov, a communist, had moved out of the village where he lived of his own volition without removing his name from the party register. He had gone to Arkhangelsk Oblast and found work at a timber industry enterprise. The kolkhoz's party organization, considering Popov's actions to be a violation of party discipline, refused to remove his name from the register, and demanded that he return to the kolkhoz. He was issued a severe reprimand, and the incident was recorded on his party registration card.[89] It is not known whether the party bureau's decision forced Popov to rethink his plans for the future, but the fact that disciplinary measures were enforced is nonetheless illustrative. It was much more difficult for a communist to leave a kolkhoz than it was for a non-party member or a Komsomol member. This, in turn, caused young people to reject offers to join the party.

The young specialist Yuri V., who was working in 1971 as the head engineer of the sovkhoz "Vorobyevsky," understood the implications of joining the party. Not wishing to face obstacles to leaving the farm, he either refused or dodged offers to become a CPSU member.[90] Membership in rural party organizations limited one's mobility, and this had a significant effect on young people's tendency to avoid the party. Thus, on the kolkhoz "Battle," Glazatovsky Village Council, Kirillovsky District, the number of party members dropped from twenty-three in 1961 to nineteen in 1969, just before "Battle" was merged with the sovkhoz "Vorobyevksy."[91] Similarly, on the kolkhoz "Red Banner," Goritsy (and later Migachevo) Village Council, Kirillovsky District, the number of communists dropped from twenty-eight in 1961[92] to twenty-seven in 1969.[93] Clearly, party membership numbers were on the decline.

Kolkhoz and sovkhoz administrations were also reluctant to release Komsomol activists, young specialists, and rank-and-file workers from the farms, but they did not have any means to seriously prevent them from leaving. There were three generally permitted reasons for leaving: "family circumstances," meaning marriage between a rural resident and a person living in a city; service in the army; or a work transfer. Theoretically, a Komsomol organization could review an individual's case at a party meeting or get in touch with the Komsomol committee for the organization to which a member wished to transfer. However, analysis of low-level sovkhoz documentation from Kirillovsky and Vologodsky Districts indicates that the Komsomol rarely implemented such measures. Sovkhoz administrations played a much more important role in the process of regulating migration than did Komsomol organizations. By refusing to return a sovkhoz worker's documents, the sovkhoz could significantly hinder that person's ability to leave and find new work.

Nevertheless, the most far-seeing Komsomol members understood the possibility that they might face disciplinary measures. Some of them tried to avoid being recorded in Komsomol registers after moving back to villages upon graduating. Some even discreetly removed their records from sovkhoz organizations before moving. Iya V., for example, secretly took his Komsomol registration card from the District Committee archive.[94]

Eugene Kh., who moved from the village of Sosunovo, part of "Vorobyevsky," to Leningrad at the beginning of the 1970s, remembers how he destroyed his work documentation because it showed his specialization as a tractor operator. On account of the push to stop workers from leaving villages at the start of the decade, the personnel departments at the majority of industrial enterprise in the USSR were forbidden to hire tractor operators in cities. When applying for new documentation at his sovkhoz's personnel department, Eugene requested that they record his profession as a "sovkhoz worker." His request was granted, and he left the sovkhoz to find work at a tram depot in Leningrad.[95] Only in this complicated way was a tractor operator able to become a metalworker at a tram depot.

Sovkhoz Komsomol organizations could not compete with urban VLKSM organizations in the eyes of district and oblast committees. With the constant outflow of young people from villages and the ever more obvious crisis in agricultural production, the rural Komsomol was not in a position to flaunt its successes. Nor could it hope to compare itself with Komsomol industrial enterprises or construction projects. It was redeemed only by the large numbers of Komsomol members in rural areas, although they were primarily schoolchildren rather than graduates who came to the sovkhoz to work.

On unequal footing with urban Komsomol organizations, and lacking the numbers and "fighting spirit" of VLKSM cells working on industrial enterprises and construction projects, rural VLKSM cells were generally viewed as weak and ineffective by party leadership. It is not by coincidence that rural organizations are hardly mentioned in the celebratory compendiums dedicated to the fiftieth anniversary of the VLKSM. Their activity was recorded only in fulfilled or exceeded work-plan targets, which paled in comparison with the various Komsomol initiatives undertaken by industrial organizations. The reason for this was not so much that rural Komsomol members lacked a fighting spirit, but rather the objective circumstances that made kolkhoz and sovkhoz work ineffective. The persistent migration of young people, constant personnel rotations, and the lack of incentives to mobilize youth made it impossible for district and oblast committees to ask for more to be done by sovkhoz organizations. Rural Komsomol members had already taken on as much work as they could. Komsomol workers worked in two shifts, first on the kolkhoz and then on their personal farms.[96] Consequently, they had no "free time" for Komsomol duties. The *trudoden*[97] system, in place until 1966, ensured that, even if they had wished to, rural Komsomol members were not in a position to accept more work.

Chapter Nine

The Invisible Komsomol: Kolkhoz and Sovkhoz VLKSM Organizations

Komsomol Reports

On 28 July 1965, a delegation of ninety-four people was sent to the city of Veliky Ustyug, a regional centre in Vologda Oblast, to identify conditions "giving rise to truancy and crime among minors."[1] The group included nine members of the Vologda CPSU Regional Committee as well as active members of the party, Komsomol, union organizations, farm administration, and youth physical education programs. According to the documentation, in the first seven months of 1965, eighty-eight crimes were committed by juvenile offenders in the region and seventy-six arrests made. Crime in the region had increased by a factor of 2.5 since 1964, and it had grown sevenfold among minors.[2] Oblast-level communists took an active interest in the situation in Veliky Ustyug. In large part, this reflected the battle against crime waged by the CPSU Central Committee in response to large-scale reforms to the Ministry of Internal Affairs and procuracy that were carried out in the 1960s and the campaign against hooliganism.[3]

The Vologda Oblast Committee representatives who were sent with the commission deemed the work carried out by regional and state institutions concerned with youth labour to be unsatisfactory. They reported that young people in the regional centre and surrounding area were "left to themselves." The Komsomol, schools, and secondary-level professional educational institutions, alongside party organization, unions, and the Soviet public sphere (represented by DOSAAF),[4] all neglected young people. The city lacked organized ·youth recreation programs, leaving them "to drink alcohol in the city park," which was apparently a cause of concern for city residents.[5] This information, which surfaced suddenly after the delegation's inspection, caught local leaders off guard. Until that time, they had relied on reports from local organizations responsible for work with youths, such as the executive committees of regional soviets, and union, party, and Komsomol organizations. The discrepancies between what had been reported and the commission's findings were so significant that they spurred a total mobilization of state institutions, from the procuracy to the Komsomol secretary, and led to the development and implementation of emergency measures to address the situation.

The divergence between what had been declared in Soviet documentation and what was discovered by officials during the regional committee raid is a clear example of how, despite the Soviet system's declared totality and solidity in the 1960s and '70s, that same system created opportunities and spaces that were uncontrolled by the state. Moreover, freedom from the state was even more evident in rural localities than in the city. Firstly, like in cities, the practice of "living *vnye*" (living "outside") flourished in rural areas. Alexei Yurchak coined that term to describe Soviet citizens' ability to live separately from the state while performing formal rituals of loyalty to it. This allowed, for example, youth subcultures to exist in the USSR in spite of bans targeting these very subcultures. Secondly, the autonomy of rural localities from the state was facilitated by geography. In the difficult-to-access backwoods, it was always possible to escape the prying gaze of the state. This was true of Veliky Ustyug, which monitoring bodies could reach only with difficulty and where oblast-level officials formed their understandings about reality on the basis of documentation created by low-level reporting bodies.

People's ability to evade the duties imposed by the state's modernization project produced two clear consequences in rural localities. On the one hand, it allowed alternative modernities to exist in Soviet society, whether oriented towards "Western" urban subcultures or "frozen-in-time" rurality. On the other hand, it granted rural youths greater scope to make choices about participation in state projects: For someone living in the countryside, refusing to complete the school curriculum or join the Komsomol did not entail serious disciplinary measures. Because such a person was already distanced from the Soviet system, it was difficult to enforce discipline by typical means such as party or Komsomol reprimands or the threat of being sent on a work assignment to a remote region.

Thus, territorial inequality in the Soviet Union produced varying conditions for communicating with the state. Although a unique relationship between rural localities and the state was not new (it is sufficient to recall the Old Believers or the practice of sending Soviet dissidents past the 101st kilometre), this continued to be the case throughout the 1960s to the 1980s, albeit in a new way. It turned out that the state had less of an ability to apply pressure on people living on the fringes of civilization and who were not attempting to occupy a prestigious position in Soviet hierarchies. An especially clear example of rural localities' relative freedom from state duties can be seen in the work of kolkhoz and sovkhoz Komsomol organizations in the 1960s and '70s.

If a reader takes reporting documentation created by party, soviet, or Komsomol organizations at face value, they will form a false impression of Soviet reality. By repeating the language of higher authorities word for word, the compilers of these documents not only classified reality in accordance with principles "imposed from above" but also copied the language and structure of higher-order state institutions.[6] This "copied" style of documentation was characteristic in the Soviet Union between the 1960s and the 1980s not only of Komsomol reports but also of party meeting protocols and work reports for various Soviet institutions.[7]

Boris Groys has argued that the philosophical principles formulated during the first decades of Soviet rule and that underpin political decisions carried much greater weight in the USSR than the economic logic of the market.[8] In his view, dialectical materialism was not merely an abstract formula in Soviet discourse; it was, rather, the "flesh and blood" of how Soviet people philosophically conceptualized reality. In other words, it necessitated that all Russian speakers bear a particular view of a given problem or phenomenon. Groys characterized this mindset as "totalistic" and argued that it allowed the Soviet subject to see phenomena in all their contradictoriness and paradoxicality. According to the "totalistic approach," reality cannot be described as purely a success or a failure. Instead, it has to described in terms of a process created by the confrontation of antagonistic forces: good and bad, progressiveness and backwardness, deliberation and spontaneity. Although progressive social elements always prevailed in official Soviet discourse, backward elements (insufficiencies, vestiges of the pre-revolutionary past, and mistakes) also received a lot of attention. Descriptions that paired successes with "individual insufficiencies" were a common feature of the conceptualization of Soviet reality. At the same time, judgments about what was considered good and bad were left to higher authorities, which could evaluate information according to an entirely different set of criteria.

Stalinism was crucial to the formation of official Soviet language. In the opinion of Alexei Yurchak, Joseph Stalin functioned as the highest source of judgment and conceptualization in Soviet culture, and after his death no leader was subsequently able to obtain a similar status.[9] As a result, official discourse began to reproduce formulas that had been tried and tested over time and deemed the most neutral and non-contradictory. The exhaustion of Soviet discourse gave rise to a unique phenomenon, what Yurchak has called a performative shift.[10] On the one hand, this shift facilitated the continuity of cultural elements, while on the other it exalted the form assumed by certain verbal expressions while minimizing the actual meaning they conveyed.[11] As a result, both Yurchak and Groys see paradoxicality as the key aspect of the Soviet political and ideological system, one that simultaneously facilitated a level of freedom in the actions of Soviet people while also formulating their dependence on a specific way of describing reality.

For these reasons, the vision of reality conveyed by Komsomol reports is deeply flawed and can provide only a distorted idea of how the Komsomol functioned and worked with Soviet youths. Someone reading the reports might be surprised to find descriptions of Komsomol organizations existing and functioning even in remote rural localities: holding regular meetings, creating youth brigades, fulfilling socialist obligations, and taking part in socialist competitions. They would read that political literacy circles were being held all across the country and that Komsomol members were taking part in *subbotnik* and *voskresnik* weekend volunteer work. However, a completely different picture emerges if one asks former Komsomol members themselves about how the Komsomol functioned during the 1960s and '70s, or if one tries to compare reports of Komsomol production activity with industrial reports created independently of the state. In that case, instead of "battle-ready" Komsomol organizations, one finds Komsomol cells that existed only on paper. At most, one might find a functioning Komsomol bureau that was able to convene a meeting once a month only with great difficulty and that harboured no illusions about fulfilling Komsomol obligations.

In other words, in the countryside in the 1960s and '70s it was sufficient to learn to write work reports rather than try to actually perform Komsomol work in practice. This was understood by party and federal-level officials. As a result, party leaders throughout this period attempted to revitalize the Komsomol by publishing resolutions and instructions aimed at improving Komsomol administration. Moreover, party organization members were required to attend Komsomol meetings. Finally, regional and district CPSU committees carried out their own inspections of low-level Komsomol cells to see local conditions with their own eyes.

However, as Iya V. remembers, locals knew about these inspections before they happened. In "Vorobyevsky" they were usually connected with selsoviet elections. The Komsomol bureau and secretary of the Komsomol organization would be informed on the eve of an inspection and could organize the *subbotnik* necessary for the inspection and work report.

Elections were the main reason for the continued existence of sovkhoz Komsomol organizations, despite low levels of bureau activity and the steady abandonment of rural areas by Komsomol members. If there was no Komsomol in a village during elections, an administrative issue (the absence of young people) became a political issue (a violation of election procedures). Thus, even if sovkhoz Komsomol organizations had been inactive all year, the VLKSM came alive in the lead-up to elections in response to party organization efforts.

Usually, Komsomol members were chosen for supervisory committees and oversaw elections in the villages. They also worked as political agitators. Most importantly, however, Komsomol organizations put their own members up for election as local selsoviet deputies. In accordance with Soviet legal norms, there were quotas for selsoviet deputies in the 1960s and '70s; these took into account one's sex, age, and participation in public organizations. VLKSM members, alongside women and non-party members, were required to be represented in the selsoviet. Without a VLKSM organization, the selsoviet would be unable to fulfil this requirement, thus meriting serious reprimands from party leadership. So long as Komsomol representation was a prerequisite for properly organized elections, party organizations and the Komsomol District Committee could not completely come to terms with a sovkhoz VLKSM organization's inactivity.

Election preparation efforts were allotted a prominent place in Komsomol work reports. Thus, it was recorded on the sovkhoz "Fruit-Tree Nursery" in 1971 that there were eleven VLKSM members who worked as deputies and three who were elected trade-union organizers.[12] On the sovkhoz "Battle" in 1967, Komsomol members nominated candidates to take part in village election commissions for elections of the Supreme Soviet of the RSFSR and of local soviet deputies within the Glazatovsky election district.[13] In addition, Sovkhoz VLKSM organizations were tasked with overseeing the election of delegates to district Komsomol conferences. However, because these were routine events, they did not typically stoke excitement among Komsomol members. Taking this state of affairs into account, it is not surprising that Iya V., as secretary of the second-branch Komsomol organization on the sovkhoz "Vorobyevsky," also managed to serve as deputy for the Migachevo Selsoviet.

The criteria according to which district Komsomol organization work was evaluated resembled those that were applied to party organization work.[14] As was the case for the party, a Komsomol organization was valued for its accurate reporting, adherence to work planning, and mass participation. In reporting documentation, the primary emphasis was placed not on the actual results of Komsomol activity in a given locality (for example, construction projects built by Komsomol members), but on descriptions of the work processes and the effort expended.[15] Thus, as in party documentation, Komsomol documentation was often filled with formulas that would later be difficult to verify, and rural Komsomol members constantly "intensified their work," "raised efficiency," "devoted more attention," and "battled with irresponsibility."

In other words, Komsomol work reports, like meeting protocols written by low-level party organizations, described reality in such a way as to, first, show that the community supported the form of Soviet discourse (that is, that people approved of Soviet policy, condemned negligent members, battled to reach socialist obligations, etc.) and, second, avoid descriptions that could incriminate the organization in failing to achieve goals set by the party or Komsomol. In order to do so, they used formulas that allowed them to conceal the ways in which reality diverged from the ideal and describe Komsomol activity so that it appeared successful to higher authorities regardless of the extent to which work was being realized on the ground.

As a result, the state, represented by district and oblast Komsomol committees, could not know for sure whether Komsomol work was being completed in rural localities. From the point of view of the documentation they received, organizations that were in fact carrying out Komsomol work as well as those that existed in name only each appeared to be flourishing. It is noteworthy that, in these conditions, rural youths could decide for themselves whether or not to participate in Komsomol work. Nevertheless, the authorities in charge of various rural localities had other means at their disposal to apply pressure on young people.

"Old Rurality" on the Sovkhoz "Vorobyevsky"

The eighteen-year-old agronomist Iya V. arrived at the village of Migachevo in the summer of 1971 after graduating from Ustyuzhensky Agricultural Technical College.[16] She had been sent to the sovkhoz "Vorobyevsky," on which Migachevo was located, by a representative of the Kirillovsky District Agricultural Department. The representative believed that the arrival of an unmarried female agronomist to a sovkhoz with a high number of bachelor tractor operators and a chief engineer would not only benefit the agricultural situation, but also potentially ease the demographic issues facing the rural locality.[17] Thus, despite having received a directive from the college to work on the sovkhoz "Komintern," whose flattering name had sparked Iya's desire to move, she set off to "Vorobyevsky."[18] As a young specialist, Iya received a salary of 120 roubles and a horse named Sailor to help her overcome the distances between the ten villages that formed Migachevo Selsoviet.

Figure 9.1. "Young specialists" on the sovkhoz "Vorobyevsky." Agronomist Iya V. is on the left, while agricultural brigade leader Galina F. is on the right. The photo was taken in Migachevo village in 1971.

Source: Photo from family archive of Iya V.

Iya never considered herself a Komsomol activist. She had joined her school's VLKSM organization along with the other schoolchildren in 1967 when she was finishing her studies at the eight-year school in Ivanovskoe, in Belozersky District.[19] After moving to Ustyuzhna in 1968, Iya was put on the register for the Komsomol organization at the agricultural technical college. She does not retain any vivid memories of Komsomol participation during her time there. In an interview, she admitted that she could not even recall for certain whether the college held Komsomol meetings. However, during her professional skills training on the sovkhoz "Bright Path," in Ustyuzhensky District, Iya had the chance to observe an active sovkhoz Komsomol. She remembers concerts organized by Komsomol youths, *subbotniks*, and sports competitions.

Iya was assigned to the sovkhoz "Vorobyevsky" alongside other young women who had graduated from various institutions of higher education across Vologda Oblast. In the year of Iya's assignment, the first branch received a new zootechnician and a building technician. The secondary branch gained a rural club and library head, a female foreman, and Iya herself.[20] A feldsher had arrived to "Vorobyevsky" a year prior.

Iya received an offer to become the secretary of the sovkhoz's second-branch Komsomol organization from Lidia Kozinova, the long-time chair of Migachevo Selsoviet and a former front-line soldier. As selsoviet chair, Kozinova oversaw the sovkhoz's first branch, ensuring that rural clubs prepared for concerts and holidays, that travelling film projectors reached villages, and that life for village residents changed for the better. Leadership took notice of Iya V., who had no notable experience but had demonstrated her strong character by battling alcoholism among tractor operators, offering her a place as secretary of the Komsomol organization.

Recounting the story of her life and work at "Vorobyevsky," within whose bounds she spent two years, Iya did not initially recall the leadership position she held in the sovkhoz Komsomol organization. Only the discovery of her Komsomol ticket in her personal archive called to mind the post she had occupied so long ago. Indeed, Iya did not assign this period of her biography great significance. In her interview, she listed her duties as follows: As secretary she attended plenums of the VLKSM District Committee in the city of Kirillov, oversaw the completion of Komsomol documentation at Komsomol meetings, and was responsible for the collection of membership fees. The Komsomol Bureau met only irregularly and on special occasions. The Komsomol organization at "Vorobyevsky" kicked into action only before selsoviet elections when they had to report to visiting district leadership on the successes that had been achieved on the eve their arrival, such as *subbotniks*, lectures, and cross-country ski trips.

As Iya remembers, "There were probably around forty-two individual Komsomol members. It was fun with us. It was really good even. There were a lot of young people, a lot of whom had come from the army. Basically, everyone was young, everyone was full of life."[21] Iya recalls locals spending their free time with young specialists who had been sent on assignment (the librarian, the agronomist, various zootechnicians, etc.). Komsomol members made an effort to distance themselves from other young people only on special occasions, and as a rule in the presence of CPSU members. For example, the Komsomol secretary for the kolkhoz "Battle" responded to party reprimands about organizational inactivity by answering that "the organization is being undermined by young people who are not part of the Komsomol [...] They drink often, come to the club drunk, disturb the peace, and although Komsomol members receive the blame, they are not the guilty ones."[22] In this case, the secretary resorted to splitting young people into groups according to Komsomol membership (and lack thereof) in order to lay the blame on "non-union" rural youths who were formally outside of the purview of Komsomol responsibility.

Far from all the young people living in the region of the sovkhoz "Vorobyevsky" were members of its rural Komsomol organizations. In the 1960s, the total number of members in the sovkhoz's first-branch Komsomol organization hovered between 13 and 15, while the second branch had between 18 and 24.[23] In 1977, the now combined "Vorobyevsky" Komsomol organization recorded its peak membership count at 65 Komsomol members across both branches.[24] This temporary spike in the sovkhoz's VLKSM membership numbers appears connected with the incorporation of new territories into the sovkhoz, in particular the village of Ivanov Bor, whose Komsomol members joined the sovkhoz organization. The Glukharevo Eight-Year School was located on the territory of Glazatovsky Selsoviet, and its Komsomol-member teachers formed the backbone of the sovkhoz Komsomol organization. In 1971, Secretary Ivanov recorded the names of all the Komsomol organization members in the sovkhoz's first branch and gave a brief description of each person.[25] Of all the members on the list for the first branch, 3 were teachers, 5 were tractor operators, 2 were "young specialists,"[26] and 2 worked in the sovkhoz administration. In 1969, the second branch of the sovkhoz "Vorobyevsky" in Migachevo Selsoviet claimed 18 members in its Komsomol organization: 5 farm machinery operators, 4 cultural workers, 2 service-sector workers, 1 milker, 2 agronomists, 1 veterinarian, 2 medical professionals, and 1 rank-and-file sovkhoz worker.[27]

Due to pressing "personnel slippage" (high turnover) issues on sovkhozes, the ranks of rural Komsomol organizations were constantly in flux. It was not incidental that the secretary of the party organization on the sovkhoz "Vorobyevsky" lamented in 1971 that "the second-branch Komsomol organization can be said to have collapsed, and this is in plain view of the secretary of the production facility's party organization. After all we have a lot of good young people who we could recommend to the party."[28] According to the statistics presented by the VLKSM secretary for the kolkhoz "Red Banner," in 1969 alone seven people left the organization and eight were added to the register.[29]

Among the impressive array of Komsomol members who worked on sovkhozes, it is striking that many were young people engaged in professions auxiliary to, rather than directly involved in, agricultural production. Teachers, economists, and club workers worked towards fulfilling personal Komsomol obligations that were tied to their professions but were unable to meet the production-related demands of district committees, such as increasing sovkhoz milk yields. As a result, when milkers joined a sovkhoz Komsomol organization, they quickly had a positive effect on its reputation.

The socialist obligations that Komsomol members adopted on the kolkhoz "Battle" in 1967 included the following: "Smirnova V. – graduate to the third course of Vologda Agricultural Technical College with good marks; Buntyakova E. – prepare for medical institute; Sergeeva R. – become a Pioneer leader at school, enrol in the pedagogical institute this year; Kuzina A. – enrol in Vologda Pedagogical Institute; Kuznitsov A. – become a Pioneer leader for first through third grades; Sokolov G. – become a Pioneer leader for second through fourth grades."[30] Only one of the Komsomol members, Valentina K., was a milker. She took on the obligation of collecting twenty-six hundred litres of milk from each cow in 1967.[31]

Alongside the individual obligations that all VLKSM members adopted, there were collective obligations that reflected the priorities of the VLKSM District Committee and sovkhoz party organization. Thus, the obligations for Komsomol members on the sovkhoz "Battle" in 1961 included the following: "raise and fatten 60 lambs, send young people into animal husbandry – 2; export manure from the farms; prepare silage – 138 tons; prepare hay – 69 tons; prepare stakes and poles – 4,600; clean leys and pastures – 11 hectares. Organize a youth night. Conduct a Q&A evening. Choose Komsomol members for the club soviet."[32] In part, these obligations were included in the sovkhoz's general work plan, but the Komsomol was expected to report on them independently.

By 1973, concrete production goals were no longer included in Komsomol members' obligations on the sovkhoz "Vorobyevsky." Instead, the Komsomol bureau meted out obligations such as increasing levels of organizational work, regularly conducting meetings, and collecting monthly membership fees. Komsomol members were required to "actively participate in production" and "demonstrate great initiative, take part in mass-cultural work."[33] Like decisions at party and Komsomol meetings, socialist obligations were being formulated in such a way that they could be formally fulfilled without the Komsomol members having to take part in burdensome work.[34]

Work reports from sovkhoz VLKSM organizations always included descriptions of *subbotniks* and *voskresniks* (volunteer weekend projects on Saturdays and Sundays, respectively). The frequency of Komsomol participation in these events depended on party leadership, who could spur the Komsomol to work, and on the level of discipline among the Komsomol members themselves. In 1950, in connection with the fiftieth anniversary of the first communist *voskresnik*, members of the kolkhoz

"Red Banner" were required to spend one Sunday sorting potatoes and then another one "filling the icehouse on the 'Vorobyevsky' farm."[35] On the kolkhoz "Battle" in 1966, Komsomol members went to work on *voskresniks* four times.[36]

Under the leadership of the selsoviet chair, all young people, not only active Komsomol members, took part in putting on concerts for Soviet holidays.[37] Nevertheless, in "Vorobyevsky" it was the Komsomol organization that was responsible for arranging them. In Migachevo Selsoviet this was considered the Komsomol's most important task and the criterion by which the organization's work was judged. Reprimands for Komsomol inactivity were usually made in connection with disruptions to holiday concert schedules.[38] The demand for mass-cultural work on sovkhozes and kolkhozes in the 1960s and '70s can be explained by an acute lack of "cultural workers" (e.g., club heads and librarians) who, in theory, were supposed to act as the organizers of "cultural recreation" in villages. However, low pay made it impossible for cultural workers to live on their salary alone. This, combined with a lack of funds that could be spent on "cultural recreation," resulted in constant and palpable labour shortages. Furthermore, whereas the central issue in the 1960s was a lack of funds, in the 1970s it was a lack of personnel. In the 1960s, for example, the kolkhoz "Battle" could not afford to spare a cabin for the club's use. As a result, at the VLKSM District Committee meeting Komsomol members lamented "the difficulties of organizing cultural recreation for young people due to not having an inside space" and asked the committee for help in "choosing a temporary space for the club and constructing a new club building."[39] But even after a club building had been built on "Battle," Komsomol concerts proved ineffective at impressing village residents, who largely ignored Komsomol performances. The situation was discussed at a joint Komsomol-party meeting on the kolkhoz "Battle" in 1967. In response to communist Boltusheva's question "why are you putting on so few concerts?" Komsomol member Sergeeva parried, "If the only ones to visit our concerts will be children, then we won't put them on at all. Adults need to attend."[40]

Sometimes, if Komsomol members refused to oversee mass-cultural work, schoolchildren from local schools would come to their assistance and prepare festive performances under the guidance of their teachers. Thus, on the same kolkhoz "Battle," it was the schoolchildren from the eight-year school in Glukharevo who organized performances for the "October holidays" and a concert for 8 March (International Women's Day) in 1966.[41]

Another problem tied to Komsomol concerts was discussed by E.V. Orekhova, the Komsomol secretary for the kolkhoz "Red Banner." In her description of Komsomol activity in 1969, she bemoaned the fact that "only young women come to repetitions, and the guys remain on the sidelines." She called the young men into action, stressing that "no one but us, the young people, can make our recreation fun and interesting."[42]

In addition to concerts, Komsomol members on "Battle" tried to organize a "Q&A evening" in 1966. This event was innovative for the time, and the intention was to collect questions from the local population and have experts answer them in a public setting. However, judging from the report, it seems that, while questions were collected by Komsomol members, there were no experts to answer them. Whether the questions were too difficult, or the Komsomol members themselves were unprepared, the result was that the event was cancelled.[43] Innovative Komsomol events were organized in the Migachevo branch of the sovkhoz as well. In 1971, at a "Vorobyevsky" Komsomol meeting, organizers conducted a debate on the topic of "maidenly pride and manly honour." The meeting protocols record the following information about the event: "The first question was answered by Ulyanova. She spoke about maidenly pride. The second question, 'What is the meaning of manly honour?,' was answered by Sokolov. The third question, 'What do we understand 'maidenly modesty' to mean?,' was answered by Vinchina. The fourth question, 'What kind of relationships should be had between young men and women?,' was answered by Khokhlov. The fifth question, 'Upon what are relationships between young men and women founded?,' was answered by Ivanova."[44] Unfortunately, the protocols do not include transcriptions of the Komsomol members' speeches. Nevertheless, such a topic would have been engaging for Komsomol members regardless of its having been chosen by Komsomol leadership. It speaks to the desire of the sovkhoz Komsomol bureau to make Komsomol meetings interesting for young people.

Theoretically, ensuring the smooth operation of village libraries was within the purview of district executive committee cultural departments and was supposed to be managed by district communists. Because the library was concerned with questions of ideology, it was placed under the careful management of the party's district committees. This allowed carefully monitoring of whether Soviet magazines reached readers in rural areas and village library catalogues were regularly restocked. Nevertheless, Komsomol organizations were viewed as partially responsible for the number of readers in rural libraries and of young people with annual subscriptions to publications like *Komsomol Truth* (*Komsomolskaya Pravda*) and *Vologda Komsomol Member* (*Vologda Komsomolets*). Thus, although it was primarily rural librarians who were tasked with setting up reader conferences, VLKSM District Committee members organized similar events when needed. For example, on the sovkhoz "Vorobyevsky," the librarian worked together with the Komsomol organization in 1971 to plan "a 'Little Light' evening dedicated to the work of Pakhmutova," a themed evening on "The Taste of Bread," a debate entitled "We Can Hold Love Dear," another "Little Light" dedicated to Sergei Yesenin, a themed evening called "And We Too Wore Grey Overcoats," a reader conference on the book *In Spite of All Deaths*, and a singing competition.[45]

There were more young people in Migachevo Selsoviet villages during the summer with the arrival of vacationing students and villagers whose parents had already managed to move into cities. These young people met in the club in the evening and sailed out to the islands by boat to have picnics. Village fistfights, common occurrences in the 1950s and associated with rural patronal holidays, gradually fell out of popularity during the 1960s and '70s, but memories of past battles, occasionally ending in fatalities and prison terms for the participants, circulated in the region for many years to come. Igor L., from the settlement Chagoda, visited relatives in Kabachino on summer holidays and remembers that patronal festivities for Crucession[46] in the 1950s often culminated in fights among local youths: "These were horrific fights – completely horrendous. I mean the whole village was surrounded by post fencing. After ten minutes there wouldn't be a post left, and all these guys with fence posts – until blood was flying, of course ... After all there were even cases where someone would be killed."[47]

A possible reason for the decline in the popularity of mass fights is that participation in them began to be punished more seriously and village troublemakers began to find themselves the subjects of police attention. The number of criminal cases for "hooliganism" jumped from thirty-four in 1960 to fifty-two in 1961.[48] But the main reason that fighting declined was that with every year there were fewer and fewer young people in the villages; there was simply no one to fight with, although isolated incidents in which "our boys" faced off against those from another village did subsequently occur. Yuri V. recalled once finding himself under a volley of stones launched by Goritsy youths at "Kabachinos" who were sailing boats to the local club.

Because there were no facilities or athletic equipment, developing a sports culture on sovkhozes was no easy task. On the kolkhoz "Battle" in 1968, the only work recorded on this front was the construction of an outdoor gym in Glukharevo, a project undertaken in response to a district directive.[49] Among the sporting events for young people recorded in Komsomol protocols were two "group overnight trips to the lake," which, evidently, could be passed off as trekking. Among village residents these events were viewed as an opportunity to have a good time and drink alcohol rather than as physical exercise or a means of promoting a healthy lifestyle.[50]

The athletic program on the kolkhoz "Red Banner" was equally prosaic. Like the Komsomol members of "Battle" in 1969, those in "Red Banner" adopted the responsibility of building an outdoor gym for the kolkhoz.[51] However, the only mention of a game actually being organized on the kolkhoz is a reference to a match of volleyball in 1973, when a net for that purpose was set up in Sosunovo.[52] The sports situation did not change after the two kolkhozes were combined into the sovkhoz "Vorobyevsky" in 1970, although one Komsomol member was tasked with overseeing athletic work and the Selsoviet Executive Committee bought skis for young people to use.[53] Generally speaking, it was no secret that "the sports program was too weak" on the territory of Migachevo Selsoviet.[54]

Nevertheless, that there are no records of the sovkhoz Komsomol organizing sporting events does not mean that young people did not partake in sports. On the contrary, judging from my interviewees' personal recollections, young people played soccer and volleyball and practised cross-country skiing independent of Komsomol leadership.[55] Modern, urban recreational practices gained in popularity among the rural population, especially because most young people on the sovkhoz, like Iya V., were not burdened by the demands of peasant labour or family life. Cross-country skiing, for example, became more widespread at a time when schoolchildren had to overcome long distances from home to school. Yuri remembers making his first skis himself when he was studying at the school in Goritsy. Around the same time, he learned to play chess by studying instructions from a magazine.[56]

Iya V. occupied the post of Komsomol organization secretary for less than two years. She met her future husband at "Vorobyevsky," and, immediately after getting married, in 1973, she ended her Komsomol career and moved away from the countryside, taking her registration card from the Komsomol archive with her. She did not register with the Komsomol at her new place of residence, the settlement Molochnoe. In effect, she removed herself from the ranks of the VLKSM at the age of twenty-one, without waiting for graduation at twenty-seven. Like many girls her age, Iya believed that VLKSM membership would hold her back from family life and that public tasks and assignments would negatively affect her ability to run the household. In view of her belief that being a wife and a mother was incompatible with being a Komsomol activist, she hid her Komsomol past from her new employers. Subsequently, after having received a higher education and starting work at a research institute, she continued to avoid party and Komsomol involvement, although she was selected to sit on various commissions for the institute's local committee and trade union committee. Taking care of her children and her home meant more to her than building her career.

Iya's experience is notable not only because it illustrates a very specific approach to Soviet activism in the era of late socialism; it also shows that Yurchak's sense of "being *vnye*" (that is, being simultaneously inside and outside of the Soviet system, fulfilling Soviet rituals without understanding their meaning while living a separate life not dictated by the state) was just as characteristic of rural localities as it was of big cities. It is notable that young people on the sovkhoz "Vorobyevsky" in the 1960s and '70s did not view VLKSM membership as a resource capable of either accelerating their escape from rural life or helping them build a career in the village. Komsomol membership, or lack thereof, was not a cardinal factor in determining the life trajectories of rural youths during this period. The crucial element determining one's life path was education, which could guarantee a job, a stable salary, and a place of residence on the sovkhoz. Komsomol membership was more like a supplement to underlying educational capital. As Benjamin Tromly has noted, education granted young people, including women, the social status of belonging to the intelligentsia, which was unequivocally regarded more highly than the status of a kolkhoz peasant.[57] Had Iya V. decided to remain on the sovkhoz, in time she undoubtedly would have come to occupy a management position. Being a VLKSM secretary and selsoviet deputy at the age of twenty, she could have made a head-spinning career for herself in a rural locality by becoming a chief specialist or working for district sovkhoz management. But, according to her system of values, these opportunities proved unattractive. A high-status specialist position in a village could not ensure her quality of life increased, and, therefore, Iya did not view this path as desirable.

In summary, the Komsomol organization on the sovkhoz "Vorobyevsky" did not play a large role in the lives of young people in the Migachevo region. Young people did not form their conceptions about life, fashion, or modernity from lectures put on by the organization "Knowledge" or district agitators who propagandized participation in sports, reading, and amateur art performances. Instead, they were influenced by trends emanating from the cities and spreading into the countryside, whether fashionable crimplene or Bologna-style fabrics, playing volleyball, or smoking cigarettes. As CPSU Committee Secretary Repin noted with distress at a party meeting for the second branch of the sovkhoz "Vorobyevsky" in 1971, "There have been multiple attempts to rally the ranks of the Komsomol organization, but these attempts have been impersistent, and, as I mentioned earlier, our Komsomol organization has fallen apart."[58] And although the practices that the Komsomol propagandized did not contradict, and at times even aligned with, youth trends more generally, there was no one to popularize these practices. Sovkhoz organizations were too weak and passive. At the same time, the existence of Komsomol organizations on sovkhozes and their work arranging holidays and recreation legitimized the rights of young people in peasant communities to their own spaces and recreational activities. In time, these activities began less and less to resemble the traditional pastimes of peasant teenagers.

The Maisky Komsomol

Unlike the party organization of "Fruit-Tree Nursery," which included communists from all over the settlement, regardless of their place of work, there were two Komsomol organizations at Maisky, a school organization and a sovkhoz organization. The two did not interact with one another and reported to different departments of the VLKSM Regional Committee: the school organization answered to the Department for Student Youths, and the sovkhoz organization answered to the Department for Rural Youths. Members of the school Komsomol were responsible for student academic success and were subordinate to teachers. The sovkhoz Komsomol members focused on production issues, mass-cultural work, and the development of sports and political education.

The Komsomol organization was far from the only institution working with young people on "Fruit-Tree Nursery" in the 1970s. There were also successful music and compulsory schools, sports activities, hobby circles, Culture House programs for children and adolescents, and yearly sovkhoz summer camps for schoolchildren in Maisky. Furthermore, the primary drivers of modernization on the sovkhoz were the administration and the director personally, who consistently preferred professional work to Komsomol initiatives.

While in the beginning of the 1960s the Komsomol still participated in setting up "Russian Winter" celebrations and concerts, by the 1970s the club and its workers were the primary organizers for holidays in the settlement. A similar shift occurred for sovkhoz amateur performances and sports competitions. Political education was overseen by the librarian and the party organization's designated party organizer. Work with children was managed by the school. In other words, the sovkhoz Komsomol was essentially left in charge of its own organizational needs: exchanging Komsomol tickets, conducting the Komsomol's "Lenin examinations,"[59] assisting during elections, and organizing *subbotniks* and *voskresniks*. The sovkhoz Komsomol at "Fruit-Tree Nursery" did not seem much more competitive than the Komsomol at "Vorobyevsky."

At the same time, greater supervision of the Komsomol by the sovkhoz administration on "Fruit-Tree Nursery" and the administration's ability to apply pressure on Komsomol members through housing distribution ensured that sovkhoz youths could not completely shirk their Komsomol duties. For example, on "Fruit-Tree Nursery," unlike on "Vorobyevsky," Komsomol members could be expelled from the VLKSM. In 1971, three Komsomol members in Maisky were stripped of their ticket for "failure to pay membership frees, nonattendance at meetings, and non-fulfilment of VLKSM member charter obligations."[60] In 1973, one instance of expulsion from the Komsomol included "a suit brought before the workers' committee and additional punitive measures."[61] Evidently, the Komsomol secretary for the sovkhoz "Maisky" was unafraid of being reprimanded by the District Committee for losing members. This was due to the large reserve of potential new members on the sovkhoz. By contrast, in 1969 on the kolkhoz "Red Banner," in Kirillovsky District, members could not be expelled even for such serious offences as drinking during the workday. Thus, the Komsomol member M., who drunkenly "used a tractor not for its intended purpose, ruined all the roads, and nearly brought down a house in Gorodishche," was merely issued a warning and allowed to retain his Komsomol membership.[62] Judging by Komsomol protocols, members were not typically expelled from the "Vorobyevsky" Komsomol either. In fact, even those who desired to exit the Komsomol voluntarily were typically not allowed to.[63]

As was common in rural localities, the Komsomol organization at "Fruit-Tree Nursery" did not always conduct regular meetings. In 1967, the sovkhoz Komsomol, which included sixty people across three departments of the sovkhoz, met only sporadically: 2 times in the first branch and 1 time in the second. The Komsomol committee of fourteen people met only 4 times.[64] In 1972, the situation with Komsomol meeting attendance improved. The Komsomol committee convened 9 times, and 6 Komsomol meetings were held.[65] The topics discussed at the meetings were for the most part the same as those discussed by the party organization – popularizing party plenum decisions, discussing socialist obligations, planning work, and discussing the results of sowing and crop harvests.

Youth participation in *subbotniks* and *voskresniks* was a critical indicator of Komsomol work in Maisky. In "Fruit-Tree Nursery" these events were held five or six times a year, although there were special cases. For example, the Komsomol work report for 1972 contains the dissatisfied remarks of the organization's secretary, who was incensed by VLKSM

Figure 9.2. Concert put on by the youth propaganda team of the sovkhoz "Maisky" for workers during a lunch break, 1977.

Source: Private collection of Alexandr Filin.

members' non-attendance at VLKSM events: "But unpaid labour for the public good is still underappreciated by many Komsomol members," she wrote. She continued: "14 May was declared a Komsomol *voskresnik* for sorting potatoes. To the great shame of everyone involved, only three of thirty Komsomol members attended. This speaks to the low level of political development among our Komsomol members."[66] In theory, *subbotniks* were voluntary and uncompensated. But when the sovkhoz could not handle the harvest on their own, it would invite not only Komsomol members but also the teachers and pupils of the Maisky school, club works, and any public servants affiliated with the sovkhoz.

As was the case with socialist obligations, the quantity of planned *subbotniks* far exceeded the number held. On the sovkhoz "Maisky," out of the five planned Komsomol *subbotniks* (to improve public and green spaces within the settlement, to collect berries, to harvest potatoes, to prepare hay, and to clean soot), only two were conducted.[67]

While activities directly connected with the work and recreation of young people tended to stimulate youth communities on kolkhozes and sovkhozes, Komsomol cells were also in charge of initiatives that did not produce a large response among organization members or the local community. However, even when the work was not carried out, it had to be reported – this was the core principle of successful rural Komsomol cell attestation.

The "Komsomol Projector" (KP), created as "a mass form of Komsomol and youth participation in the realm of public supervision, the battle against mismanagement and wastefulness, infringements upon socialist property, and against everything that is damaging to the national economy and the building of socialism,"[68] was actively embedded into the sovkhoz Komsomol in the 1960s and '70s. Descriptions of KP raids are commonplace in Komsomol documentation from this time. An organization's participation in the KP lent credence to the quality of the Komsomol's work and was seen as evidence of active Komsomol participation in sovkhoz affairs. In theory, a KP raid participant was supposed to visit farms and production facilities and then write up announcements for wall newspapers about any shortcomings that were discovered. In addition, Komsomol members were required to report these deficiencies to the farm leadership and selsoviet administration, in addition to making efforts to address them.

The conflicts that subsequently arose – a near certainty thanks to the intrusive nature of these Komsomol inspections – were the main reason that "projectors" never caught on in rural localities. The sovkhoz Komsomol was no less dependent on the party organization than it was on the sovkhoz leadership or selsoviet administration, and anything that threatened to destroy the harmony of these organizations' coexistence was interpreted negatively by all parties. KP units were created in low-level organizations on the orders of Komsomol district committees, but the inspections they occasionally conducted served a purely formal function and had little impact outside of being recorded in Komsomol committee reporting documentation.

This was the case for kolkhozes in Kirillovsky District as well as for the sovkhoz "Maisky." For example, during the first half of 1965, the Komsomol members of the kolkhoz "Red Banner" conducted four raids during which they "inspected the level of preparation for spring sowing," monitored the organization of bookselling, and oversaw "agriculture machine repair carried out by the 'Agrotechnical' association."[69] The first mention of a KP in reports from the kolkhoz "Battle" in Kirillovsky District are from the year 1967. A KP crew consisting of three Komsomol members was selected at a Komsomol meeting. However, judging by the fact that there is no mention of the results of the raid in either Komsomol organization reports or in party cell documentation, it can be assumed with a fair degree of certainty that the KP's activity was limited to this.[70]Moreover, Komsomol members themselves typically made no effort to hide the fact that KP work was poorly set up on sovkhozes.

In fact, there are reports in which they made suggestions about how the KP could be improved. Even on the sovkhoz "Fruit-Tree Nursery," where Komsomol leadership tried to meet all the demands of their higher-ups, they were often forced to report that work was not being completed. The only evidence attesting to the role played by the KP in this rural locality can be found in sovkhoz documentation from 1973, where it was reported that KP members regularly issued wall newspapers with descriptions of problems on the sovkhoz's farms. The authors ridiculed the practice of collecting food waste for cattle, the slow production of organic fertilizers, and drunkenness among tractor operators during the sowing season.[71]

An obligatory but not very popular form of Komsomol activity in rural areas in the 1960s and '70s were educational programs. In a system designed to prepare the USSR's party and Komsomol ranks, political education was given high official priority. The political education system created in the 1960s included a sprawling network of "politinstruction" schools, people's universities, and various levels of political discussion circles where Komsomol and party members were acquainted with socialist history and theory. Judging by a report from the consultant for the Vologda Politinstruction House, out of the total number of working young people, there were 68,616 young men and women who were involved in the political education system. Of these, 13,983 studied in the party system and 24,366 studied in the Komsomol. Moreover, 30,267 attended mass propaganda group events and 28,572 took courses on politinstruction-related topics offered at evening classes, part-time public schools, technical colleges, and institutions of higher education.[72] Theoretically, political studies were supposed to reach all the young people working and studying in the oblast, including "non-union" youths. In practice, however, even the extremely formalized count made by V.A. Nutrikhin, the Politinstruction House consultant, revealed a large portion of "untapped" youths, amounting to around 15 to 30 per cent of the young people living in the oblast's various districts.[73] Successful completion of these various courses, discussion circles, and schools would be recorded on a person's Komsomol membership card, thereby qualifying them to work as a propogandist or political agitator. Such a career path was no doubt remote from the desires of most rural youths. Nevertheless, Komsomol members were required to organize and attend these schools and discussion circles.

Typically, schools were the primary institutions where political studies were implemented in rural localities, and teachers were responsible for combining political education and propaganda with their core professional duties. The propaganda efforts of Komsomol organizations were evaluated not so much by the quality of the information members took away from discussion circles, but by levels of attendance and membership participation numbers.

On the sovkhoz "Fruit-Tree Nursery," politinstruction was discussed alongside issues of general education. In 1967, there was discussion of creating a "consulting point" that would provide school courses for young people without a seven-year education and allow them to raise their level of education and pass exams for school completion. However, as the sovkhoz's VLKSM secretary noted, none of the Komsomol members wanted to continue their studies. At another time, two "Outlook" discussion circles were organized on the sovkhoz in 1967, but these were immediately disbanded "because Komsomol members did not want to attend."[74] In 1972, the settlement's Komsomol organized a political circle under the name "Discussing the Party," and twelve people attended, according to a report.[75] However, a 1973 report stated that political education was completely neglected on the sovkhoz: "Tarustina, who was responsible [for political education], made a plan and prepared topics for every lesson, but it was not possible even once to bring together Komsomol members. Then Tarustina left the Komsomol," and work on this front stopped.[76]

Nevertheless, despite the unpopularity of political education among rural Komsomol members, VLKSM district committees stubbornly insisted that it be organized. Therefore, on the sovkhoz "Maisky," where Komsomol activity was carefully monitored, it appears that politinstruction circles were organized and held; at the very least, they were reported at Komsomol meetings. By contrast, on farms like "Vorobyevsky," where there was a greater outflow of young people and the leadership was concerned with more pressing issues, no political education circles were mentioned.

As was the case on "Vorobyevsky," young people in the Maisky settlement were not in a rush to become Komsomol members. In 1967, the VLKSM secretary for "Fruit-Tree Nursery" wrote about insufficient levels of among with "non-union" youth and reprimanded the organization, stating "there are non-union youths on the sovkhoz, and they still have yet to be drawn into the Komsomol."[77] In any case, a contrast between those who belonged to the Komsomol members and those who declined to join was rarely drawn in reports from sovkhoz Komsomol organizations. Even Komsomol secretaries themselves understood the illusory nature of making a clear distinction between members and non-members. Thus, the Komsomol organizer for "Fruit-Tree Nursery" stated, "we have many such Komsomol members on the sovkhoz who, when they begin their employment, forget to put their names on the Komsomol register and essentially forget that they are Komsomol members altogether. Nor is work discipline at the necessary level among Komsomol members. There are cases when Komsomol members are found to be inebriated during work hours."[78]

Unlike the sovkhoz "Vorobyevsky" in the 1960s and '70s, where there was neither an active Komsomol task unit nor a volunteer public-order squad, measures for the maintenance of public order found support among the population of "Fruit-Tree Nursery." Although the Komsomol task unit on the Sovkhoz was not formed until 1980,[79] before that nearly half of the sovkhoz's Komsomol members participated in a volunteer public-order squad that supervised discotheques and patrolled the settlement on weekends.[80] Additionally, the battle against hooliganism in the settlement was waged by the Police Department for Juvenile Crime, which had been created in the 1970s, and the school's "Police Assistance Youth Unit." Judging by the high number of cases in the Vologodsky District Department for Juvenile Affairs involving teenagers from Maisky, it can be surmised that the settlement police department was also active.

Another important criterion used to assess Komsomol organizations on sovkhozes and kolkhozes was whether the Komsomol bureau, a management body elected at Komsomol general meetings, actively functioned. The Komsomol bureau ensured that Komsomol and committee meetings were regularly held, planned organizational activities, checked that Komsomol members paid their fees and exchanged their tickets, certified that election procedures were observed during the selection of secretaries, and was responsible for Komsomol documentation.[81] Even if no actual work was undertaken by a Komsomol organization, proper documentation and carefully composed reports from bureau meetings were considered a sufficient basis for a district committee to grant a sovkhoz Komsomol "battle-ready" status. For this reason, membership fee collection and Komsomol session regularity were given a prominent place in reporting documentation.

Describing the sovkhoz Komsomol's mass-cultural work on "Fruit-Tree Nursery" in 1967, the secretary offered a list of events that had been held in the previous year: "organized amateur performances (performed in clubs and drove out to perform for work brigades in the fields), organized and held the 'Blue Flame' celebration for New Year's, organized *voskresniks* for planting potatoes and working on green spaces and public spaces in the settlement, held a Komsomol wedding, culture trips to the theatre and circus."[82] In 1971, sovkhoz Komsomol members put on a "'Russian Winter' celebration with music, prizes, and horse riding," held five concerts, made three tips with the agitation brigade, "organized a masquerade for New Year's, a 'Little Light' for 8 March, and a literary-musical composition 'The Year 1917' for 7 November 7"[83] Apart from these, they held competitions for volleyball and hockey.[84] A 1973 report records that the Komsomol members on "Fruit-Tree-Nursery" had a choir and an ensemble that performed at amateur public showings: "Komsomol members organized evenings, holidays, and concerts dedicated to the fiftieth anniversary of the USSR and the tenth anniversary of the sovkhoz, as well as a 'celebration of the passing of winter.'"[85] In 1980, the idea of creating a "Young Families' Club" was discussed at a sovkhoz Komsomol meeting.[86]

Construction of the Culture House and the sports complex by paid workers evidently transformed life in Maisky. Before this time Komsomol members were prone to announce, like their peers in "Vorobyevsky," that "our Komsomol members ... do not know how to spend their downtime."[87] With four rural clubs on the territory of "Fruit-Tree Nursery" by 1967, the primary pastime of Komsomol youths was not putting on amateur art performances but watching films.[88]

Komsomol work organizing sports on "Fruit-Tree Nursery" was equally prosaic. Judging by the sovkhoz documentation, athletic work in 1973 was still considered the "Achilles' Heel of the organization's work."[89] In accordance with the demands of Soviet leadership, sovkhoz Komsomol organizations and selsoviets were expected to play a fundamental role in raising and supervising rural youths. While sovkhoz and kolkhoz VLKSM organizations were originally evaluated on tasks related to the economic needs of farms and the conscientious fulfilment of professional duties, by the 1970s the character of rural Komsomol work had changed. Milk yields and the area of cultivated land surrendered their place at the top of Komsomol meeting agendas to discussions of organizational and mass-cultural work.

Despite the unpopularity of the majority of official Komsomol initiatives in villages, some did align with the desires of rural youths, such as for the organization of recreational activities. In localities such as Migachevo and Glazatovsky Selsoviets, which rarely saw visits by artists from district and oblast centres, the participation of young people in concerts for Soviet holidays was not merely a "Komsomol affair" – it was also an outlet for everyone who wanted to add colour to village life. Given that Komsomol performances at clubs were booked to capacity throughout the 1960s and '70s, it can be surmised that these events garnered wide public support and kolkhoz workers gladly attended Komsomol concerts.[90] At the same time, unpopular Komsomol initiatives never took root in villages, even when they were reported in Komsomol documentation. Moreover, the threat of being punished for not fulfilling district committee demands was for the most part insignificant. Sovkhoz Komsomol personnel were in a state of constant flux, and finding a new Komsomol secretary among the rapidly thinning youth population of Vologda selsoviets was extremely difficult.

As was the case in cities, belonging to a sovkhoz Komsomol organization did not guarantee either Komsomol-style "work on oneself" or the fulfilment of district and oblast CPSU directives. For official structures, the formal existence of a Komsomol organization on a sovkhoz was enough to consider it successful and capable of answering the needs of the era. Membership in rural VLKSM organizations was as formal and straightforward as was membership in other voluntary public organizations such as the Red Cross and the Red Crescent, the All-Union Book Lovers Society, or the DOSAAF sports organization. Moreover, in most cases expulsion from the organization did not entail dramatic consequences.

VLKSM organizations had different functions in different rural settlements. On the sovkhoz "Vorobyevsky," the Komsomol was essentially the only institution dedicated to young people, meaning that the Komsomol bureau could initiate various important undertakings. However, unequal governmental distribution of resources between cities and the countryside left them without a chance: Young people did not want to remain in villages even if the sovkhoz provided them with a club for dances and bought them sports equipment.

In Maisky, sovkhoz leadership did not rely on Komsomol initiatives and instead created the infrastructure for youth recreation itself. Sports groups, a musical school, and amateur arts programs were managed by professionals rather than Komsomol activists. And although many undertakings were implemented from the "top down" in villages and faced resistance and passivity from the local population, for the children and adolescents growing up in these villages sovkhoz initiatives were a chance to become acquainted with modern, urban ways of life. Nevertheless, both the "Vorobyevsky" and "Maisky" Komsomol organizations were faced with quite similar tasks and a similar repertoire of possibilities for building socialism in a rural area. The varied "rurality" of Vologda settlements and villages ultimately led to various results.

Like city youth, young people in the two Vologda Oblast rural settlements I have described did not consider the Komsomol to be "their organization," and very rarely demonstrated interest in it. As a rule, either Komsomol workers or a bureau specially assigned by the sovkhoz administration and usually comprised of the most responsible young workers and public servants were in charge of organizing Komsomol work. Rural VLKSM cells were more important for state structures like sovkhoz administrations, selsoviets, and schools than for rural youths themselves, who preferred activities "without an order from above." And although

Komsomol initiatives did not elicit significant backlash from the rural population in the 1960s '70s, it was rare for a young person from either "Vorobyevsky" or Maisky to voluntarily join Komsomol initiatives.

The rural Komsomol in this era was a vehicle for the transmission of CPSU decisions and never became a voice for the interests of rural youths, not because the latter did not share Soviet values, but because they viewed Komsomol activity as an ineffective means of changing life in the village and did not see it as a guarantee of social mobility. The limits placed on rural Komsomol organizations were also counterproductive in garnering popularity for the VLKSM during this period. Rural youths were justifiably cautious about the VLKSM because it could use its power as an instrument of pressure at any moment, whether by issuing a Komsomol work assignment to a faraway kolkhoz, publicly criticizing member behaviour at meetings, or demanding work on the weekends. Although such measures were far less common in rural localities than in cities, young people tended to feel more comfortable keeping their distance from the organization.

In other words, Komsomol work was in many cases a burden to young workers and distracted them from their family lives and the leisure activities typical of young sovkhoz workers. Ultimately, the VLKSM organization was not very useful for young people in the old villages of the sovkhoz "Vorobyesvky" because its initiatives frequently disrupted the flow of rural life and took away valuable time that otherwise could have been used to tend the farm. Nor did the VLKSM organization become popular in urban-type settlements such as Maisky, where it was viewed as a quasi-state institution for disciplining youths.

Nevertheless, sovkhoz Komsomol work proved easier to organize in settlements with urban-type cultural infrastructure, such as clubs, stadiums, union committees, etc. As a result, the Maisky Komsomol remained functional until the end of the 1980s, while the "Vorobyevsky" Komsomol became defunct by the end of the 1970s, after the sovkhoz's final Komsomol member left.

Soviet modernity, advocated by the Komsomol, had to compete with both peasant culture (Komsomol members consistently left the organization when they entered marriage, and "Komsomol weddings" were often reminiscent of rural traditions) and a youth urban culture that made the Komsomol seem excessively disciplinary and aesthetically uninteresting by comparison. Only when Komsomol initiatives corresponded to youth expectations or overlapped with general modernizing trends (for example, in organizing sports or amateur hobby groups) did young people show an interest in the organization. But even then, the Komsomol did not so much initiate these trends as adjust itself to them.

Conclusion

Every year I visit my parents in Kabachino. Unlike urban vacationers retiring to their summer dachas, my parents return to the countryside to work. They cultivate vegetables and prepare fish, berries, and mushrooms for the long winter ahead. For my parents, as for many former villagers from Vologda Oblast, the countryside remains a source of sustenance, as it had been in the past. In the 1980s, people supplemented their diets during food shortages with vegetables from their garden plots. During the 1990s, produce from village gardens became foundational to people's diets. Throughout my entire childhood, the menu for family lunches and dinners was comprised of boiled potatoes with fermented cabbage, salted mushrooms, and vegetable salads prepared in the fall. In the 2000s, when fruit and vegetables ceased to be a rarity even in village stores, my parents continued to cultivate them, explaining that "our" produce is organic and healthier than what is available in stores. I know, however, that the authentic reason they continue to labour over their produce lies elsewhere.

Only to a small extent can my parents' assiduousness in preserving their village home and peasant custom of living off the land be attributed to nostalgia for the past. Most crucially, former villagers do not want to lose their ability to survive autonomously in a rapidly changing world. Peasant labour and local knowledge preserved families on kolkhozes during the numerous disasters brought down upon them by state initiatives. It is for this reason that, no matter how technologized production becomes, and no matter how far science advances, the humble village plot remains the guarantor of self-preservation. Peasant logic is simple: What I have grown on my plot, I eat. Even villagers who move to the city remember this basic formula, despite their education and urban socialization.

A stubborn attachment to peasant agricultural practices capable of supporting an autonomous existence remained strong among former Vologda Oblast village residents despite the state program to build socialism. By proclaiming socialism to be the sole possible technologized and urbanized future, Soviet leadership threw down a challenge to rural communities and denied their importance. Thus, preserving rural identity can be seen as an act of resistance and distrust towards the vision of the future offered by socialism. After years of experimentation, it became clear that rural culture, autonomy, and identity help people feel secure in the difficult conditions of contemporary Russian politics and a globalized world.

It is possible that modern Russians seem uninterested in solving pressing political questions for a simple reason: They know that they are incapable of influencing the state. By maintaining a connection with autonomous life in the countryside, however, they are able to achieve a sense of security that allows life to go on.

The rural settlements I described in this book have each followed dramatically different trajectories over the last fifty years. The Molochnoe settlement eventually lost its status as an urban-type settlement and was reclassified as a village in the early 2000s in order to reduce property values ahead of the sales carried out by settlement leadership at the turn of the twenty-first century. With time, Molochnoe ceased to be an administrative centre and turned into one the district's run-of-the-mill small communities where large stores moved in to serve dacha vacationers from Vologda and tourists taking trips "to nature," otherwise known as dacha cooperatives established in the surrounding region.

The research institute in Molochnoe has been preserved but barely makes ends meet after the majority of the region's farms went bankrupt and it lost government funding. The dairy factory is still functioning, as are a few farms from the former breeding plant that are now owned by a large agricultural concern. However, the biggest change to the settlement came with the sharp decline in the student population of the Vologda State Dairy Farming Academy, the successor to VDI. The remaining population of young people who would potentially study and receive a diploma in Molochnoe has been practically exhausted. There are almost no rural young people in the Russian North-West. An aging population, half-empty dormitories, and the university's old asphalt paths overrun with weeds are all that remains of a once thriving and dynamic modernization project.

The Maisky settlement proved to be more resilient than Molochnoe in the face of changing conditions, although its continued viability was not connected with the businesses or economic structures preserved from the USSR. It survived because of its proximity to the city of Vologda. The settlement's fortuitous location, the infrastructure built under the Soviet system including schools, stores, a sports complex, and the unusual construction of individual cottages, as well as the sovkhoz fields that were parcelled out as land for dachas, allowed Maisky residents to weather crises in the agricultural sector and the redistribution of property that occurred during the 1990s and 2000s. The price of former sovkhoz land just outside of the city allowed the settlement to survive even after the sovkhoz went bankrupt. Currently, there is a functioning agricultural nursery in Maisky where a small portion of the settlement population works, but most people commute to Vologda for work. In the 2000s, Maisky replaced Molochnoe as the district's administrative centre.

The villages in Kirillovsky District described in this study underwent a more predictable process of rural decline. Now, fifty years after the events described in this book, the combined population of these villages, which are now part of the Aleshinsky Rural Settlement, hardly exceed one hundred permanent residents. The fields of the former sovkhoz "Vorobyevsky" have been subsumed by the forest, and the Glukharevskaya Secondary School shut its doors. The river crossing that once connected the local villages with the village of Goritsy was closed down at the end of the 1990s, and a new bridge was built over the Sheksna a dozen kilometres away from the old crossing. As a result, the only way residents could reach the villages of the Migachevo and Glazatovsky Selsoviets was to take personal transport. Nevertheless, the residents who left these villages for the cities have been slow to cut ties with their family homes and garden plots. During the summer months they flock to the countryside like migratory birds. As was the case for the sovkhoz "Maisky," the lands of the former "Vorobyevsky" sovkhoz fell into the hands of realtors and have been gradually sold off to city dwellers who want to build houses with a view of the river or lake.

The Soviet project of creating a "new rurality" proved to be just as unsuccessful as the government's belated attempts in the 1980s to preserve rural social and economic structures. The aid program for the Russian Non-Black Earth region adopted in 1977 quickly collapsed during the crises of perestroika.

Far-sighted village youths had already made their fateful choice. By tying progress with socialism, young villagers, unsatisfied even with the "new rurality" represented by urban-type settlements, moved to the city. Although they did not harbour illusions about attaining equal opportunities with urban residents, when the chance arose to leave the countryside and raise their social status through urban education, they were forced to choose global progress over loyalty. Only cities are believed capable of producing a modern person, and only they can offer the chance of a better life.

In his 2017 book *Où atterrir?* (translated into the English the following year as *Down to Earth*), the French philosopher Bruno Latour addresses the question of progress in the modern era.[1] He argues that the current model of social evolution, which focuses on levels of development and colonization, as well as on the opposition between the global and the local, is irrelevant because, in Latour's view, the main issue of our time is the question of survival on planet Earth in the face of limited natural resources, serious changes to the climate, and war. Latour intended to draw attention to new possibilities in understanding the dichotomy of the local and the global, which is pertinent to research about rural areas. According to the philosophy of the modern era, knowledge means understanding the signs of modernity and progress. People believe that knowledge brings the best components of civilization to the village, whether in the form of higher education levels, new agricultural technologies, or improved sanitary conditions for rural dwellings. In the modern age, notions of progress presupposed that the "rural" lagged behind the "urban" and that technology would provide a panacea for all ills. In time, however, it has become clear that not every experiment and form of radical interference in the lives of local communities for the sake of progress has had the desired effects. As I show in this book about Vologda villages, the unintended consequences can be quite dramatic.

The thirst for progress, manifested in a state initiative to complete the project of building socialism in the countryside and create equal rights for all Soviet citizens, irreparably altered local worlds within Vologda villages and the fates of their inhabitants. The state modernization system revealed to rural youths the limitations of their social position, and they chose the most accessible path to escape these constraints: receiving an education and migrating to the city. The Soviet socialist world view during the 1960s and '70s stopped associating inequality with the problems of the Soviet social structure. Instead, it reconceptualized inequality in terms of cultural geography. In this context, changing one's place of residence became a viable method for battling inequality. Nevertheless, inequality was not eradicated by this shift in official priorities; it was merely veiled and hidden, following those who sought to change their social status by relocating to the city. Those who left the countryside still had opportunities, albeit extremely limited ones, for upward social mobility, and the state continued to view these opportunities as a means of justifying the existence of socialism, urbanization, and industrially oriented progress.

The Program for Building Communism announced at the Twenty-Second CPSU Congress in 1961 was based on Soviet leadership's belief that eradicating class distinctions would lead to equal rights for all Soviet people, especially those who were deprived of such rights by their social origin. First and foremost, this applied to the sovkhoz peasantry, who until this time were not granted the rights held by other social groups, such as workers and public servants. However, the plan for equalizing all social classes lacked measures that would have allowed the peasantry to become full participants in the socialist future, where their "rural" conceptions about life would be taken into account, and they would be granted personal farms, cultural autonomy, and a lifestyle attuned to the specificities of their local environment. Instead, peasants were given access to the previously inaccessible privileges that other classes enjoyed, and which defined Soviet mainstream culture. In essence, there was no class parity on the table. In order to avoid discrimination based on social origin, rural people had to become part of a different class and change their identity. This was the ultimate cost of socialist development for the rural population of the USSR in the 1960s and '70s.

In Soviet discourse during this period, peasant kolkhoz workers were viewed as full members of the Soviet state; the only problem was that they were born into inadequately developed localities that needed to be transformed. It was for this reason that the key task of Soviet socialism in the countryside in the 1960s and '70s became the creation of a new rurality, one resembling Soviet cities.

The realization of this program was possible only with the help of enormous financial infusions, an endless supply of which was guaranteed by the post-war USSR's access to global markets and the development of global energy. This new reality reduced the value of autonomous rural economies in the USSR. The exploitation of the kolkhoz population was reduced significantly during the 1960s and '70s in comparison with previous decades, but the price for this was the abandonment of any attempt to find a compromise between the state and the peasantry, which, although it had taken a severe blow from collectivization, nonetheless managed to preserve rural worlds. In the 1960s, the peasantry had the opportunity to fully reject its cultural, economic, and political subjecthood. The village become a symbol of underdeveloped socialism that had to be turned into the city, just as peasants had to be turned into workers. Rural youths were assigned the primary role in this project.

The desire of Soviet leadership to build a classes society in the 1960s and '70s was based on a profoundly humanistic ideal. Nikita Khrushchev, who had deep empathy for the peasantry, sincerely believed that rejecting policies of economic and political discrimination towards the kolkhoz population would provide socialism with a new vitality. Slogans about equality took on a renewed impetus during the years of his leadership, but in the 1960s and '70s they were directed not towards the class origin of Soviet citizens but to the equality of urban and rural territories, an ideal the government strove to reach by providing access to general compulsory education for all. Soviet society in developed socialism was only formally divided between workers, peasants, and the intelligentsia. The most important fault lines in the Soviet social structure ran along geographical boundaries. In the 1960s, the belief in progress and the power of education and science appeared to be capable of changing the world for the better. It was precisely for this reason that the mission to finish building socialism seemed not to meet opposition among either the Soviet post-war elites, who felt the need for a democratized society after Stalin's "cult of personality," or residents of rural regions, who interpreted the push to make life easier in the countryside as a new stage of progress. Ironically, however, it was this faith in progress that became the impetus for the disappearance of rural worlds and agricultural production in the Russian North-West.

The new, urbanized rurality, although it was recognized as an alternative to the traditional village, nevertheless could not compete with industrial cities in the arena of socialist progress. New rural structures in the 1960s and '70s, urban-type settlements, held up as seats of progress, debased the cardinal virtues of rural existence – namely, the collective nature of the community and the ability of the rural world to maintain economic and cultural autonomy in the globally changing world. In essence, the vitality of rural communities was offered as a sacrifice to globalism, a phenomenon born from faith in the limitless possibilities of social progress. This faith, which appealed to people with promises of justice, as a rule, facilitated even more deep-rooted types of discrimination.

Inequality between the city and the countryside was not exclusive to the Soviet state in the 1960s and '70s. However, in the USSR it was based not so much on the geography of modernity (where levels of access to transportation infrastructure and markets varied among developed and undeveloped territories) as upon a whole complex of limitations bound tightly with social discrimination against a large number of the country's inhabitants and the belief that their class conceptions about property were dangerous to socialism. In this regard, Soviet idealogues in the post-war USSR were extremely thorough in their policy of "depeasantization," the origins of which can be traced back to collectivization. However, unlike in the 1930s, when only one segment of the peasant population was to be destroyed by the state as a group, in the 1960s the threat hung above the entire class, whose class consciousness was disallowed along with its right to independence in shaping its own future. In becoming the faceless "rural population" in the eyes of the state, the kolkhoz peasantry lost the ability to stand up for its way of life, its right to its culture, and its own vision of the future in the countryside.

Notes

Introduction

1 The *sovkhoz*, or state farm, was a form of organized agricultural production in the USSR that replaced the earlier collective farms (*kolkhozes*) and was widespread in the 1970s and '80s. In contrast to collective farms, state farms were large state enterprises with less economic autonomy.

2 Juliane Fürst, *Stalin's Last Generation: Soviet Post-War Youth and the Emergence of Mature Socialism* (Oxford University Press, 2010); Alexey Golubev, *The Things of Life: Materiality in Late Soviet Russia* (Cornell University Press, 2021); Elena Omelchenko, *Molodezh': Otkrytyy Vopros* (Simbirskaya kniga, 2004); Hilary Pilkington, *Russia's Youth and Its Culture: A Nation's Constructors and Constructed* (Routledge, 1994); Donald J. Raleigh, *Soviet Baby Boomers: An Oral History of Russia's Cold War Generation* (Oxford University Press, 2011); Benjamin Tromly, *Making the Soviet Intelligentsia: Universities and Intellectual Life Under Stalin and Khrushchev* (Cambridge University Press, 2015); Gleb Tsipursky, *Socialist Fun: Youth, Consumption, and State-Sponsored Popular Culture in the Soviet Union, 1945–1970* (University of Pittsburgh Press, 2016); Alexei Yurchak, *Everything Was Forever, Until It Was No More: The Last Soviet Generation* (Princeton University Press, 2006); Sergeĭ Ivanovich Zhuk, *Rock and Roll in the Rocket City: The West, Identity, and Ideology in Soviet Dniepropetrovsk, 1960–1985* (Woodrow Wilson Center Press, 2010).

3 Dmitry Kozlov, "Sotsializatsiya Sovetskoy Molodezhi Perioda 'ottepeli': Varianty Al'ternativnykh Identichnostey (Na Primere Arkhangel'skoy Oblasti)," *Laboratorium: Russian Review of Social Research* 4, no. 2 (2012): 115–29, www.soclabo.org/index.php/laboratorium/article/view/6/111.

4 Liubov' Nikolaevna Denisova, *Ischezayushchaya Derevnya Rossii: Nechernozem'ye v 1960–1980-Ye Gody* (Moscow: IRIRAN, 1996); Katja Bruisch, "The Soviet Village Revisited," *Cahiers Du Monde Russe* 57, no. 1 (2016): 81–100, https://doi.org/10.4000/MONDERUSSE.8332; Mikhail Alekseyevich Beznin

and Tatiana Mikhaylovna Dimoni, *Kapitalizatsiya v Rossiyskoy Derevne 1930–1980kh Godov* (Knizhnyy dom Librokom, 2009); Yuriy Afanas'ev, ed., *Sud'by Rossiyskogo Krest'yanstva* (Rossiyskiy gosudarstvenniy gumanitarniy universitet, 1996).

 5 The Program for Building Communism, also known as Third Program of the CPSU, became the central document for the Communist Party of the Soviet Union after its adoption at the Twenty-Second Congress on 31 October 1961. The program included an extended explanation of the political, economic, and social reforms adopted at the congress. The realization of the program's primary goal, the creation of a communist society, was intended to be achieved by 1980. Unlike other CPSU programs, the Third Program included concrete descriptions of the communist society of the future, which shaped Nikita Khrushchev's speech at the Twentieth Congress, and set out concrete timelines for the development of the communist future. Cf. Xenia A. Cherkaev, *Gleaning for Communism: The Soviet Socialist Household in Theory and Practice* (Cornell University Press, 2023), 97–115; P'otr Vail' and Alexandr Genis, *60-e. Mir sovetskogo cheloveka* (ACT, Corpus, 2001), 12–18.

 6 Oleg Popzov, *Zhizn' Vopreki* (Algoritm, 2018).

 7 A *kolkhoz*, or collective farm, was a form of organized agricultural production in the USSR. It combined private peasant lands into a single entity with common ownership. See Caroline Humphrey, *Marx Went Away – But Karl Stayed Behind* (University of Michigan Press, 1999).

 8 Catriona Kelly, "The End of Childhood and/or the Discovery of the *Tineidzher*? Adolescence in Soviet and Post-Soviet Culture," in *Eastern European Youth Cultures in a Global Context*, ed. Matthias Schwartz and Heike Winkel (Palgrave Macmillan, 2016), 23.

 9 Kelly, "The End of Childhood and/or the Discovery of the *Tineidzher*?"

10 Marshall Berman, *All That Is Solid Melts Into Air: The Experience of Modernity* (Simon and Schuster, 1982); Peter Wagner, *Moderne als Erfahrung und Interpretationen: Eine neue Soziologie zur Moderne* (UVK Universitätsverlag Konstanz, 2009).

11 Anna Krylova, "Soviet Modernity: Stephen Kotkin and the Bolshevik Predicament," *Contemporary European History* 23, no. 2 (2014): 167–92.

12 Reinhart. Koselleck, *Futures Past: On the Semantics of Historical Time* (Columbia University Press, 2004), 222.

13 Neringa Klumbyte and Gulnaz Sharafutdinova, eds., *Soviet Society in the Era of Late Socialism, 1964–1985* (Lexington Books, 2012), 4.

14 Shmuel N. Eisenstadt, "Multiple Modernities," *Daedalus* 129, no. 1 (2000): 1–29; Peter Wagner, "Multiple Trajectories of Modernity: Why Social Theory Needs Historical Sociology", *Thesis Eleven*, 100, no. 1 (2010): 53–60, https://doi.org/10.1177/0725513609353705.

15 Anthony Giddens, *The Consequences of Modernity* (Stanford University Press, 1990); Berman, *All That Is Solid Melts Into Air,* 7–10.

16 Katja Bruisch and Klaus Gestwa, "Expertise and the Quest for Rural Modernization in the Russian Empire and the Soviet Union," *Cahiers Du Monde Russe* 57, no. 1 (2016): 7–30, https://doi.org/10.4000/MONDERUSSE.8324.

17 David L. Hoffmann and Yanni Kotsonis, eds., *Russian Modernity: Politics, Knowledge, Practices* (St. Martin's Press, 2000); Ilya Gerasimov, *Modernism and Public Reform in Late Imperial Russia: Rural Professionals and Self-Organization, 1905–30* (Palgrave Macmillan, 2009); Michael David-Fox, *Crossing Borders: Modernity, Ideology, and Culture in Russia and the Soviet Union* (University of Pittsburgh Press, 2015); Stephen Kotkin, "Modern Times: The Soviet Union and the Interwar Conjecture," *Kritika: Explorations in Russian and Eurasian History* 2, no. 1 (2001): 111–64.

18 Tatiana Voronina, "Space and Time in the Socialist Countryside: All-Union Anniversaries in Vologda Rural Schools during the 1960s and 1970s," *Canadian Slavonic Papers* 65, no. 1 (2023): 7–29, https://doi.org/10.1080/00085006.2023.2168422.

19 Teodor Shanin, *Defining Peasants: Essays Concerning Rural Societies, Expolary Economies, and Learning from Them in the Contemporary World* (Basil Blackwell, 1990), 3.

20 James Scott introduced the term "high modernity" to describe how state policy interacts with rural communities. He contrasts "high modernity" with Mêtis, which he associates with local knowledge. James C. Scott, *Seeing Like a State: How Certain Schemes to Improve the Human Condition Have Failed* (Yale University Press, 1998), 311.

21 Ralph A. Thaxton Jr., *Salt of the Earth: The Political Origins of Peasant Protest and Communist Revolution in China* (University of California Press, 1997).

22 Koselleck, *Futures Past : On the Semantics of Historical Time,* 255.

23 David-Fox, *Crossing Borders,* 104–33.

24 Scott, *Seeing Like a State,* 309.

25 Michel Foucault, *Power/Knowledge: Selected Interviews and Other Writings, 1972–1977,* ed. Colin Gordon et al. (New York: Pantheon Books, 1980).

26 Foucault, *Power/Knowledge.*

27 Stephen J. Ball, *Foucault and Education: Disciplines and Knowledge* (Routledge, 2012); Pierre Bourdieu, "Systems of Education and Systems of Thought," in *Knowledge and Control: New Directions for the Socioloay of Education,* ed. Michael F.D. Young (Macmillan, 1971), 189–207.

28 Shanin, *Defining Peasants,* 150–6.

29 Yurchak, *Everything Was Forever,* 132–4.

30 Alexandr Kamkin, "Pyat' vekov eparchil," *Russkiy Sever,* 11 August 1992, 3.

31 Olga Naumova, "Istoria russkoy pravoslavnoy tserkvi v documentach sovetskich organizatsiy noveyshego vremeni (1918–1990 gg)," in

Regional'nyye aspekty istoricheskogo puti pravoslaviya: Arkhivy, istochniki, metodologiya issledovaniy: [sbornik], ed. Alexandr Kamkin (Istoricheskoe kraevedenie, 2001), 1:80.

32 Oleg Molodov, "Pravoslavnoe duchovenstvo Vologodskoy eparchii v 1960–1980 gody (po dokumentam GAVO)," in *Istoricheskoe kraevedenie I archivy*, ed. Alexandr Kamkin et al. (Vologda, 2002), 8:190–4.

33 Molodov, "Pravoslavnoe duchovenstvo," 190.

34 Victoria Smolkin *A Sacred Space Is Never Empty: A History of Soviet Atheism* (Princeton University Press, 2018).

35 Margaret Paxson, *Solovyovo: The Story of Memory in a Russian Village* (Woodrow Wilson Center Press; Indiana University Press, 2005); Elizabeth Warner and Svetlana Adonyeva, *We Remember, We Love, We Grieve: Mortuary and Memorial Practice in Contemporary Russia* (University of Wisconsin Press, 2021); Oleg Molodov, "Sovetskoe gosudarstvo I Russkaya pravoslavnaya tserkov' na Euvropeyskom Severe v 1960–1980 gody" (PhD diss., Cherepovetskiy Gosudarstvenniy Universitet, 2006), 12.

36 Denisova, *Ischezayushchaya Derevnya Rossii*, 4.

37 Denisova, 16.

38 Denisova, 16.

39 Vlasova Irina Vladimirovna, "Etnicheskaya istoriya i formirovaniye naseleniya Russkogo Severa," in *Russkiy Sever: Etnicheskaya Istoriya i Narodnaya Kul'tura. XII-XX Veka* (Nauka, 2001), 16–37. The Non-Black Earth region is an agricultural and economic region of north-western European Russia that received its name because its soil differs from the fertile soil of the Black Earth region to the south.

40 Mikhail Alekseyevich Beznin, *Krest'yanskiy Dvor v Rossiyskom Nechernozem'ye 1950–1965 Gody* (Vologodskiy pedagogocheskiy institut, 1991), 3.

41 "Vsesoyuznaya Perepis' Naseleniya 1979 g. Chislennost' Nalichnogo Naseleniya RSFSR, Avtonomnykh Respublik, Avtonomnykh Oblastey i Okrugov, Krayev, Oblastey, Rayonov, Gorodskikh Poseleniy, Sel-Raytsentrov i Sel'skikh Poseleniy s Naseleniyem Svyshe 5000," *Демоскоп Weekly*, accessed 27 December 2024, https://www.demoscope.ru/weekly/ssp/ussr_nac _79.php.

42 Denisova, *Ischezayushchaya Derevnya Rossii*, 121.

43 Elena Bogdanova, "Antropologiya derevenskoy dvukhetazhki: Ot issledovaniya zhilishcha k issledovaniyu soobshchestva," in *Vdali ot gorodov. Zhizn' postsovetskoy derevni*, ed. Elena Bogdanova, Olga Brednikova (Aleteyya, 2013): 105–26.

44 Sergey Alymov, "Nesluchaynoye Selo: Sovetskiye Etnografy i Kolkhozniki Na Puti ot Starogo k Novomu i Obratno," *Novoye Literaturnoye Obozreniye* 110, no. 1 (2010): 110–29

45 *Narodnoye Khozyaystvo Vologodskoy Oblasti Za Gody Sovetskoy Vlasti: Statisticheskiy Sbornik* (Statistika, 1967), 12.

46 *Narodnoye Khozyaystvo Vologodskoy Oblasti Za Gody Sovetskoy Vlasti*, 13.

47 Denisova, *Ischezayushchaya Derevnya Rossii*, 120.

48 *Narodnoye Khozyaystvo Vologodskoy Oblasti Za Gody Sovetskoy Vlasti*, 15.

49 GAVO, f. 1703, op. 20, d. 8618, l. 10.

50 Tatiana Voronina and Anna Sokolova, "Myslit' Kak Kommunisty: Protokoly Sel'skikh Partsobraniy 'epokhi Razvitogo Sotsializma,'" *Novoe Literaturnoe Obozrenie* 4, no. 164 (2020): 1–15.

1. Ruralism in the State Discourse of Developed Socialism

1 Sergey Alymov, "Ponyatiye 'Perezhitok' i Sovetskiye Sotsial'nyye Nauki v 1950–1960-Ye Gody," *Antropologicheskiy Forum* 16 (2012): 261–87.

2 Robert J. Balfour, Claudia Mitchell, and Relebohile Moletsane, "View of Troubling Contexts: Toward a Generative Theory of Rurality as Education Research," *Journal of Rural and Community Development* 3, no. 3 (2008): 100–11.

3 Keith Halfacree, "Rural Space: Constructing a Three-Fold Architecture," in *Handbook of Rural Studies*, ed. Paul Cloke, Terry Marsden, and Patrick Mooney (SAGE Publications, 2006), 57.

4 Paul Cloke, "Conceptualizing Rurality," in Cloke et al., *Handbook of Rural Studies*, 18.

5 Mitchell, Balfour, and Moletsane, "View of Troubling Contexts."

6 Anne Martin Matthews, "Variations in the Conceptualization and Measurement of Rurality: Conflicting Findings on the Elderly Widowed," *Journal of Rural Studies* 4, no. 2 (1988): 145.

7 Cloke, "Conceptualizing Rurality."

8 Boris Doktorov and Aleksandr Nikulin, "Teodor Shanin: Krest'yanovedeniye i Rossiya," *Krest'yanovedeniye* 5, no. 3 (2020): 146–72.

9 Mark Shucksmith and David L. Brown, *Routledge International Handbook of Rural Studies* (Routledge, 2019).

10 Stephen E. Hanson, *Time and Revolution: Marxism and the Design of Soviet Institutions* (University of North Carolina Press, 1997): 20.

11 Neil Melvin, *Soviet Power and the Countryside: Policy Innovation and Institutional Decay* (Palgrave Macmillan, 2003), 32.

12 Stanislav Petryashin, "Rabochiye v Sovetskoy Muzeynoy Etnografii 1950-Kh Godov: Klassovyy Analiz i Politika Vremeni," *Etnograficheskoye obozreniye* 4 (2021): 157–75; Ilya Gerasimov, *Plebeian Modernity: Social Practices, Illegality, and the Urban Poor in Russia, 1906–1916* (University of Rochester Press, 2018), 3.

13 Alymov, "Ponyatiye 'Perezhitok' i Sovetskiye Sotsial'nyye Nauki v 1950–1960-Ye Gody," 261–87; Alymov, "Nesluchaynoye Selo," 109–29

14 Henry Bernstein, "The 'Peasant Problem' in the Russian Revolution(s), 1905–1929," *Journal of Peasant Studies* 45, nos. 5–6 (2018): 1127–50.

15 Benno Ennker, "Sovetskiy Narod, Stalinskiy Rezhim i Konstitutsiya 1936 Goda v Politicheskoy Istorii Sovetskogo Soyuza," Perspectivia.net, accessed 28 December 2024, https://perspectivia.net/receive/ploneimport _mods_00011427.

16 Pitirim Sorokin and Carle C. Zimmerman, *Principles of Rural-Urban Sociology* (Henry Holt and Company, 1969).

17 Albert Baiburin, *Sovetskiy Pasport: Istoriya, Struktura, Praktika* (European University at St. Petersburg, 2019).

18 Baiburin, *Sovetskiy Pasport*, 104.

19 Melvin, *Soviet Power and the Countryside*, 32; Alexandr Nikulin, *Agrarniki, Vlast' i Selo: Ot Proshlogo k Nastoyashchemu* (Rossiyskaya akademiya narodnogo khozyaystva i gosudarstvennoy sluzhby pri Prezidente Rossiyskoy Federatsii, 2014), 6; Carol S. Leonard, *Agrarian Reform in Russia: The Road from Serfdom* (Cambridge University Press, 2010), 13–17.

20 Auri C. Berg, "Reform in the Time of Stalin: Nikita Khrushchev and the Fate of the Russian Peasantry" (PhD diss., University of Toronto, 2012), 4.

21 Katja Bruisch, "Knowledge and Power in the Making of the Soviet Village," in *Governing the Rural in Interwar Europe*, ed. Liesbeth Van de Grift and Amalia Ribi Forclaz (Routledge, 2018), 155.

22 Denisova, *Ischezayushchaya Derevnya Rossii*, 152.

23 Sheila Fitzpatrick, *Stalin's Peasants: Resistance and Survival in the Russian Village after Collectivization* (Oxford University Press, 1994), 7.

24 Many scholars have noted the principal importance of the Program for Building Communism for Soviet society. Xenia Cherkaev, for example, considers the program the primary manifestation of "Khrushchev's collective ethics" in the USSR, and argues that it profoundly affected socialist property policy over the following decades. See Cherkaev, *Gleaning for Communism*, 97–115. Stefan Guth has written in depth about how the Program for Building Communism influenced ideas about progress and temporality. In his view, the program's explicit declaration that the communist society of the future would be achieved in twenty years created a temporal framework and temporal limits for the interpretation of socialism. Stefan Guth, "One Future Only: The Soviet Union in the Age of the Scientific-Technical Revolution." *Journal of Modern European History* 13, no. 3 (2015): 355–76, doi:10.17104/1611-8944-2015-3-355.

25 "O Programme Kommunisticheskoy Partii Sovetskogo Soyuza. Doklad Tovarishcha N. S. Khrushcheva 18 Oktyabrya 1961. In 3 Vol. Part 1," in *XX s'yezd Kommunisticheskoy Partii Sovetskogo Soyuza 17–31 Oktyabrya 1961. Stenograficheskiy Otchet* (Izdatel'stvo Politicheskoy literatury, 1962), 167.

26 Bruisch and Gestwa, "Expertise and the Quest for Rural Modernization in the Russian Empire and the Soviet Union," 11.

27 Melvin, *Soviet Power and the Countryside*, 32; Alymov, "Ponyatiye 'Perezhitok' i Sovetskiye Sotsial'nyye Nauki v 1950–1960-Ye Gody," 262–3.

28 Alymov, "Ponyatiye 'Perezhitok' i Sovetskiye Sotsial'nyye Nauki v 1950–1960-Ye Gody," 261–87.

29 *Kinozhurnal Novosti Dnya. №46* (USSR, 1954), YouTube, uploaded 25 May 2020, www.youtube.com/watch?v=b97uxc7rJBA.

30 Melvin, *Soviet Power and the Countryside.*

31 Melvin, 34.

32 Aleksandr Ivanovich Alekseyev, "Sel'skoye Rasseleniye i Sel'skoye Khozyaystvo Nechernozemnoy Zony RSFSR: Problemy Izucheniya Vzaimosvyazey," in *Territorial' noye Planirovaniye Naseleniya: 4-Ye Mezhvedomstvennoye Soveshchaniye Po Geografii Naseleniya. Tbilisi, Noyabr' 1979 G* (GO SSSR, 1979), 125–6.

33 Vladimir Nikolaevich Gorlov, "Neudachnaya Popytka N.S. Khrushcheva Sozdat' Agrogoroda v Moskovskoy Oblasti v Poslevoyennyye Gody," *Vestnik Moskovskogo Gosudarstvennogo Oblastnogo Universiteta. Seriya Istoriya i Politicheskiye Nauki* 4 (2019): 227–8, https://doi.org/10.18384/2310-676X-2019-4-226-229.

34 *Narodnoye Khozyaystvo Vologodskoy Oblasti Za Gody Sovetskoy Vlasti.*

35 *O Merakh Po Dal' neyshemu Razvitiyu Sel' skogo Khozyaystva v Nechernozemnoy Zone RSFSR Postanovleniye TSK KPSS i Soveta Ministrov SSSR Ot 20 Marta 1974* (Politizdat, 1977).

36 Denisova, *Ischezayushchaya Derevnya Rossii.*

37 Aleksandr Ivanovich Alekseyev, "Chelovek i Priroda v Razvitii Sel'skoy Mestnosti Nechernozem'ya," *Regional'nyye Issledovaniya,* no. 4 (2014): 81–7.

38 Denisova, *Ischezayushchaya Derevnya Rossii.*

39 Sergey Vasilievich Vikulov, *Vstat' Poran'she, Shagnut' Podal'she: Ocherki i Stat'i* (Sovremennik, 1980).

40 GAVO, f. 70, op. 1, d. 11, l. 110.

41 GAVO, f. 70, op. 3, d. 222, l. 7.

42 A document that contained fundamental statistical information about the sovkhoz: number of workers, founding date, the existence of farms and sowed land, crop yields, etc.

43 GAVO, f. 70, op. 3, d. 222, l. 7.

44 VOANPI, f. 2959, op. 25, d. 12, l. 123.

45 Bruisch, "The Soviet Village Revisited," 82.

46 Melvin, *Soviet Power and the Countryside,* 81.

47 Afanas'ev, *Sud'by Rossiyskogo Krest'yanstva.*

2. Staying Rural: Ex-Peasants and Identities

1 Interview with Valentina B. (1948, Molochnoe, 2021).

2 *Sortuchastki* were special fields where plant varieties, called *sortovye,* were cultivated and tested for durability and yield in various local environments.

3 Matthews, "Variations in the Conceptualization and Measurement of Rurality."

4 Beznin and Dimoni, *Kapitalizatsiya v Rossiyskoy Derevne 1930–1980kh Godov.*

5 Ekaterina Mel'nikova, "'Odnazhdy v Studenuyu Zimnyuyu Poru … '
 Ideal'noye Detstvo v Ustnoy Biografii," *Neprikosnovennij Zapas* 73, no. 5
 (2010): 139–57.

6 Irina Paperno, *Stories of the Soviet Experience: Memoirs, Diaries, Dreams*
 (Cornell University Press, 2009), 1–55.

7 This was demonstrated most expressively by Adrian Toporov, who organized
 public readings of world literature in the peasant commune "May Morning"
 near Barnaul, and compiled a book based on the statements of the peasants.
 See Adrian Mitrofanovich Toporov, *Krest'yane o Pisatelyakh* (Konstanta,
 2015), 5–9.

8 Fitzpatrick, *Stalin's Peasants.*

9 Kathleen Parthé, *Russian Village Prose: The Radiant Past* (Princeton
 University Press, 1992), 48–50.

10 Laura J. Olson and Svetlana B. Adonyeva, *The Worlds of Russian Village
 Women: Tradition, Transgression, Compromise* (University of Wisconsin Press,
 2013).

11 Mikhail Lazarevich Lur'ye, "Poteryannyy Ray: Nostal'giya i Kommemoratsiya
 v Pesnyakh o Rodnoy Derevne," *Etnograficheskoye Obozreniye* 6 (2020): 31–51,
 https://doi.org/10.31857/S086954150013120-2.

12 Olson and Adonyeva, *Worlds of Russian Village Women,* 8–9.

13 Sergey Shtyrkov, *Predaniya ob inozemnom nashestvii: Krest'yanskiy narrativ i
 mifologiya landshafta (na materialakh Severo-Vostochnoy Novgorodchiny)* (Nauka,
 2012), 35.

14 Paxson, *Solovyovo,* 142–7.

15 Aleksandr Panchenko, *Ivan i Yakov – neobychnyye svyatyye iz bolotistoy mestnosti*
 (Novoye literaturnoye obozreniye, 2012), 315–16.

16 Parthé, *Russian Village Prose,* 48–64.

17 Paxson, *Solovyovo,* 89.

18 Richard Bradley, "Ritual, Time and History," *World Archaeology* 23, no. 2
 (1991): 209.

19 Sergey Shubin,"Istoriya Trudodnya (1930–1966) Kak Mery Truda i
 Instrument Yego Stimulirovaniya," *Vestnik Severnogo (Arkticheskogo) Federal'nogo
 Universiteta. Seriya: Gumanitarnyye i Sotsial'nyye Nauki,* no. 6 (2013): 31.

20 Stephen Lovell, "Dosug v Rossii: 'Svobodnoye' Vremya i Yego
 Ispol'zovaniye," *Antropologicheskiy Forum,* no. 2 (2005): 136–73.

21 Panchenko, *Ivan i Yakov,* 315; Shtyrkov, *Predaniya ob inozemnom nashestvii,*
 33; Olson and Adonyeva, *Worlds of Russian Village Women,* 23–43; Paxson,
 Solovyovo, 14.

22 Fedor Dudyrev, Ol'ga Romanova, and Aleksey Shabalin, *Starshaya shkola i
 yeye al'ternativy v sovetskoy i rossiyskoy praktike* (Natsional'nyy issledovatel'skiy
 universitet "Vysshaya shkola ekonomiki," 2017), 13.

23 Inreview with Valentina B. (1948, Molochnoe 2021).

24 Olson and Adonyeva, *Worlds of Russian Village Women*, 4.

25 Paxson, *Solovyovo*.

26 Giddens, *The Consequences of Modernity*.

27 Foucault, *Power/Knowledge*, 93.

28 Ann Hartman, "In Search of Subjugated Knowledge," *Journal of Feminist Family Therapy* 11, no. 4 (2000): 19–23, https://doi.org/10.1300/J086v11n04_03.

29 Ruth Panelli, Samantha Punch, and Elsbeth Robson, eds., *Global Perspectives on Rural Childhood and Youth: Young Rural Lives* (Routledge, 2010), 4.

30 Serguei Alex. Oushakine, "Pole Boya Na Lone Prirody: Ot Kakogo Nasledstva My Otkazyvalis," *Novoe Literaturnoe Obozrenie* 71 (2005): 263–98.

31 Berman, *All That Is Solid Melts Into Air*, 174.

32 Oushakine, "Pole Boya Na Lone Prirody," 274.

33 Rebecca Friedman, *Modernity, Domesticity and Temporality in Russia: Time at Home* (Bloomsbury Academic, 2020).

34 Krylova, "Soviet Modernity," 186.

35 Catriona Kelly, "Ob Izuchenii Istorii Detstva v Rossii XIX–XX Vekov," in *Kakoreya. Iz Istorii Detstva v Rossii i Drugikh Stranakh: Sbornik Statey i Materialov*, ed. Galina Makarevich (Nauchnaya kniga, 2008), 10.

36 Hugh Matthews, Mark Taylor, Kenneth Sherwood, and Faith Tucker, "Growing-Up in the Countryside: Children and the Rural Idyll," *Journal of Rural Studies*, no. 16 (2000): 141–53.

37 Kelly, "Ob Izuchenii Istorii Detstva v Rossii XIX–XX Vekov," 17.

38 Hugh Matthews and Melanie Limb, "Defining an Agenda for the Geography of Children: Review and Prospect," *Progress in Human Geography* 23, no. 1 (1999): 61–90.

39 Mary Ann Powell, Nicola Taylor, and Anne Smith, "Constructions of Rural Childhood: Challenging Dominant Perspectives," *Children's Geographies* 11, no. 1 (2013): 117.

40 Paul Thomson, *The Voice of the Past: Oral History* (Oxford University Press, 1978); Melissa Walker, *Southern Farmers and Their Stories: Memory and Meaning in Oral History* (University Press of Kentucky, 2006); Elizabeth Warner and Svetlana Borisovna Adonyena, *We Remember, We Love, We Grieve: Mortuary and Memorial Practice in Contemporary Russia* (University of Wisconsin Pres, 2020).

41 Panelli, Punch, and Robson, *Global Perspectives on Rural Childhood and Youth*; Powell et al., "Constructions of Rural Childhood," 117–31.

42 Nadezhda Konstantinovna Krupskaya, "Detskiy Trud v Kolkhoze," in *Pedagogicheskiye Sochineniya: Trudovoye Vospitaniye i Politekhnicheskoye Obrazovaniye*, vol. 4, ed. Nikolay Kirillovich Gincharov (Akademiya pedagogicheskikh nauk, 1959), 44–5.

43 Krupskaya, "Detskiy Trud v Kolkhoze," 44.

44 Maria Mayofis, "Pansiony Trudovykh Rezervov: Formirovaniye Sistemy Shkol-Internatov v 1954–1964 Godakh," *Novoe Literaturnoe Obozrenie* 142, no. 6 (2016): 292–324.

45 Yevgeniya Yegorovna Solov'yeva, ed., *Rodnaya Rech'. Kniga Dlya Chteniya v 4 Klasse* (Sovetskiye uchebniki, 1949), 96.

46 Interview with Alexandr K. (1955, Kargach 2018).

47 Interview with Alexandr K.

48 Interview with Yuri V. (1949, Molochnoe, 2018). In contrast to the condescending connotations attached to the word *muzhik*, or peasant man, in nineteenth-century literary sources, in the discourse of villagers the term has a neutral, or even positive, connotation. In this case, the speaker is emphasizing that the young boy works as well as an adult man. For more information of the word *muzhik*, see Irina Bashkova, "Semantika slova muzhik v diskurse V.P. Astaf'yeva," *Mir nauki, kul'tury, obrazovaniya* 5, no. 48 (2014): 105.

49 Interview with Yuri V. A word on the treatment of quotations here and below: When quoting from oral interviews, I use bracketed ellipses to indicate where a portion of the interviewee's original statement has been deliberately omitted, as opposed to interrupted or faltering speech on the part of the speaker, instances of which are indicated by unbracketed ellipses. However, when quoting from written sources (books, articles, various primary source documents, etc.), I have retained the convention of using unbracketed ellipses to indicate deliberate elisions.

50 Interview with Yuri V.

51 Interview with Alexandr K. (1955, Kargach, 2018).

52 Aleida Assmann, *Dlinnaya Ten' Proshlogo: Memorial'naya Kul'tura i Istoricheskaya Politika* (Novoe literaturnoe obozrenie, 2014), 223–5.

53 Matthews et al., "Growing-Up in the Countryside," 121.

54 Owain Jones, "Little Figures, Big Shadows," in *Contested Countryside Culture. Rurality and Socio-Cultural Marginalisation*, ed. Paul Cloke and Jo Little (London: Routledge, 1997), 158–79.

55 Powell et al., "Constructions of Rural Childhood," 118–19.

56 Göran Therborn, *Ot Marksizma k Postmarksizmu?* (Izdatel'skiy dom NIU VSHE, 2021), 141–4.

57 Alla Bolotova, "Colonization of Nature in the Soviet Union," *Historical Social Research* 29, no. 3 (2004): 104–23.

58 Douglas Weiner, *A Little Corner of Freedom: Russian Nature Protection from Stalin to Gorbachev* (University of California Press, 1999), 1–8.

59 Katerina Clark, *The Soviet Novel: History as Ritual* (Chicago University Press, 1981), 100–6.

60 Valentin Petrovich Katayev, "Beleyet Parus Odinokiy," in *Rodnaya Literatura: Khrestomatiya Dlya 5 Klassa*, ed. Nikolay Vladimirovich Kolokol'tsev

(Prosveshcheniye, 1969), 5–8; Mikhail Mikhaylovich Prishvin, "Kladovaya Solntsa," in Kolokol'tsev, *Rodnaya Literatura*, 120–50.

61 Anna Razuvalova, *Pisateli-"derevenshchiki" Literatura i Konservativnaya Ideologiya 1970-h Godov* (Novoe literaturnoe obozrenie, 2015).

62 "Rech' Sekretarya Stavropol'skogo Kraykoma Komsomola Vasiliya Kurilova," *Sel'skaya Molodezh*, no. 1 (1972): 5.

63 Margaret Paxson, *Solovyovo*, 122–47.

64 Interview with Tatyana K. (1958, Kabachino, 2018).

65 Interview with Yuri V. (1949, Molochnoe, 2018).

66 Interview with Tatyana K. (1958, Kabachino, 2018).

67 Baiburin, *Sovetskiy Pasport*, 179, 289.

68 Charles Taylor, "Chto Takoye Sotsial'noye Voobrazhayemoye?," *Neprekosnovenniy Zapas* 69, no. 1 (2010): 19–26.

69 Interview with Antonina K. (1942, Goritsy, 2018).

70 A *lespromkhoz* was a type of timber production enterprise in the USSR. People who worked in the logging sector had the status of workers rather than that of peasants, unlike those working on collective farms. This was reflected in the better food and grocery supplies available in logging settlements and timber industry enterprises as compared to villages. Anna Sokolova, "Invading the Void: Social Time Production as a Developmental Tool in the Late Soviet Periphery," *Canadian Slavonic Papers* 65, no. 1 (2023): 52–71.

71 Collective interview with Elena A., Tat'yana R., Irina, Alena, Ol'ga B. (Molochnoe, 2018).

72 Interview with Yuri V. (1949, Molochnoe, 2018).

73 Interview with Luda M. (1946, Molochnoe, 2021).

74 Interview with Luda M.

75 Interview with Luda M.

76 Interview with Vlad and Tatiana S. (1947, 1949, Kabachino, 2019). Names have been changed.

3. The Colonization of Rural Knowledge Begins

1 Michel Foucault, *Dits et écrits: Articles politiques conférences interviews, 1970–1984* (Praxis, 2002), 120.

2 Ball, *Foucault and Education*.

3 Bourdieu, "Systems of Education and Systems of Thought"; Greg Dimitriadis, "Popular Culture and the Sociology of Education," in *The Routledge International Handbook of the Sociology of Education*, ed. Michael W. Apple, Stephen J. Ball, and Luis Armando Gandin (Routledge, 2010), 190–9.

4 Karen Robson, *Sociology of Education in Canada* (Pearson Canada, 2013).

5 Simone White and Downey Jayne, "International Trends and Patterns in Innovation in Rural Education," in *Rural Education Across the World Models*

of Innovative Practice and Impact, ed. Simone White and Jayne Downey (Springer International, 2021), 3–21; Kai A. Schafft and Alecia Youngblood Jackson, eds., *Rural Education for the Twenty-First Century Identity, Place, and Community in a Globalizing World* (Penn State University Press, 2010); Vincent L. Griffiths, *The Problems of Rural Education* (International Institute for Educational Planning, 1968), https://unesdoc.unesco.org/ark:/48223/pf0000076492; William M. Reynolds, ed., *Forgotten Places: Critical Studies in Rural Education* (Lang, 2017); Cath Gristy, Linda Hargreaves, and Silvie R. Kučerová, eds., *Educational Research and Schooling in Rural Europe: An Engagement with Changing Patterns of Education, Space and Place* (Springer International, 2020).

6 George D. Spindler, ed., *Education and Anthropology* (Stanford University Press, 1955).

7 Sheila Fitzpatrick, *Education and Social Mobility in the Soviet Union: 1921–1934* (Cambridge University Press, 1979); Yevgeniy Mikhaylovich Balashov, *Shkola v Rossiyskom Obshchestve 1917–1927 Gg. Stanovleniye "novogo Cheloveka"* (Dmitriy Bulanin, 2003); Robert Vafich Shakirov, "Shkola i Obshchestvo: Sistemno-Kontseptual'nyy Analiz Reform Obrazovaniya v Rossii v XX Veke" (PhD diss., Kazan' State University, 1997); Oskar Anweiler and Friedrich Kuebart, *Die Sowjetische Schul – Und Berufsbildungsreform: Vorbereitung, Schwerpunkte, Beginn Der Realisierung* (Bundesinst. für Ostwiss. u. Internat. Studien, 1958).

8 David L. Ransell, "Russia and USSR," in *Children in Historical and Comparative Perspective: An International Handbook and Research Guide*, ed. Joseph M. Hawes and Ray N. Hiner (Greenwood Press, 1991), 471–90; Catriona Kelly, *Children's World: Growing Up in Russia, 1890–1991* (Yale University Press, 2007); Ilya Kukulin, Maria Mayofis, and Petr Safronov, eds., *Ostrova Utopii. Pedagogicheskoye i Sotsial'noye Proyektirovaniye Poslevoyennoy Shkoly (1940–1980-E)* (Novoe literaturnoe obozrenie, 2015); Kirill Maslinskiy and Svetlana Leont'yeva, eds., *Uchebnyy Tekst v Sovetskoy Shkole: Sbornik Statey* (Institut logiki, kognitologii i razvitiya lichnosti, 2008).

9 Dimitriadis, "Popular Culture and the Sociology of Education"; Kirill Maslinsky, "Sovetskaya Shkola v Svete Teorii Soprotivleniya, Ili Britanskiye Rostki Na Postsovetskoy Pochve," in *Gorodskiye Teksty i Praktiki. Tom I: Simvolicheskoye Soprotivleniye*, ed. Alexandra Archipova, Daria Radchenko, and Alexey Titkov (Izdatel'skiy dom "Delo" RANKhiGS, 2017), 264–82.

10 Some aspects of educational inequality under socialism are discussed in the following studies: Michal Šimáně, "Socialist Egalitarianism in Everyday Life of Secondary Technical Schools in Czechoslovakia During the Normalization Period (1969–89)," *Communist and Post-Communist Studies* 56, no. 1 (2023): 129–51; Irena Stonkuvienė, "The Equal and the More Equal: Pupils' Experiences of School in Lithuania in the Late Soviet Era," *Journal of Education Culture and Society* 14, no. 1 (2023): 124–42.

11 Catriona Kelly, "Shkol'nyy Val's: Povsednevnaya Zhizn' Sovetskoy Shkoly v Poslestalinskoye Vremya," *Antropologicheskiy Forum* 1 (2004): 104–55.

12 Kelly, "Shkol'nyy Val's," 149.

13 Leont'yeva and Maslinskiy, eds., *Uchebnyy Tekst v Sovetskoy Shkole*, 7.

14 For analysis and discussion of Soviet schools and the history of childhood, see Kelly, "Ob Izuchenii Istorii Detstva v Rossii XIX–XX Vekov."

15 Larry E. Holmes, *Stalin's School: Moscow's Model School No. 25, 1931–1937* (University of Pittsburgh Press, 1999); Slava Gerovitch, "'We Teach Them to Be Free': Specialized Math Schools and the Cultivation of the Soviet Technical Intelligentsia," *Kritika* 20, no. 4 (2019): 717–54, https://doi.org/10.1353/KRI.2019.0066; Maria Mayofis and Ilya Kukulin, "Matematicheskiye Shkoly v SSSR: Genezis Institutsii i Tipologiya Utopiy," in Kukulin et al., *Ostrova Utopii*, 241–316.

16 Ilya Kukulin, Maria Mayofis, and Piotr Safronov, "Namyvaya Ostrova: Pozdnesovetskaya Obrazovatel'naya Politika v Sotsial'nykh Kontekstakh," in Kukulin, *Ostrova Utopii*, 5–35.

17 "Obsuzhdeniye Stat'i Katriony Kelli Shkol'nyy Val's," *Antropologicheskiy Forum* 4 (2006): 7–128.

18 The school report compiled by the Vologodsky District Department of Public Education for the 1973–4 academic year stated that the number of students in cities and rural areas was almost equal. At that time, there were 105,257 urban students and 105,377 rural students attending school in Vologda Oblast. However, the number of rural schools in Vologda Oblast still far exceeded the number of urban ones, with 1,176 rural schools and 150 urban ones. GAVO, f. 2360, Op. 5, d. 282, l. 2.

19 Fridrich Filippov, *Vseobshcheye Sredneye Obrazovaniye v SSSR (Sotsiologicheskiye Problemy)* (Mysl', 1976); Liubov' Denisova, *Vseobshcheye Sredneye Obrazovaniye i Sotsial'nyy Progress Sela* (Nauka, 1988).

20 T.Yu. Trukhanovich, "O Primenenii 'klassovogo Podkhoda' v Sovetskoy Sisteme Obrazovaniya vo Vtoroy Polovine 1920-Kh Godov: (Po Dokumentam Cherepovetskogo Tsentra Khraneniya Dokumentatsii)," *Istoricheskoye Krayevedeniye i Arkhivy. Vologda* 8 (2002): 74–8.

21 Larisa Leonidovna Shpakovskaya, "Sovetskaya Obrazovatel'naya Politika: Sotsial'naya Inzheneriya i Klassovaya Bor'ba," *Journal Issledovaniy Socialnoy Politiki* 7, no. 1 (2010): 39–64.

22 GAVO, f. 2360, op. 5, d. 126, l. 42; GAVO, f. 2360, op. 5, d. 260, l. 2.

23 GAVO, f. 2360, op. 5, d. 94, l. 2.

24 Gerber and Hout, "Educational Stratification in Russia During the Soviet Period," 611.

25 Gerber and Hout, 613.

26 Theodore P. Gerber and Michael Hout, "Tightening Up: Declining Class Mobility During Russia's Market Transition," *American Sociological Review* 69, no. 5 (October 2004): 677, www.jstor.org/stable/3593034?seq=1.

27 GAVO, f. 2360, op. 5, d. 310, l. 110, 83.

28 RGASPI, f. 1, op. 41, d. 254, l. 64, 65.

29 GAVO, f. 2360, op. 5, d. 310, l. 110, 111.

30 GAVO, f. 2360, op. 5, d. 283, l. 61.

31 Zhanna Vladimirovna Chernova, "Sovremennyye Modeli Genderno-Segregirovannogo Obrazovaniya," *Zhurnal Issledovaniy Sotsial'noy Politiki* 4, no. 1 (2006): 56.

32 Chernova, "Sovremennyye Modeli Genderno-Segregirovannogo Obrazovaniya."

33 Yelena Zdravomyslova and Anna Temkina, "Gosudarstvennoye Konstruirovaniye Gendera v Sovetskom Obshchestve," *Zhurnal Issledovaniy Sotsial'noy Politiki* 1, nos. 3–4 (2010): 304.

34 Kukulin et al., "Namyvaya Ostrova"; Galina Ivanova, *Sovetskaya Shkola v 1950–1960-Ye Gody* (Fond "Moskovskoye vremya," 2018).

35 Gerber and Hout, "Educational Stratification in Russia During the Soviet Period."

36 Anna Temkina and Anna Rotkirkh, "Sovetskiye Gendernyye Kontrakty i Ikh Transformatsiya v Sovremennoy Rossii," in *Gendernyy Poryadok: Sotsiologicheskiy Podkhod*, ed. Elena Zdravomyslova and Anna Temkina (Europeyskiy Universiet v Sankt-Peterburge, 2007), 169–200.

37 Liubov' Denisova, *Rural Women in the Soviet Union and Post-Soviet Russia*, ed. and trans. Irina Mukhina (Routledge, 2010), 219.

38 Ilhan Dulger, "Compulsory Education and Learning," in *Encyclopedia of the Sciences of Learning*, ed. Norbert M. Seel (Springer, 2012), 697–700; Andy Green, *Education and State Formation: The Rise of Education Systems in England, France and the USA* (Macmillan, 1990).

39 VOANPI, f. 2522, op. 42, d. 88, l. 27.

40 Alexandr Vladimirovich Pyzhikov, "Reformirovanie Sistemy Obrazovania SSSR v Period Ottepeli (1953–1964)," *Voprosy Istorii*, no. 9 (2004): 99–103.

41 Pyzhikov, "Reformirovanie Sistemy Obrazovania," 100.

42 Ann Livschiz, "Pre-Revolutionary in Form, Soviet in Content? Wartime Educational Reforms and the Postwar Quest for Normality," *History of Education* 35, nos. 4–5 (2006): 541–60; Maria Mayofis, "Reshayushiy Rezept: Avtonomizatsia Shkol'noy Sistemy v Pozdnestalinskom SSSR," *Vestnik Pravoslavnogo Sviato-Tochonovskogo Gumanitarnogo Universiteta. Seria IV: Pedagogika.Psichologia* 4, no. 2 (2014): 65–82.

43 GAVO, f. 2360, op. 5, d. 49, l. 18.

44 VOANPI, f. 25, op. 66, d. 46, l. 101.

45 RGASPI, f. 1, op. 36, d. 63, l. 12, 15.

46 Filippov, *Vseobshcheye Sredneye Obrazovaniye v SSSR (Sotsiologicheskiye Problemy)*, 34.

47 Denisova, *Vseobshcheye Sredneye Obrazovaniye i Sotsial'nyy Progress Sela*, 35.

48 Filippov, *Vseobshcheye Sredneye Obrazovaniye v SSSR (Sotsiologicheskiye Problemy)*, 34–8.

49 Denisova, *Vseobshcheye Sredneye Obrazovaniye i Sotsial'nyy Progress Sela*, 41–53.

50 GAVO, f. 2360, op. 2a, d. 797, l. 1.

51 GAVO, f. 2360, op. 2a, d. 797, l. 2.

52 GAVO, f. 5031, op. 1, d. 46, l. 4.

53 GAVO, f. 2360, op. 2a, d. 797, l. 4.

54 GAVO, f. 2360, op. 2a, d. 797, l. 4.

55 Interview with Tatyana K. (1958, Kabachino, 2018).

56 Interview with Antonina K. (1942, Goritsy, 2018).

57 Interview with Tatyana K. (1958, Kabachino, 2018).

58 VOANPI, f. 1428, op. 27, d. 11, l. 1.

59 GAVO, f. 2202, op. 3, d. 193, l. 1.

60 GAVO, f. 2360, op. 5, d. 357, l. 6.

61 GAVO, f. 2360, op. 5, d. 49, l. 1; GAVO, f. 2360, op. 5, d. 451, l. 2.

62 GAVO, f. 2360, op. 5, d. 49, l. 1; GAVO, f. 2360, op. 5, d. 451, l. 2.

63 GAVO, f. 2360, op. 5, d. 49, l. 1; GAVO, f. 2360, op. 5, d. 451, l. 2.

64 Tatiana Ivanovna Zaslavskaya, "Kakoy Bit' Derevne?," *Molodoy Kommunist* 11 (1973): 91.

65 VOANPI, f. 2445, op. 25, d. 4, l. 52.

66 *Voprosy Ideologicheskoy Raboty KPSS: Sbornik Dokumentov (1965–1973)* (Politizdat, 1973), 558–64.

67 *Voprosy Ideologicheskoy Raboty KPSS*, 10.

68 *Voprosy Ideologicheskoy Raboty KPSS*.

69 GAVO, f. 2360, op. 5, d. 357, l. 56.

70 GAVO, f. 2360, op. 5, d. 357, l. 14.

71 GAVO, f. 2360, op. 5, d. 357, l. 14.

72 Mayofis, "Pansiony Trudovykh Rezervov."

73 GAVO, f. 2360, op. 5, d. 72, l. 2; GAVO, f. 2360, op. 5, d. 163, l. 32.

74 Ol'ga Pavlovna Ilyukha, "Karel'skiy Filipok: Regional'nyye Osobennosti Sotsiokul'turnogo Oblika Sel'skogo Shkol'nika Kontsa XIX – Nachala," *Antropologicheskiy Forum* 13 (2010): 242–70.

75 GAVO, f. 2360, Op. 5, d. 260, l. 5.

76 Mayofis, "Pansiony Trudovykh Rezervov."

77 GAVO, f. 2360, op. 5, d. 72, l. 2.

78 Judging by reports on schools in Vologda Oblast from the 1975–6 academic year, 19,463 people, or 54.7 per cent of the total number of rural students, lived in 345 school dormitories. GAVO, f. 2360, op. 5, d. 334, l. 4.

79 GAVO, f. 2360, op. 5, d. 126, l. 15.

80 VOANPI, f. 2445, op. 25, d. 4, l. 12.

81 GAVO, f. 2360, op. 5, d. 126, l. 16.

82 GAVO, f. 2360, op. 5, d. 334, l. 4.

83 Interview with Tatyana K. (1958, Kabachino, 2018).

84 Interview with Sergei A. (1954, Migachevo, 2019).

85 Interview with Vlad and Tatiana S. (1949, 1947, Kabachino, 2019);
    interview with Sergei A. (1954, Migachevo, 2019).

86 Interview with Sergey T. (1967, Vologda, 2018).

87 GAVO, f. 2360, op. 5, d. 357, l. 86.

88 According to Oblono statistics presented to the CPSU regional committee,
    there were 63 routes actively transporting children to schools in the
    Vologda region in 1980. Farms in the region allocated 32 buses, 7
    equipped vehicles, and 4 tractors for this purpose. VOANPI, f. 2522,
    op. 96, d. 53, l. 81.

89 GAVO, f. 2360, op. 5, d. 282, l. 8.

90 GAVO, f. 2360, op. 5, d. 334, l. 6.

91 GAVO, f. 2360, op. 5, d. 260, l. 5; GAVO, f. 2360, op. 5, d. 334, l. 6.

92 GAVO, f. 2360, op. 5, d. 260, l. 5; GAVO, f. 2360, op. 5, d. 334, l. 6.

93 GAVO, f. 2360, op. 5, d. 334, l. 4.

94 VOANPI, f. 2445, op. 25, d. 4, l. 15.

95 VOANPI, f. 2522, op. 73, d. 357, l. 1.

96 Shpakovskaya, "Sovetskaya Obrazovatel'naya Politika," 58.

97 Gerber and Hout, "Educational Stratification in Russia During the Soviet
    Period"; Shpakovskaya, "Sovetskaya Obrazovatel'naya Politika."

98 GAVO, f. 2360, op. 5, d. 234, l. 22, 23, 24, 25.

99 GAVO, f. 2360, op. 5, d. 357, l. 5.

100 GAVO, f. 2360, op. 5, d. 415, l. 19.

101 GAVO, f. 504, op. 3, d. 314, l. 54.

102 VOANPI, f. 4039, op. 35, d. 8, l. 65 ob., 66.

103 GAVO, f. 3, op. 314, l. 13.

104 Sergey Ivanovich Shubin, "Istoriya Trudodnya (1930–1966) Kak Mery
    Truda i Instrument Yego Stimulirovaniya," *Vestnik Severnogo (Arkticheskogo)
    Federal'nogo Universiteta. Seriya: Gumanitarnyye i Sotsial'nyye Nauki*, no. 6
    (2013): 34.

105 Interview with Alexandr K. (1955, Kargach, July 2018).

106 GAVO, f. 2360, op. 5, d. 52, l. 89.

107 GAVO, f. 2360, op. 5, d. 52, l. 79.

108 GAVO, f. 2360, op. 5, d. 357, l. 61.

109 GAVO, f. 2360, op. 5, d. 357, l. 61.

110 GAVO, f. 2202, op. 3, d. 86, l. 19.

111 Aleksandra Aleksandrovna Nesterova, "Rol' Komsomola v Organizatsii
    Trudovogo Vospitaniya Shkol'nikov Na Rubezhe 1950-Kh–1960-Kh Godov,"
    Politika i Obshchestvo 8 (2015): 178.

112 GAVO, f. 2360, op. 5, d. 357, l. 16.

113 GAVO, f. 521, op. 8, d. 335, l. 18.

114 GAVO, f. 521, op. 8, d. 335, l. 18.

115 GAVO, f. 521, op. 8, d. 335, l. 18, 22.

116 Interview with Galina Sh. (1949, Molochnoe, 2018).

117 Interview with Yuri V. (1949, Molochnoe, 2018).

118 VOANPI, f. 2522, op. 63, d. 82, l. 1.

119 GAVO, f. 2360, op. 5, d. 357, l. 67.

120 GAVO, f. 521, op. 8, d. 714, l. 52.

121 Interview with Elena V. (1950, Vologda, 2018).

122 Interview with Elena V.

123 Interview with Elena V.

124 Olson and Adonyeva, *Worlds of Russian Village Women*, 49.

125 Galina Michailovna Ivanova, "Sotsial'nyye Aspekty Razvitiya Sovetskoy Sistemy Obrazovaniya v 1960–1980e Gody," *Vesntik Slavianskich Kultur* 3 (2013): 25–31.

126 Interview with Galina Sh. (1949, Molochnoe, 2018).

127 Interview with Antonina K. (1942, Goritsy, 2018).

128 GAVO, f. 2360, op. 5, d. 357, l. 52.

129 Filippov, *Vseobshcheye Sredneye Obrazovaniye v SSSR (Sotsiologicheskiye Problemy)*, 107.

130 GAVO, f. 2360, op. 5, d. 357, l. 18.

131 VOANPI, f. 2445, op. 25, d. 4, l. 12.

132 Michael Corbett, "Rural Youth Out-Migration and Education: Challenges to Aspirations Discourse in Mobile Modernity," *Discourse: Studies in the Cultural Politics of Education* 38, no. 3 (2017): 429–44, https://doi.org /10.1080/01596306.2017.1308456, 430.

4. Education Is Enlightenment, Ignorance Is Darkness

1 Filippov, *Vseobshcheye Sredneye Obrazovaniye v SSSR (Sotsiologicheskiye Problemy)*; Denisova, *Vseobshcheye Sredneye Obrazovaniye i Sotsial'nyy Progress Sela*; David Konstantinovskiy, *Neravenstvo i Obrazovaniye. Opyt Sotsiologicheskikh Issledovaniy Zhiznennogo Starta Rossiyskoy Molodezhi (1960-Ye Gody–Nachalo 2000-Kh)* (SFC, 2008).

2 Griffiths, *The Problems of Rural Education*; White and Jayne, "International Trends and Patterns in Innovation in Rural Education."

3 Denisova, *Vseobshcheye Sredneye Obrazovaniye i Sotsial'nyy Progress Sela*; Filippov, *Vseobshcheye Sredneye Obrazovaniye v SSSR (Sotsiologicheskiye Problemy)*.

4 Griffiths, *The Problems of Rural Education*; Julia Weiss and Christin Heinz-Fischer, "The More Rural the Less Educated? An Analysis of National Policy Strategies for Enhancing Young Adults' Participation in Formal and Informal Training in European Rural Areas," *Youth* 2, no. 3 (2022): 405–21, https://doi.org/10.3390/YOUTH2030030; Chad Gaffield, "Children's Lives

and Academic Achievement in Canada and the United States," *Comparative Education Review* 38, no. 1 (1994): 36–64.

5 Andrew Brantlinger, Laureland Cooley, and Ellen Brantlinger, "Families, Values, and Class Relations: The Politics of Alternative Certifcation," in Apple et al., *Routledge International Handbook of the Sociology of Education,* 179–89; Stephen J. Ball, *Education Policy and Social Class: The Selected Works of Stephen Ball* (Routledge, 2006).

6 James Collins, "Social Reproduction in Classrooms and Schools," *Annual Review of Anthropology* 38 (October 2009): 33–48, https://doi.org/10.1146/ANNUREV.ANTHRO.37.081407.085242.

7 Ball, *Education Policy and Social Class.*

8 Annette Lareau, *Unequal Childhoods: Class, Race, and Family Life, with an Update a Decade Later* (University of California Press, 2011), 3–7.

9 Paul E. Willis, *Learning to Labor: How Working Class Kids Get Working Class Jobs,* 2nd ed. (Columbia University Press, 1977), 1; Lareau, *Unequal Childhoods,* 7; Collins, "Social Reproduction in Classrooms and Schools."

10 Geoge Konrad and Ivan Szelenyi, *The Intellectuals on the Road to Class Power* (Harvester Press, 1979); Anna Paretskaya, "A Middle Class Without Capitalism? Socialist Ideology and Post-Collectivist Discourse in the Late-Soviet Era," in *Soviet Society in the Era of Late Socialism, 1964–1985,* ed. Neringa Klumbyte and Gulnaz Sharafutdinova (Lexington Books, 2012), 43–66.

11 Sheila Fitzpatrick, "Ascribing Class," *Journal of Modern History* 65, no. 4 (1993): 745–70, https://doi.org/10.1086/244724.

12 Paretskaya, "A Middle Class Without Capitalism?"

13 Isak Froumin and Oleg Leshukov, "The Soviet Flagship University Model and Its Contemporary Transition," in *The New Flagship University: Changing the Paradigm from Global Ranking to National Relevancy,* ed. John Aubrey Douglass (Palgrave Macmillan, 2016), 173–89.

14 Gerber and Hout, "Tightening Up."

15 Sergey Alymov, "Intellektualy Zastoya: Mezhdu Ofitsial'nym Kollektivizmom i Vystradannoy Elitarnost'yu," in *Eto Bylo Navsegda 68/85* (Gosudarstvennaya tret'yakovskaya galereya, 2020), 19.

16 Shubin, "Istoriya Trudodnya (1930–1966) Kak Mery Truda i Instrument Yego Stimulirovaniya," 34.

17 Alymov, "Nesluchaynoye Selo," 110.

18 Petr Iosifovich Simush, *Socialniy Portret Sovetskogo Krest'yanstva* (Poligrafist, 1976); Rozalina Vladimirovna Ryvkina, *Obraz Zhizni Sel'skogo Naseleniya: Metodologiya, Metodika i Rezul'taty Izucheniya Sotsial'no-Ekonomicheskikh Aspektov Zhiznedeyatel'nosti* (Nauka, 1978).

19 Alymov, "Nesluchaynoye Selo," 109–29.

20 "Rossiyskaya Povsednevnost': Elektronnyy Arkhiv," Fotoarkhiv Y.A. Galeva, accessed 26 December 2024, http://daytodaydata.ru/type/themgroups?dv=3437194&at=3394299&ot=3393999&cd=10.

21 Oleg Gorbachev, *Na Puti k Gorodu: Sel'skaya Migratsiya v Tsentral'noy Rossii (1946–1985) i Sovetskaya Model' Urbanizatsii* (MPGU, 2002), 5.

22 Olson and Adonyeva, *Worlds of Russian Village Women.*

23 Filippov, *Vseobshcheye Sredneye Obrazovaniye v SSSR (Sotsiologicheskiye Problemy),* 6–7.

24 Gerber and Hout, "Educational Stratification in Russia During the Soviet Period," 611–60.

25 Gerber and Hout, 611.

26 Weiss and Heinz-Fischer, "The More Rural the Less Educated?"

27 Gaffield, "Children's Lives and Academic Achievement in Canada and the United States," 44.

28 Mikhail Alekseyevich Beznin and Tatiana Mikhaylovna Dimoni, "Intellektualy v Sel'skom Khozyaystve Rossii 1930–1980-Kh Gg," *Yaroslavskiy Pedagogicheskiy Vestnik* 1 (2013): 29–41.

29 Interview with Elena V. (1950, Vologda, July 2018).

30 Interview with Yuri V. (1949, Molochnoe, 2018).

31 Interview with Tatyana K. (1958, Kabachino, 2018).

32 Interview with Sergey T. (1967, Vologda, 2018).

33 Judith Pallot, "Rural Depopulation and the Restoration of the Russian Village Under Gorbachev," *Soviet Studies* 42, no. 4 (2019): 655–74; Gorbachev, *Na Puti k Gorodu.*

34 RGASPI, f. 1, op. 36, d. 63, l. 15.

35 RGASPI, f. 1, op. 36, d. 63, l. 15.

36 GAVO, f. 2360, op. 5, d. 72, l. 17.

37 GAVO, f. 2360, op. 5, d. 163, l. 11.

38 Denisova, *Vseobshcheye Sredneye Obrazovaniye i Sotsial'nyy Progress Sela.*

39 Interview with Iya V. (1953, Molochnoe, 2018).

40 Sue Bridger, "Rural Youth," in *Soviet Youth Culture* (Macmillan, 1989), 83–102.

41 Interview with Yuri V. (1949, Molochnoe, 2018).

42 Interview with Tatyana K. (1958, Kabachino, 2018).

43 Interview with Tatyana K.

44 GAVO, f. 504, op. 3, d. 506, l. 247.

45 GAVO, f. 504, op. 3, d. 506, l. 1, 2.

46 GAVO, f. 504, op. 3, d. 506, l. 1, 2.

47 Holmes, *Stalin's School*; Gerovitch, "'We Teach Them to Be Free.'"

48 Yuriy L'vovich Slezkin, *Dom Pravitel'stva. Saga o Russkoy Revolyutsii* (Corpus, 2019).

49 Raleigh, *Soviet Baby Boomers,* 117; Maria Mayofis, "Strakh Vliyaniya: K Ranney Istorii Sovetskikh Yazykovykh Spetsshkol (Konets 1940-Kh–Nachalo 1960-Kh Godov)," *Voprosy Obrazovania* 2 (2016): 287.

50 "Iz Istorii Razvitiya Obrazovaniya. Istoriya Obrazovaniya v Vologodskom Kraye," Vek Obrazovania, accessed 26 December 2024, https://www.booksite.ru/education/main/history/1.htm.

51 "Sozdaniye Sovetskoy Shkoly. 1930–1940-Ye Gody," *Kraevedenie, Istoria Cherepovza*, 12 December 2017, https://cherkray.ru/?page =cherprosvet&view=3.

52 GAVO, f. 2360, op. 5, d. 357, l. 153.

53 GAVO, f. 2202, op. 3, d. 42, l. 7.

54 Interview with Galina Sh. (1949, Molochnoe, 2018).

55 Kirill Maslinsky, "Uchitel' Zheleznodorozhnoy Shkoly (k Tipologii Sovetskikh Pedagogicheskikh Soobshchestv)," *Antropologicheskiy Forum* 16 (2012): 403–18.

56 Interview with Vladimir and Tatiana S. (1949, 1947, Kabachino, 2019).

57 GAVO, f. 504, op. 3, d. 401, l. 8.

58 GAVO, f. 504, op. 3, d. 506, l. 38.

59 GAVO, f. 504, op. 3, d. 506, l. 44, 45.

60 GAVO, f. 504, op. 3, d. 506, l. 65.

61 GAVO, f. 2202, op. 3, d. 57, l. 206 ob.

62 GAVO, f. 2202, op. 3, d. 57, l. 206 ob.

63 GAVO, f. 2202, op. 3, d. 57, l. 206.

64 GAVO, f. 2202, op. 3, d. 57, l. 205.

65 GAVO, f. 2202, op. 3, d. 218, l. 17 ob.

66 GAVO, f. 2202, op. 3, d. 218, l. 17 ob.

67 Interview with Elena V. (1950, Vologda, 2018).

68 Interview with Zinaida S. (1949, Kabachino, 2018).

69 Lovell, "Dosug v Rossii," 136–73.

70 Lovell, 146.

71 Lovell, 170.

72 RGASPI, f. 1, op. 36, d. 78, l. 96.

73 Ryvkina, *Obraz Zhizni Sel'skogo Naseleniya*, 211.

74 Ryvkina, 211.

75 Interview with Yuri V. (1949, Molochnoe, 2018).

76 GAVO f. 2202, op. 3, d. 57, l. 185 ob.

77 Interview with Antonina K. (1942, Goritsy, 2018).

78 GAVO, f. 2202, op. 3, d. 57, l. 184 ob.

79 Interview with Alexandr K. (1955, Kargach, 2018).

80 Interview with Yuri V. (1949, Molochnoe, 2018).

81 GAVO, f. 2360, op. 5, d. 415, l. 32.

82 Interview with Antonina K. (1942, Goritsy, 2018).

83 Interview with Yuri V. (1949, Molochnoe, 2018).

84 Interview with Nina S. (1963, Mayskiy, 2018).

85 GAVO, f. 2360, op. 5, d. 72, l. 71.

86 GAVO, f. 2360, op. 5, d. 163, l. 33.

87 Filippov, *Vseobshcheye Sredneye Obrazovaniye v SSSR (Sotsiologicheskiye Problemy)*, 9.

5. On the Margins of Vologda Villages: Poor-Performing and "Mentally Deficient" Students

1 GAVO, f. 521, op. 8, d. 266, l. 47.

2 GAVO, f. 521, op. 8, d. 316, l. 89 ob.

3 GAVO, f. 521, op. 8, d. 220, l. 44.

4 GAVO, f. 521, op. 8, d. 220, l. 33.

5 GAVO, f. 521, op. 8, d. 316, l. 82 ob.

6 GAVO, f. 2202, op. 3, d. 42, l. 6.

7 GAVO, f. 2202, op. 3, d. 139, l. 4.

8 VOANPI, f. 2522, op. 65, d. 69, l. 4, 5

9 Ball, *Foucault and Education.*

10 Kirill Maslinsky, "Sovetskaya Shkola v Svete Teorii Soprotivleniya, Ili Britanskiye Rostki Na Postsovetskoy Pochve," 264–82.

11 Mark G. McFadden, "Resistance to Schooling and Educational Outcomes: Questions of Structure and Agency," *British Journal of Sociology of Education* 16, no. 3 (1995): 293–308, www.jstor.org/stable/1393261?searchText =&searchUri=&ab_segments=&searchKey=&refreqid=fastly-default%3A9244 f23d33db882c300939785c7cf3fc.

12 Willis, "Learning to Labor."

13 Maslinsky, "Sovetskaya Shkola v Svete Teorii Soprotivleniya, Ili Britanskiye Rostki Na Postsovetskoy Pochve," 264.

14 Maria Cristina Galmarini-Kabala, *The Right to Be Helped: Deviance, Entitlement, and the Soviet Moral Order* (Northern Illinois University Press, 2016).

15 Willis, "Learning to Labor"; Dimitriadis, "Popular Culture and the Sociology of Education"; Ball, *Education Policy and Social Class.*

16 Bourdieu, "Systems of Education and Systems of Thought."

17 Mayofis, "Pansiony Trudovykh Rezervov."

18 Kirill Maslinsky, "The New Powers of the Pedsovet: Social Control during the Thaw and the Transformation of Disciplinary Practice in a Town School, 1953–68," *Russian Review* 79, no. 2 (2020): 227–45, https://doi.org /10.1111/russ.12264; Yuriy Alekseyevich Sadovnikov, "Gosudarstvennyye i Obshchestvennyye Struktury i Komissiya Po Delam Nesovershennoletnikh Chuvashii v 1960-Ye Gody," in *Nuzhda i Poryadok: Istoriya Sotsial'noy Raboty v Rossii,* ed. Pavel Vasil'yevich Romanov and Yelena Rostislavovna Yarskaya-Smirnova (Nauchnaya kniga, 2005), 353–74.

19 Willis, *Learning to Labor.*

20 Ilyukha, "Karel'skiy Filipok"; Natal'ya Sergeyevna Vorotnikova, "Otnosheniye Krest'yan k Nachal'nomu Obrazovaniyu v Vologodskoy Gubernii vo Vtoroy Polovine XIX–Nachale XX Vv," in *Ledentsovskiye Chteniya. Biznes. Nauka. Obrazovaniye. Materialy Mezhdunarodnoy Nauchno-Prakticheskoy Konferentsii, 22 Aprelya 2009 Goda,* ed. Irina Ivanovna Lyutova

and Tamara Vladimirovna Lodkina (Moskovskiy gumanitarnyy universitet, 2009), 342–7.

21 Examples of village residents who left the Migachevo region before the start of the Khrushchev reforms include Valentina B., who left Kabachino to work as a nanny in the 1950s; Zinaida V., who was sent by her parents at the age of ten to work as a nanny in Leningrad in the 1930s; and Alexander S., who was mobilized to Leningrad in 1945 through the "labour recruitment" program. The primary cities that attracted migration from Vologda Oblast villages were Leningrad, Cherepovets, Murmansk, Arkhangelsk, and Vorkuta.

22 VOANPI, f. 2522, op. 68, d. 109, l. 114.

23 Inteview with Eugeniy and Galina Ch. (1948, Sosunovo, July 2018).

24 Yuliya Yur'yevna Marinicheva, "Tekhnika Tela: Istoriya, Pamyat' i Metis," in *Pervichnyye Znaki/Naznachennaya Real'nost'*, ed. Svetlana Borisovna Adon'yeva (Proppovskiy tsentr, 2017), 47–74.

25 During a 1972 inspection of the Kirillovsky District Department of Public Education, inspector Sokolova wrote that the district "failed to make decisive improvements in labor education issues for school students." Only in the Charozerskaya and Kirillovskaya Secondary Schools was "labour training on par with obtaining a profession." As for the rest, either "labour training was not conducted," or it was limited to workshops. GAVO, f. 2207, op. 3, d. 139, l. 3.

26 RGASPI, f. 1, op. 39, d. 44, l. 25, 26.

27 Scott, *Seeing Like a State*.

28 Leonard, *Agrarian Reform in Russia*, 85–121; Alec Nove, *An Economic History of the USSR, 1917–1991* (Penguin Books, 1992), 377–82.

29 Jenny Leigh Smith, *Works in Progress: Plans and Realities on Soviet Farms, 1930–1963* (Yale University Press, 2014); Julia Obertreis, *Imperial Desert Dreams: Cotton Growing and Irrigation in Central Asia, 1860–1991* (V&R Unipress, 2017).

30 Beznin and Dimoni, "Intellektualy v Sel'skom Khozyaystve Rossii 1930–1980-Kh Gg," 29–41.

31 Bruisch, "The Soviet Village Revisited," 81–100.

32 Mikhail Alekseyevich Beznin, *Krest'yanskiy Dvor v Rossiyskom Nechernozem'ye 1950–1965 Gody* (Vologodskiy pedagogocheskiy institut, 1991), 107, 108.

33 GAVO, f. 1703, op. 19, d. 59, l. 1–3

34 Interview with Galina and Evgeny H. (1948, 1952, Sosunovo, 2018).

35 Maslinsky, "The New Powers of the Pedsovet."

36 GAVO, f. 2360, op. 5, d. 235, l. 73.

37 GAVO, f. 2360, op. 5, d. 235, l. 74.

38 In a 1962 report on restructuring the public education system in Kirillovsky District, it was recorded that "the material base of most schools does not meet requirements. It is necessary to build educational structures and

boarding schools in response to the growth of the student body. Currently there is an acute shortage of classrooms. There is a real possiblity of a transition to teaching in two shifts during the 1962–3 academic year in the Kuzinskaya, Kirillovskaya, and Vognemskaya Eight-Year Schools, as well as in other schools that still need to be reorganized from the seven-year to the eight-year model. These schools lack classrooms, gyms, canteens, and small buildings for workshops." VOANPI, f. 2522, op. 66, d. 102, l. 53.

39 GAVO, f. 504, op. 3, d. 322, l. 9.

40 GAVO, f. 504, op. 3, d. 329, l.89.

41 GAVO, f. 521, op. 1, d. 2, l. 60.

42 Interview with Elena V. (1950, Vologda, July 2018).

43 GAVO, f. 504, op. 3, d. 506, l. 219.

44 GAVO, f. 504, op. 3, d. 506, l. 219.

45 GAVO, f. 504, op. 3, d. 506, l. 219.

46 GAVO, f. 504, op. 3, d. 506, l. 219.

47 During the 1960s and '70s, student grades in the Soviet Union were assessed according to a 5-point scale, with 5 as the highest result and 1 the lowest. A 2, *dvoika*, or a 1, *edinitsa*, were considered unsatisfactory grades. Thus, students who performed poorly were known as *dvoichniki*, derived from the word for the number 2.

48 GAVO, f. 504, op. 3, d. 506, l. 219.

49 GAVO, f. 2202, op. 3, d. 139, l. 4.

50 GAVO, f. 2202, op. 3, d. 139, l. 4.

51 Sadovnikov, "Gosudarstvennyye i Obshchestvennyye Struktury i Komissiya Po Delam Nesovershennoletnikh Chuvashii v 1960-Ye Gody," 353–74.

52 GAVO, f. 521, op. 8, d. 134, l. 78.

53 GAVO, f. 521, op. 8, d. 316, l. 36.

54 GAVO, f. 521, op. 8, d. 266, l. 13–17.

55 Maria Cristina Galmarini-Kabala, "'Moral'no Defektivnyi, Prestupnik Ili Psikhicheskii Bol'noi? Detskie Povedencheskie Deviatsii i Sovetskie Distsipliniruiushchie Praktiki: 1935–1957,'" in Kukulin et al., *Ostrova Utopii*, 107–51.

56 Fürst, *Stalin's Last Generation*; Brian LaPierre, *Hooligans in Khrushchev's Russia* (University of Wisconsin Press, 2012).

57 GAVO, f. 521, op. 8, d. 316, l. 19.

58 Interview with Galina Sh. (1949, Molochnoe, 2018).

59 Interview with Antonina K. (1942, Goritsy, 2018).

60 For example, the Vologodsky District General Education Fund for the 1962–3 academic year spent 12,977 of its 15,018-rouble budget providing students with material assistance. This included 3,567 roubles that were spent on the purchase of shoes and clothes, and 7, 503 roubles spent on food. GAVO, f. 504, op. 3, d. 306, l. 3.

61 GAVO, f. 2202, op. 3, d. 57, l. 173.

62 Maslinsky, "The New Powers of the Pedsovet."

63 GAVO, f. 521, op. 8, d. 316, l. 86 ob.

64 GAVO, f. 521, op. 8, d. 379, l. 7.

65 GAVO, 521, op. 8, d. 316, l. 89 ob.

66 GAVO, f. 2202, op. 3, d. 42, l. 16.

67 Kelly, *Children's World*; Galmarini-Kabala, *The Right to Be Helped*; Fürst, *Stalin's Last Generation*.

68 GAVO, f. 521, op. 8, d. 316, l. 32, 33.

69 GAVO, f. 521, op. 8, d. 316, l. 32, 33.

70 Interview with Antonina K. (1942, Goritsy, July 2018).

71 After the reforms of 1958, all rural elementary schools were attached to an eight-year or secondary school. This arrangement was called a "bush-like" network. The more senior teachers who worked at eight-year and secondary schools were supposed to mentor their colleagues from elementary schools.

72 Dmitry Kozlov, "Neofitsial'nyye Gruppy Sovetskikh Shkol'nikov 1940–1960-Kh Godov: Tipologiya, Ideologiya, Praktik," in Kukulin et al., *Ostrova Utopii*, 451–95; Gleb Tsipursky, "Ulichnyy Mir i Molodyye Khuligany v Post-Stalinskom Sovetskom Soyuze," in *Molodezhnyye Ulichnyye Gruppirovki: Vvedeniye v Problematiku*, ed. Dmitry Gromov and Natal'a Pushkareva (Institut rossiyskoy istorii RAN, 2009), 73–93.

73 Galmarini-Kabala, *The Right to Be Helped*.

74 Matthias Neumann, "'Youth, It's Your Turn!': Generations and the Fate of the Russian Revolution (1917–1932)," *Journal of Social History* 46, no. 2 (2012): 273–304, https://doi.org/10.1093/jsh/shs098; Anne E. Gorsuch, *Youth in Revolutionary Russia* (Indiana University Press, 2000); Alan M. Ball, *And Now My Soul Is Hardened: Abandoned Children in Soviet Russia, 1918–1930* (University of California Press, 1994).

75 Kelly, *Children's World*; David R. Shearer, *Policing Stalin's Socialism: Repression and Social Order in the Soviet Union, 1924–1953* (Yale University Press, 2009).

76 Galmarini-Kabala, *The Right to Be Helped*.

77 Miriam Dobson, *Khrushchev's Cold Summer: Gulag Returnees, Crime, and the Fate of Reform After Stalin* (New York: Cormell University Press, 2009).

78 Galmarini-Kabala, "'Moral'no Defektivnyi, Prestupnik Ili Psikhicheskii Bol'noi?," 110.

79 Galmarini-Kabala, 118.

80 LaPierre, *Hooligans in Khrushchev's Russia*.

81 GAVO, f. 504, op. 3, d. 321, l. 53.

82 GAVO, f. 521, op. 8, d. 220, l. 29.

83 GAVO, f. 521, op. 8, d. 316, l. 17.

84 GAVO, f. 504, op. 3, d. 426, l. 5.

85 GAVO, f. 504, op. 3, d. 426, l. 5.

86 GAVO, f. 521, op. 8, d. 110, l. 105.

87 In a 1977 Vologda Oblast Executive Committee report on juvenile affairs commissions, it was indicated that "higher juvenile delinquency was observed" in Kubensky Selsoviet, where Specialized Professional Technical College 2 was located. GAVO, f. 521, op. 8, d. 379, l. 121.

88 "O Vvedenii v Deystviye Tipovogo Polozheniya o Spetsial'noy Obshcheobrazovatel'noy Shkole-Internate (Shkole) Dlya Umstvenno Otstalykh Detey (Vspomogatel'noy Shkole)" [1978], Garant, accessed 26 December 2024, https://base.garant.ru/70587788/.

89 GAVO, f. 2360, op. 5, d. 72, l. 1a.

90 GAVO, f. 2360, op. 5, d. 94, l. 2.

91 GAVO, f. 2360, op. 5, d. 94, l. 7.

92 GAVO, f. 2360, op. 5, d. 235, l. 2.

93 GAVO, f. 2360, op. 5, d. 415, l. 2.

94 GAVO, f. 1703, op. 20, d. 7526, l. 10, 10 ob.

95 GAVO, f. 504, op. 3, d. 329, l. 150.

96 GAVO, f. 504, op. 3, d. 329, l. 150 ob.

97 GAVO, f. 504, op. 3, d. 329, l. 150 ob.

98 GAVO, f. 504, op. 3, d. 329, l. 150 ob.

99 GAVO, f. 504, op. 3, d. 329, l. 150 ob.

100 GAVO, f. 504, op. 3, d. 329, l. 150 ob.

101 GAVO, f. 504, op. 3, d. 329, l. 150 ob.

102 GAVO, f. 504, op. 3, d. 329, l. 148.

103 Yelena Aleksandrovna Zotova, Marina Yevgen'yevna Baskakova, and Yelena Borisovna Mezentseva, "Gendernyye Voprosy Prestupnosti," in *Gendernyye Problemy Sovremennoy Rossii (Po Dannym Ofitsial'noy Statistiki)*, ed. Yelena Zotova, Marina Baskakova, and Yelena Mezentseva (Alex, 2006), 205.

104 Agnes R. Quisumbing et al., *Gender in Agriculture: Closing the Knowledge Gap, Gender in Agriculture: Closing the Knowledge Gap* (Springer Netherlands, 2014).

105 Olson and Adonyeva, *Worlds of Russian Village Women*.

106 Zdravomyslova and Temkina, "Gosudarstvennoye Konstruirovaniye Gendera v Sovetskom Obshchestve"; Melanie Ilic, Susan E. Reid, and Lynne Attwood, eds., *Women in the Khrushchev Era* (Palgrave Macmillan, 2004).

107 Olson and Adonyeva, *Worlds of Russian Village Women*; Anna Kushkova, *Krest'yanskaya Ssora. Opyt Izucheniya Derevenskoy Povsednevnosti* (European University at St.Petersburg, 2016).

108 Natasha Kolchevska, "Angels in the Home and at Work: Russian Women in the Khrushchev Years," *Women's Studies Quarterly* 33, nos. 3–4 (2005): 114–37.

109 Liubov' Nikolaevna Denisova, *Sud'ba Russkoy Krest'yanki* (ROSSPEN, 2007), 20.

110 Stephen K. Wegren et al., "Gender Inequality in Russia's Rural Formal Economy," *Post-Soviet Affairs* 31, no. 5 (2015): 367–96.

111 Yelena Andreyevna Zdravomyslova and Anna Adrianovna Temkina, "Patriarkhat i Zhenskaya Vlast," in *Rossiyskiy Gendernyy Poryadok: Sotsiologicheskiy Podkhod,* ed. Elena Zdravomyslova and Anna Temkona (Izdatel'stvo Europeyskiy Universitet v Sankt-Peterburge, 2007), 68–96; Denisova, *Sud'ba Russkoy Krest'yanki,* 396–9.

112 Wegren et al., "Gender Inequality in Russia's Rural Formal Economy," 374.

113 Denisova and Mukhina, "Rural Women in the Soviet Union and Post-Soviet Russia," 54–64.

114 VOANPI, f. 4039, op. 43, d. 7, l. 13.

115 VOANPI, f. 3892, op. 38, d. 282, l. 10.

116 VOANPI, f. 3892, op. 38, d. 282, l. 10.

117 GAVO, f. 504, op. 3, d. 597, l. 39.

118 GAVO, f. 521, op. 8, d. 335, l. 18–22.

119 GAVO, f. 521, op. 8, d. 335, l. 22.

120 Sergey Vladimirovich Zakharov, "Menyayushchiyesya Parametry Matrimonial'nogo Povedeniya," in *Demograficheskaya Modernizatsiya Rossii 1900–2000,* ed. Anatoliy Grigor'yevich Vishnevskiy (Moscow: Novoe Izdatelstvo, 2006), 90.

121 Denisova and Mukhina, "Rural Women in the Soviet Union and Post-Soviet Russia," 85.

122 "'Zakon RSFSR Ot 30 Iyulya 1969 g. Ob Utverzhdenii Kodeksa o Brake i Sem'ye RSFSR,'" *Vedomosti Verkhovnogo Soveta RSFSR,* no. 32 (1969): 1397.

123 Interview with Galina Sh. (1949, Molochnoe, 2018).

124 Interview with Antonina K. (1942, Goritsy, 2018).

125 Interview with Galina Sh. (1949, Molochnoe, 2018).

126 GAVO, f. 521, op. 8, d. 316, l. 86 ob.

127 GAVO, f. 521, op. 8, d. 220, l. 45.

128 Interview with Antonina K. (1942, Goritsy, 2018).

129 Interview with Galina Sh. (1949, Molochnoe, 2018).

130 Interview with Elena V. (1950, Vologda, 2018).

6. Cadres for the Village

1 Loren R. Graham, *The Ghost of the Executed Engineer: Technology and the Fall of the Soviet Union* (Harvard University Press, 1993); David-Fox, *Crossing Borders*; Michael David-Fox and Gyorgy Peteri, *Academia in Upheaval: Origins, Transfers, and Transformations of the Communist Academic Regime in Russia and East Central Europe* (Bloomsbury Academic, 2000).

2 Filippov, *Vseobshcheye Sredneye Obrazovaniye v SSSR (Sotsiologicheskiye Problemy).*

3 Tatyana Afrikanovna Siplova, Lyubov' Dmitriyevna Belyayeva, and Margarita Aleksandrovna Rukavishnikova, *Vologodskoy Gosudarstvennoy*

Molochnokhozyaystvennoy Akademii Imeni N.V. Vereshchagina – 100 Let. Stranitsy Istorii (Yaroslavl', 2012), 106.

4 Siplova et al., *Vologodskoy Gosudarstvennoy Molochnokhozyaystvennoy Akademii Imeni N.V. Vereshchagina*, 13.

5 GAVO, f. 1703, op. 20, d. 8618, l. 7, 8.

6 GAVO, f. 1703, op. 20, d. 8618, l. 7, 8.

7 GAVO, f. 1703, op. 20, d. 8618, l. 7, 8.

8 Clark Kerr, *The Uses of the University*, 5th ed. (Harvard University Press, 2001); John Aubrey Douglass, "How Rankings Came to Determine World Class," in Douglass, *The New Flagship University*, 9–30; Bourdieu, "Systems of Education and Systems of Thought."

9 Bourdieu, "Systems of Education and Systems of Thought."

10 Filippov, *Vseobshcheye Sredneye Obrazovaniye v SSSR (Sotsiologicheskiye Problemy)*.

11 Shpakovskaya, "Sovetskaya Obrazovatel'naya Politika"; Andrey Ivanovich Savin, "Vyssheye Obrazovaniye v RSFSR Kak Lift Sotsial'noy Mobil'nosti (1918–1936)," *Gumanitarnyye Nauki v Sibiri* 23, no. 4 (2016): 43–9.

12 Fitzpatrick, "Ascribing Class."

13 Konrad and Szelenyi, *The Intellectuals on the Road to Class Power*.

14 Bourdieu, "Systems of Education and Systems of Thought"; Ball, *Foucault and Education*.

15 Lareau, *Unequal Childhoods*; Douglass, "How Rankings Came to Determine World Class."

16 RGASPI, f. 1, op. 39, d. 44, l. 9.

17 RGASPI, f. 1, op. 39, d. 44, l. 9.

18 RGASPI, f. 1, op. 39, d. 44, l. 12.

19 Froumin and Leshukov, "The Soviet Flagship University Model and Its Contemporary Transition," 180.

20 Ol'ga Gerasimova, *"Ottepel'," "zamorozki" i Studenty Moskovskogo Uni-Versiteta* (AIRO-XXI, 2015); Lada Vladimirovna Silina, *Nastroyeniya Sovetskogo Studenchestva: 1945–1964 Gg.* (Russkiy Mir, 2004).

21 Tromly, *Making the Soviet Intelligentsia*, 8.

22 Paretskaya, "A Middle Class Without Capitalism?"; Shpakovskaya, "Sovetskaya Obrazovatel'naya Politika."

23 Konrad and Szelenyi, *The Intellectuals on the Road to Class Power*; Paretskaya, "A Middle Class Without Capitalism?"; Nikolay Mitrochin, *Russkaya Partiya: Dvizheniye Russkikh Natsionalistov v SSSR. 1953–1985 Gody* (NLO, 2003); Beznin and Dimoni, "Intellektualy v Sel'skom Khozyaystve Rossii 1930–1980-Kh Gg"; Polly Jones, *Revolution Rekindled: The Writers and Readers of Late Soviet Biography* (Oxford University Press, 2019).

24 Interview with Yuri V. (1949, Molochnoe, 2018).

25 Aleksandr Valer'yevich Ivanov, "Problemy Kooperativnogo Dvizheniya v Dorevolyutsionnoy Rossii i Ikh Izucheniye v Sovet·skoy Istoriografii Vtoroy Poloviny XX Veka," *Vestnik KrasGAU* 10 (2006): 366–70.

26 Kendra Smith-Howard, *Pure and Modern Milk: An Environmental History Since 1900* (Oxford University Press, 2017).

27 Erna Melanie DuPuis, *Nature's Perfect Food: How Milk Became America's Drink* (New York University Press, 2002), 46–66.

28 Smith-Howard, *Pure and Modern Milk*, 14.

29 Andrea S. Wiley, *Re-Imagining Milk: Cultural and Biological Perspectives* (Routledge, 2016), 49–50.

30 Elena Kochetkova, "Milk and Milk Packaging in the Soviet Union: Technologies of Production and Consumption, 1950s–70s," *Russian History* 46, no. 1 (2019): 33.

31 Kochetkova, "Milk and Milk Packaging in the Soviet Union," 33.

32 Kochetkova, 35.

33 Loren R. Graham, ed., *Science and the Soviet Social Order* (Harvard University Press, 1990); Graham, *The Ghost of the Executed Engineer.*

34 Isak Froumin, Yaroslav Kouzminov, and Dmitry Semyonov, "Institutional Diversity in Russian Higher Education: Revolutions and Evolution," *European Journal of Higher Education* 4, no. 3 (2014): 209–34.

35 Siplova et al., *Vologodskoy Gosudarstvennoy Molochnokhozyaystvennoy Akademii Imeni N.V. Vereshchagina,* 53–4.

36 Stephan Merl, "Why Did the Attempt Under Stalin to Increase Agricultural Productivity Prove to Be Such a Fundamental Failure?," *Cahiers Du Monde Russe* 57, no. 1 (2016): 191–220.

37 Interview with Evelina M. (1940, Molochnoe, 2021).

38 Siplova et al., *Vologodskoy Gosudarstvennoy Molochnokhozyaystvennoy Akademii Imeni N.V. Vereshchagina,* 29, 41.

39 Siplova et al., 61–2.

40 Siplova et al., 55–7.

41 Siplova et al., 51.

42 Kochetkova, "Milk and Milk Packaging in the Soviet Union," 32.

43 Interview with Evelina M. (1940, Molochnoe, 2021).

44 VOANPI, f. 2522, op. 63, d. 85, l. 70.

45 VOANPI, f. 2522, op. 63, d. 85, l. 69.

46 VOANPI, f. 3892, op. 29, d. 201, l. 40.

47 VOANPI, f. 3892, op. 29, d. 201, l. 41.

48 Gerber and Hout, "Educational Stratification in Russia During the Soviet Period."

49 Gerber and Hout, 612.

50 VOANPI, f. 3892, op. 29, d. 201, l. 320.

51 VOANPI, f. 2522, op. 63, d. 85, l. 70.

52 VOANPI, f. 2522, op. 72, d. 263, l. 38.

53 Interview with Yuri V. (1949, Molochnoe, March 2018).

54 VOANPI, f. 2522, op. 73, d. 63, l. 38. In the USSR, "public services
   combines" provided various quotidian services such as clothing and item
   repair, hair dressing, dry cleaning, etc.
55 VOANPI, f. 2522, op. 73, d. 63, l. 37
56 RGASPI, f. 1, op. 41, d. 171, l. 1, 1 ob.
57 RGASPI, f. 1, op. 41, d. 171, l. 2.
58 VOANPI, f. 3892, op. 29, d. 201, l. 11.
59 Interview with Yuri V. (1949, Molochnoe, March 2018).
60 Interview with Yuri V.
61 Interview with Kapitalina (1948, Molochnoe, 2021).
62 Yuliya Viktorovna Ukhanova, "Intellektualy Sel'skogo Khozyaystva
   Evropeyskogo Severa Rossii v 1930–1960-Ye Gg," *Yaroslavskiy Pedagogicheskiy
   Vestnik* 1, no. 2 (2012): 50.
63 GAVO f. 1703, op. 20, d. 8618, l. 1.
64 GAVO f. 1703, op. 20, d. 8618, l. 1.
65 RGASPI, f. 1, op. 36, d. 125, l. 5.
66 Interview with Yuri V. (1949, Molochnoe, March 2018).
67 VOANPI, f. 2522, op. 63, d. 84, l. 33.
68 VOANPI, f. 2522, op. 63, d. 85, l. 69.
69 VOANPI, f. 2522, op. 63, d. 84, l. 33.
70 RGASPI, f. 1, op. 39, d. 44, l. 58.
71 Gerber and Hout, "Educational Stratification in Russia During the Soviet
   Period"; Scott, *Seeing Like a State.*
72 *Narodnoye Khozyaystvo Vologodskoy Oblasti Za Gody Sovetskoy Vlasti,* 118.
73 *Narodnoye Khozyaystvo Vologodskoy Oblasti Za Gody Sovetskoy Vlasti,* 118.
74 Olga A. Khasbulatova, "Professional'noye Obrazovaniye Muzhchin i
   Zhenshchin v Rossii v 1918–2015 Godakh. Istoriko-Sotsiologicheskiy Analiz,"
   Zhenzhiny v Rossiyskom Obshchestve 3–4, nos. 76–7 (2015): 3–16.
75 Interview with Kapitalina (1948, Molochnoe, 2021).
76 Interview with Yuri V. (1949, Molochnoe, 2018).
77 RGASPI, f. 1, op. 39, d. 44, l. 55.
78 RGASPI, f. 1, op. 39, d. 44, l. 55.
79 VOANPI, f. 2522, op. 63, d. 85, l. 69.
80 RGASPI, f. 1, op. 39, d. 44, l. 54, 55.
81 Siplova et al., *Vologodskoy Gosudarstvennoy Molochnokhozyaystvennoy Akademii
   Imeni N.V. Vereshchagina,* 110.
82 Interview with Evelina M. (1940, Molochnoe, 2021).
83 GAVO f. 1703, op. 20, d. 8618, l. 7, 8.
84 Mikhail Alekseyevich Beznin and Tatiana Mikhaylovna Dimoni,
   "Intellektualy v Sel'skom Khozyaystve Rossii 1930–1980-h godach,"
   Yaroslavskiy Pedagogicheskiy Vestnik 1 (2013): 29.

85 Beznin and Dimoni, "Intellektualy v Sel'skom Khozyaystve Rossii 1930–1980-h godach," 29.

86 GAVO, f. 165, op. 10, d. 271, l. 13, 25, 29a.

87 GAVO, f. 165, op. 10, d. 331, l. 21.

88 GAVO, f. 165, op. 10, d. 331, l. 21.

89 VOANPI, f. 2522, op. 63, d. 85, l. 72.

90 Alena V. Ledeneva, *Russia's Economy of Favours:* Blat, *Networking and Informal Exchange* (Cambridge University Press, 1998).

91 GAVO, f. 165, op. 10, d. 271, l. 25.

92 GAVO, f. 165, op. 10, d. 271, l. 20.

93 GAVO, f. 165, op. 10, d. 271, l. 29a.

94 GAVO, f. 165, op. 10, d. 271, l. 40, 41.

95 Tromly, *Making the Soviet Intelligentsia,* 4.

96 Mikhail Nikolayevich Rutkevich, "Izmeneniye Sotsial'noy Struktury Sovetskogo Obshchestva i Intelligentsiya," in *Sotsiologiya v SSSR,* ed. Gennadiy Vasil'yevich Osipov (Moscow: Mysl', 1966), 1:392; Vadim Sergeyevich Semenov, "Ob Izmenenii Intelligentsii i Sluzhashchikh v Protsesse Stroitel'stva Kommunizma," in Osipov, *Sotsiologiya v SSSR,* 1: 417–18; Ovsey Irmovich Shkaratan, *Problemy sotsial'noy struktury rabochego klassa SSSR (istoriko-sotsiologicheskoye issledovaniye)* (Mysl', 1970), 4–5.

97 Gerasimov, *Modernism and Public Reform in Late Imperial Russia,* 48.

98 Vadim Volkov, "The Concept of Kul'turnost': Notes on the Stalinist Civilizing Process," in *Stalinism: New Directions,* ed. Sheila Fitzpatrick (Routledge, 1999), 210–30.

99 Beznin and Dimoni, "Intellektualy v Sel'skom Khozyaystve Rossii 1930–1980-Kh Gg," 29–41.

100 Graham, *Science and the Soviet Social Order.*

101 Froumin and Leshukov, "The Soviet Flagship University Model and Its Contemporary Transition," 170.

102 "Chleny Izbiratel'noy Komissii Vologodskoy Oblasti. Valyuzhenich Anatoliy Ivanovich," Izbiratel'naya Komissiya Vologodskoy Oblasti, accessed 27 December 2024, www.vologod.izbirkom.ru/docs/4266/.

103 Siplova et al., *Vologodskoy Gosudarstvennoy Molochnokhozyaystvennoy Akademii Imeni N.V. Vereshchagina,* 103.

104 VOANPI, f. 2522, op. 73, d. 386, l. 11.

105 VOANPI, f. 3892, op. 29, d. 201, l. 14.

106 VOANPI, f. 3892, op. 29, d. 201, l. 14.

107 VOANPI, f. 2522, op. 63, d. 85, l. 71.

108 Yurchak, *Everything Was Forever.*

109 Interview with Yuri V. (1949, Molochnoe, March 2018).

110 However, indirect sources provide only approximate information about how exactly institute party organization meetings were conducted, and

what kind of issues were decided there. Minutes from VMI party and Komsomol organization meetings have yet to be issued by the Vologda archive.

111 GAVO, f. 165, op. 10, d. 229, l. 13, 30, 61, 107, 127, 139; GAVO, f. 165, op. 10, d. 254, l. 1–140.

112 GAVO, f. 165, op. 10, d. 229, l. 217, 218.

113 RGASPI, f. 1, op. 39, d. 44, l. 48.

114 RGASPI, f. 1, op. 39, d. 44, l. 48.

115 RGASPI, f. 1, op. 39, d. 44, l. 48.

116 VOANPI, f. 3892, op. 29, d. 201, l. 12.

117 VOANPI, f. 2522, op. 63, d. 85, l. 70.

118 GAVO, f. 165, op. 10, d. 225, l. 42.

119 VOANPI, f. 3892, op. 29, d. 201, l. 12.

120 Siplova et al., *Vologodskoy Gosudarstvennoy Molochnokhozyaystvennoy Akademii Imeni N.V. Vereshchagina*, 111.

121 "Akademgorodok," *Akademgorodok* 2508, no. 10 (2016): 6.

122 VOANPI, f. 3892, op. 29, d. 201, l. 10.

123 VOANPI, f. 3892, op. 29, d. 201, l. 10.

124 Interview with Yuri V. (1949, Molochnoe, March 2018).

125 Interview with Kapitalina (1948, Molochnoe, 2021).

126 Tsipursky, *Socialist Fun.*

127 Viktor Alexandrovich Kozlov, ed., *Kramola: Inakomysliye v SSSR Pri Khrushcheve i Brezhneve: 1953–1982 Gg.: Rassekrechennyye Dokumenty Verkhovnogo Suda i Prokuratury SSSR* (Materik, 2005); Kozlov, "Neofitsial'nyye Gruppy Sovetskikh Shkol'nikov 1940–1960-Kh Godov"; Gerasimova, *"Ottepel'," "zamorozki" i Studenty Moskovskogo Uni-Versiteta.*

128 Interview with Vladimir P. (1954, Molochnoe, 2021).

129 VOANPI, f. 2522, op. 63, d. 85, l. 73.

130 VOANPI, f. 2522, op. 63, d. 85, l. 74.

131 Yurchak, *Everything Was Forever*; Zhuk, *Rock and Roll in the Rocket City.*

132 Gerasimova, *"Ottepel'," "zamorozki" i Studenty Moskovskogo Uni-Versiteta.*

133 Nikolay Mitrochin, *Ocherki Sovetskoy Ekonomicheskoy Politiki v 1965–1989 Godakh. In 2 Volums* (Novoe literaturnoe obozrenie, 2023).

134 Interview with Yuri V. (1949, Molochnoe, March 2018).

135 GAVO f. 1703, op. 20, d. 8618, l. 7, 8.

136 VOANPI, f. 2522, op. 77, d. 34, l. 68.

137 VOANPI, f. 2522, op. 77, d. 34, l. 68.

138 Lyubov' Dmitriyevna Belyayeva, "Iz Istorii Stroyotryadovskogo Dvizheniya VMI," *Akademgorodok*, 2015, 8.

139 Belyayeva, "Iz Istorii Stroyotryadovskogo Dvizheniya VMI," 8.

140 Belyayeva, 8.

141 "Kak Eto Bylo," *Akademgorodok* 2496, no. 8 (2015): 8.

142 "Kak Eto Bylo," 8.

143 Belyayeva, "Iz Istorii Stroyotryadovskogo Dvizheniya VMI," 8.

144 "Kak Eto Bylo," 8.

145 Lyubov' Dmitriyevna Belyayeva and Angelina Sergeyevna Serova, "Ko Dnyu Rossiyskikh Studencheskikh Otryadov," *Akademgorodok* 2500, no. 2 (2016): 13.

146 Belyayeva and Serova, 13.

147 GAVO f. 1703, op. 20, d. 8618, l. 5.

7. Molochnoe: Urban Meets Rural

1 Interview with Valentina B. (1948, Molochnoe, 2021).

2 Siplova et al., *Vologodskoy Gosudarstvennoy Molochnokhozyaystvennoy Akademii Imeni N.V. Vereshchagina.*

3 Interview with Kapitalina (1948, Molochnoe, 2021).

4 Interview with Kapitalina.

5 Interview with Evelina M. (1940, Molochnoe, 2021).

6 For example, the École nationale supérieure agronomique de Rennes was formed near Paris in 1849 as an institution of higher education that trained specialists in the field of agriculture. It was an architectural complex that included, in addition to educational premises and buildings, outbuildings, dormitories, rooms for inventory, training herds, etc.

7 Lefebvre, *Proizvodstvo Prostranstva.*

8 Appadurai, "The Production of Locality," 204–25.

9 Appadurai, 210.

10 Pierre Bourdieu, *Algeria 1960: The Disenchantment of the World; The Sense of Honour; The Kabyle House or the World Reversed: Essays* (Cambridge University Press, 1979), 133–54.

11 Bourdieu, *Algeria 1960*, 133–54.

12 Alexandra Kasatkina, "Poetics and Practice of Modern Urbanism: 'Garden City' as a Technology of Social Integration in Obninsk in the 1960s," *Laboratorium: Russian Review of Social Research* 14, no. 1 (2022): 32.

13 Moisey Ginzburg, *Stil' i Epokha: Problemy Sovremennoy Arkhitektury* (Strelka Press, 2021), 160.

14 El' Lisitskiy, *Rossiya: Rekonstruktsiya Arkhitektury v Sovetskom Soyuze* (Izdatel'stvo European University at Sankt-Petersburg, 2019), 55.

15 Lisitskiy, *Rossiya*, 54.

16 Mikhail Timofeyev, "Predchuvstviye Utopii: Reprezentatsii Goroda Budushchego v Povesti A.V. Chayanova 'Puteshestviye Moyego Brata Alekseya v Stranu Krest'yanskoy Utopii' (1920) i v Gazetnom Romane Vl. Fedorova 'Chudo Greshnogo Pitirima' (1925)," *Novoe Literaturnoe Obozrenie* 167, no. 1 (2021): 5–6.

17 Michail Alexandrovich Ochitovich, "K Probleme Goroda," *Sovremennaya Arkhitektura* 4 (1929): 130–4.

18 Alexanrd Vasilievich Chayanov, "Puteshestviye Moyego Brata Alekseya v Stranu Krest'yanskoy Utopii," in *Venetsianskoye Zerkalo: Povesti* (Moscow, 1989), 161–208.

19 A twentieth-century urban planning concept, the "garden city" promoted satellite settlements separated by green belts encircling the main metropolis. These garden cities were to have proportionately sized residential, commercial, and agricultural districts.

20 Mark Meerovich, "Rozhdenie i smert' sovetskogo goroda-sada: Deistvuiushchie litsa i motivy ubiistva," *Vestnik Evrazii* 1 (2007): 118–66.

21 Melvin, *Soviet Power and the Countryside*, 63.

22 RGASPI, f. 1, op. 39, d. 44, l. 15.

23 VOANPI, f. 2522, op. 63, d. 85, l. 69.

24 VOANPI, f. 3892, op. 30, d. 181, l. 25.

25 Scott, *Seeing Like a State*.

26 Scott, 104.

27 Siplova et al., *Vologodskoy Gosudarstvennoy Molochnokhozyaystvennoy Akademii Imeni N.V. Vereshchagina*, 12–13.

28 Gleb Nikolayevich Trofimov, *"Institut v Molochnom," Kinozhurnal Nash Kray, № 32*, Leningradskaya studiya dokumental'nykh fil'mov, 1961, YouTube, uploaded 3 August 2019, www.youtube.com/watch?v=JffvrbLYNkg; Vasiliy Petrovich Vasilenko, *Vologodskaya Oblast. Poselok Molochnoye. Studenty Molochnogo Instituta v Tsekhakh Molokozavoda. Kinozhurnal Nash Kray, № 12*, Leningradskaya studiya dokumental'nykh fil'mov, 1959, YouTube, uploaded 3 August 2019, www.youtube.com/watch?v=JffvrbLYNkg.

29 Alexandra Kasatkina, "Poetics and Practice of Modern Urbanism," 30–59; Ksenia Tartachenko, *Soviet SCI_BERIA: Novosibirsk Science City and the Politics of Expertise, 1957–1991* (Bloomsbury Academic, 2024).

30 Georgiy Andreyevich Dudchenko, *Molochnoye – Poselok Uchenykh. Ocherki* (Severo-zapadnoye knizhnoye izdatel'stvo, 1984).

31 Siplova et al., *Vologodskoy Gosudarstvennoy Molochnokhozyaystvennoy Akademii Imeni N.V. Vereshchagina*, 6–15.

32 Georgiy Sergeyevich Inikhov, *Zapiski o Vologodskom Molochnom Institute* (Tipografiya Severosoyuza, 1919).

33 Inikhov, *Zapiski o Vologodskom Molochnom Institute*.

34 Siplova et al., *Vologodskoy Gosudarstvennoy Molochnokhozyaystvennoy Akademii Imeni N.V. Vereshchagina*, 17.

35 Olga Vladimirovna Ochrimenko (Krylova), "'Kazhdiy Professorskiy Dom … ,'" in Plastinina (Makarova) et al., *Molochnoye – Dom, v Kotorom My Zhivem*, 80–93.

36 Andey Georgievich Titov, "'Na Ploshchadke Mezhdu Korpusom Instituta … ,'" in Plastinina (Makarova) et al., *Molochnoye – Dom, v Kotorom My Zhivem*, 32.

37 Lyudmila Nikolayevna Makarova, "Ulitsa Parkovaya, Dom № 6," in Plastinina (Makarova) et al., *Molochnoye – Dom, v Kotorom My Zhivem*, 23.

38 Viktoriya Il'inichna Ruchenkova (Abramova), "'V 1946 Godu Nasha Sem'ya … ,'" in Plastinina (Makarova) et al., *Molochnoye – Dom, v Kotorom My Zhivem*, 94.

39 Ol'ga Yur'yevna Martinovich (Levinskaya) and Natal'ya Vladimirovna Artomova (Soboleva), "Rasskaz Zapisan so Slov Margarity Aleksandrovny Talashovoy," in Plastinina (Makarova) et al., *Molochnoye – Dom, v Kotorom My Zhivem*, 122.

40 Ol'ga Aleksandrovna Plastinina (Makarova) and Tatiana Yulievna Berman, "'V Opisanii Doma … ,'" in Plastinina (Makarova) et al., *Molochnoye – Dom, v Kotorom My Zhivem*, 285.

41 Collective interview with Elena A., Tat'yana R., Irina, Alena, Ol'ga B. (Molochnoe, 2018).

42 GAVO, f. 1822, op. 5, d. 136, l. 15, 16.

43 Ochrimenko (Krylova), "'Kazhdiy Professorskiy Dom … ,'" 89.

44 "Ostroumov Lev Aleksandrovich," *Izvestnyye Uchonyye: Biograficheskiye Dannyye Uchenykh i Spetsialistov*, Proyekt Rossiyskoy Akademii Yestestvoznaniya, accessed 26 december 2024, https://famous-scientists.ru/anketa /ostroumov-lev-aleksandrovich-1213.

45 Valentina Stepanovna Kuznetsova, "'Ja Prozhivayu v Etom Dome s Sentyabrya 1964 … ,'" in Plastinina (Makarova) et al., *Molochnoye – Dom, v Kotorom My Zhivem*, 147.

46 Lareau, *Unequal Childhoods*.

47 Lareau, 3.

48 Makarova, "Ulitsa Parkovaya, Dom № 6," 21.

49 Makarova, 21.

50 Sergey Yevgen'yevich Tyapugin and Irina Vasil'yevna Serebrova, "Severo-Zapadnomu NII Molochnogo i Lugopastbishchnogo Khozyaystva – 90 Let," *Dostizheniya Nauki i Tekhniki APK* 1 (2011): 3–4.

51 Anna Klepikovskaya, "100-Letnemu Yubileyu Meditsinskoy Sluzhby Sela Molochnoye Posvyashchayetsya," *Akademgorodok*, 2014, 4.

52 Yelena Anatol'yevna Litvina, "Domik Arkhitektora," in Plastinina (Makarova) et al., *Molochnoye – Dom, v Kotorom My Zhivem*, 266, 268.

53 Anatoliy Yekhalov, *"Rodina" Nasha. Yest' Li Budushcheye u Severnoy Derevni?* (Izdatel'skie resheniya, 2019), 25.

54 Aleksey Stepanovich Yemel'yanov, *O Rekordistke Korove Vene* (Oblastnaya tipografia, 1956).

55 Collective interview with Elena A., Tat'yana R., Irina, Alena, Ol'ga B. (Molochnoe, 2018).

56 Interview with Yuri V. (1949, Molochnoe, 2018).

57 Makarova, "Ulitsa Parkovaya, Dom № 6," 19–21.

58 Viktor Vasil'yevich Krasavtsev, "'Kazhdyy Raz, Prokhodya Mimo Etogo Doma … ,'" in Plastinina (Makarova) et al., *Molochnoye – Dom, v Kotorom My Zhivem*, 302.

59 A *krushchevka* was a type of low-cost, three- to five-storey apartment building that rose to prominence in the Soviet Union under the rule of Nikita Khrushchev, who presided over the Soviet government from 1953 to 1964.

60 Nadezhda Simonova (Malikova), "'Zaselyalsya Nash Dom … ,'" in Plastinina (Makarova) et al., *Molochnoye – Dom, v Kotorom My Zhivem*, 304.

61 "Vsesoyuznaya Perepis' Naseleniya 1959 g. Chislennost' Gorodskogo Naseleniya RSFSR, Yeye Territorial'nykh Yedinits, Gorodskikh Poseleniy i Gorodskikh Rayonov Po Polu," Demoskop Weekly, n.d., www.demoscope.ru /weekly/ssp/rus59_reg2.php.

62 "Vsesoyuznaya Perepis' Naseleniya 1970 g. Chislennost' Gorodskogo Naseleniya RSFSR, Yeye Territorial'nykh Yedinits, Gorodskikh Poseleniy i Gorodskikh Rayonov Po Polu," *Демоскоп Weekly*, last moified 18 January 2011, https://www.demoscope.ru/weekly/ssp/rus70_reg1.php.

63 "Vsesoyuznaya Perepis' Naseleniya 1979 g. Chislennost' Nalichnogo Naseleniya RSFSR, Avtonomnykh Respublik, Avtonomnykh Oblastey i Okrugov, Krayev, Oblastey, Rayonov, Gorodskikh Poseleniy, Sel-Raytsentrov i Sel'skikh Poseleniy s Naseleniyem Svyshe 5000," *Демоскоп Weekly*, accessed 27 December 2024, https://www.demoscope.ru/weekly/ssp/ussr_nac_79.php.

64 Yelena Pavlovna Drozd and Valentina Feodos'yevna Shabalina, "Posle Voyny Na Ulitse Proizoshli Izmenenia … ,'" in Plastinina (Makarova) et al., *Molochnoye – Dom, v Kotorom My Zhivem*, 245.

65 Kuznetsova, "'Ja Prozhivayu v Etom Dome s Sentyabrya 1964 … ,'" 146.

66 Kuznetsova, 148.

67 Kuznetsova, 148.

68 Kuznetsova, 147, 150.

69 Elena Vladimirovna Britvina, "'Vot Uzhe 33 Goda Proshlo s Tekh Por, Kak Nasha Sem'ya Pereyekhala … ,'" in Plastinina (Makarova) et al., *Molochnoye – Dom, v Kotorom My Zhivem*, 152.

70 Margarita Mikhaylovna Kazanskaya, "Vospominaniya o Molochnom," in Plastinina (Makarova) et al., *Molochnoye – Dom, v Kotorom My Zhivem*, 70.

71 Britvina, "'Vot Uzhe 33 Goda Proshlo s Tekh Por, Kak Nasha Sem'ya Pereyekhala … ,'" 152.

72 Plastinina (Makarova) and Berman, "'V Opisanii Doma … ,'" 154.

73 Plastinina (Makarova) and Berman, 155.

74 Nadezhda Andreyevna Seregicheva (Yanina), "'Eto Byl Dvukhetazhnyy Iz Tolstykh Breven … ,'" in Plastinina (Makarova) et al., *Molochnoye – Dom, v Kotorom My Zhivem*, 60.

75 Elena Stanislavovna Zolotova, "'Ulitsa Shmidta, Dom № 3 – Eto Babushkin Dom … ,'" in Plastinina (Makarova) et al., *Molochnoye – Dom, v Kotorom My Zhivem*, 79.

76 *Lapta* is a Russian folk game of the bat-and-ball type.

77 *Gorodki* is a Russian folk sport. Similar in concept to bowling and also somewhat to horseshoes, the aim of the game is to knock out groups of

wooden pins arranged in various patterns by throwing a bat at them. The pins are called *gorodki* (literally "little cities" or "townlets"), and the square zone in which they are arranged is called the *gorod* (city).

78 Ochrimenko (Krylova), "'Kazhdiy Professorskiy Dom … ,'" 87.

79 Ochrimenko (Krylova), 92

80 Interview with Eugeniy G. (1949, Molochnoe, 2018).

81 Ol'ga Aleksandrovna Plastinina (Makarova) and Elena Aleksandrovna Makarova, "Ulitsa Shmidta, Dom № 14," in Plastinina (Makarova) et al., *Molochnoye – Dom, v Kotorom My Zhivem*, 41.

82 "Obkoms" were the oblast committees of the Communist Party, regional branches of the CPSU.

83 Interview with Evgeniy G. (1949, Molochnoe, 2018).

84 Interview with Iya V. (1953, Molochnoe, 2018).

85 Galina Vasilievna Guseva, "Dom № 14 Na Ulitse Shmidta – Eto Neobychnyy Dom," in Plastinina (Makarova) et al., *Molochnoye – Dom, v Kotorom My Zhivem*, 45.

86 Interview with Iya V. (1953, Molochnoe, 2018).

87 For more about *blat*, see Ledeneva, *Russia's Economy of Favours*.

88 Interview with Evgeniy G. (1949, Molochnoe, 2018).

89 Plastinina (Makarova) and Makarova, "Ulitsa Shmidta, Dom № 14," 43.

90 Guseva, "Dom № 14 Na Ulitse Shmidta – Eto Neobychnyy Dom," 45.

91 Kazanskaya, "Vospominaniya o Molochnom," 70.

92 Interview with Evgeniy G. (1949, Molochnoe, 2018).

93 "Kak Eto Bylo."

94 Makarova, "Ulitsa Parkovaya, Dom № 6," 325.

95 Lyubov' Dmitriyevna Belyayeva (Biryukova), "Ulitsa i Dom Moyego Detstva," in Plastinina (Makarova) et al., *Molochnoye – Dom, v Kotorom My Zhivem*, 358–62.

96 Belyayeva (Biryukova), "Ulitsa i Dom Moyego Detstva," 359.

97 Ol'ga Yur'yevna Martinovich (Levinskaya), "'Na Ulitse Podlesnoy … ,'" in Plastinina (Makarova) et al., *Molochnoye – Dom, v Kotorom My Zhivem*, 334.

98 Sergey Alexandrovich Shishigin and Tatiana Alexandrovna Shishigina, "'Dom Byl Dvuchetazhniy, Dvuchpod'ezdniy … ,'" in Plastinina (Makarova) et al., *Molochnoye – Dom, v Kotorom My Zhivem*, 49.

99 Belyayeva (Biryukova), "Ulitsa i Dom Moyego Detstva," 361.

100 Litvina, "Domik Arkhitektora," 271.

101 Interview with Yuri V. (1949, Molochnoe, 2018).

102 Ochrimenko (Krylova), "'Kazhdiy Professorskiy Dom … ,'" 92.

103 Galina Yukhimovna Tsaregorodtseva (Povshednaya), "'Pered Tem, Kak Nasha Semya Poluchila Kvartiru … ,'" in Plastinina (Makarova) et al., *Molochnoye – Dom, v Kotorom My Zhivem*, 110.

104 Natalia Konstantinovna Chuglova, "'Istoriya Doma – Eto Istoriya Sem'i … ,'" in Plastinina (Makarova) et al., *Molochnoye – Dom, v Kotorom My Zhivem*, 349.

105 Yuriy Leonidovich Zyuzin, "Ulitsa Shmidta, Dom № 9," in Plastinina
     (Makarova) et al., *Molochnoye – Dom, v Kotorom My Zhivem*, 106.
106 Martinovich (Levinskaya), "'Na Ulitse Podlesnoy … ,'" 336.
107 Martinovich (Levinskaya), 336.
108 Plastinina (Makarova) and Berman, "'V Opisanii Doma … ,'" 35.
109 Interview with Alexandr A. (1953, Molochnoe, 2021).
110 Chuglova, "'Istoriya Doma – Eto Istoriya Sem'i … ,'" 346, 348.

8. Modernity's Conduit and Hostages of Backwardness

1   Interview with Ludmila S. (1954, Molochnoe, 2021).
2   Interview with Ludmila S.
3   Pilkington, *Russia's Youth and Its Culture*, 5–6.
4   Jim Riordan, "The Komsomol," in *Soviet Youth Culture*, ed. Jim Riordan
    (Macmillan Press, 1989), 16–44; Uhl, "Pokoleniye Mezhdu 'Geroicheskim
    Proshlym' i 'Svetlym Budushchim,'" 279–326.
5   VOANPI, f. 3892, op. 38, d. 282, l. 13.
6   Pilkington, *Russia's Youth and Its Culture*, 37–40.
7   Riordan, "The Komsomol," 26.
8   Yurchak, *Everything Was Forever*, 79–85.
9   Yurchak, 93.
10 Tsipursky, *Socialist Fun*; Fürst, *Stalin's Last Generation*; Pilkington, *Russia's
    Youth and Its Culture*.
11 Robert Hornsby, "Strengthening Friendship and Fraternal Solidarity: Soviet
    Youth Tourism to Eastern Europe Under Khrushchev and Brezhnev,"
    Europe-Asia Studies 71, no. 7 (2019): 1205–32, https://doi.org/10.1080
    /09668136.2019.1624690; Robert Hornsby, "Soviet Youth on the March: The
    All-Union Tours of Military Glory, 1965–87," *Journal of Contemporary History*
    52, no. 2 (J2017): 418–45, https://doi.org/10.1177/0022009416644666.
12 Sergei I. Zhuk, "Détente and Western Cultural Products in Soviet Ukraine
    during the 1970s," in *Youth and Rock in the Soviet Bloc: Youth Cultures, Music,
    and the State in Russia and Eastern Europe*, ed. William Jay Risch (Rowman
    and Littlefield, 2012), 118–19.
13 The term *stylagi* describes members of a Soviet youth subculture between
    the 1940s and the 1960s who listened to Western pop music and wore showy,
    Western clothing.
14 David Burg, *Oppozitsionnye Nastroeniiya Molodezhi v Gody Posle "Ottepeli"*
    (University of Virginia, 1960), 25; Silina, *Nastroyeniya Sovetskogo
    Studenchestva*; Izrail Mazus, *Podpol'nye Molodezhnye Organizatsii, Gruppy
    i Kruzhki (1926–1953 Gg.): Spravochnik* (Vozvrasheniye, 2014); Kozlov,
    Kramola.
15 Kozlov, "Sotsializatsiya Sovetskoy Molodezhi Perioda 'ottepeli,'" 115–29.
16 Kozlov, 115–29.

17 Pilkington, *Russia's Youth and Its Culture*, 8.

18 David Farrugia, "Young People and Structural Inequality: Beyond the Middle Ground," *Journal of Youth Studies* 16, no. 5 (2013): 679, https://doi .org/10.1080/13676261.2012.744817.

19 Tatiana Ivanovna Zaslavskaya, *Raspredeleniye Po Trudu v Kolkhozakh* (Economika, 1966); Vladimir Grigorievich Venzher, *Kolkhoznyy Stroy Na Sovremennom Etape* (Economika, 1966); Tatiana Ivanovna Zaslavskaya, ed., *Migratsiya Sel'skogo Naseleniya* (Mysl', 1970); Vladimir Ivanovich Staroverov, *Sotsial'no-Demograficheskiye Problemy Derevni: Metodologiya, Metodika, Opyt Analiza Migratsii Sel'skogo Naseleniya* (Nauka, 1975); Ryvkina, *Obraz Zhizni Sel'skogo Naseleniya.*

20 Interview with Olga and Alexandr B. (1950, 1950, Cherepovets, 2020).

21 Interview with Olga and Alexandr B.

22 Wiliam Chase, "Voluntarism, Mobilisation and Coercion: *Subbotniki* 1919–1921," *Soviet Studies* 41, no. 1 (1989): 116, www.jstor.org/stable /152380?seq=1#metadata_info_tab_contents.

23 A *Komsomolsky prizyv* was an appeal to Komsomol members, usually from the party but sometimes from the Komsomol itself, to take part in an initiative. In the 1960s and '70s, when agricultural work fell out of favour with the young, announcements were published in newspapers encouraging young people to go work on farms.

24 VOANPI, f. 4039, op. 43, d. 7, l. 65.

25 VOANPI, f. 3892, op. 30, d. 21, l. 96.

26 VOANPI, f. 4039, op. 45, d. 6, l. 70.

27 VOANPI, f. 3892, op. 30, d. 181, l. 11.

28 *Imya Tvoye Komsomol: Ocherki Istorii Vologodskoy Oblastnoy Organizatsii VLKSM. 1918–1982* (Archangelskoe Severo-zapadnoe issledovanie, 1983), 177.

29 VOANPI, f. 4039, op. 43, d. 7, l. 15.

30 *Imya Tvoye Komsomol*, 201.

31 Vasiliy Stepanovich Yaroshovets, "Udarnaya Komsomolskaya Zona," in *Vsesoyusnaya Udarnaya v Moem Rodnom Sele*, ed. I. Danchenko (Molodaya gvardia, 1977), 26.

32 *Imya Tvoye Komsomol*, 235.

33 Clubs, bathhouses, stores, libraries – anything intended for people rather than industry.

34 Yaroshovets, "Udarnaya Komsomolskaya Zona," 26.

35 A *komsomolskaya putyovka* was a document issued by a VLKSM District Committee sending a Komsomol member on a short- or long-term work project.

36 *Imya Tvoye Komsomol*, 203–4.

37 VOANPI, f. 4039, op. 43, d. 7, l. 1.

38 VOANPI, f. 4039, op. 43, d. 7, l. 103.

39 Raymond Williams, *The Country and the City* (Chatto and Windus; Spokesman Books, 1973), 4.

40 Astrid Van Oyen, "Rural Time," *World Archaeology* 51, no. 2 (2019): 192.

41 Isabel A. Tirado, "The Komsomol's Village Vanguard: Youth and Politics in the NEP Countryside," *Russian Review* 72, no. 3 (2013): 343.

42 Isabel A. Tirado, "Peasants Into Soviets: Reconstructing Komsomol Identity in the Russian Countryside of the 1920s," *Acta Slavica Iaponica*, no. 18 (2001): 46–7.

43 Isabel A. Tirado, "The Komsomol and Young Peasants: The Dilemma of Rural Expansion, 1921–1925," *Slavic Review* 52, no. 3 (1993): 463.

44 Tirado, "The Komsomol and Young Peasants," 463.

45 Paxson, *Solovyovo*, 52–5.

46 Omelchenko, *Molodezh'*, 17.

47 VOANPI, f. 3892, op. 29, d. 201, l. 397.

48 VOANPI, f. 4039, op. 40, d. 13, l. 32 ob.

49 VOANPI, f. 3892, op. 30, d. 21, l. 107.

50 *Politodeli*, or political departments, were structures created in the 1930s that sent party and Komsomol members to oversee various governmental organizations and enterprises. The assignments could last for as long as a year and could not be declined. "Difficult assignments" were those assignments generally considered to be undesirable.

51 Kuznetskov, *Komsomol v Zakrytom Gorode*.

52 VOANPI, f. 3892, op. 30, d. 181, l. 5.

53 VOANPI, f. 3892, op. 30, d. 181, l. 6.

54 Anatoliy Slezin, *Fenomen Komsomola: Seredina 1950-Kh–Pervaya Polovina 1960-Kh Gg*, ed. A.A. Slezin (Gramota, 2017), 100.

55 Interview with Lyuda M. (1946, Molochnoe, 2021).

56 Interview with Lyuda M.

57 Paxson, *Solovyovo*, 66.

58 VOANPI, f. 3892, op. 30, d. 181, l. 8.

59 RGASPI, f. 1, op. 36, d. 131, l. 1.

60 RGASPI, f. 1, op. 36, d. 131, l. 1.

61 RGASPI, f. 1, op. 36, d. 125, l. 14.

62 RGASPI, f. 1, op. 36, d. 125, l. 15.

63 RGASPI, f. 1, op. 36, d. 125, l. 18.

64 VOANPI, f. 3892, op. 30, d. 181, l. 11.

65 Neverov, "Ukrepit' Malochislennyye Organizatsii VLKSM."

66 RGASPI, f. 1, op. 36, d. 63, l. 17.

67 RGASPI, f. 1, op. 36, d. 131, l. 65.

68 *Agrarnaya Politika KPSS i Komsomol* (Molodaya gvardia, 1975), 19–26.

69 Voronina and Sokolova, "Myslit' Kak Kommunisty," 4.

70 Interview with Alexandr K. (1955, Kargach, 2018).

71 Russian school mark roughly equivalent to an American C.
72 Interview with Alexandr K. (1955, Kargach, 2018)
73 Interview with Rimma F. (1949, Vologda, 2021)
74 VOANPI, f. 4039, op. 43, d. 7, l. 93–95.
75 VOANPI, f. 2959, op. 25, d. 27, l. 20.
76 VOANPI, f. 4039, op. 34, d. 2, l. 12.
77 VOANPI, f. 5230a, op. 1, d. 32, l. 11.
78 Interview with Iya V. (1953, Molochnoe, 2018).
79 Oleg Kharkhordin, *Oblichat' i Litsemerit': Genealogija Rossijskoj Lichnosti* (Letniy Sad, 2002), 364.
80 VOANPI, f. 520 a, op. 1, d. 33, l. 26.
81 At the Vologda VLKSM Regional Committee bureau, Secretary Shcherbakov outlined four ways in which the Vytegra Komsomol District Committee had worked together with "non-union youth." First, Shcherbakov talked about how the VLKSM "engaged [non-union youth] in communist labour," and illustrated his point with statistics on youth participation in communist labour brigades. Next, he cited VLKSM history propaganda projects as an example of cooperation between the VLKSM and non-union youth: "In 1960, 280 lectures and reports were delivered about the Komsomol and the upbringing of young people." Third, he discussed how non-union youths in Vytegra District had taken part in neighbourhood patrols and maintaining public order. The speaker explained that, in the district's sixty-two patrols, 150 of the 373 members were "non-union youth." Lastly, he pointed out that, under the leadership of the VLKSM, the district's young people were taking part in physical education and sport, receiving technical training, and "mastering new professions." Furthermore, the district committee secretary explained, "for the last few years all tenth-graders have left school as Komsomol members" (VOANPI, f. 3892, op. 30, d. 21, l. 35). Judging from the secretary's speech, the Komsomol's work with non-union youth did not differ greatly from its work with VLKSM members.
82 VOANPI, f. 2522, op. 68, d. 109, l. 53.
83 A yearly tax requiring a kolkhoz to hand over products such as meat, milk, and eggs from its farms.
84 VOANPI, f. 3892, op. 30, d. 221, l. 6.
85 VOANPI, f. 3892, op. 30, d. 21, l. 108.
86 VOANPI, f. 5230a, op. 1, d. 25, l. 5; VOANPI, f. 520a, op. 1, d. 33, l. 27; VOANPI, f. 3245, op. 1, d. 1, l. 34 ob.
87 Bridger, "Rural Youth," 90.
88 VOANPI, f. 3245, op. 1, d. 3, l. 5 ob.
89 VGANPI, f. 2522, op. 48, d. 62, l. 97.
90 Interview with Yuriy V. (1949, Molochnoe, 2018).
91 VGANPI, f. 5230a. op. 1, d. 26, l. 15.

92 VOANPI, f. 3245, op. 1, d. 1, l. 15.

93 VOANPI, f. 3245, op. 1, d. 6, l. 1.

94 Interview with Iya V. (1953, Molochnoe, 2020).

95 Interview with Evgeniy (1953, Molochnoe, 2028).

96 After communes failed to take hold in the Soviet countryside, the government returned some small plots of land to kolkhoz workers starting in 1932. In effect, kolkhoz workers had to labour on state farms during the day and then work a "second shift" on their own land to sustain themselves. When Khrushchev tried to end this system by limiting personal farms, it sparked an agricultural crisis.

97 Under the *trudoden* system, Kolkhoz workers were not paid a salary. Instead, their compensation was measured in "workdays," on the basis of which they were given grain or livestock feed for their personal farms.

9. The Invisible Komsomol: Kolkhoz and Sovkhoz VLKSM Organizations

1 VOANPI, f. 2522, op. 68, 109, l. 53.

2 VOANPI, f. 2522, op. 68, 109, l. 53.

3 LaPierre, *Hooligans in Khrushchev's Russia*; Dmitriy Krasnov, "Charasteristika sistemy borby s podrostkovoy prestupnostiyu I prestupleniyami nesovershennoletnich v RSFSR za 1965–1969," *Sotsialno-poloticheskie nauki* 3 (2013): 84.

4 DOSAAF is the acronym for the Volunteer Society for Cooperation with the Army, Aviation, and Navy (Russian: Добровольное общество содействия армии, авиации и флоту), a Soviet paramilitary sport organization concerned primarily with weapons, automobiles, and aviation. The society was established in 1927 as OSOAVIAKhIM but from 1951 to 1991 carried the name of DOSAAF.

5 VOANPI, f. 2522, op. 68, 109, l. 53.

6 Sonja Luehrmann, *Religion in Secular Archives: Soviet Atheism and Historical Knowledge* (Oxford University Press, 2015).

7 Voronina and Sokolova, "Myslit' kak kommunisty."

8 Boris Groys, *Kommunisticheskiy postskriptum* (Ad Marginem PresMoscow, 2014).

9 Yurchak, *Everything Was Forever*, 36–77.

10 Yurchak, 71–6.

11 Yurchak, 159.

12 VOANPI, f. 2959, op. 25, d. 12, l. 24 ob.

13 VOANPI, f. 4039, op. 38, d. 11, l. 67.

14 Voronina and Sokolova, "Myslit' kak kommunisty."

15 Voronina and Sokolova.

16 Interview with Iya V. (1953, Molochnoe, 2018).

17 Despite the overall similarities between the position of sovkhozes and kolkhozes within the Soviet economy, kolkhozes had slightly more economic and political autonomy than sovkhozes. More on the difference in status in Humphrey, *Marx Went Away*, 3.

18 This was a system in which graduates from colleges and technical schools received job assignments to state or collective farms and were required to work there for at least three years.

19 Interview with Iya V. (1953, Molochnoe, 2018).

20 Interview with Iya V.

21 Interview with Iya V.

22 VOANPI, f. 4039, op. 35, d. 10, l. 66.

23 VOANPI, f. 4039, op. 39, d. 9, l. 60; VOANPI, f. 4039, op. 38, d. 11, l. 73.

24 VOANPI, f. 4039, op. 45, d. 13, l. 148.

25 VOANPI, f. 4039, op. 40, d. 13, l. 25, 25 ob.

26 "Young specialist" is a Russian title for a young trained professional. The term was used to denote the graduates of colleges, universities, and technical schools who were sent to work in rural areas between the 1960s and the 1980s. They could be people with agricultural professions but also teachers, librarians, or medical professionals.

27 VOANPI, f. 4039, op. 39, d. 9, l. 60.

28 VOANPI, f. 9594, op. 1, d. 361, l. 34.

29 VOANPI, f. 4039, op. 39, d. 9, l. 60.

30 VOANPI, f. 4039, op. 38, d. 11, l. 68 ob.

31 The socialist obligation for milk yield, which appeared in the annual report on work for the same year, was ultimately reduced from 2,600 to 2,100 litres per year. Judging by the report, Valentina K. milked only 2,530 litres, a little short of the declared norm. However, by a simple juggling of numbers (replacing the social obligation indicator from 2,600 to 2,100 litres), it turned out that she exceeded the plan, for which she was awarded a washing machine. See VOANPI, f. 4039, op. 38, d. 11, l. 76.

32 VOANPI, f. 4039, op. 35, d. 10, l. 3.

33 VOANPI, f. 4039, op. 41, d. 14, l. 94 ob.

34 Voronina and Sokolova, "Myslit' kak kommunisty," 13.

35 VOANPI, f. 4039, op. 39, d. 9, l. 55 ob.

36 VOANPI, f. 4039, op. 38, d. 11, l. 79.

37 GAVO, f. 5031, op. 1, d. 59, l. 7.

38 VOANPI, f. 4039, op. 38, d. 11, l. 74 ob.

39 VOANPI, f. 4039, op. 35, d. 10, l. 28 ob.

40 VOANPI, f. 4039, op. 35, d. 10, l. 65.

41 VOANPI, f. 4039, op. 38, d. 11, l. 74.

42 VOANPI, f. 4039, op. 39, d. 9, l. 53.

43 VOANPI, f. 4039, op. 38, d. 11, l. 75.

44 VOANPI, f. 4039, op. 40, d. 13, l. 21.

45 VOANPI, f. 4039, op. 40, d. 13, l. 21.

46 The "Day of Procession" (*krestniy khod*) was a village-day holiday in Kabachino celebrated on the last Sunday in July. In neighbouring settlements, village days were celebrated on Ivanov's Day (24 June), Ilyin's Day (2 August), Peter's Day (12 July), or on the dates of other religious holidays.

47 Interview with Igor L. (1945, Kabachino, 2019).

48 VOANPI, f. 2522, op. 47, d. 41, l. 94.

49 VOANPI, f. 4039, op. 38 d. 11, l. 69.

50 VOANPI, f. 4039, op. 38, d. 11, l. 79.

51 VOANPI, f. 4039, op. 39, d. 9, l. 56.

52 VOANPI, f. 4039, op. 41. d. 14, l. 100.

53 Interview with Yuri V. (1949, Molochnoe, 2018).

54 VOANPI, f. 4039, op. 39, d. 9, l. 57 ob.

55 Interview with Evgeny and Galina Kh. (1950, 1948, Sosunovo, 2018).

56 Interview with Yuri V. (1949, Molochnoe, 2018).

57 Tromly, *Making the Soviet Intelligentsia*, 53–76.

58 VOANPI, f. 9594, op. 1, d. 1, l. 44.

59 An exam on the fundamentals of Marxism and the works of Lenin required of Komsomol members and implemented on the one hundredth anniversary of Lenin's birth in 1970.

60 VOANPI, f. 2958, op. 25, d. 12, l. 118.

61 VOANPI, f. 2950, op. 26, d. 15, l. 59.

62 VOANPI, f. 4039, op. 39, d. 9, l. 54.

63 For example, the rejection of an application for withdrawal from the Komsomol was discussed at the general Komsomol meeting of the Vorobyevsky state farm's second branch on 3 December 1971. VOANPI, f. 4039, op. 40, d. 13, l. 32 ob.

64 VOANPI, f. 2959, op. 23, d. 13, l. 33.

65 VOANPI, f. 2959, op. 25, d. 38, l. 9.

66 VOANPI, f. 2959, op. 25, d. 38, l. 12.

67 VOANPI, f. 2959, op. 25, d. 38, l. 12, 58 ob., 71 ob.

68 Geral'd Aleksandrovich Solov'yev, ed., *Spravochnik Komsomol'skogo Aktivista Armii i Flota* (Voenizdat, 1976), 94.

69 VOANPI, f. 2522, op. 63, d. 60, l. 46.

70 VOANPI, f. 4039, op. 38, d. 11, l. 80.

71 VOANPI, f. 2950, op. 26, d. 15, l. 61.

72 VOANPI, f. 2522, op. 77, d. 127, l. 55, 56, 57.

73 VOANPI, f. 2522, op. 77, d. 127, l. 56.

74 VOANPI, f. 2959, op. 23, d. 13, l. 36.

75 VOANPI, f. 2959, op. 25, d. 38, l. 9.

76 VOANPI, f. 2959, op. 26, d. 15, l. 66 ob.

77 VOANPI, f. 2959, op. 23, d. 13, l. 32 ob.

78 VOANPI, f. 2959, op. 25, d. 12, l. 126.

79 VOANPI, f. 2959, op. 34, d. 15, l. 61 ob.

80 VOANPI, f. 2959, op. 29, d. 23, l. 32 ob.

81 "Vnutrisoyuznaya Rabota – Osnova Deyatel'nosti Pervichnoy Organizatsii," in *Osnovy Deyatel'nosti "Komsomol'skogo Prozhektora": (V Pomoshch' Sekretaryu Pervichnoy Komsomol'skoy Organizatsii, Nachal'niku Shtaba "K.P."* (Vologda, 1976), 2–6.

82 VOANPI, f. 2959, op. 23, d. 13, l. 30.

83 VOANPI, f. 2959, op. 25, d. 12, l. 114.

84 VOANPI, f. 2959, op. 25, d. 18, l. 125.

85 VOANPI, f. 2959, op. 26, d. 15, l. 66 ob.

86 VOANPI, f. 2959, op. 34, d. 15, l. 59 ob.

87 VOANPI, f. 2959, op. 23, d. 13, l. 34 ob.

88 VOANPI, f. 2959, op. 23, d. 13, l. 34 ob.

89 VOANPI, f. 2959, op. 26, d. 15, l. 66 ob.

90 The popularity of Komsomol concerts held at rural clubs on the sovkhoz "Vorobyevsky" was attested to during interviews with Alexander K. and Iya V. Interview with Alexander K. (1956, Kargach, July 2018); interview with Iya V. (1953, Molochnoe, March 2018).

Conclusion

1 Bruno Latour, *Down to Earth: Politics in the New Climatic Regime* (Polity Press, 2018).

Bibliography

State Archive of Vologda Oblast (GAVO): Title of Fonds

1. State farm "Podopitomnichesky," Vologda District, Vologda Oblast: f. 70, op. 1, d. 11, 57; f. 70, op. 2, d. 1, 8; f. 70, op. 3, d. 222, 260.
2. Vologda Dairy Institute: f. 165, op. 10, d. 331, 271, 229, 254, 225.
3. Vologda Oblast Regional Committee of Education: f. 504, op. 3, d. 306, 314, 321, 322, 329, 337, 401, 426, 506, 597, 2979.
4. Vologda District Executive Committee of Working People's Deputies: f. 521, op. 8, d. 110, 134, 220, 316, 335, 379, 714; op. 4, d. 2.
5. Statistical Office, Vologda Oblast: f. 1703, op. 19, d. 59; op. 20, d. 7526, 8618.
6. Kirillovsky District Regional Committee of Education: f. 2202, op. 3, d. 42, 47, 57, 86, 139, 193, 218, 248, 278.
7. Vologda Regional Committee of Public Education: f. 2207, op. 3, d. 139.
8. Vologda Regional Department of Public Education. School sector: f. 2360, op. 5, 49, 52, 72, 94, 95, 126, 163, 182, 183, 205, 235, 260, 282, 283, 310, 334, 357, 385, 415, 451.
9. Executive Committee of the Migachevsky Village Council, Kirillovsky District, Vologda Oblast: f. 5031, op. 1, d. 43, 59, 104, 142, 255.

Vologda Regional Archive of Recent Political History (VOANPI)

1. Kirillovsky District Committee of the Komsomol: f. 4039, op. 40, d. 40; op. 43, d. 7.
2. Party organization of the collective farm "Fight": f. 5230a, op. 1, d. 25, 26, 32, 34.
3. Kirillovsky District Committee of the CPSU. Department of Propaganda and Agitation: f. 1428, op. 27, d. 11.

4. Vologda Regional Department of the CPSU. Common Department: f. 2445, op. 25, d. 4, 52.

5. Reception sector of the Vologda Regional Committee of the CPSU: f. 2522, op. 42, d. 88; op. 48, d. 62; op. 65, d. 69; op. 63, d. 60; op. 68, d. 85, 109; op. 73, d. 357, 386; op. 77, d. 34, 127; op. 96, d. 53; op. 47, d. 41; op. 72, d. 263; op. 63, d. 84; op. 66, d. 84, 102; op. 63, d. 84; op. 45, d. 106; op. 73, d. 63; op. 83, d. 98, 104.

6. Vologda District Committee of the Komsomol. Protocols of general and departmental meetings of primary Komsomol meetings of state farms: f. 2958, op. 25, d. 12.

7. Vologda District Committee of the Komsomol. Protocols of general and departmental meetings of primary Komsomol meetings of state farms: f. 2950, op. 26, d. 15.

8. Vologda District Committee of the Komsomol. Protocols of general and departmental meetings of primary Komsomol meetings of state farms: f. 2959, op. 23, d. 7, 12, 13, 15, 18, 23, 29, 34, 38; op. 34, d. 14; op. 28, d. 12; op. 24, d. 18.

9. Kirillovsky District Committee of the CPSU. Minutes of general meetings of the primary party organizations of the state farm "Red Banner": f. 3245, op. 1, d. 1, 3, 6.

10. Vologda Regional Committee of the Komsomol: f. 3892, op. 29, d. 114, 201, 204; op. 30, d. 21, 22, 181, 221; op. 35, d. 8, 10; op. 38, d. 11, 282; op. 39, d. 9; op. 40, d. 2, 13; op. 41, d. 14; op. 43, d. 7; op. 45, d. 13.

11. Kirillovsky District Committee of the Komsomol: f. 4039, op. 38, d. 11; op. 43, d. 7; op. 45, d. 6.

12. The primary organization of the CPSU state farm "Vorobyevsky": f. 9594, op. 1, d. 1, 361.

Russian State Archive of Socio-Political History (RGASPI)

1. Central Committee of the Komsomol: f. 1, op. 36, d. 49, 63, 78, 273, 131, 125; op. 41, d. 171; op. 39, d. 44.

Archival Sources

GAVO, f. 165, op. 10, d. 225, l. 42
GAVO, f. 165, op. 10, d. 254, l. 1–140
GAVO, f. 165, op. 10, d. 271, l. 13
GAVO, f. 165, op. 10, d. 271, l. 29a
GAVO, f. 165, op. 10, d. 271, l. 25
GAVO, f. 165, op. 10, d. 331, l. 21
GAVO, f. 1703, op. 19, d. 59, l. 1–3

GAVO, f. 1703, op. 20, d. 7526, l. 10–10 ob.
GAVO, f. 2202, op. 3, d. 218, l. 17 ob.
GAVO, f. 2202, op. 3, d. 42, l. 6
GAVO, f. 2202, op. 3, d. 42, l. 7
GAVO, f. 2202, op. 3, d. 57, l. 173
GAVO, f. 2202, op. 3, d. 57, l. 206 ob.
GAVO, f. 2202, op. 3, d. 86, l. 19
GAVO, f. 2207 op. 3, d. 139, l. 3
GAVO, f. 2360, op. 5, d. 126, l. 15
GAVO, f. 2360, op. 5, d. 126, l. 16
GAVO, f. 2360, op. 5, d. 126, l. 42
GAVO, f. 2360, op. 5, d. 163, l. 11
GAVO, f. 2360, op. 5, d. 235, l. 73
GAVO, f. 2360, op. 5, d. 235, l. 74
GAVO, f. 2360, op. 5, d. 260, l. 2
GAVO, f. 2360, op. 5, d. 282, l. 2
GAVO, f. 2360, op. 5, d. 282, l. 8
GAVO, f. 2360, op. 5, d. 334, l. 4
GAVO, f. 2360, op. 5, d. 334, l. 6
GAVO, f. 2360, op. 5, d. 357, l. 14
GAVO, f. 2360, op. 5, d. 357, l. 153
GAVO, f. 2360, op. 5, d. 357, l. 16
GAVO, f. 2360, op. 5, d. 357, l. 18
GAVO, f. 2360, op. 5, d. 357, l. 56
GAVO, f. 2360, op. 5, d. 357, l. 61
GAVO, f. 2360, op. 5, d. 357, l. 67
GAVO, f. 2360, op. 5, d. 415, l. 14
GAVO, f. 2360, op. 5, d. 49, l. 18
GAVO, f. 2360, op. 5, d. 52, l. 79
GAVO, f. 2360, op. 5, d. 52, l. 89
GAVO, f. 2360, op. 5, d. 72, l. 17
GAVO, f. 2360, op. 5, d. 72, l. 2
GAVO, f. 2360, op. 5, d. 94, l. 2
GAVO, f. 2360, op. 5, d. 260, l. 5
GAVO, f. 3, op. 314, l. 13
GAVO, f. 5031, op. 1, d. 59, l. 7
GAVO, f. 504, op. 3, d. 306, l. 9, 10
GAVO, f. 504, op. 3, d. 314, l. 54
GAVO, f. 504, op. 3, d. 321, l. 53
GAVO, f. 504, op. 3, d. 322, l. 9
GAVO, f. 504, op. 3, d. 329, l. 148
GAVO, f. 504, op. 3, d. 329, l. 150

GAVO, f. 504, op. 3, d. 401, l. 8
GAVO, f. 504, op. 3, d. 426, l. 5
GAVO, f. 504, op. 3, d. 506, l. 1, 2
GAVO, f. 504, op. 3, d. 506, l. 219
GAVO, f. 504, op. 3, d. 506, l. 247
GAVO, f. 504, op. 3, d. 506, l. 38
GAVO, f. 504, op. 3, d. 597, l. 39
GAVO, f. 521, op. 1, d. 2, l. 60
GAVO, f. 521, op. 8, d. 110, l. 105
GAVO, f. 521, op. 8, d. 134, l. 78
GAVO, f. 521, op. 8, d. 220, l. 29
GAVO, f. 521, op. 8, d. 220, l. 44
GAVO, f. 521, op. 8, d. 266, l. 13–17
GAVO, f. 521, op. 8, d. 266, l. 47
GAVO, f. 521, op. 8, d. 316, l. 17
GAVO, f. 521, op. 8, d. 316, l. 19
GAVO, f. 521, op. 8, d. 316, l. 32, 33
GAVO, f. 521, op. 8, d. 316, l. 36
GAVO, f. 521, op. 8, d. 316, l. 82 ob.
GAVO, f. 521, op. 8, d. 316, l. 86 ob.
GAVO, f. 521, op. 8, d. 316, l. 89 ob.
GAVO, f. 521, op. 8, d. 335, l. 18, 19, 20, 21, 22
GAVO, f. 521, op. 8, d. 335, l. 18
GAVO, f. 521, op. 8, d. 379, l. 121
GAVO, f. 521, op. 8, d. 714, l. 52
GAVO, f. 70, op. 1, d. 11, l. 110
GAVO, f. 70, op. 2, d. 1, l. 10
GAVO, f. 70, op. 2, d. 1, l. 14 ob.
GAVO, f. 70, op. 2, d. 1, l. 36
GAVO, f. 70, op. 2, d. 8, l. 25
GAVO, f. 70, op. 3, d. 222, l. 7
GAVO, f. 70, op. 3, d. 260, l. 5
GAVO, f. 165, op. 10, d. 229, l. 13, 30, 61, 107, 127, 139
GAVO, f. 1703, op. 20, d. 7526, l. 10–10 ob.
GAVO, f. 1822, op. 5, d. 136, l. 15, 16
GAVO, f. 2202, op. 3, d. 139, l. 4
GAVO, f. 2202, op. 3, d. 193, l. 1
GAVO, f. 2360, op. 5, d. 357, l. 52
GAVO, f. 2360, op. 5, d. 357, l. 86
GAVO, f. 2360, op. 5, d. 451, l. 2
GAVO, f. 2360, op. 5, d. 49, l. 1
GAVO, f. 2360, op. 2a, d. 797, l. 1

GAVO, f. 2360, op. 2a, d. 797, l. 4
GAVO, f. 2360, op. 5, d. 163, l. 32
GAVO, f. 2360, op. 5, d. 234, l. 22, 23, 24, 25
GAVO, f. 2360, op. 5, d. 283, l. 55, 56, 57, 58, 59, 60
GAVO, f. 2360, op. 5, d. 310, l. 110, 111
GAVO, f. 2360, op. 5, d. 357, l. 5
GAVO, f. 2360, op. 5, d. 357, l. 6
GAVO, f. 2360, op. 5, d. 415, l. 19
GAVO, f. 2360, op. 5, d. 94, l. 70
GAVO, f. 2360, op. 5, d. 94, l. 69
GAVO, f. 5031, op. 1, d. 46, l. 4
GAVO, f. 504, op. 3, d. 306, l. 3
GAVO, f. 504, op. 3, d. 329, l. 89
GAVO, f. 521, op. 8, d. 379, l. 7
GAVO, f. 70, op. 2, d. 1, l. 16
GAVO, f. 2202, op. 3, d. 57, l. 186
GAVO, f. 1703, op. 20, d. 8618, l. 10
RGASPI, f. 1, op. 36, d. 63, l. 12, 15
RGASPI, f. 1, op. 36, d. 78, l. 96
RGASPI, f. 1, op. 36, d. 63, l. 15
RGASPI, f. 1, op. 41, d. 171, l. 1, 1 ob.
RGASPI, f. 1, op. 36, d. 125, l. 18
RGASPI, f. 1, op. 39, d. 44, l. 25, 26
RGASPI, f. 1, op. 41, d. 254, l. 64, 65
VOANPI, f. 1428, op. 27, d. 11, l. 1
VOANPI, f. 2445, op. 25, d. 4, l. 12
VOANPI, f. 2445, op. 25, d. 4, l. 15
VOANPI, f. 2522, op. 42, d. 88, l. 27
VOANPI, f. 2522, op. 47, d. 41, l. 94
VOANPI, f. 2522, op. 63, d. 84, l. 33
VOANPI, f. 2522, op. 63, d. 85, l. 70
VOANPI, f. 2522, op. 65, d. 69, l. 4, 5
VOANPI, f. 2522, op. 66, d. 102, l. 53
VOANPI, f. 2522, op. 68, d. 109, l. 114
VOANPI, f. 2522, op. 72, d. 263, l. 27, 28
VOANPI, f. 2522, op. 73, d. 63, l. 38
VOANPI, f. 2522, op. 73, d. 357, l. 1
VOANPI, f. 2522, op. 73, d. 386, l. 11
VOANPI, f. 2522, op. 77, d. 34, l. 68
VOANPI, f. 2522, op. 77, d. 127, l. 55, 56, 57
VOANPI, f. 2950, op. 26, d. 15, l. 61
VOANPI, f. 2958, op. 25, d. 12, l. 118

VOANPI, f. 2959, op. 23, d. 13, l. 33
VOANPI, f. 2959, op. 23, d. 13, l. 34 ob.
VOANPI, f. 2959, op. 23, d. 13, l. 36
VOANPI, f. 2959, op. 25, d. 12, l. 114
VOANPI, f. 2959, op. 25, d. 12, l. 123
VOANPI, f. 2959, op. 25, d. 12, l. 126
VOANPI, f. 2959, op. 25. d. 12, l. 24 ob.
VOANPI, f. 2959, op. 25, d. 18, l. 125
VOANPI, f. 2959, op. 29, d. 23, l. 32 ob.
VOANPI, f. 3892, op. 38, d. 282, l. 10
VOANPI, f. 4039, op. 35, d. 10, l. 28 ob.
VOANPI, f. 4039, op. 35, d. 10, l. 65
VOANPI, f. 4039, op. 35, d. 10, l. 66
VOANPI, f. 4039, op. 35, d. 10, l. 3
VOANPI, f. 4039, op. 35, d. 8, l. 65 ob., 66
VOANPI, f. 4039, op. 38, d. 11, l. 67
VOANPI, f. 4039, op. 38, d. 11, l. 74 ob.
VOANPI, f. 4039, op. 38, d. 11, l. 75
VOANPI, f. 4039, op. 38, d. 11, l. 79
VOANPI, f. 4039, op. 38, d. 11, l. 80
VOANPI, f. 4039, op. 38, d. 11, l. 73
VOANPI, f. 4039, op. 38, d. 11, l. 76
VOANPI, f. 4039, op. 38, d. 11, l. 68 ob.
VOANPI, f. 4039, op. 39, d. 9, l. 53
VOANPI, f. 4039, op. 39, d. 9, l. 54
VOANPI, f. 4039, op. 39, d. 9, l. 55 ob.
VOANPI, f. 4039, op. 39, d. 9, l. 56
VOANPI, f. 4039, op. 39, d. 9, l. 60
VOANPI, f. 4039, op. 40, d. 13, l. 21
VOANPI, f. 4039, op. 40, d. 13, l. 32 ob.
VOANPI, f. 4039, op. 40, d.13, l. 25, 25 ob.
VOANPI, f. 4039, op. 41, d. 14, l. 94 ob.
VOANPI, f. 4039, op. 41. d. 14, l. 100
VOANPI, f. 4039, op. 43, d. 7, l. 13
VOANPI, f. 4039, op. 45, d. 13, l. 148
VOANPI, f. 9594, op. 1, d. 361, l. 34
VOANPI, f. 2445, op. 25, d. 4, l. 12
VOANPI, f. 2445, op. 25, d. 4, l. 52
VOANPI, f. 25, op. 66, d. 46, l. 101
VOANPI, f. 2522, op. 63, d. 60, l. 46
VOANPI, f. 2522, op. 96, d. 53, l. 81
VOANPI, f. 2522, op. 63, d. 82, l. 1

VOANPI, f. 2950, op. 26, d. 15, l. 59
VOANPI, f. 2959, op. 23, d. 13, l. 30
VOANPI, f. 2959, op. 23, d. 13, l. 32 ob.
VOANPI, f. 2959, op. 25, d. 38, l. 12, 58 ob., 71 ob.
VOANPI, f. 2959, op. 25, d. 38, l. 9
VOANPI, f. 2959, op. 26, d. 15, l. 66 ob.
VOANPI, f. 2959, op. 34, d. 15, l. 59 ob.
VOANPI, f. 2959, op. 34, d. 15, l. 61 ob.
VOANPI, f. 3892, op. 29, d. 201, l. 397
VOANPI, f. 3892, op. 29, d. 201, l. 383
VOANPI, f. 3892, op. 30, d. 181, l. 8
VOANPI, f. 3892, op. 29, d. 201, l. 383
VOANPI, f. 4039, op. 38 d. 11, l. 69
VOANPI, f. 4039, op. 39, d. 9, l. 57 ob.
VOANPI, f. 9594, op. 1, d. 1. l. 44.

Interviews

Collective interview with Elena A., Tat'yana R., Irina, Alena, Olga B. (1964, 1970, 1969, 1970, 1970, Molochnoe, 2018)
Interview with Alexandr A. (1953, Molochnoe, 2021)
Interview with Alexandr K. (1955, Kargach, 2018)
Interview with Antonina K. (1942, Goritsy, 2018)
Interview with Elena V. (1950, Vologda, 2018)
Interview with Evelina M. (1940, Molochnoe, 2021)
Interview with Evgeniy G. (1949, Molochnoe, 2018, 2019)
Interview with Galina Sh. (1949, Molochnoe, 2018)
Inteview with Galina and Eugeniy H. (1948, 1952, Sosunovo, 2018)
Interview with Irina B. (1942, Mayskiy, 2018)
Interview with Iya V. (1953, Molochnoe, 2018, 2019, 2021)
Interview with Kapitalina (1948, Molochnoe, 2021)
Interview with Ludmila S. (1954, Molochnoe, 2021)
Interview with Lyuda M. (1946, Molochnoe, 2021)
Interview with Nina S. (1963, Mayskiy, 2018)
Interview with Olga and Alexandr B. (1950, 1950, Cherepovets, 2020)
Interview with Sergei and Valentina A. (1954, Migachevo, 2019)
Interview with Sergey K. (1959, Kabachino, 2019)
Interview with Sergey T. (1967, Vologda, 2018)
Interview with Tatyana K. (1958, Kabachino, 2018)
Interview with Valentina B. (1948, Molochnoe, 2020)
Interview with Vlad and Tatiana S. (1949, 1947, Kabachino, 2019)
Interview with Vladimir P. (1954, Molochnoe, 2021)

310   Bibliography

Interview with Vladislav (1949, Molochnoe, 2018)
Interview with Yuri V. (1949, Molochnoe, 2018, 2019, 2021)
Interview with Zinaida S. (1949, Kabachino, 2018)
Interview with Zoya L. (1941, Mayskiy, 2018)

Secondary Sources

Afanas'ev, Yuriy, ed. *Sud'by Rossiyskogo Krest'yanstva.* Rossiyskiy gosudarstvenniy
    gumanitarniy universitet, 1996.
Agrarnaya Politika KPSS i Komsomol. Molodaya gvardia, 1975.
"Akademgorodok: Istoriya Glavnoy Gazety Akademii." *Akademgorodok* 2508,
    no. 10 (2016): 6.
Alekseyev, Aleksandr Ivanovich. "Chelovek i Priroda v Razvitii Sel'skoy
    Mestnosti Nechernozem'ya." *Regional'nyye Issledovaniya,* no. 4 (2014): 81–7.
–. "Sel'skoye Rasseleniye i Sel'skoye Khozyaystvo Nechernozemnoy
    Zony RSFSR: Problemy Izucheniya Vzaimosvyazey." In *Territorial'noye
    Planirovaniye Naseleniya: 4-Ye Mezhvedomstvennoye Soveshchaniye Po Geografii
    Naseleniya. Tbilisi, Noyabr' 1979 G,* 125–6. GO SSSR, 1979.
Alymov, Sergey. "Intellektualy Zastoya: Mezhdu Ofitsial'nym Kollektivizmom
    i Vystradannoy Elitarnost'yu." In *Eto Bylo Navsegda 68/85,* 18–23.
    Gosudarstvennaya tret'yakovskaya galereya, 2020.
–. "Nesluchaynoye Selo: Sovetskiye Etnografy i Kolkhozniki Na Puti "ot
    Starogo k Novomu" i Obratno." *Novoye literaturnoye obozreniye* 110, no. 1
    (2010): 109–29.
–. "Ponyatiye 'Perezhitok' i Sovetskiye Sotsial'nyye Nauki v 1950–1960-Ye
    Gody." *Antropologicheskiy Forum* 16 (2012): 261–87.
Anweiler, Oskar, and Friedrich Kuebart. *Die Sowjetische Schul – Und
    Berufsbildungsreform: Vorbereitung, Schwerpunkte, Beginn Der Realisierung.*
    Bundesinstitut für Ostwissenschaftliche und Internationale Studien, 1958.
Appadurai, Arjun. "The Production of Locality." In *Counterworks: Managing the
    Diversity of Knowledge,* edited by Richard Fardon, 204–25. Routledge, 1995.
Assmann, Aleida. *Dlinnaya Ten' Proshlogo: Memorial'naya Kul'tura i Istoricheskaya
    Politika.* Novoe literaturnoe obozrenie, 2014.
Baiburin, Albert. *Sovetskiy Pasport: Istoriya, Struktura, Praktika.* European
    University at St. Petersburg, 2019.
Balashov, Yevgeniy Mikhaylovich. *Shkola v Rossiyskom Obshchestve 1917–1927 Gg.
    Stanovleniye "novogo Cheloveka."* Dmitriy Bulanin, 2003.
Balfour, Robert J., Claudia Mitchell, and Relebohile Moletsane. "View of
    Troubling Contexts: Toward a Generative Theory of Rurality as Education
    Research." *Journal of Rural and Community Development* 3, no. 3 (2008): 100–11.
Ball, Alan M. *And Now My Soul Is Hardened: Abandoned Children in Soviet Russia,
    1918–1930.* University of California Press, 1994.

Ball, Stephen J. *Education Policy and Social Class: The Selected Works of Stephen Ball.* Routledge, 2006.

–. *Foucault and Education : Disciplines and Knowledge.* Routledge, 2012. https://www.routledge.com/Foucault-and-Education-Disciplines-and-Knowledge/Ball/p/book/9780415521581.

Belyayeva, Lyubov' Dmitriyevna. "Iz Istorii Stroyotryadovskogo Dvizheniya VMI." *Akademgorodok* 507, no. 9 (2016): 8–9.

Belyayeva (Biryukova), Lyubov' Dmitriyevna. "Ulitsa i Dom Moyego Detstva." In Plastinina (Makarova) et al., *Molochnoye – Dom, v Kotorom My Zhivem,* 358–62.

Belyayeva, Lyubov' Dmitriyevna, and Angelina Sergeyevna Serova. "Ko Dnyu Rossiyskikh Studencheskikh Otryadov." *Akademgorodok* 2500, no. 2 (2016): 12–13.

Berg, Auri C. "Reform in the Time of Stalin: Nikita Khrushchev and the Fate of the Russian Peasantry." PhD diss., University of Toronto, 2012.

Berman, Marshall. *All That Is Solid Melts Into Air: The Experience of Modernity.* Simon and Schuster, 1982.

Bernstein, Henry. "The 'Peasant Problem' in the Russian Revolution(s), 1905–1929." *Journal of Peasant Studies* 45, nos. 5–6 (2018): 1127–50. https://doi.org/https://doi.org/10.1080/03066150.2018.1428189.

Beznin, Mikhail Alekseyevich. *Krest'yanskiy Dvor v Rossiyskom Nechernozem'ye 1950–1965 Gody.* Vologodskiy Pedagogocheskiy Institut, 1991.

Beznin, Mikhail Alekseyevich, and Tatiana Mikhaylovna Dimoni. *Kapitalizatsiya v Rossiyskoy Derevne 1930–1980kh Godov.* Knizhnyy Dom Librokom, 2009.

–, "Intellektualy v Sel'skom Khozyaystve Rossii 1930–1980-Kh Gg." *Yaroslavskiy Pedagogicheskiy Vestnik* 1 (2013): 29–41.

Bogdanova, Elena. "Antropologiya derevenskoy dvukhetazhki: Ot issledovaniya zhilishcha k issledovaniyu soobshchestva." In *Vdali ot gorodov: Zhizn' postsovetskoy derevni,* edited by Elena Bogdanova and Olga Brednikova, 105–26. Aleteyya, 2013.

Bourdieu, Pierre. *Algeria 1960: The Disenchantment of the World; The Sense of Honour; The Kabyle House or the World Reversed: Essays.* Cambridge University Press, 1979.

–. "Systems of Education and Systems of Thought." In *Knowledge and Control: New Directions for the Socioloay of Education,* edited by Michael F.D. Young, 189–207. Macmillan, 1971.

Bradley, Richard. "Ritual, Time and History." *World Archaeology* 23, no. 2 (1991): 209–19.

Brantlinger, Andrew, Laureland Cooley, and Ellen Brantlinger. "Families, Values, and Class Relations: The Politics of Alternative Certifcation." In *The Routledge International Handbook of the Sociology of Education,* edited by Andrew Brantlinger, Laurel Cooley, and Ellen Brantlinger, 179–89. Routledge, 2009.

Bridger, Sue. "Rural Youth." In *Soviet Youth Culture*, edited by Jim Riordan, 83–102. Macmillan, 1989.

Britvina, Elena Vladimirovna. "'Vot Uzhe 33 Goda Proshlo s Tekh Por, Kak Nasha Sem'ya Pereyekhala … '" In Plastinina (Makarova) et al., *Molochnoye – Dom, v Kotorom My Zhivem*, 150–2.

Bruisch, Katja. "Knowledge and Power in the Making of the Soviet Village." In *Governing the Rural in Interwar Europe*, edited by Liesbeth Van de Grift and Amalia Ribi Forclaz, 139–63. Routledge, 2018.

–. "The Soviet Village Revisited: Household Farming and the Changing Image of Socialism in the Late Soviet Period." *Cahiers Du Monde Russe* 57, no. 1 (2016): 81–100. www.tara.tcd.ie/handle/2262/89671.

Bruisch, Katja, and Klaus Gestwa. "Expertise and the Quest for Rural Modernization in the Russian Empire and the Soviet Union." *Cahiers Du Monde Russe* 57, no. 1 (2016): 7–30. https://doi.org/10.4000/MONDERUSSE.8324.

Burg, David. *Oppozitsionnye Nastroeniiya Molodezhi v Gody Posle "Ottepeli."* University of Virginia, 1960.

Chase, Wiliam. "Voluntarism, Mobilisation and Coercion: *Subbotniki* 1919–1921." *Soviet Studies* 41, no. 1 (1989): 111–28. www.jstor.org/stable/152380?seq=1#metadata_info_tab_contents.

Chayanov, Alexanrd Vasilievich. "Puteshestviye Moyego Brata Alekseya v Stranu Krest'yanskoy Utopii." In *Venetsianskoye Zerkalo: Povesti*, edited by V.M. Muraviev, 161–208. Moscow, 1989.

Cherkaev, Xenia A. *Gleaning for Communism: The Soviet Socialist Household in Theory and Practice.* Cornell University Press, 2023.

Chernova, Zhanna Vladimirovna. "Sovremennyye Modeli Genderno-Segregirovannogo Obrazovaniya." *Zhurnal Issledovaniy Sotsial'noy Politiki* 4, no. 1 (2006): 58–80.

"Chleny Izbiratel'noy Komissii Vologodskoy Oblasti. Valyuzhenich Anatoliy Ivanovich." Izbiratel'naya Komissiya Vologodskoy Oblasti, accessed 27 December 2024. www.vologod.izbirkom.ru/docs/4266/.

Chuglova, Natalia Konstantinovna. "'Istoriya Doma – Eto Istoriya Sem'i … '" In Plastinina (Makarova) et al., *Molochnoye – Dom, v Kotorom My Zhivem*, 246–351.

Clark, Katerina. *The Soviet Novel: History as Ritual.* Chicago University Press, 1981.

Cloke, Paul. "Conceptualizing Rurality." In *Handbook of Rural Studies*, edited by Paul Cloke, Terry Marsden, and Patrick Mooney, 18–28. SAGE Publications, 2006.

Collins, James. "Social Reproduction in Classrooms and Schools." *Annual Review of Anthropology* 38 (October 2009): 33–48. https://doi.org/10.1146/ANNUREV.ANTHRO.37.081407.085242.

Corbett, Michael. "Rural Youth Out-Migration and Education: Challenges to Aspirations Discourse in Mobile Modernity." *Discourse: Studies in the Cultural Politics of Education* 38, no. 3 (2017): 429–44. https://doi.org/10.1080/01596306.2017.1308456.

David-Fox, Michael. *Crossing Borders: Modernity, Ideology, and Culture in Russia and the Soviet Union.* University of Pittsburgh Press, 2015.

David-Fox, Michael, and Gyorgy Peteri. *Academia in Upheaval: Origins, Transfers, and Transformations of the Communist Academic Regime in Russia and East Central Europe.* Bloomsbury Academic, 2000.

Denisova, Liubov'. *Ischezayushchaya Derevnya Rossii. Nechernozem'ye v 1960–1980-Ye Gody.* Institut Rossiyskoz Istorii RAN, 1996.

–. *Rural Women in the Soviet Union and Post-Soviet Russia.* Edited and translated by Irina Mukhina. Routledge, 2010.

–. *Sud'ba Russkoy Krest'yanki.* ROSSPEN, 2007.

–. *Vseobshcheye Sredneye Obrazovaniye i Sotsial'nyy Progress Sela.* Nauka, 1988.

Dimitriadis, Greg. "Popular Culture and the Sociology of Education." In *The Routledge International Handbook of the Sociology of Education*, edited by Michael W. Apple, Stephen J. Ball, and Luis Armando Gandin, 190–9. Routledge, 2010.

Dobson, Miriam. *Khrushchev's Cold Summer: Gulag Returnees, Crime, and the Fate of Reform After Stalin.* Cormell University Press, 2009. www.cornellpress.cornell.edu/book/9780801477485/khrushchevs-cold-summer/.

Doktorov, Boris, and Aleksandr Nikulin. "Teodor Shanin: Krest'yanovedeniye i Rossiya." *Krest'yanovedeniye* 5, no. 3 (2020): 146–72.

Douglass, John Aubrey. "How Rankings Came to Determine World Class." In *The New Flagship University: Changing the Paradigm from Global Ranking to National Relevancy*, edited by John Aubrey Douglass, 9–30. Palgrave Macmillan, 2016.

Drozd, Yelena Pavlovna, and Valentina Feodos'yevna Shabalina. "'Posle Voyny Na Ulitse Proizoshli Izmenenia ... '" In Plastinina (Makarova) et al., *Molochnoye – Dom, v Kotorom My Zhivem*, 244–6.

Dudchenko, Georgiy Andreyevich. *Molochnoye – Poselok Uchenykh. Ocherki.* Severo-zapadnoye knizhnoye izdatel'stvo, 1984.

Dudyrev Fedor, Romanova Olga, Shabalin Aleksey. *Starshaya shkola i yeye al'ternativy v sovetskoy i rossiyskoy praktike.* Natsional'nyy issledovatel'skiy universitet "Vysshaya shkola ekonomiki," 2017.

Dulger, Ilhan. "Compulsory Education and Learning." In *Encyclopedia of the Sciences of Learning*, edited by Norbert M. Seel, 697–700. Springer, 2012.

DuPuis, E. Melanie [Erna Melanie]. *Nature's Perfect Food: How Milk Became America's Drink.* New York University Press, 2002.

Eisenstadt, Shmuel N. "Multiple Modernities." *Daedalus* 129, no. 1 (2000): 1–29.

Ennker, Benno. "Sovetskiy Narod, Stalinskiy Rezhim i Konstitutsiya 1936 Goda v Politichcskoy Istorii Sovetskogo Soyuza." Perspectivia.net, accessed

28 December 2024. https://perspectivia.net/receive/ploneimport
_mods_00011427.

Farrugia, David. "Young People and Structural Inequality: Beyond the Middle
Ground." *Journal of Youth Studies* 16, no. 5 (August 2013): 679–93. https://
doi.org/10.1080/13676261.2012.744817.

Filippov, Fridrich. *Vseobshcheye Sredneye Obrazovaniye v SSSR (Sotsiologicheskiye
Problemy)*. Mysl', 1976.

Fitzpatrick, Sheila. "Ascribing Class." *Journal of Modern History* 65, no. 4
(December 1993): 745–70. https://doi.org/10.1086/244724.

–. *Education and Social Mobility in the Soviet Union: 1921–1934*. Cambridge
University Press, 1979.

–. *Stalin's Peasants: Resistance and Survival in the Russian Village after
Collectivization*. Oxford University Press, 1994.

Foucault, Michel. *Dits et écrits: Articles politiques conférences interviews, 1970–1984*.
Praxis, 2002.

–. *Power/Knowledge: Selected Interviews and Other Writings, 1972–1977*. Edited by
Colin Gordon, Leo Marshall, John Merpham, and Kate Soper. Pantheon
Books, 1980.

Friedman, Rebecca. *Modernity, Domesticity and Temporality in Russia: Time at
Home*. Bloomsbury Academic, 2020.

Froumin, Isak, Yaroslav Kouzminov, and Dmitry Semyonov. "Institutional
Diversity in Russian Higher Education: Revolutions and Evolution."
European Journal of Higher Education 4, no. 3 (2014): 209–34.

Froumin, Isak, and Oleg Leshukov. "The Soviet Flagship University Model and
Its Contemporary Transition." In *The New Flagship University: Changing the
Paradigm from Global Ranking to National Relevancy*, edited by John Aubrey
Douglass, 173–89. Palgrave Macmillan, 2016.

Fürst, Juliane. *Stalin's Last Generation: Soviet Post-War Youth and the Emergence of
Mature Socialism*. Oxford University Press, 2010.

Gaffield, Chad. "Children's Lives and Academic Achievement in Canada and
the United States." *Comparative Education Review* 38, no. 1 (1994): 36–64.

Galmarini-Kabala, Maria Cristina. "'Moral'no Defektivnyi, Prestupnik
Ili Psikhicheskii Bol'noi? Detskie Povedencheskie Deviatsii i Sovetskie
Distsipliniruiushchie Praktiki: 1935–1957.'" In *Ostrova Utopii:
Pedagogicheskoye i Sotsial'noye Proyektirovaniye Poslevoyennoy Shkoly (1940–1980-
E)*, edited by Ilya Kukulin, Maria Mayofis, and Piotr Safronov, 107–51. NLO,
2015.

–. *The Right to Be Helped: Deviance, Entitlement, and the Soviet Moral Order*.
Northern Illinois University Press, 2016.

George D., Spindler, ed. *Education and Anthropology*. Stanford University Press,
1955.

Gerasimov, Ilya V. *Modernism and Public Reform in Late Imperial Russia: Rural
Professionals and Self-Organization, 1905–30*. Palgrave Macmillan, 2009.

–. *Plebeian Modernity: Social Practices, Illegality, and the Urban Poor in Russia, 1906–1916*. University of Rochester Press, 2018.

Gerasimova, Ol'ga. *"Ottepel'," "zamorozki" i Studenty Moskovskogo Uni-Versiteta*. AIRO-XXI, 2015.

Gerber, Theodore P., and Michael Hout. "Educational Stratification in Russia during the Soviet Period." *American Journal of Sociology* 101, no. 3 (November 1995): 611–60.

–. "Tightening Up: Declining Class Mobility During Russia's Market Transition." *American Sociological Review* 69, no. 5 (October 2004): 677–703. https:// www.jstor.org/stable/3593034?seq=1.

Gerovitch, Slava. "'We Teach Them to Be Free': Specialized Math Schools and the Cultivation of the Soviet Technical Intelligentsia." *Kritika* 20, no. 4 (September 2019): 717–54. https://doi.org/10.1353/KRI.2019.0066.

Giddens, Anthony. *The Consequences of Modernity*. Stanford University Press, 1990.

Ginzburg, Moisey. *Stil' i Epokha: Problemy Sovremennoy Arkhitektury*. Strelka Press, 2021.

Golubev, Alexey. *The Things of Life: Materiality in Late Soviet Russia*. Cornell University Press, 2021.

Gorbachev, Oleg. *Na Puti k Gorodu: Sel'skaya Migratsiya v Tsentral'noy Rossii (1946–1985) i Sovetskaya Model' Urbanizatsii*. MPGU, 2002.

Gorlov, Vladimir Nikolaevich. "Neudachnaya Popytka N.S. Khrushcheva Sozdat' Agrogoroda v Moskovskoy Oblasti v Poslevoyennyye Gody." *Vestnik Moskovskogo Gosudarstvennogo Oblastnogo Universiteta: Seriya Istoriya i Politicheskiye Nauki* 4 (2019): 226–9. https://doi.org/10.18384/2310 -676X-2019-4-226-229.

Gorsuch, Anne E. *Youth in Revolutionary Russia*. Indiana University Press, 2000.

Graham, Loren R., ed. *The Ghost of the Executed Engineer: Technology and the Fall of the Soviet Union*. Harvard University Press, 1993.

–. *Science and the Soviet Social Order*. Harvard University Press, 1990.

Green, Andy. *Education and State Formation: The Rise of Education Systems in England, France and the USA*. Macmillan, 1990.

Griffiths, Vincent L. *The Problems of Rural Education*. International Institute for Educational Planning, 1968. https://unesdoc.unesco.org/ark:/48223 /pf0000076492.

Gristy, Cath, Linda Hargreaves, and Silvie R. Kučerová, eds. *Educational Research and Schooling in Rural Europe: An Engagement with Changing Patterns of Education, Space and Place*. Springer International, 2020.

Groys, Boris. *Kommunisticheskiy postskriptum*. Ad Marginem PresMoscow, 2014.

Guseva, Galina Vasilievna. "Dom №14 Na Ulitse Shmidta – Eto Neobychnyy Dom." In Plastinina (Makarova) et al., *Molochnoye – Dom, v Kotorom My Zhivem*, 44–6.

Guth, Stefan. "One Future Only: The Soviet Union in the Age of the Scientific-Technical Revolution." *Journal of Modern European History* 13, no. 3 (2015): 355–76. doi:10.17104/1611-8944-2015-3-355.

Halfacree, Keith. "Rural Space: Constructing a Three-Fold Architecture." In *Handbook of Rural Studies*, edited by Paul Cloke, Terry Marsden, and Patrick Mooney, 44–52. SAGE Publications, 2006.

Hanson, Stephen E. *Time and Revolution: Marxism and the Design of Soviet Institutions.* University of North Carolina Press, 1997.

Hartman, Ann. "In Search of Subjugated Knowledge." *Journal of Feminist Family Therapy* 11, no. 4 (2000): 19–23. https://doi.org/10.1300/J086v11n04_03.

Holmes, Larry E. *Stalin's School: Moscow's Model School No. 25, 1931–1937.* University of Pittsburgh Press, 1999.

Hornsby, Robert. "Soviet Youth on the March: The All-Union Tours of Military Glory, 1965–87." *Journal of Contemporary History* 52, no. 2 (2017): 418–45. https://doi.org/10.1177/0022009416644666.

–. "Strengthening Friendship and Fraternal Solidarity: Soviet Youth Tourism to Eastern Europe Under Khrushchev and Brezhnev." *Europe-Asia Studies* 71, no. 7 (2019): 1205–32. https://doi.org/10.1080/09668136.2019.1624690.

Humphrey, Caroline. *Marx Went Away – But Karl Stayed Behind.* University of Michigan Press, 1999.

Ilic, Melanie, Susan E. Reid, and Lynne Attwood, eds. *Women in the Khrushchev Era.* Palgrave Macmillan, 2004.

Ilyukha, Ol'ga Pavlovna. "Karel'skiy Filipok: Regional'nyye Osobennosti Sotsiokul'turnogo Oblika Sel'skogo Shkol'nika Kontsa XIX – Nachala." *Antropologicheskiy Forum* 13 (2010): 242–70.

Imya Tvoye Komsomol: Ocherki Istorii Vologodskoy Oblastnoy Organizatsii VLKSM. 1918–1982. Archangelskoe Severo-zapadnoe issledovanie, 1983.

Inikhov, Georgiy Sergeyevich. *Zapiski o Vologodskom Molochnom Institute.* Tipografiya Severosoyuza, 1919. www.booksite.ru/fulltext/inih/hov/1.htm.

Ivanov, Aleksandr Valer'yevich. "Problemy Kooperativnogo Dvizheniya v Dorevolyutsionnoy Rossii i Ikh Izucheniye v Sovet·skoy Istoriografii Vtoroy Poloviny XX Veka." *Vestnik KrasGAU* 10 (2006): 366–70.

Ivanova, Galina Michailovna. "Sotsial'nyye Aspekty Razvitiya Sovetskoy Sistemy Obrazovaniya v 1960–1980e Gody." *Vesntik Slavianskich Kultur* 3 (2013): 25–31.

–. *Sovetskaya Shkola v 1950–1960-Ye Gody.* Fond "Moskovskoye vremya," 2018.

"Iz Istorii Razvitiya Obrazovaniya. Istoriya Obrazovaniya v Vologodskom Kraye." Vek Obrazovania, accessed 26 December 2024. https://www.booksite.ru/education/main/history/1.htm.

Jones, Owain. "Little Figures, Big Shadows." In *Contested Countryside Culture: Rurality and Socio-Cultural Marginalisation*, edited by Paul Cloke and Jo Little, 158–79. Routledge, 1997.

Jones, Polly. *Revolution Rekindled: The Writers and Readers of Late Soviet Biography.* Oxford University Press, 2019.

"Kak Eto Bylo." *Akademgorodok* 2496, no. 8 (2015): 8.

Kamkin, Alexandr. "Pyat' vekov eparchii." *Russkiy Sever,* 11 August 1992, 3.

Kasatkina, Alexandra. "Poetics and Practice of Modern Urbanism: 'Garden City' as a Technology of Social Integration in Obninsk in the 1960s." *Laboratorium: Russian Review of Social Research* 14, no. 1 (2022): 30–59. https://doi.org/10.25285/2078-1938-2022-14-1-30–59.

Katayev, Valentin Petrovich. "Beleyet Parus Odinokiy." In *Rodnaya Literatura: Khrestomatiya Dlya 5 Klassa,* edited by Nikolay Vladimirovich Kolokol'tsev, 5–8. Prosveshcheniye, 1969.

Kazanskaya, Margarita Mikhaylovna. "Vospominaniya o Molochnom." In Plastinina (Makarova) et al., *Molochnoye – Dom, v Kotorom My Zhivem,* 67–73.

Kelly, Catriona. *Children's World: Growing Up in Russia, 1890–1991.* Yale University Press, 2007.

–. "The End of Childhood and/or the Discovery of the *Tineidzher?* Adolescence in Soviet and Post-Soviet Culture." In *Eastern European Youth Cultures in a Global Context,* edited by Matthias Schwartz and Heike Winkel, 21–44. Palgrave Macmillan, 2016.

–. "Ob Izuchenii Istorii Detstva v Rossii XIX–XX Vekov." In *Kakoreya. Iz Istorii Detstva v Rossii i Drugikh Stranakh: Sbornik Statey i Materialov,* edited by Galina Makarevich, 8–46. Nauchnaya kniga, 2008.

–. "Shkol'nyy Val's: Povsednevnaya Zhizn' Sovetskoy Shkoly v Poslestalinskoye Vremya." *Antropologicheskiy Forum* 1 (2004): 104–55.

Kerr, Clark. *The Uses of the University.* 5th ed. Harvard University Press, 2001.

Kharkhordin, Oleg. *Oblichut' i Litsemerit': Genealogija Rossijskoj Lichnosti.* Letniy Sad, 2002.

Khasbulatova, O.A. "Professional'noye Obrazovaniye Muzhchin i Zhenshchin v Rossii v 1918–2015 Godakh. Istoriko-Sotsiologicheskiy Analiz." *Zhenzhiny v Rossiyskom Obshchestve* 3–4, nos. 76–7 (2015): 3–16.

Kinozhurnal Novosti Dnya. № 46. USSR, 1954. YouTube, uploaded 25 May 2020. www.youtube.com/watch?v=b97uxc7rJBA.

Klepikovskaya, Anna. "100-Letnemu Yubileyu Meditsinskoy Sluzhby Sela Molochnoye Posvyashchayetsya." *Akademgorodok* 2487, no. 28 (2014): 4.

Klumbyte, Neringa, and Gulnaz Sharafutdinova, eds. *Soviet Society in the Era of Late Socialism, 1964–1985.* Lexington Books, 2012.

Kochetkova, Elena. "Milk and Milk Packaging in the Soviet Union: Technologies of Production and Consumption, 1950s–70s." *Russian History* 46, no. 1 (2019): 29–52. https://doi.org/10.1163/18763316-04601002.

Kolchevska, Natasha. "Angels in the Home and at Work: Russian Women in the Khrushchev Years." *Women's Studies Quarterly* 33, nos. 3–4 (2005): 114–37.

Konrad, Geoge, and Ivan Szelenyi. *The Intellectuals on the Road to Class Power.* Harvester Press, 1979.

Konstantinovskiy, David. *Neravenstvo i Obrazovaniye. Opyt Sotsiologicheskikh Issledovaniy Zhiznennogo Starta Rossiyskoy Molodezhi (1960-Ye Gody–Nachalo 2000-Kh).* SFC, 2008.

Koselleck, Reinhart. *Futures Past: On the Semantics of Historical Time.* Columbia University Press, 2004.

Kotkin, Stephen. "Modern Times: The Soviet Union and the Interwar Conjecture." *Kritika: Explorations in Russian and Eurasian History* 2, no. 1 (2001): 111–64.

Kozlov, Dmitry. "Neofitsial'nyye Gruppy Sovetskikh Shkol'nikov 1940–1960-Kh Godov: Tipologiya, Ideologiya, Praktik." In *Ostrova Utopii: Pedagogicheskoye i Sotsial'noye Proyektirovaniye Poslevoyennoy Shkoly (1940–1980-E)*, edited by Ilya Kukulin, Maria Mayofis, and Piotr Safronov, 451–95. Novoe literaturnoe obozrenie, 2015.

–. "Sotsializatsiya Sovetskoy Molodezhi Perioda 'ottepeli': Varianty Al'ternativnykh Identichnostey (Na Primere Arkhangel'skoy Oblasti)." *Laboratorium: Russian Review of Social Research* 4, no. 2 (2012): 115–29. https://www.soclabo.org/index.php/laboratorium/article/view/6/111.

Kozlov, Viktor Alexandrovich, ed. *Kramola: Inakomysliye v SSSR Pri Khrushcheve i Brezhneve: 1953–1982 Gg.: Rassekrechennyye Dokumenty Verkhovnogo Suda i Prokuratury SSSR.* Materik, 2005.

Krasavtsev, Viktor Vasil'yevich. "'Kazhdyy Raz, Prokhodya Mimo Etogo Doma … '" In Plastinina (Makarova) et al., *Molochnoye – Dom, v Kotorom My Zhivem*, 302–4.

Krasnov, Dmitriy. "Charasteristika sistemy borby s podrostkovoy prestupnostiyu I prestupleniyami nesovershennoletnich v RSFSR za 1965–1969." *Sotsialno-poloticheskie nauki* 3 (2013): 84.

Krupskaya, Nadezhda Konstantinovna. "Detskiy Trud v Kolkhoze." In *Pedagogicheskiye Sochineniya: Trudovoye Vospitaniye i Politekhnicheskoye Obrazovaniye*, vol. 4, edited by Nikolay Kirillovich Goncharov, 44–5. Akademiya pedagogicheskikh nauk, 1959.

Krylova, Anna. "Soviet Modernity: Stephen Kotkin and the Bolshevik Predicament." *Contemporary European History* 23, no. 2 (2014): 167–92.

Kukulin, Ilya, Maria Mayofis, and Petr Safronov, eds. *Ostrova Utopii: Pedagogicheskoye i Sotsial'noye Proyektirovaniye Poslevoyennoy Shkoly (1940–1980-E).* Novoe literaturnoe obozrenie, 2015.

Kukulin, Ilya, Maria Mayofis, and Piotr Safronov. "Namyvaya Ostrova: Pozdnesovetskaya Obrazovatel'naya Politika v Sotsial'nykh Kontekstakh." In *Ostrova Utopii: Pedagogicheskoye i Sotsial'noye Proyektirovaniye Poslevoyennoy Shkoly (1940–1980-E)*, edited by Ilya Kukulin, Maria Mayofis, and Piotr Safronov, 5–35. Novoe literaturnoe obozrenie, 2015.

Kushkova, Anna. *Krest'yanskaya Ssora: Opyt Izucheniya Derevenskoy Povsednevnosti.* European University at St. Petersburg, 2016.

Kuznetsova, Valentina Stepanovna. "'Ja Prozhivayu v Etom Dome s Sentyabrya 1964 … '" In Plastinina (Makarova) et al., *Molochnoye – Dom, v Kotorom My Zhivem,* 145–50.

LaPierre, Brian. *Hooligans in Khrushchev's Russia.* University of Wisconsin Press, 2012.

Lareau, Annette. *Unequal Childhoods: Class, Race, and Family Life, with an Update a Decade Later.* University of California Press, 2011.

Latour, Bruno. *Down to Earth: Politics in the New Climatic Regime.* Polity Press, 2018.

Ledeneva, Alena V. *Russia's Economy of Favours:* Blat, *Networking and Informal Exchange.* Cambridge University Press, 1998.

Lefebvre, Henri. *Proizvodstvo Prostranstva.* Strelka Press, 2015.

Leonard, Carol S. *Agrarian Reform in Russia: The Road from Serfdom.* Cambridge University Press, 2010.

Leont'yeva, Svetlana Gennad'yevna, and Kirill Aleksandrovich Maslinskiy, eds. *Uchebnyy Tekst v Sovetskoy Shkole: Sbornik Statey.* Institut Logiki, kognitologii i razvitiya lichnosti, 2008.

Lisitskiy, El'. *Rossiya: Rekonstruktsiya Arkhitektury v Sovetskom Soyuze.* Izdatel'stvo Europeyskogo Universiteta v Sankt-Petersburge, 2019.

Litvina, Yelena Anatol'yevna. "Domik Arkhitektora." In Plastinina (Makarova) et al., *Molochnoye – Dom, v Kotorom My Zhivem,* 266–9.

Livschiz, Ann. "Pre-Revolutionary in Form, Soviet in Content? Wartime Educational Reforms and the Postwar Quest for Normality." *History of Education* 35, nos. 4–5 (2006): 541–60.

Lovell, Stephen. "Dosug v Rossii: 'Svobodnoye' Vremya i Yego Ispol'zovaniye." *Antropologicheskiy Forum* 2 (2005): 136–73.

Luehrmann, Sonja. *Religion in Secular Archives: Soviet Atheism and Historical Knowledge.* Oxford University Press, 2015.

Lur'ye, Mikhail Lazarevich. "Poteryannyy Ray: Nostal'giya i Kommemoratsiya v Pesnyakh o Rodnoy Derevne." *Etnograficheskoye Obozreniye* 6 (2020): 31–51. https://doi.org/10.31857/S086954150013120-2.

Makarova, Lyudmila Nikolayevna. "Ulitsa Parkovaya, Dom № 6." In Plastinina (Makarova) et al., *Molochnoye – Dom, v Kotorom My Zhivem,* 325–8.

Marinicheva, Yuliya Yur'yevna. "Tekhnika Tela: Istoriya, Pamyat' i Metis." In *Pervichnyye Znaki/Naznachennaya Real'nost',* edited by Svetlana Borisovna Adon'yeva, 47–74. Proppovskiy tsentr, 2017.

Martinovich (Levinskaya), Ol'ga Yur'yevna. "'Na Ulitse Podlesnoy … '" In Plastinina (Makarova) et al., *Molochnoye – Dom, v Kotorom My Zhivem,* 331–9.

Martinovich (Levinskaya), Ol'ga Yur'yevna, and Natal'ya Vladimirovna Artomova (Soboleva). "Rasskaz Zapisan so Slov Margarity Aleksandrovny

Talashovoy." In Plastinina (Makarova) et al., *Molochnoye – Dom, v Kotorom My Zhivem*, 122–4.

Matthews, Hugh, Taylor, Mark, Sherwood Kenneth, and Tucker Faith, "Growing-Up in the Countryside: Children and the Rural Idyll," Journal of Rural Studies, no. 16 (2000): 141–3.

Matthews, Hugh and Limb, Melanie, "Defining an Agenda for the Geography of Children: Review and Prospect," *Progress in Human Geography* 23, no. 1 (1999): 61–90.

Maslinsky, Kirill. "The New Powers of the Pedsovet: Social Control During the Thaw and the Transformation of Disciplinary Practice in a Town School, 1953–68." *Russian Review* 79, no. 2 (2020): 227–45. https://doi.org/10.1111 /russ.12264.

–. "Sovetskaya Shkola v Svete Teorii Soprotivleniya, Ili Britanskiye Rostki Na Postsovetskoy Pochve." In *Gorodskiye Teksty i Praktiki. Tom I: Simvolicheskoye Soprotivleniye*, edited by Alexandra Archipova, Daria Radchenko, and Alexey Titkov, 264–82. Izdatel'skiy dom "Delo" RANKhiGS, 2017.

–. "Uchitel' Zheleznodorozhnoy Shkoly (k Tipologii Sovetskikh Pedagogicheskikh Soobshchestv)." *Antropologicheskiy Forum* 16 (2012): 403–18.

Maslinskiy, Kirill, and Svetlana Leont'yeva, eds. *Uchebnyy Tekst v Sovetskoy Shkole: Sbornik Statey*. Institut logiki, kognitologii i razvitiya lichnosti, 2008.

Matthews, Anne Martin. "Variations in the Conceptualization and Measurement of Rurality: Conflicting Findings on the Elderly Widowed." *Journal of Rural Studies* 4, no. 2 (1988): 141–50.

Mayofis, Maria. "Pansiony Trudovykh Rezervov: Formirovaniye Sistemy Shkol-Internatov v 1954–1964 Godakh." *Novoe Literaturnoe Obozrenie* 142, no. 6 (2016): 292–324.

–. "Reshayushiy Rezept: Avtonomizatsia Shkol'noy Sistemy v Pozdnestalinskom SSSR." *Vestnik Pravoslavnogo Sviato-Tochonovskogo Gumanitarnogo Universiteta. Seria IV: Pedagogika. Psichologia* 4, no. 2 (2014): 65–82.

–. "Strakh Vliyaniya: K Ranney Istorii Sovetskikh Yazykovykh Spetsshkol (Konets 1940-Kh–Nachalo 1960-Kh Godov)." *Voprosy Obrazovania* 2 (2016): 286–310.

Mayofis, Maria, and Ilya Kukulin. "Matematicheskiye Shkoly v SSSR: Genezis Institutsii i Tipologiya Utopiy." In *Ostrova Utopii. Pedagogicheskoye i Sotsial'noye Proyektirovaniye Poslevoyennoy Shkoly (1940–1980-E)*, edited by Ilya Kukulin, Maria Mayofis, and Petr Safronov, 241–316. Novoe literaturnoe obozrenie, 2015.

Mazus, Izrail. *Podpol'nye Molodezhnye Organizat͡sii, Gruppy i Kruzhki (1926–1953 Gg.): Spravochnik*. Vozvrasheniye, 2014.

McFadden, Mark G. "Resistance to Schooling and Educational Outcomes: Questions of Structure and Agency." *British Journal of Sociology of Education* 16, no. 3 (1995): 293–308.

Meerovich, Mark. "Rozhdenie i smert' sovetskogo goroda-sada:
    Deistvuiushchie litsa i motivy ubiistva," *Vestnik Evrazii* 1 (2007): 118–66.
Mel'nikova, Ekaterina. "'Odnazhdy v Studenuyu Zimnyuyu Poru … '
    Ideal'noye Detstvo v Ustnoy Biografii." *Neprikosnovennij Zapas* 73, no. 5
    (2010): 139–57.
Melvin, Neil. *Soviet Power and the Countryside: Policy Innovation and Institutional
    Decay.* Palgrave Macmillan, 2003.
Merl, Stephan. "Why Did the Attempt Under Stalin to Increase Agricultural
    Productivity Prove to Be Such a Fundamental Failure ?" *Cabiers Du
    Monde Russe* 57, no. 1 (2016): 191–220. https://doi.org/10.4000
    /MONDERUSSE.8343.
Mitrochin, Nikolay. *Ocherki Sovetskoy Ekonomicheskoy Politiki v 1965–1989
    Godakh.* 2 vols. Novoe literaturnoe obozrenie, 2023.
–. *Russkaya Partiya: Dvizheniye Russkikh Natsionalistov v SSSR. 1953–1985 Gody.*
    NLO, 2003.
Molodov, Oleg. "Pravoslavnoe duchovenstvo Vologodskoy eparchii v 1960–
    1980 gody (po dokumentam GAVO)." In *Istoricheskoe kraevedenie I archivy,*
    vol. 8, edited by Alexandr Kamkin, Olga Naumova, Olga Artemova, Nina
    Golikova, Sergey Tsvetkov, Ilia Kuznetzov, and Natalia Polikarpova, 190–4.
    Vologda, 2002.
–. "Sovetskoe gosudarstvo I Russkaya pravoslavnaya tserkov' na Euvropeyskom
    Severe v 1960–1980 gody." PhD diss., Cherepovetskiy Gosudarstvenniy
    Universitet, 2006.
*Narodnoye Khozyaystvo Vologodskoy Oblasti Za Gody Sovetskoy Vlasti: Statisticheskiy
    Sbornik.* Statistika, 1967.
Naumova, Olga. "Istoria russkoy pravoslavnoy tserkvi v documentach
    sovetskich organizatsiy noveyshego vremeni (1918–1990 gg)." In
    *Regional'nyye aspekty istoricheskogo puti pravoslaviya: Arkhivy, istochniki,
    metodologiya issledovaniy: [sbornik],* vol. 1, edited by Alexandr Kamkin.
    Istoricheskoe kraevedenie, 2001.
Nesterova, Aleksandra Aleksandrovna. "Rol' Komsomola v Organizatsii
    Trudovogo Vospitaniya Shkol'nikov Na Rubezhe 1950-Kh–1960-Kh Godov."
    Politika i Obshchestvo 8 (2015): 1076–87.
Neumann, Matthias. "'Youth, It's Your Turn!': Generations and the Fate of the
    Russian Revolution (1917–1932)." *Journal of Social History* 46, no. 2 (2012):
    273–304. https://doi.org/10.1093/jsh/shs098.
Nikulin, Alexandr. *Agrarniki, Vlast' i Selo: Ot Proshlogo k Nastoyashchemu.*
    Rossiyskaya akademiya narodnogo khozyaystva i gosudarstvennoy sluzhby
    pri Prezidente Rossiyskoy Federatsii, 2014.
Nove, Alec. *An Economic History of the USSR, 1917–1991.* Penguin Books, 1992.
*O Merakh Po Dal'neyshemu Razvitiyu Sel'skogo Khozyaystva v Nechernozemnoy Zone
    RSFSR Postanovleniye TSK KPSS i Soveta Ministrov SSSR Ot 20 Marta 1974.*
    Politizdat, 1977.

"O Programme Kommunisticheskoy Partii Sovetskogo Soyuza. Doklad Tovarishcha N.S. Khrushcheva 18 Oktyabrya 1961. In 3 Vols. Part 1." In *XXII s'yezd Kommunisticheskoy Partii Sovetskogo Soyuza 17–31 Oktyabrya 1961. Stenograficheskiy Otchet*, 148–258. Izdatel'stvo Politicheskoy literatury, 1962.

"O vvedenii v deystviye tipovogo polozheniya o spetsial'noy obshcheobrazovatel'noy shkole-internate (shkole) dlya umstvenno otstalykh detey (vspomogatel'noy shkole)" [1978]. Garant, accessed 26 December 2024. https://base.garant.ru/70587788/.

Obertreis, Julia. *Imperial Desert Dreams: Cotton Growing and Irrigation in Central Asia, 1860–1991*. V&R Unipress, 2017.

"Obsuzhdeniye Stat'i Katriony Kelli Shkol'nyy Val's." *Antropologicheskiy Forum* 4 (2006): 7–128.

Ochitovich, Michail Alexandrovich. "K Probleme Goroda." *Sovremennaya Arkhitektura* 4 (1929): 130–4.

Ochrimenko (Krylova), Olga Vladimirovna. "'Kazhdiy Professorskiy Dom … '" In Plastinina (Makarova) et al., *Molochnoye – Dom, v Kotorom My Zhivem*, 80–93.

Olson, Laura J., and Svetlana B. Adonyeva. *The Worlds of Russian Village Women: Tradition, Transgression, Compromise*. University of Wisconsin Press, 2013.

Omelchenko, Elena. *Molodezh': Otkrytyy Vopros*. Simbirskaya kniga, 2004.

"Ostroumov Lev Aleksandrovich." *Izvestnyye Uchonyye: Biograficheskiye Dannyye Uchenykh i Spetsialistov*. Proyekt Rossiyskoy Akademii Yestestvoznaniya, accessed 26 december 2024. https://famous-scientists.ru/anketa /ostroumov-lev-aleksandrovich-1213.

Oushakine, Serguei Alex. "Pole Boya Na Lone Prirody: Ot Kakogo Nasledstva My Otkazyvalis." *Novoe Literaturnoe Obozrenie* 71 (2005): 263–98.

Oyen, Astrid Van. "Rural Time." *World Archaeology* 51, no. 2 (2019): 191–207. https://doi.org/10.1080/00438243.2019.1601461.

Pallot, Judith. "Rural Depopulation and the Restoration of the Russian Village Under Gorbachev." *Soviet Studies* 42, no. 4 (2019): 655–74.

Panchenko, Aleksandr. *Ivan i Yakov – neobychnyye svyatyye iz bolotistoy mestnosti*. Novoye literaturnoye obozreniye, 2012.

Panelli, Ruth, Samantha Punch, and Elsbeth Robson, eds. *Global Perspectives on Rural Childhood and Youth: Young Rural Lives*. Routledge, 2010.

Paretskaya, Anna. "A Middle Class Without Capitalism? Socialist Ideology and Post-Collectivist Discourse in the Late-Soviet Era." In *Soviet Society in the Era of Late Socialism, 1964–1985*, edited by Neringa Klumbyte and Gulnaz Sharafutdinova, 43–66. Lexington Books, 2012.

Parthé, Kathleen. *Russian Village Prose: The Radiant Past*. Princeton University Press, 1992.

Paxson, Margaret. *Solovyovo: The Story of Memory in a Russian Village*. Woodrow Wilson Center Press; Indiana University Press, 2005.

Petryashin, Stanislav. "Rabochiye v Sovetskoy Muzeynoy Etnografii 1950-Kh Godov: Klassovyy Analiz i Politika Vremeni," *Etnograficheskoye obozreniye* 4 (2021): 157–75.

Pilkington, Hilary. *Russia's Youth and Its Culture: A Nation's Constructors and Constructed*. Routledge, 1994.

Plastinina (Makarova), Ol'ga Aleksandrovna, and Tatiana Yulievna Berman. "'V Opisanii Doma … '" In Plastinina (Makarova) et al., *Molochnoye – Dom, v Kotorom My Zhivem*, 152–62.

Plastinina (Makarova), Ol'ga Aleksandrovna, and Elena Aleksandrovna Makarova. "Ulitsa Shmidta, Dom № 14." In Plastinina (Makarova) et al., *Molochnoye – Dom, v Kotorom My Zhivem*, 39–44.

Plastinina (Makarova), Ol'ga Aleksandrovna, Olga Vladimirovna Ochrimenko (Krylova), and Lyubov' Dmitriyevna Belyayeva, eds. *Molochnoye – Dom, v Kotorom My Zhivem*. Poligraf-Periodika, 2019.

Popzov, Oleg. *Zhizn' Vopreki*. Algoritm, 2018.

Powell, Mary Ann, Nicola Taylor, and Anne B. Smith. "Constructions of Rural Childhood: Challenging Dominant Perspectives." *Children's Geographies* 11, no. 1 (2013): 117–31. https://doi.org/10.1080/14733285.2013.743285.

Prishvin, Mikhail Mikhaylovich. "Kladovaya Solntsa." In *Rodnaya Literatura: Khrestomatiya Dlya 5 Klassa*, edited by Nikolay Vladimirovich Kolokol'tsev, 120–50. Prosveshcheniye, 1969.

Pyzhikov, Alexandr Vladimirovich. "Reformirovanie Sistemy Obrazovania SSSR v Period Ottepeli (1953–1964)." *Voprosy Istorii*, no. 9 (2004): 99–135.

Quisumbing, Agnes R., Ruth Meinzen-Dick, Terri L. Raney, André Croppenstedt, Julia A. Behrman, and Amber Peterman. *Gender in Agriculture: Closing the Knowledge Gap*. Springer Netherlands, 2014.

Raleigh, Donald J. *Soviet Baby Boomers: An Oral History of Russia's Cold War Generation*. Oxford University Press, 2011.

Ransell, David L. "Russia and USSR." In *Children in Historical and Comparative Perspective: An International Handbook and Research Guide*, edited by Joseph M. Hawes and Ray N. Hiner, 471–90. Greenwood Press, 1991.

Razuvalova, Anna. *Pisateli-"derevenshchiki" Literatura i Konservativnaya Ideologiya 1970-h Godov*. Novoe literaturnoe obozrenie, 2015.

"Rech' Sekretarya Stavropol'skogo Kraykoma Komsomola Vasiliya Kurilova." *Sel'skaya Molodezh*, no. 1 (1972): 5.

Reynolds, William M., ed. *Forgotten Places: Critical Studies in Rural Education*. Peter Lang, 2017.

Riordan, Jim. "The Komsomol." In *Soviet Youth Culture*, edited by Jim Riordan, 16–44. Macmillan Press, 1989.

Robson, Karen. *Sociology of Education in Canada*. Pearson Canada, 2013.

"Rossiyskaya Povsednevnost': Elektronnyy Arkhiv." Fotoarkhiv Y.A. Galeva, accessed 26 December 2024. https://daytodaydata.ru/catalog?filter=person %3D5528408.

Ruchenkova (Abramova), Viktoriya Il'inichna. "'V 1946 Godu Nasha Sem'ya … '" In Plastinina (Makarova) et al., *Molochnoye – Dom, v Kotorom My Zhivem*, 94–8.

Rutkevich, Mikhail Nikolayevich. "Izmeneniye Sotsial'noy Struktury Sovetskogo Obshchestva i Intelligentsiya." In *Sotsiologiya v SSSR*, vol. 1., edited by Gennadiy Vasil'yevich Osipov. Mysl', 1966.

Ryvkina, Rozalina Vladimirovna. *Obraz Zhizni Sel'skogo Naseleniya: Metodologiya, Metodika i Rezul'taty Izucheniya Sotsial'no-Ekonomicheskikh Aspektov Zhiznedeyatel'nosti.* Nauka, 1978.

Sadovnikov, Yuriy Alekseyevich. "Gosudarstvennyye i Obshchestvennyye Struktury i Komissiya Po Delam Nesovershennoletnikh Chuvashii v 1960-Ye Gody." In *Nuzhda i Poryadok: Istoriya Sotsial'noy Raboty v Rossii*, edited by Pavel Vasil'yevich Romanov and Yelena Rostislavovna Yarskaya-Smirnova, 353–74. Nauchnaya kniga, 2005.

Savin, Andrey Ivanovich. "Vyssheye Obrazovaniye v RSFSR Kak Lift Sotsial'noy Mobil'nosti (1918–1936)." *Gumanitarnyye Nauki v Sibiri* 23, no. 4 (2016): 43–9.

Schafft, Kai A., and Alecia Youngblood Jackson, eds. *Rural Education for the Twenty-First Century: Identity, Place, and Community in a Globalizing World.* Penn State University Press, 2010.

Scott, James C. *Seeing Like a State: How Certain Schemes to Improve the Human Condition Have Failed.* Yale University Press, 1998.

Semenov, Vadim Sergeyevich. "Ob Izmenenii Intelligentsii i Sluzhashchikh v Protsesse Stroitel'stva Kommunizma." In *Sotsiologiya v SSSR*, vol. 1, edited by Gennadiy Vasil'evich Osipov. Mysl', 1966.

Seregicheva (Yanina), Nadezhda Andreyevna. "'Eto Byl Dvukhetazhnyy Iz Tolstykh Breven … '" In Plastinina (Makarova) et al., *Molochnoye – Dom, v Kotorom My Zhivem*, 60–5.

Shakirov, Robert Vafich. "Shkola i Obshchestvo: Sistemno-Kontseptual'nyy Analiz Reform Obrazovaniya v Rossii v XX Veke." PhD diss., Kazan' State University, 1997.

Shanin, Teodor. *Defining Peasants: Essays Concerning Rural Societies, Expolary Economies, and Learning from Them in the Contemporary World.* Basil Blackwell, 1990.

Shearer, David R. *Policing Stalin's Socialism Repression and Social Order in the Soviet Union, 1924–1953.* Yale University Press, 2009.

Shishigin, Sergey Alexandrovich, and Tatiana Alexandrovna Shishigina. "'Dom Byl Dvuchetazhniy, Dvuchpod'ezdniy … '" In Plastinina (Makarova) et al., *Molochnoye – Dom, v Kotorom My Zhivem*, 48–9.

Shkaratan, Ovsey Irmovich. *Problemy sotsial'noy struktury rabochego klassa SSSR (istoriko-sotsiologicheskoye issledovaniye).* Mysl', 1970.

Shpakovskaya, Larisa Leonidovna. "Sovetskaya Obrazovatel'naya Politika: Sotsial'naya Inzheneriya i Klassovaya Bor'ba." *Journal Issledovaniy Socialnoy Politiki* 7, no. 1 (2010): 39–64.

Shtyrkov, Sergey. *Predaniya ob inozemnom nashestvii: Krest'yanskiy narrativ i mifologiya landshafta (na materialakh Severo-Vostochnoy Novgorodchiny).* Nauka. 2012.

Shubin, Sergey Ivanovich. "Istoriya Trudodnya (1930–1966) Kak Mery Truda i Instrument Yego Stimulirovaniya." *Vestnik Severnogo (Arkticheskogo) Federal'nogo Universiteta. Seriya: Gumanitarnyye i Sotsial'nyye Nauki,* no. 6 (2013): 31–7.

Shucksmith, Mark, and David L. Brown. *Routledge International Handbook of Rural Studies.* Routledge, 2019.

Silina, Lada Vladimirovna. *Nastroyeniya Sovetskogo Studenchestva: 1945–1964 Gg.* Russkiy Mir, 2004.

Šimáně, Michal. "Socialist Egalitarianism in Everyday Life of Secondary Technical Schools in Czechoslovakia During the Normalization Period (1969–89)." *Communist and Post-Communist Studies* 56, no. 1 (2023): 129–51.

Simonova (Malikova), Nadezhda. "'Zaselyalsya Nash Dom … '" In Plastinina (Makarova) et al., *Molochnoye – Dom, v Kotorom My Zhivem,* 304–7.

Simush, Petr Iosifovich. *Socialniy Portret Sovetskogo Krest'yanstva.* Poligrafist, 1976.

Siplova, Tatyana Afrikanovna, Lyubov' Dmitriyevna Belyayeva, and Margarita Aleksandrovna Rukavishnikova. *Vologodskoy Gosudarstvennoy Molochnokhozyaystvennoy Akademii Imeni N.V. Vereshchagina – 100 Let. Stranitsy Istorii.* Yaroslavl', 2012.

Slezin, Anatoliy. *Fenomen Komsomola: Seredina 1950-Kh–Pervaya Polovina 1960-Kh Gg.* Edited by A.A Slezin. Gramota, 2017.

Slezkin, Yuriy L'vovich. *Dom Pravitel'stva. Saga o Russkoy Revolyutsii.* Corpus, 2019.

Smith, Jenny Leigh. *Works in Progress: Plans and Realities on Soviet Farms, 1930–1963.* Yale University Press, 2014.

Smith-Howard, Kendra. *Pure and Modern Milk: An Environmental History Since 1900.* Oxford University Press, 2017.

Smolkin, Victoria. *A Sacred Space Is Never Empty: A History of Soviet Atheism.* Princeton University Press, 2018.

Sokolova, Anna. "Invading the Void: Social Time Production as a Developmental Tool in the Late Soviet Periphery." *Canadian Slavonic Papers* 65, no. 1 (2023): 52–71.

Solov'yev, Geral'd Aleksandrovich, ed. *Spravochnik Komsomol'skogo Aktivista Armii i Flota.* Voenizdat, 1976.

Solov'yeva, Yevgeniya Yegorovna, ed. *Rodnaya Rech'. Kniga Dlya Chteniya v 4 Klasse.* Sovetskiye uchebniki, 1949.

Sorokin, Pitirim, and Carle C. Zimmerman. *Principles of Rural-Urban Sociology.* Henry Holt and Company, 1969.

"Sozdaniye Sovetskoy Shkoly. 1930–1940-Ye Gody." *Kraevedenie, Istoria Cherepovza,* 12 December 2017. https://cherkray.ru/?page=cherprosvet&view=3.

Staroverov, Vladimir Ivanovich. *Sotsial'no-Demograficheskiye Problemy Derevni: Metodologiya, Metodika, Opyt Analiza Migratsii Sel'skogo Naseleniya.* Nauka, 1975.

Stonkuvienė, Irena. "The Equal and the More Equal: Pupils' Experiences of School in Lithuania in the Late Soviet Era." *Journal of Education Culture and Society* 14, no. 1 (2023): 124–42.

Tartachenko, Ksenia. *Soviet SCI_BERIA: Novosibirsk Science City and the Politics of Expertise, 1957–1991.* Bloomsbury Academic, 2024.

Taylor, Charles. "Chto Takoye Sotsial'noye Voobrazhayemoye?" *Neprekosnovenniy Zapas* 69, no. 1 (2010): 19–26.

Temkina, Anna, and Anna Rotkirkh. "Sovetskiye Gendernyye Kontrakty i Ikh Transformatsiya v Sovremennoy Rossii." In *Gendernyy Poryadok: Sotsiologicheskiy Podkhod*, edited by Elena Zdravomyslova and Anna Temkina, 169–200. Europeyskiy Universiet v Sankt-Peterburge, 2007.

Thaxton, Ralph A., Jr. *Salt of the Earth: The Political Origins of Peasant Protest and Communist Revolution in China.* University of California Press, 1997.

Therborn, Göran. *Ot Marksizma k Postmarksizmu?* Izdatel'skiy dom NIU VSHE, 2021.

Thompson, Edward Palmer. *The Making of the English Working Class.* Victor Gollancz, 1963.

Thompson, Paul, and Joanna Bornat. *The Voice of the Past: Oral History.* 4th ed. Oxford University Press, 2017.

Timofeyev, Mikhail. "Predchuvstviye Utopii: Reprezentatsii Goroda Budushchego v Povesti A.V. Chayanova 'Puteshestviye Moyego Brata Alekseya v Stranu Krest'yanskoy Utopii' (1920) i v Gazetnom Romane Vl. Fedorova 'Chudo Greshnogo Pitirima' (1925)." *Novoe Literaturnoe Obozrenie* 167, no. 1 (2021): 1–13.

Tirado, Isabel A. "The Komsomol's Village Vanguard: Youth and Politics in the NEP Countryside," *Russian Review* 72. no. 3 (2013): 427–46.

–. "The Komsomol and Young Peasants: The Dilemma of Rural Expansion, 1921–1925." *Slavic Review* 52, no. 3 (1993): 460–76.

–. "Peasants Into Soviets: Reconstructing Komsomol Identity in the Russian Countryside of the 1920s." *Acta Slavica Iaponica*, no. 18 (2001): 42–63.

Titov, Andey Georgievich. "'Na Ploshchadke Mezhdu Korpusom Instituta … '" In Plastinina (Makarova) et al., *Molochnoye – Dom, v Kotorom My Zhivem*, 30–2.

Toporov, Adrian Mitrofanovich. *Krest'yane o Pisatelyakh.* Konstanta, 2015.

Trofimov, Gleb Nikolayevich. *"Institut v Molochnom," Kinozhurnal Nash Kray, № 32.* Leningradskaya studiya dokumental'nykh fil'mov, 1961. YouTube, uploaded 3 August 2019. https://www.youtube.com/watch?v=JffvrbLYNkg.

Tromly, Benjamin. *Making the Soviet Intelligentsia: Universities and Intellectual Life Under Stalin and Khrushchev.* Cambridge University Press, 2015.

Trukhanovich, T.Yu. "O Primenenii 'klassovogo Podkhoda' v Sovetskoy Sisteme Obrazovaniya vo Vtoroy Polovine 1920-Kh Godov: (Po Dokumentam

Cherepovetskogo Tsentra Khraneniya Dokumentatsii)." *Istoricheskoye Krayevedeniye i Arkhivy. Vologda* 8 (2002): 74–8.

Tsaregorodtseva (Povshednaya), Galina Yukhimovna. "'Pered Tem, Kak Nasha Semya Poluchila Kvartiru … '" In Plastinina (Makarova) et al., *Molochnoye – Dom, v Kotorom My Zhivem*, 110–11.

Tsipursky, Gleb. *Socialist Fun: Youth, Consumption, and State-Sponsored Popular Culture in the Soviet Union, 1945–1970.* University of Pittsburgh Press, 2016.

–. "Ulichnyy Mir i Molodyye Khuligany v Post-Stalinskom Sovetskom Soyuze." In *Molodezhnyye Ulichnyye Gruppirovki: Vvedeniye v Problematiku*, edited by Dmitry Gromov and Natal'a Pushkareva, 73–93. Institut rossiyskoy istorii RAN, 2009.

Tyapugin, Sergey Yevgen'yevich, and Irina Vasil'yevna Serebrova. "Severo-Zapadnomu NII Molochnogo i Lugopastbishchnogo Khozyaystva – 90 Let." *Dostizheniya Nauki i Tekhniki APK* 1 (2011): 3–4.

Ukhanova, Yuliya Viktorovna. "Intellektualy Sel'skogo Khozyaystva Evropeyskogo Severa Rossii v 1930–1960-Ye Gg." *Yaroslavskiy Pedagogicheskiy Vestnik* 1, no. 2 (2012): 49–56.

Vail', P'otr, and Alexandr Genis. *60-e. Mir sovetskogo cheloveka.* ACT, Corpus, 2001.

Vasilenko, Vasiliy Petrovich. *Vologodskaya Oblast. Poselok Molochnoye. Studenty Molochnogo Instituta v Tsekhakh Molokozavoda. Kinozhurnal Nash Kray, № 12.* Leningradskaya studiya dokumental'nykh fil'mov, 1959. YouTube, uploaded 3 August 2019. www.youtube.com/watch?v=JffvrbLYNkg.

Venzher, Vladimir Grigorievich. *Kolkhoznyy Stroy Na Sovremennom Etape.* Economika, 1966.

Vikulov, Sergey Vasilievich. *Vstul' Poran'she, Shagnut' Podal'she: Ocherki i Stat'i.* Sovremennik, 1980.

Vlasova, Irina Vladimirovna. "Etnicheskaya istoriya i formirovaniye naseleniya Russkogo Severa." In *Russkiy Sever: Etnicheskaya Istoriya i Narodnaya Kul'tura. XII XX Veka*, edited by Irina Vlasova. Nauka, 2001.

"Vnutrisoyuznaya Rabota – Osnova Deyatel'nosti Pervichnoy Organizatsii." In *Osnovy Deyatel'nosti "Komsomol'skogo Prozhektora": (V Pomoshch' Sekretaryu Pervichnoy Komsomol'skoy Organizatsii, Nachal'niku Shtaba "K.P.").* Vologda, 1976.

Volkov, Vadim. "The Concept of Kul'turnost': Notes on the Stalinist Civilizing Process." In *Stalinism: New Directions*, edited by Sheila Fitzpatrick, 210–30. Routledge, 1999.

Voprosy Ideologicheskoy Raboty KPSS: Sbornik Dokumentov (1965–1973). Politizdat, 1973.

Voronina, Tatiana. "Space and Time in the Socialist Countryside: All-Union Anniversaries in Vologda Rural Schools during the 1960s and 1970s." *Canadian Slavonic Papers* 65, no. 1 (2023): 7–29. https://doi.org/10.1080 /00085006.2023.2168422.

Voronina, Tatiana, and Anna Sokolova. "Myslit' Kak Kommunisty: Protokoly Sel'skikh Partsobraniy 'epokhi Razvitogo Sotsializma.'" *Novoe Literaturnoe Obozrenie* 4, no. 164 (2020): 1–15.

Vorotnikova, Natal'ya Sergeyevna. "Otnosheniye Krest'yan k Nachal'nomu Obrazovaniyu v Vologodskoy Gubernii vo Vtoroy Polovine XIX–Nachale XX Vv." In *Ledentsovskiye Chteniya. Biznes. Nauka. Obrazovaniye. Materialy Mezhdunarodnoy Nauchno-Prakticheskoy Konferentsii, 22 Aprelya 2009 Goda*, edited by Irina Ivanovna Lyutova and Tamara Vladimirovna Lodkina, 342–7. Moskovskiy gumanitarnyy universitet, 2009.

"Vsesoyuznaya Perepis' Naseleniya 1959 g. Chislennost' Gorodskogo Naseleniya RSFSR, Yeye Territorial'nykh Yedinits, Gorodskikh Poseleniy i Gorodskikh Rayonov Po Polu." *Демоскоп Weekly*, last modified 17 May 2011. https://www.demoscope.ru/weekly/ssp/rus59_reg1.php.

"Vsesoyuznaya Perepis' Naseleniya 1970 g. Chislennost' Gorodskogo Naseleniya RSFSR, Yeye Territorial'nykh Yedinits, Gorodskikh Poseleniy i Gorodskikh Rayonov Po Polu." *Демоскоп Weekly*, last moified 18 January 2011. https://www.demoscope.ru/weekly/ssp/rus70_reg1.php.

"Vsesoyuznaya Perepis' Naseleniya 1979 g. Chislennost' Nalichnogo Naseleniya RSFSR, Avtonomnykh Respublik, Avtonomnykh Oblastey i Okrugov, Krayev, Oblastey, Rayonov, Gorodskikh Poseleniy, Sel-Raytsentrov i Sel'skikh Poseleniy s Naseleniyem Svyshe 5000." *Демоскоп Weekly*, accessed 27 December 2024. https://www.demoscope.ru/weekly/ssp/ussr_nac_79.php.

Wagner, Peter. *Moderne Als Erfahrung Und Interpretationen. Eine Neue Soziologie Zur Moderne – Perlentaucher.* UVK Universitätsverlag Konstanz, 2009.

–. "Multiple Trajectories of Modernity: Why Social Theory Needs Historical Sociology." *Thesis Eleven* 100, no. 1 (2010): 53–60. https://doi.org/10.1177/0725513609353705.

Warner, Elizabeth, and Svetlana Adonyeva. *We Remember, We Love, We Grieve: Mortuary and Memorial Practice in Contemporary Russia.* University of Wisconsin Press, 2021.

Wegren, Stephen K., Alexander Nikulin, Irina Trotsuk, Svetlana Golovina, and Marina Pugacheva. "Gender Inequality in Russia's Rural Formal Economy." *Post-Soviet Affairs* 31, no. 5 (2015): 367–96. https://doi.org/10.1080/1060586X.2014.986871.

Weiner, Douglas. *A Little Corner of Freedom: Russian Nature Protection from Stalin to Gorbachev.* University of California Press, 1999.

Weiss, Julia, and Christin Heinz-Fischer. "The More Rural the Less Educated? An Analysis of National Policy Strategies for Enhancing Young Adults' Participation in Formal and Informal Training in European Rural Areas." *Youth* 2, no. 3 (2022): 405–21. https://doi.org/10.3390/YOUTH2030030.

White, Simone, and Downey Jayne. "International Trends and Patterns in Innovation in Rural Education." In *Rural Education Across the World Models of Innovative Practice and Impact*, edited by Simone White and Jayne Downey, 3–21. Springer International, 2021.

Wiley, Andrea S. *Re-Imagining Milk: Cultural and Biological Perspectives.* Routledge, 2016.

Williams, Raymond. *The Country and the City.* Chatto and Windus; Spokesman Books, 1973.

Willis, Paul E. *Learning to Labor: How Working Class Kids Get Working Class Jobs.* 2nd ed. Columbia University Press, 1977.

Yaroshovets, Vasiliy Stepanovich. "Udarnaya Komsomolskaya Zona." In *Vsesoyusnaya Udarnaya v Moem Rodnom Sele*, edited by I. Danchenko, 23–40. Molodaya gvardia, 1977.

Yekhalov, Anatoliy. *"Rodina" Nasha. Yest' Li Budushcheye u Severnoy Derevni?* Izdatel'skie resheniya, 2019.

Yemel'yanov, Aleksey Stepanovich. *O Rekordistke Korove Vene.* Oblastnaya tipografia, 1956.

Yurchak, Alexei. *Everything Was Forever, Until It Was No More: The Last Soviet Generation.* Princeton University Press, 2006.

Zakharov, Sergey Vladimirovich. "Menyayushchiyesya Parametry Matrimonial'nogo Povedeniya." In *Demograficheskaya Modernizatsiya Rossii 1900–2000*, edited by Anatoliy Grigor'yevich Vishnevskiy, 96–134. Novoe Izdatelstvo, 2006.

"'Zakon RSFSR Ot 30 Iyulya 1969 g. Ob Utverzhdenii Kodeksa o Brake i Sem'ye RSFSR.'" *Vedomosti Verkhovnogo Soveta RSFSR*, no. 32 (1969): 1397.

Zaslavskaya, Tatiana Ivanovna. "Kakoy Bit' Derevne?" *Molodoy Kommunist* 11 (1973): 86–93.

–, ed. *Migratsiya Sel'skogo Naseleniya.* Mysl', 1970.

–. *Raspredeleniye Po Trudu v Kolkhozakh.* Economika, 1966.

Zdravomyslova, Yelena Andreyevna, and Anna Adrianovna Temkina. "Gosudarstvennoye Konstruirovaniye Gendera v Sovetskom Obshchestve." *Zhurnal Issledovaniy Sotsial'noy Politiki* 1, nos. 3–4 (2010): 299–322.

–. "Patriarkhat i Zhenskaya Vlast." In *Rossiyskiy Gendernyy Poryadok: Sotsiologicheskiy Podkhod*, edited by Elena Zdravomyslova and Anna Temkona, 68–96. Izdatel'stvo Europeyskiy Universitet v Sankt-Peterburge, 2007.

Zhuk, Sergeĭ Ivanovich. "Détente and Western Cultural Products in Soviet Ukraine During the 1970s." In *Youth and Rock in the Soviet Bloc: Youth Cultures, Music, and the State in Russia and Eastern Europe*, edited by William Jay Risch, 184–242. Rowman and Littlefield , 2012. https://rowman.com /ISBN/9780739178232/Youth-and-Rock-in-the-Soviet-Bloc-Youth-Cultures -Music-and-the-State-in-Russia-and-Eastern-Europe.

–. *Rock and Roll in the Rocket City: The West, Identity, and Ideology in Soviet Dniepropetrovsk, 1960–1985.* Woodrow Wilson Center Press, 2010.

Zolotova, Elena Stanislavovna. "'Ulitsa Shmidta, Dom № 3 – Eto Babushkin Dom … '" In Plastinina (Makarova) et al., *Molochnoye – Dom, v Kotorom My Zhivem*, 74–80.

Zotova, Yelena Aleksandrovna, Marina Yevgen'yevna Baskakova, and Yelena Borisovna Mezentseva. "Gendernyye Voprosy Prestupnosti." In *Gendernyye Problemy Sovremennoy Rossii (Po Dannym Ofitsial'noy Statistiki)*, edited by Yelena Zotova, Marina Baskakova, and Yelena Mezentseva, 205–16. Alex, 2006.

Zyuzin, Yuriy Leonidovich. "Ulitsa Shmidta, Dom № 9." In Plastinina (Makarova) et al., *Molochnoye – Dom, v Kotorom My Zhivem*, 105–7.